UNEASY ALLIES

UNEASY ALLIES

WORKING FOR LABOR REFORM IN
NINETEENTH-CENTURY BOSTON

David A. Zonderman

University of Massachusetts Press
AMHERST AND BOSTON

Copyright © 2011 by David A. Zonderman
All rights reserved
Printed in the United States of America

LC 2010050526
ISBN 978-1-55849-866-2 (paper); 865-5 (library cloth)

Designed by Dennis Anderson
Set in Minion Pro with Berthold Walbaum Book display
by Westchester Book
Printed and bound by Thomson-Shore, Inc.

Library of Congress Cataloging-in-Publication Data
Zonderman, David A.
Uneasy allies : working for labor reform in nineteenth-century Boston /
David A. Zonderman.
  p.   cm.
Includes bibliographical references and index.
ISBN 978-1-55849-866-2 (pbk. : alk. paper)—ISBN 978-1-55849-865-5 (library cloth : alk. paper)
 1. Labor policy—Massachusetts—Boston—History—19th century.
 2. Working class—Massachusetts—Boston—History—19th century.
 3. Labor movement—Massachusetts—Boston—History—19th century.   I. Title.
HD8070.Z66 2011
331.8809744'6109034—dc22
2010050526

British Library Cataloguing in Publication data are available.

For my mother and the memory of my father

CONTENTS

List of Maps	ix
Acknowledgments	xi
Introduction	1

Part I: 1830s–1870s — 25

1 Awakenings
  The First Cross-Class Labor Reform Organizations,
  1832–1848 — 27

2 Keeping the Flame Alive
  The Enduring Vision of Antebellum Labor Reform,
  1848–1865 — 64

3 Acts of Commission
  Labor Reformers, Activists, and the Levers of
  Political Power, 1865–1870 — 82

4 The Generation of 1869
  Two Leagues, a Bureau, and a Party — 114

Part II: 1870s–1900 — 169

5 Piety and Protest
  Labor Reform, Religion, and Mass Demonstrations,
  1872–1898 — 173

6 Spaces, Places, and Headquarters
Workers, Reformers, and the Search for Common
Ground, 1879–1900 212

7 New Models for a New Century
Labor Reform and the Origins of the Progressive
Movement, 1891–1900 240

Epilogue 261

Abbreviations 265

Notes 267

Index 307

MAPS

Boston, 1842   29

"Boston in 1880. Showing All Ground Occupied by Buildings"   171

"Chief Institutions & Meeting Places . . . South End Boston," 1898   213

ACKNOWLEDGMENTS

THIS BOOK has been many years in the making and I have amassed many debts in bringing it to completion. Generous support from the American Antiquarian Society, American Council of Learned Societies, American Historical Association, American Philosophical Society, Massachusetts Historical Society, and the National Endowment for the Humanities facilitated research for this project. Both the University of Wisconsin–Madison and North Carolina State University granted me research leaves to complete significant portions of the manuscript.

Staff at the following archives and libraries helped me immensely in finding a wealth of sources, and granting me permission to publish material in their collections where applicable: Boston Public Library, Houghton Library at Harvard University, Library of Congress, Massachusetts Historical Society, Massachusetts State Archives, National Archives, New York Public Library, Schlesinger Library at Harvard University, and the State Historical Society of Wisconsin. The librarians at North Carolina State University deserve a special thank-you for tracking down many unusual and obscure interlibrary loan requests.

Several graduate student research assistants worked long hours combing through reels of microfilm and cartons of uncatalogued nineteenth-century pamphlets: Robert Avery, Steven Chudnick, Maureen Conklin, Javan Frazier, Corinne Glover, Daniel Graff, and Paul Taillon all have my deepest gratitude for their hard work.

Colleagues here at North Carolina State University—past and present—read various chapters in multiple stages of revision. I am especially grateful to David Ambaras, Jim Banker, Ross Bassett, Matthew Booker, Holly Brewer, Jim Crisp, Alex DeGrand, Craig Friend, David Gilmartin, Bill Harris, Joe Hobbs, Owen Kalinga, Akram Khater, Mimi Kim, Will Kimler, Tony Lavopa, Keith Luria, Steve Middleton, Nancy Mitchell, Gail O'Brien, Jonathan Ocko,

Tom Parker, John Riddle, Rich Slatta, John David Smith, Jerry Surh, Ken Vickery, and Steve Vincent for all their wise counsel.

Other scholars also read portions of the manuscript and offered very constructive criticism that I hope made this a better book: thanks to Mary Blewett, Ardis Cameron, Mary Ann Clawson, Sarah Deutsch, Ileen DeVault, Rebecca Edwards, Eric Foner, Kenneth Fones-Wolf, William Freehling, Lawrence Glickman, Brian Greenberg, Gregory Kaster, Jama Lazerow, Timothy Messer-Kruse, David Roediger, Sal Salerno, Richard Schneirov, Shelton Stromquist, and an anonymous reader for University of Massachusetts Press. Jonathan Prude merits extra special recognition because he read this entire book in several drafts, and each time pressed me to sharpen my arguments and see the big picture.

At University of Massachusetts Press, Clark Dougan saw the promise in this project and encouraged me to complete the work, Carol Betsch shepherded the manuscript through the production process, and Pat Sterling provided a deft hand at copyediting.

Finally, this book is dedicated to my mother—who kept asking me when I was ever going to finish this darn thing—and the memory of my father—who first nurtured my desire to learn about history and so many other things in the world.

UNEASY ALLIES

INTRODUCTION

I

FROM THE early 1830s until the end of the nineteenth century, more than a dozen labor reform organizations emerged and later disappeared in the streets, halls, and tenements of Boston.[1] These groups brought together men and women from widely divergent economic and educational backgrounds—including ministers, "millgirls," and machinists—to campaign for better working conditions and dignity for all who labored. This book is the first study to analyze comprehensively how these workers and reformers struggled to build cross-class labor reform alliances in a nineteenth-century American city. In particular, this monograph pursues fundamental historical questions about the impact of class, gender, and ethnicity on the ideological arguments and institutional structures and strategies of this reform impulse as it evolved throughout the nineteenth century. What motivated working-class activists and middle-class reformers to join together and create cross-class organizations devoted to the cause of labor reform? What internal debates and external pressures caused these groups to break down (even as new alliances formed); and how did these forces change over the course of the nineteenth century? What did workers and reformers learn about building coalitions, exercising political power, and struggling for social change within these complex and volatile alliances; and can those lessons still speak to activists and reformers today?

American historians have been studying nineteenth-century labor reform organizations ever since the nineteenth century; but they have never developed a comprehensive analytical framework for understanding these groups, nor have they rigorously traced their evolution over the entire century. Pioneers in the field of American labor history placed cross-class labor reform organizations in the context of much broader institutional studies of trade union development. These "old" labor historians emphasized conflict between pragmatic union leaders and utopian reformers who distracted organized labor from basic workplace issues—wages, hours, collective bargaining rights—with unrealistic radical schemes.

The "new" labor history broke down the old dichotomy of workers versus reformers and argued for a more nuanced understanding of these complex cross-class labor reform coalitions. More recent studies were often narrower in their chronological scope but far more encompassing in their analysis of both the tensions and the cooperative bonds between working-class activists and middle-class reformers. These historians clearly demonstrated that the static bipolar model of practical workers and idealistic reformers does not apply to nineteenth-century labor reform groups in which men and women often shared organizational leadership, pragmatic goals, and visionary ideals. But these new explanatory frameworks still did not provide a coherent chronological scheme for tracing historical development throughout the nineteenth century or offer a rigorous analysis of the campaign's evolving structures and strategies.

This book, by tracing cross-class labor reform organizations in Boston from the 1830s to 1900, provides just such a chronological account across much of the nineteenth century and explains organizational changes over time. What emerges from this investigation is a narrative of both progress and declension that spans nearly three-quarters of a century. The backdrop to this story is the ebb and flow of struggle year upon year to assemble and hold together cross-class alliances. Labor reform organizations existed in a continual state of formation, disintegration, and reconstitution decade after decade. Individual activists and reformers reappeared constantly in an ever shifting constellation of leagues and associations. Endlessly debating the very meaning of labor reform and the best strategy to secure justice for workers, wrestling with questions of religious influence and labor protest, facing constant external political opposition and economic constraints, and searching for a place to call home, these coalitions endured enormous ongoing strain.

This continual organizational struggle, however, was not entirely inchoate. As the nineteenth century progressed, both workers and reformers searched for strategies that would give more political and moral leverage to the labor reform crusade. They argued about focusing on the workplace itself and the hours of labor, on direct action more than just debate, on legislative lobbying, and on the city of Boston and its poorest neighborhoods. But such ideological consistency and clarity, and organizational coherence and continuity, were not easily achieved—and, once secured, often came with unintended costs and limitations.

To be specific, this study reveals that the labor reform campaign in nineteenth-century Boston had two phases: one from its origins in the early

1830s through the 1870s, and the second beginning in the 1870s and extending to the end of the century. The earliest cross-class labor reform organizations often built broad coalitions based on wide-open meetings and generous platforms with a resolution for virtually every reformer and activist in the audience. Yet out of this seeming cacophony of competing schemes for labor reform emerged one issue that commanded increasing attention—the hours of labor. Starting with those first alliances in the 1830s and 1840s, and becoming stronger in the 1850s and 1860s, the demand for a shorter workday became the pivot point for much labor reform activism in Boston. Whether it was the ten-hour day, especially for factory workers, or the growing insistence on an eight-hour day for all labor, the shorter workday was seen not as a simple end in itself but as the crucial first step on the road to broad social transformation. Beginning in the 1870s and continuing to the century's end, Boston's eight-hour movement was intersected frequently by other labor reform ideas and organizations. Eight-hour leagues now had to compete for public and political support with labor churches, settlement houses, consumer leagues, and even unemployment marches. Many labor reform groups chose to look beyond a near-exclusive focus on the eight-hour day; to construct alliances that would address other workplace problems (such as tenement house manufacturing, or shop conditions for employees in retail stores); and to seek carefully crafted solutions.

Why did Boston's labor reform campaign start to shift, around the 1870s, away from its main focus on the hours of labor and toward a more complex, variegated world of labor reform organizations? Part of the answer probably lies in two events: in 1874, the Massachusetts legislature finally passed a ten-hour law for factory workers; and in 1880, Ira Steward—the leading theorist and tactician for the eight-hour day in Boston—left the city as a broken man over the death of his wife Mary. Steward's departure, in particular, robbed the labor reform community of its most passionate (some might say monomaniacal) advocate for the primacy of the shorter workday. Without Steward's constant goading to place the eight-hour day front and center in all labor reform activities, the doors opened to alternative alliances and strategies. Moreover, Gilded Age Boston was filled with many such crosscurrents of social change—Christian Socialists confronting mass labor protest; the growing population of Catholic and Jewish immigrants from southern and eastern Europe living and working in cramped, airless tenements—all of whom clamored for labor reformers and activists to craft new coalitions and new remedies. To be sure, the demand for the eight-hour day continued to be heard across the city, but other pressing needs also insisted on their place in the public forum.

Even as the world of labor reform in post Civil War Boston became more complex and variegated, some of the emerging organizations individually became narrower in their membership, leadership, and social vision. New associations pushed labor reformers and activists in new directions and into unfamiliar neighborhoods, yet these groups could also have more limited goals and more structured organizational hierarchies than the eight-hour leagues that had previously dominated the conversation. By the end of the century, middle-class (mostly Protestant) reformers often grew more distant from a laboring class increasingly populated by Catholic and Jewish immigrants. Labor reform, for these men and women of some means, became more an effort to solve particular problems associated with the urban poor than a process of building cross-class alliances around a shared vision of social justice.

The growing variety and specialization of later nineteenth-century labor reform groups offered both benefits and costs, especially for those workers committed to this campaign. The earlier emphasis on actively recruiting workers across a spectrum of skill and status, and having those workers share leadership roles with reformers, eventually often yielded to a growing reliance on middle-class expertise and economic leverage channeled down the organizational hierarchy to workers below (frequently recent immigrants). Thus, workers may have gained improvements at particular worksites, such as tenements and mercantile stores, but they often lost the opportunity to continue sharing in the leadership of a broader cross-class labor reform agenda. Reformers, for their part, increasingly came to see labor more as an object of social engineering than as a partner in a struggle for social change.

With the book's chronological structure and arguments sketched out, several definitions and explanations are in order here. The terms *worker* (or working-class activist, or activist) and *reformer* (or middle-class reformer) are used throughout this book. Needless to say, these terms refer to specific men and women who joined organizations and shared goals; they are not archetypes or representatives of entire classes. For example, not all workers were activists, but workers who joined labor reform groups did make a commitment to activism in that cause. Moreover, to make the use of such terminology even more challenging, determining who was working-class or middle-class in nineteenth-century Boston was never an exact science. Economic status could be quite fluid and volatile during decades of dramatic booms and busts. Men and women might shift occupations and lose or gain significant amounts of property; others might move from job to job and never see any real material change in their standard of living. Several working-class activists in Boston, for example, eventually left their manual trades and sought jobs in emerging state agencies or the federal customs house. They did not move upward significantly in their income or wealth; but they hoped to use their modest political connections to find a "white-collar" occupation that would give them more time to devote to the labor reform struggle—which included the campaign for a shorter workday for all who labored! Furthermore, class—and the perceptions of class—was more than just a measure of wages and wealth. A man or woman's family background and education could contribute to his or her class position; so might a person's race, ethnicity, and religion. Martin Burke cautions scholars to remember that "class has [always] been a mobile and unstable social category." There has never "been a single true meaning of the concept of 'class' in the nation's public discourse; there was always diversity and disagreement." In the end, historians should "recognize," though they probably will "not resolve, the conundrum of class in American culture."[2]

With all these caveats in mind, and making no claim that my definitions offer any resolution to this centuries-old conundrum, I use the term *worker* (or working-class activist or activist) to refer to men and women in manual occupations—such as mill operatives, seamstresses, machinists, or carpenters. And the term *reformer* (or middle-class reformer) refers to men and women usually with a higher level of education (often college or divinity school) in professional positions—such as ministers, teachers, lawyers, or physicians. It is also important to note that most labor reformers in nineteenth-century Boston did not come from the city's economic, political, or cultural elite—the so-called Boston "Brahmins." Rather, most labor reformers were part of an emerging urban professional class, and some were newcomers to the city without long-established family ties to the wealthier circles of charitable work.

"Worker" and "reformer" are not always correlated to measures of income or wealth, but the terms do echo nineteenth-century distinctions between manual and "mental" labor. For example, in the nineteenth century (and even sometimes today) a machinist might earn more money than a teacher. But, across the century, those professions that relied increasingly on higher education (and less on physical exertion) also became recognized as middle-class jobs. Cross-class alliances usually acknowledged the existence of such distinctions in education and status, even as they made a conscious effort not to ascribe prestige or power to any one job but to bring together men and women from divergent backgrounds who would all participate in a shared struggle for social justice. These labels were not, and are not, precise markers; but they remain useful for highlighting the diversity of occupations encompassed in the labor reform groups of nineteenth-century Boston.[3]

One other term that needs to be clarified is cross-class labor reform organizations. This study analyzes more than a dozen groups in nineteenth-century Boston which brought workers and reformers together to campaign for improved working conditions and dignity for labor. Some of the organizations selected, such as the Massachusetts Bureau of the Statistics of Labor (BSL), may not seem at first glance to fit the definition. But a close inspection of each institution reveals that every one of them did draw on both workers and reformers to press their case for labor reform, even as each one had its own particular take on *how* to reform the conditions and circumstances of labor in Boston. Each of these associations also left behind some record of its reform activities, though some of these materials reveal increasingly feeble attempts to recruit working-class members. (And increasingly restricted membership, especially in the 1890s, supports the arguments at the conclusion of this book.) Meanwhile, some likely prospects for inclusion in this investigation—such as the city's Central Labor Union or the District Assembly of the Knights of Labor—rarely appear in these pages. Either those organizations did not make a sustained effort to recruit middle-class reformers, or, in the Knights' case, their district records are little more than technical accounts of jurisdictional disputes with little to say about larger issues of labor reform.

Another basic question: why focus on Boston? To be sure, Boston did not experience the same explosive growth as New York City or Chicago in the nineteenth century. Yet Boston was certainly not immune to the pressures and challenges facing most American cities: a large influx of immigrants from Europe and Canada, growing exploitation of labor in sweatshops, increasingly crowded tenements in neighborhoods without adequate sanitation or utilities. Thus, although this study makes no claim that Boston should stand as the prototypical nineteenth-century American city (what city can?), it is not anomalous, so its experiences with a plethora of cross-class labor reform organizations over nearly seventy years can offer some lessons about coalition-building in the struggle for social change.

I focus on Boston also because that city was so vibrant a center for labor reform organizations throughout the nineteenth century. Why was it such a magnet for activists and reformers interested in labor's cause? Why did some men and women move to Boston to join other long-term residents in this struggle, or at least visit regularly to take part in conventions and rallies? Part of the answer to these questions lies in the community's long history of enthusiasm for all kinds of reform schemes. Boston's distinctive reform tradition was rooted in Puritan ideals of social responsibility, Enlightenment concepts of human reason, and more recent Unitarian beliefs in the possibility of progress and improvement. By the time the first cross-class labor reform organization emerged in the early 1830s, Boston was already home to a slew of societies devoted to the reform of prisons, asylums, and schools, as well as to the elimination of drunkenness and war. Perhaps it is no coincidence that

William Lloyd Garrison began to publish *The Liberator* just a few months before and a few blocks away from the hotel where Boston's first cross-class labor reform organization was born. Demands for social change were in the air, and Bostonians continued to imbibe this rarified atmosphere throughout the nineteenth century, as the city built a reputation for cultural and educational innovation, new technology, and even what might be called alternative lifestyles. Labor reform organizations and ideologies continually sprouted in such an environment of intellectual questioning and experimentation—though such fertile soil certainly did not ensure long-term stability, as many groups also quickly withered and disappeared. Nor did Boston's reputation for reform guarantee success in the political arena, where legislators often looked askance at what they considered outlandish or dangerous forms of social protest.

II

The early historians of labor reform often participated in the campaigns they chronicled. They filled their accounts with firsthand information and detail, but they also wrote to defend their positions in complex internal debates over leadership and political tactics. Thus, these early studies have a richness and immediacy, but they also tend to be polemical rather than analytical. Trying to make sense of cross-class organizations that were often unstable, early chroniclers looked for someone to blame when groups failed to thrive. Many early historical narratives eventually concluded that reformers were the villains, the source of so many unrealistic dreams and disappointments.

In 1886 the Knights of Labor reached the pinnacle of their strength; the American Federation of Labor was established; and a series of strikes for the eight-hour workday swept the nation. That same year Richard Ely published what scholars regard as the first academic treatment of American labor history: *The Labor Movement in America*. Ely—then an assistant professor of political economy at Johns Hopkins University—searched for the American labor movement's roots in the decades preceding the Civil War, and in his quest he brought renewed attention to some of the earliest cross-class labor reform groups in antebellum Boston. Though Ely rescued these organizations from obscurity, he also mischaracterized them as primitive forms of trade unions: a problematic label that other subsequent scholars would also adopt.[4]

One year after Ely published his pathbreaking work, George McNeill provided detailed documentation on many labor reform groups in his edited collection *The Labor Movement: The Problem of Today*. McNeill played a key role in Boston's postwar labor reform community. He served as an officer in cross-class organizations such as the Boston Eight Hour League, and the Church of the Carpenter. His book assembled convention proceedings and proclamations from many groups that he helped to lead, as well as material on earlier antebellum organizations. Today, McNeill's book still stands as an important resource on the man himself (he left behind no personal papers) and the campaigns he devoted so much of his life to. Yet readers must also approach this compendium with caution, because the book is a product of the very cross-class political and organizational struggles that it recorded and McNeill's desire to tell an optimistic story of triumph against long odds. Thus, the collection often obscures conflicts within coalitions so as to paint a deceptive image of near-continuous harmony in the campaign for labor reform.[5]

Friedrich Sorge, following Ely and McNeill, included cross-class labor reform activism in his more comprehensive history, *Labor Movement in the United States,* originally published as a series of newspaper articles from 1891 to 1895. Sorge too wrote both as a student of labor history and as an activist involved intimately in shaping that history, forging his book in the cauldron of late nineteenth-century ideological conflict. But Sorge also did something different: his work offered a clearer chronological framework then either Ely or McNeill's compendious volumes, and he placed organizational and ideological disputes at the center of his analysis.

Sorge discussed, more than McNeill, the complexities and tensions within postwar cross-class labor reform organizations. He pointedly criticized middle-class labor reformers, labeling them as interlopers meddling in workers' affairs. Sorge was the first historian to draw this sharp distinction between working-class activists and middle-class reformers within labor reform groups, and to blame reformers for distracting workers from organizing and agitating for both better working conditions and more radical social change. Twentieth-century labor historians often reiterated this stark contrast between workers and reformers. But Sorge saw middle-class reformers as often timid and unfocused in their commitment to radicalism—in effect, not passionate enough to stir the workers' latent revolutionary spirit. Later historians would condemn these reformers for the opposite reason—being too radical in their utopian schemes.[6]

Charles Persons was the first twentieth-century scholar to examine cross-class labor reform groups in nineteenth-century Boston. In his 1911 study "The Early History of Factory Legislation in Massachusetts from 1825 to the Passage of the Ten Hour Law in 1874," writing a generation removed from the struggles of the nineteenth century, Persons was a more detached observer of these debates in the labor reform community. His extended article provided a detailed account of the political agitation surrounding proposed legislation for the ten-hour and eight-hour workdays in nineteenth-century Massachusetts. He also drew a sharp distinction between working-class activists and middle-class reformers, especially in his discussion of the New England Workingmen's Association (NEWA) in the 1840s. Persons saw cross-class organizations, particularly the NEWA, as contested terrain where workers and reformers constantly fought for control of the agenda. Each meeting brought a continually shifting set of leaders and priorities as the association ricocheted from faction to faction. Thus, Persons echoed Sorge's model of antagonism between workers and reformers. Persons, however, portrayed workers as pragmatic proto-unionists interested mainly in bread-and-butter issues, such as shorter hours, and with little enthusiasm for revolutionary ideas. Persons then blamed the ethereal utopian reformers for diverting these practical workers from their sensible goals.[7]

In 1914, Frank Carlton's "Ephemeral Labor Movements, 1866–1889," injected a modicum of analytical subtlety into the discussion of cross-class labor reform organizing. Carlton—a student of John R. Commons at the University of Wisconsin and later a professor at DePauw University—characterized various labor reform organizations as "unstable" and "undisciplined"; but he did not ascribe all problems to inherent class antagonisms within the groups. He noted that these organizations had their own political strategies for pursuing labor reform and that these alliances did not always divide into hostile camps of workers versus reformers. Carlton's argument for a more balanced appraisal of both the tensions and the opportunities for cooperation embedded in postwar labor reform groups lay buried in this brief and little-read article. A half-century would pass before scholars would again seriously consider his ideas as a useful conceptual framework for understanding cross-class labor reform organizations.[8]

Most contemporary historians ignored Carlton's essay because in 1918 his mentor John R. Commons and a group of Commons's students published the first two volumes of *The History of Labour in the United States*. This massive encyclopedic work's great strength lay in its descriptive presentation of information about a welter of labor reform groups, rather than a careful explication of how those organizations changed over time. Here again, cross-class labor reform organizations became just more entries in a sweeping compendium of all organized labor. When Commons and his students tried to analyze the historical record of labor reform, their strict economic and trade union models of workers' behavior, their stringent dichotomy between workers and reformers, and their patrician perspective prevented them from exploring the intriguing organizational complexities and subtleties that Carlton had alluded to just a few years earlier.

Commons and his students' discussion of labor reform, much like Persons's, centered on the struggle between radical utopians and pragmatic trade unionists for political and organizational control of cross-class alliances. Workers again appeared to have an interest in only basic questions of wages, hours, working conditions, and union organizing, whereas the Commons school condemned reformers for their radical schemes to pursue broader social and political change. The authors usually dismissed any worker's or reformer's demand that transcended narrow class interests as a panacea or a utopian dream. When reformers (or intellectuals, as Commons often labeled them) steered workers toward cross-class alliances and away from trade unions, Commons concluded that the results were frequently disastrous for labor. Himself an intellectual and reformer, he may have been particularly hard on his nineteenth-century predecessors because they did not follow his own professional stance as advisor and consultant to organized labor. What many earlier reformers would have seen as a great strength—their openness to sharing authority with workers in a common struggle for social change—Commons took to be unrealistic dreaming and scheming that filled workers' heads with unattainable notions of radical social transformation. *The History of Labour in the United States* became an enormously influential work, and made the sharp distinction between idealistic radical reformers and pragmatic moderate workers the dominant model for several generations of twentieth-century historians studying nineteenth-century labor reform.[9]

Norman Ware's *The Industrial Worker, 1840–1860* (published in 1924) was the first post-Commons study of labor reform. Ware's concise book presented the starkest portrait yet of alliances torn asunder by the antagonism between workers and reformers. He characterized the reform campaigns of the 1840s as conservative and defensive; Associationists (American followers of the French utopian socialist Charles Fourier) and land reformers wanted to return to some mythic lost past. In his introduction, Ware decried the way reformers distanced themselves from the realities of working-class life. Ware's accusation had some merit, yet he was extremely harsh in his conclusions. "Too often these self-constituted exponents had little appreciation of the necessities and compulsions of the poor themselves. It was this economic transcendentalism of the reformers, their denial of the necessity of the industrial revolution that made them blind leaders of the blind. The workers, of necessity, were realists. For them there was no withdrawal into any inner sanctuary, Phalanx, Republican Township, or what not." Ware went on to urge that "care must be exercised in distinguishing between the authentic voice of the worker and that of his advocate and advisor." Ware criticized Commons—who always claimed that he did recognize the distinction between labor leaders and intellectual advisors—for assuming that cross-class labor groups were at the center of working-class agitation in the 1840s and 1850s, and that middle-class reformers often spoke for workers.

Ware, like Persons, argued that key antebellum labor reform organizations—such as the NEWA—and the growing ten-hour movement were inherently unstable alliances where urban artisans, factory operatives, and reformers constantly fought for control. Ware believed that these competing groups pulled apart the labor reform effort in antebellum Boston because, once again, reformers' utopian schemes deflected workers' efforts to confront the industrial order on its own terms.

Ware's conclusions reinforced the Commons school's arguments for the historical superiority of trade union demands over reformist ideals, even as Ware criticized some of Commons's specific observations about the antebellum labor movement. Ware's praise for early unions and criticism of reformers, however, was not simply a restatement of Commons's pragmatist-idealist dichotomy. Ware argued that the reformers failed not because they were radical, as Commons would have it, nor because they were timid, as Sorge labeled them, because they were too intellectual and theoretical; they looked down on workers and knew nothing about the daily struggles of working-class life; and they promoted their own pet projects rather than tapping into the working class's latent economic and political power. Ware believed that reformers diverted workers from organizations and strategies that offered a chance not only for basic workplace gains such as shorter hours and better wages but also for a more fundamental transformation of industrial capitalism itself. Thus Ware, like Sorge, saw great possibilities in workers' organizing themselves at the point of production to challenge the power of capital; the antebellum working class had the potential to achieve *both* immediate improvements in working conditions *and* a long-term vision for social change—a portrait of working women and men that many nineteenth-century reformers and activists could have also embraced.[10]

III

Four decades after Ware published his revision of the Commons model, "new" labor historians started to criticize those earlier scholars who placed the institutional development of trade unions at the center of labor history, and privileged bread-and-butter demands for shorter hours and higher wages over all other alternatives for social change. Influenced by radical British historians, especially E. P. Thompson and Eric Hobsbawm, these historians developed broader and more nuanced readings of working-class culture, communities, and politics. One element of their "new" labor history was a renewed appreciation for nineteenth-century cross-class labor reform organizations.

In 1967, David Montgomery's massive exploration of labor in the Reconstruction Era—*Beyond Equality: Labor and the Radical Republicans, 1862–1872*—directly confronted the old dichotomy that classified "types of labor leaders into wage-conscious trade unionists and antimonopoly reformers" and "obscured . . . the ideological affinity between the then-prominent trade unionists and the Radicals." Montgomery's work presented the richest and most complex portrait of cross-class labor reform ever published up to that date, although it focused on only one decade in the nineteenth century. Picking up a line of reasoning from Carlton's nearly forgotten article of more than half a century earlier, Montgomery refused to pigeonhole workers and reformers into rigidly antagonistic camps. Drawing on his own background as both an active trade unionist and a committed social radical, Montgomery recognized both the opportunities for cooperation and the tensions that developed in postbellum labor reform groups. Like Ware, he saw in workers the desire to change conditions on the job and to reshape the broader social structure, but Montgomery argued that many middle-class labor reformers also shared this dual vision for both immediate improvements and long term transformations. He insisted that both workers and reformers could be both pragmatic and idealistic, and could strive to create a unified labor reform agenda within cross-class alliances.[11]

Montgomery never denied that there could also be sharp disagreements between middle-class reformers and working-class activists, especially over specific questions of strategy and tactics. But the old labor history's false dichotomy between pragmatic unionists and utopian reformers obscured crucial commonalities as workers and their allies all searched for alternatives to industrial capitalism. The labor reform campaign was a place where class conflict and attempts at cross-class cooperation were in a dialectical relationship with each other.

Within the complex personal, political, ideological, and organizational interactions of labor reform groups, Montgomery saw fascinating case studies of ideas cutting across class lines even as they were often reshaped in the process.

> To look for—or to look at—labor leaders through blinders imposed by a preconception of "pure and simple trade unionism" distorts our understanding of these men. Tribunes of the working classes employed several forums and did not necessarily "desert their class" when they moved into legislative halls. . . . The fact that active trade unionists pursued their organizational goals in a social setting that brought them into constant contact

with politicians or other reformers, of both working-class and middle-class origins, and that these men were both locally eminent and friendly to the cause of labor reform meant that the latter became educators of the rising trade unionist.... The most active workingmen readily became the most thoroughly indoctrinated with the outlook of middle-class reformers. The labor-reform movement itself became an institutional funnel for the transmission of Radical ideas to the working classes.

As ideas and tactics flowed between workers and reformers, cross-class labor reform organizations constantly emerged, disintegrated, and coalesced again to continue the struggle for social change. Montgomery's emphasis on this rich, complex, and ever shifting world of labor reform broke the back of the earlier models based solely on simplistic views of class antagonism.[12]

Montgomery's work reconceptualized the history of labor reform in the era of Reconstruction. Nearly a quarter of a century later, Carl Guarneri's *The Utopian Alternative: Fourierism in Nineteenth-Century America* (1991) directed scholarly attention back to the world of antebellum labor reform. Guarneri's book laid to rest, once and for all, the old labor history's sharp dichotomy between workers and reformers battling for control of labor reform efforts in the 1840s. In this first modern treatment of the entire Fourierist utopian movement in America, the chapter "Campaigns with Labor" stands out as the most comprehensive recent discussion of key antebellum labor reform organizations and their legacy to the post Civil War labor reform effort in Boston. Guarneri's book offered a compelling portrait of emerging labor reformers and activists who were creative thinkers, and anxious to transcend narrow assumptions about class and politics. Guarneri demonstrated convincingly that workers could be as visionary as reformers, and reformers could be as hard-nosed as workers.

> Labor reformers ... often found a ready hearing as "friends" of workingmen. More important, many Associationists ... were themselves working class in origin. Some of these, far from being diverted from labor agitation by utopian socialism, brought Associationist ideas into the labor movement.... Workers of the period were not uniformly or solely interested in bread-and-butter issues.... Many workers favored pragmatic labor measures but also listened readily to general reform schemes that put their plight in larger perspective and promised long-range benefits.... Especially when strikes and legislation failed to improve conditions workers turned naturally to self-help schemes and social reform....
>
> It is a mistake to judge the labor movement of the 1840s by either the militant standards of Marxism or the expectations of conventional trade unionism. What has been viewed as an anachronistic, unfortunate decade

of agitation was in fact a creative period of labor organization when, at the onset of industrial capitalism, intriguing alternatives to "wage slavery" were promoted in a broad agitation that gathered workers and reformers in productive alliances.... While they sometimes argued over strategy, they shared enough ideas, interests, and goals to cooperate in campaigns to consolidate worker resistance.[13]

In conjunction with Guarneri's monograph, Teresa Murphy's *Ten Hours' Labor: Religion, Reform, and Gender in Early New England* (1992) also shed important new light on early labor reform groups, and placed these organizations in the context of a rich and subtle argument about the impact of religion, gender, and moral reform on working-class activism in antebellum New England. Murphy complicated concepts of cross-class labor reform by arguing that workers used middle-class moral reform strategies even as they challenged middle-class reformers' control of these ideas. Murphy saw the NEWA as encouraging not only the cross-class alliances that Guarneri delineated but also the cross-gender organizational dynamics embodied in the legislative petition campaign for a ten-hour workday. This crusade drew women into labor reform efforts as they testified to the Massachusetts legislature, led signature drives, and moved into the NEWA's leadership ranks.[14]

In more than a decade and a half since the publication of Guarneri's and Murphy's books, other scholars have also contributed to a more nuanced understanding of cross-class labor reform organizations in nineteenth-century Boston. For example, Bruce Laurie's recent study of antislavery and social reform in antebellum Massachusetts included a chapter with an extensive discussion of the politics surrounding the ten-hour movement in the 1840s and 1850s. Sarah Deutsch's monograph on women's political power and gendered space in Boston across the end of the nineteenth century (and into the twentieth) shed important new light on the cross-class labor agitation in the city's settlement houses. These books continued to limn a portrait of an ongoing labor reform campaign that tried to bridge class divides and evolved with the city's shifting economic and political climate. Yet most of these studies are relatively limited in chronological scope, so the processes by which the Boston labor reform community evolved across nearly three-quarters of the nineteenth century still remains to be explicated fully and rigorously in one coherent account.[15]

IV

The historiography of cross-class labor reform in nineteenth-century Boston is both exceedingly rich in its lineage and yet often curiously attenuated in its analysis. More than forty years ago, Montgomery demolished the model of an overwhelming, inherent conflict between practical workers and utopian reformers. He painted a more complex portrait of cross-class labor reform organizations in the Reconstruction era, shaped by crosscurrents of both cooperation and tension between workers and reformers who were themselves complex individuals. Subsequent historians applied this more nuanced understanding of labor reform to organizations in the antebellum period and at the end of the nineteenth century. Yet no scholar has put all these isolated historical epochs together and traced the process of organizational evolution across the century's span to see how this intricate amalgam of alliances and divisions changed as the urban-industrial economy grew and transformed. By both narrowing the geographic focus to one city and expanding the chronological coverage across the century, this study strives to paint a more complete historical portrait of nineteenth-century labor reform organizations' shifting membership, leadership, organizational structure, tactics, and goals as these groups labored decade after decade to hold coalitions together and press forward with the campaign for social justice at the workplace and beyond. In tracking that struggle to build stable cross-class alliances for labor reform across nineteenth-century Boston, what emerges is an even more complex campaign than previous scholars have depicted, one that was constantly mutating in its efforts to establish effective organizations for public activism.

This book focuses on those men and women who not only talked and wrote about labor reform but also rolled up their sleeves and joined hands in cross-class alliances to agitate publicly and politically for social change. Labor reformers did more than reach out to individuals living in poverty; they often shared leadership roles and decision-making power with workers. Working-class activists, for their part, also often embraced the notion of creating genuine cross-class organizations where authority was held equally and "horizontally" between men and women of varying social backgrounds. Cross-class labor reform groups built bridges across boundaries of occupation, skill, education, status, and gender—fragile though these bridges sometimes were—and searched constantly for political and economic solutions to stop the exploitation of labor in the rapidly changing urban economy. In a society where definitions of class were often debated yet were also becoming more sharply delineated, these coalitions cut across not only differences in wealth and income but also the perceived gap between manual and "mental" labor. Given this diverse constituency, these groups—such as ten-hour conventions, eight-hour leagues, labor reform associations, and even some churches and settlement houses—are excellent "laboratories" for studying potential strengths and limitations of cross-class, cross-gender, and (sometimes) cross-ethnic coalitions in the midst of a developing industrial economy.

Though these organizations did not make any effort to work with people of color—whether by a deliberate practice of exclusion or as a matter of indifference—Boston's labor reform community certainly swirled with the rhetoric of race, slavery, and abolition. Especially in the decades leading up to, during, and immediately following the Civil War, labor reformers and activists often supported antislavery campaigns and welcomed former abolitionists (such as Wendell Phillips) into their ranks. Advocates for the shorter workday, and other labor reform campaigns, frequently couched their struggle in terms of a fight against the specter of slavery and for the abolition of exploitive economic institutions. Labor reform lay at the heart of a transformed—some might say genuinely reconstructed—society where all workers were to be treated fairly and justly.

Cross-class labor reform organizations filled a particular niche in the ecology of social change, distinct from working-class entities—such as mechanics' societies, trade unions, and workingmen's parties—and from charitable institutions such as employment exchanges and industrial schools. Reformers and activists wanted to advocate social change more than provide social services; they believed they could solve the injustices of modern industrial life rather than just treat symptoms of economic dislocation. Workers and reformers insisted that genuine social justice lay in questioning the prevailing economic system, finding the root causes of chronic problems such as unemployment, and reorganizing society so that everyone shared in the labor to be done and the rewards to be gained. Creating such an equitable society would do more to improve workers' lives than all the partial, ameliorative efforts of the city's many philanthropic agencies. Labor reformers also thought it was far more important to improve working conditions than to regulate workers' personal behavior and mores. Men and women who made fair wages and worked reasonable hours would usually see to their own moral improvement and advancement.

Thus, labor reformers *and* activists in nineteenth-century Boston often embraced both basic demands for better working conditions *and* broader ideals for social change to improve workers' status, even if they did not always agree on specific strategies and priorities for accomplishing the goals they might agree upon. Moreover, the very definition of what was labor reform could expand or contract, depending on which individual or organization was defining the concept. For example, some antebellum labor reform organizations stated their goals in broad, sweeping terms that might encompass land reform schemes and even communitarian socialism. But labor reform should not be defined, as some previous scholars have done, as merely any reform (such as temperance, abolition, woman suffrage) that attracted some workers' attention even when it did not try to alleviate problems at the workplace or elevate the status of working people. The challenge for this study is neither to lose sight of labor reform's larger vision (which, in some organizations, narrowed by century's end) nor to stretch the definition over so many issues that it loses any historical comprehensibility or analytical coherence. The focus should remain on how workers and reformers defined the term in the context of their shared struggles. These alliances strove, though not always successfully, to craft labor reform agendas in a dialogue across class lines. Labor reform was not supposed to be designed merely by middle-class sympathizers and imposed on workers.[16]

Furthermore, although labor reform groups were often interested in many of the same issues as trade unions—higher wages, shorter working hours, safer workplaces, fewer child laborers—labor reform should not be defined as a subset of organized labor in general. Over the course of the nineteenth century, unions increasingly used strikes to gain contractual guarantees for their members, but many labor reform organizations continued to believe that every worker's right to a reasonable workday and a safe workplace could be secured through public education and political agitation leading to legislative regulation. These reformers and activists wanted to bring the state (and they often literally meant the state of Massachusetts) into the world of work as an arbiter and enforcer of fair play and equity.

Thus, across much of the nineteenth century, no yawning chasm opened between workers and reformers in Boston on questions of social change and justice for labor. Workers believed that by helping themselves they were working toward changing society; and reformers believed that by helping workers (who might not be able to secure their rights entirely on their own) they were also building a better community. But it is also true that tensions often developed over particular tactics for labor reform—including key questions about political activism and public protest. Cross-class organizations often broke apart because they reproduced—within their meetings and their campaigns—some of the very class divisions between activists and reformers that they hoped to transcend. The parties involved could not be labeled merely as pragmatic workers and middle-class utopians, however, nor as radical workers and moderate reformers. Shared ideals and interests often brought arguing factions and disparate individuals back together in new coalitions to try yet again, decade after decade, to press onward with the campaign for labor reform.

The process of constantly building alliances across class lines was both a means and an end for labor reformers and activists—creating networks necessary for public agitation, and giving the public a glimpse of what a cooperative society might look like. These cross-class organizations premised their existence on the idea that class lines were not always hardened or insurmountable, even as workers and reformers often struggled to overcome such obstacles.

The quest for new alliances and alternatives often had an experimental quality, rather than a sharply delineated pattern of institutional and ideological change. Reformers and activists groped for successful strategies and felt their way toward possible solutions to the labor problem—trying to find just the right mixture of just the right people with just the right message to secure justice for workers. Thus, shifts in arguments, organizational structures, and political behavior were not always dramatic; old forms of labor reform activism sometimes intertwined with the new. Moreover, the labor reform effort as it evolved through the nineteenth century was certainly not victorious in all its new endeavors. And even its accomplishments sometimes came at the expense of individuals' commitment to the cause and of the internal cohesion of cross-class alliances. By the end of the century, the horizontal structure of many labor reform groups—where leadership was often shared across class lines—was yielding to more vertical, top-down organizations where professional experts claimed the authority to speak for labor's best interests.

V

This book's organizational structure reflects the Boston labor reform community's transformations across the nineteenth century; and the two phases of that historical change. Part I (chapters 1 through 4) is essentially a chronological account of the campaign from the early 1830s through the 1870s. This was the period when the struggle for the ten-hour workday, and then the eight-hour day, emerged as the dominant issue for labor reformers and activists working to define the central goals for their endeavor. Part II (chapters 5 through 7) focuses on the final three decades of the nineteenth century from a series of topical perspectives. The expanding universe of potential labor reform groups in this period, often with overlapping chronologies, makes a more selective thematic approach necessary for analytical clarity and coherence. In these decades, Boston labor reformers and activists increasingly displaced the eight-hour day as the unchallenged center of the labor reform campaign, created alternative institutions (such as labor churches and settlement houses), and moved toward more hierarchical organizational structures that often excluded recent immigrants.

Chapter 1 examines the first cross-class labor reform organizations that emerged in the 1830s and 1840s. These early associations laid some of the organizational and ideological foundations of a cross-class effort that would struggle yet endure for nearly three-quarters of a century. These groups championed both the immediate issue of working hours and broader ideas such as land reform and utopian socialism. They also endorsed political action for legislation but showed little interest in recreating a workingmen's party that would exclude working women. These pioneering cross-class, cross-gender coalitions often had ambitious ideals yet few accomplishments. Frustrated workers and reformers tended to blame each other for failing to enact an agenda they supposedly shared. The devil was in the details of organizational activism—which reform should be pursued first? Workers often said that improving conditions on the shop floor was the first step toward sweeping social change; reformers countered that bold structural changes would necessarily *include* better working conditions. Nascent class conflict disrupted coalitions trying to bridge growing gaps in education and wealth. Yet the early cross-class labor reform community emerged from these years of shared struggle—sometimes within their own coalitions—to fight new battles in the midst of sectional crisis and civil war.

Chapter 2 explores exactly how the labor reform cause survived and evolved through nearly two decades of sectional conflict and war. During this period, workers and reformers experimented with producer cooperatives, and reoriented the ten-hour movement's political strategy from legislative petitioning to the endorsing of specific candidates. The campaign for the shorter workday was now based on a more precisely defined legislative proposal and on new arguments connecting shorter hours, higher wages, and economic expansion. At the height of the war, workers and reformers began to articulate the first sustained demand for the eight-hour workday (a central tenet of labor activism for another three-quarters of a century). This new campaign linked eight hours with a rising standard of living and the imperative for bold social change at the very moment when slavery was destroyed, the Union restored, and the nation setting its course for a postwar future where the rights of free labor had to be defined and enshrined.

Chapter 3 analyzes labor reform agitation in the years immediately following the Civil War. Reformers and activists saw Reconstruction itself as something more than legal reunification; Reconstruction had to encompass a restructuring of the nation's economy and work relations. A new generation of leaders made the eight-hour day the centerpiece of the postwar labor reform campaign. Legislators scrambled to respond somehow to this growing demand for legal regulation of the workday, without necessarily passing any such law. A series of committees and commissions held hearings and issued reports in the late 1860s, and workers and reformers plunged deeper than ever into the political process. Ira Steward emerged as the leading thinker and organizer of this postwar effort. His consumption-based arguments for the shorter workday reinforced the idea that fewer hours on the job was the crucial first step on the road to far-reaching social change. Steward also insisted that an unwavering focus on securing the eight hour day was the glue that would hold cross-class labor reform coalitions together. Yet despite Steward's ceaseless efforts, no eight-hour law passed in the 1860s; activists and reformers had to look beyond the legislative process for new organizations and strategies. One option was to build a labor reform headquarters that would serve as a central location for ongoing education, agitation, and coalition-building. Such an institution could generate and sustain public pressure and political mobilization beyond the fleeting enthusiasm of occasional conventions and rallies. Yet establishing such a stable organization and meeting place proved to be no easy task; chronic financial uncertainty and continuing debates about the efficacy of political lobbying undermined efforts to keep the doors open.

Chapter 4 looks at four organizations that constitute the "Generation of 1869." The New England Labor Reform League (NELRL) and the Boston Eight Hour League stood on opposite ends of an increasingly bitter debate about how to sustain cross-class alliances. The NELRL harked back to antebellum models of wide-open discussions on broad platforms with a cause for everyone. This league also put extra emphasis on financial reform and anti-monopoly libertarianism—and put itself on a collision course with Ira Steward and his Eight Hour League's continued lobbying for legislation regulating the hours of labor. Curiously, both groups claimed to have the solution to the crisis of industrial capitalism, but their solutions remained radically different from each other. The Massachusetts Bureau of the Statistics of Labor and the Massachusetts Labor Reform Party looked beyond organization-building within the labor reform community and tapped directly into the power of state agencies and third-party politics. The BSL, at its inception, forged strong bonds with Boston eight-hour advocates. This alliance quickly provoked opposition from legislators, businessmen, and even rival reformers. Within four years, the agency dropped its activist posture and severed its connections to the labor reform community. The Labor Reform Party enjoyed a surprising early electoral success, drawing on years of frustration with do-nothing legislatures. Yet again, within a few years, this party weakened under pressure from the mainstream political players and internecine fights over platform planks and gubernatorial nominations. The promise of unifying the labor reform movement through the electoral process succeeded only in driving wedges deeper between factions.

Chapter 5 explores how religion, especially liberal Protestantism and its more radical offshoot, Christian Socialism, assumed an increasingly influential role in labor reform efforts over the last three decades of the nineteenth century. In these same decades, deep economic downturns and broad strike waves forced sympathetic ministers and other allies to confront mass protest and its challenge to their ideals of Christian brotherhood and cross-class cooperation. Religiously inspired workers and supporters began their postwar efforts by creating openly Christian labor reform groups. By 1890, labor preachers were assembling cross-class religious congregations. Finally, at century's end, a labor church by and for workers proclaimed that ministers should not mediate between classes but champion labor's own unique moral vision. Building a new Jerusalem in Gilded Age Boston—racked by economic instability and class conflict—was never simple. The alliance between labor reform and religious commitment, so natural to some activists and reformers, still looked too radical for many churchgoers and too clerical for many secular workers.

Chapter 6 returns to the final two decades of the nineteenth century, and the labor reform campaign's renewed quest to create central meeting places in Boston. Four institutions staked some claim to this role of labor reform headquarters. The Wells Memorial Workingmen's Institute evolved from a moral improvement society into an open forum for cross-class dialogue on the labor question, but never endorsed particular campaigns or legislation. The Wendell Phillips Union took the opposite strategy of proclaiming openly its desire to be the center for all social reform in the city. In the 1890s, two new settlement houses also created space for ongoing engagement between workers and reformers (and sometimes employers). The men at Andover House saw themselves as honest brokers between labor and capital, and their settlement as a place where class conflict could be defused. The college-educated women at Denison House believed that wage-earning women first had to be organized, and that their organizations had to be recognized by male union leaders and employers, before genuine cross-class dialogue could be nurtured. As the Denison House residents dove deeper into the world of labor agitation, they often found themselves wrestling with their conflicting roles as organizers, advocates, and mediators.

Chapter 7 examines two organizations created in the 1890s: the Anti-Tenement House League and the Consumers' League of Massachusetts. Each of these leagues drew on nearly three-quarters of a century of experience in building cross-class labor reform alliances, and transformed those earlier models in ways that reflected new structures and strategies from the emerging Progressive movement. In particular, faced with a growing population of immigrant workers from southern and eastern Europe, these organizations shifted away from cross-class alliances where leadership was shared across occupational and social hierarchies, and toward structures where formally educated experts tried to solve the city's problems by using elite economic and political power. The Anti-Tenement House League championed the new immigrants' right to work under something better than sweatshop conditions but made few efforts to recruit these newcomers into the league itself. The Consumers' League mobilized middle-class women's growing purchasing power and demanded that merchants and legislators ensure the sale of high-quality products manufactured in safe workplaces. But working-class women and children remained outside objects of this league's attention as well, not active participants in the organization's political and retail campaigns. At the dawn of the twentieth century, some of Boston's labor reform organizations looked very different from their antebellum ancestors—their social vision was often constricted, and their leadership had become more elitist.

VI

This book offers a fuller and perhaps more sympathetic appraisal than many previous scholars have afforded these cross-class labor reform organizations in nineteenth-century Boston, but the flaws and failures of these alliances cannot be overlooked. The middle-class and working-class men and women who filled their ranks and offices all had their biases and limitations. Reformers sometimes made condescending remarks about workers, and workers sometimes questioned the reformers' dedication to the cause. And the groups as a whole often failed to accomplish their economic or political goals. The constant internal debates, which on one level speak to the vibrant intellectual exchanges within these organizations, also reveal that these groups often could not resolve their disagreements and create effective organizations. Weakened by differences over strategy and tactics, even as they strove to fashion a shared vision of social change and a more engaged movement, these alliances were usually no match for the powerful economic and political forces arrayed against them. By century's end, the desire to address workplace issues other than just the eight-hour day, coupled with a workforce increasingly populated by Catholic and Jewish immigrants from southern and eastern Europe, transformed many ostensibly cross-class coalitions into increasingly hierarchical organizations where experts studied various labor problems and formulated specialized legislative solutions. Labor reform became less a discussion of options for activism across class lines than a program to cure particular social ills of the urban poor.

Yet even in their limitations and failures, Boston's labor reformers and activists did something that many other nineteenth-century Americans never did. More than talking about the "labor problem," these men and women confronted injustices at the workplace and throughout the entire urban industrial economy. And they never stopped searching for solutions to eliminate the exploitation of working men, women, and children. Their persistence sometimes masked an inability to understand fully how their own divergent worldviews were rooted in differences in wealth and status. Middle-class reformers could not comprehend completely the physical dangers and economic constraints that workers faced every day on and off their jobs. When the going got tough, reformers had the luxury of abandoning a particular campaign and contemplating other options for social change—without fear of job loss and imminent hardship. Workers, on the other hand, usually had little margin for error; they were driven by necessity to demand concrete solutions to immediate problems at the workplace. Yet this existential gap never stopped men and women of good faith from trying to rebuild alliances, redouble efforts at public agitation, and offer a vision of a world where workers would earn the full value of their labor and create a better future for their families. In the end, workers who joined hands with reformers cannot be cynically dismissed as traitors to their class, nor can reformers be condemned as merely manipulative meddlers.

Taken as a whole, the nineteenth-century labor reform campaign in Boston was a constant struggle to transcend the perceived barriers of class, gender, and ethnicity and to fashion a common strategy among workers and reformers for change at the workplace. But the effort was ultimately unsuccessful in surmounting boundaries that became increasingly contentious as the century progressed, especially the growing sense of class and ethnic conflict that pervaded Boston (and all of industrial America). Cross-class alliances kept forming, only to succumb to the recurring problems of internal friction and external opposition. Yet activists and reformers did demonstrate remarkable resiliency in the face of such obstacles; they created an ever wider constellation of new alliances and campaigns, even as their organizations' social vision and leadership structures often narrowed. These men and women in nineteenth-century Boston left a legacy of persistence that offers important lessons about the possibilities and limitations of coalition-building for social change organizations today.

Part I
1830s–1870s

BOSTON'S first cross-class labor reform organizations emerged in the early 1830s as alternatives to the city's struggling trade unions and workingmen's party, stagnated during the economic depression of the late 1830s, then reappeared with renewed vigor in the mid-1840s as part of a vibrant outpouring of reform enthusiasm. The early cross-class alliances debated fundamental questions concerning goals, strategies, and tactics, questions that the labor reform community would continue to wrestle with throughout the nineteenth century. Would labor reform be defined as immediate improvements in working conditions (especially the shorter workday), or as long-term change in the nation's social structure? Would organizations focus on discussion and education, or on action? Would an activist agenda be framed at worksites or in the legislature? If the campaign for labor reform became openly political, would it enter the electoral arena in an organized fashion? And, finally, would the effort encompass the city, the state, or the entire New England region?

Labor reform activism survived the years of sectional crisis and civil war by focusing much of its campaign on shorter working hours, as activists and reformers articulated new economic arguments and political strategies in support of the ten-hour day. Before the war's end, emerging leaders such as Ira Steward began to press for the eight-hour workday—a demand that would help define the American labor movement well into the twentieth century.

The years immediately following the Civil War saw Steward and his allies press a bold consumption-based economic model for the eight-hour day. The Massachusetts legislature responded with a series of committees and commissions that held hearings, took testimony from workers and reformers, and wrote lengthy reports; yet lawmakers never passed any bill regulating working hours for men and women. Thus labor reformers and activists plunged deeper into the political process than ever before but had few legislative gains to show for all their lobbying efforts.

The 1860s closed with a flurry of activity in the Boston labor reform community as four new organizations all appeared on the scene in 1869. (Each of these groups would remain active into the 1870s, if not longer.) The New England Labor Reform League (NELRL) and the Boston Eight Hour League stood at opposite poles of an increasingly intense debate over defining and achieving labor reform. The NELRL held the ideal that public discussion itself, and wide-open conventions with reformers of all stripes stepping up to the podium, gave breath and strength to the struggle for labor reform. Ira Steward's Eight Hour League insisted that securing shorter working hours was the undisputed first priority. A focused public campaign for legislation would provide the necessary organizational and ideological glue to hold together fractious coalitions. The Massachusetts Bureau of the Statistics of Labor (BSL), a new state agency, quickly built links with eight-hour advocates in Boston. But within less than five years, the bureau severed those connections under pressure from angry businessmen, suspicious legislators, and jealous rival reformers. Finally, the Labor Reform Party, tapping into years of frustration with do-nothing legislatures, achieved surprising early electoral success. Yet here again, within five years the party that hoped to galvanize labor reform advocates into a unified political force splintered under pressure from Republican and Democratic pols, and internecine squabbles over platforms and nominations that drove wedges ever deeper between competing factions.

1

AWAKENINGS

The First Cross-Class Labor Reform Organizations,
1832–1848

ON FEBRUARY 16, 1832, at the Marlborough Hotel on Washington Street in Boston's central commercial district, "a General Convention of Mechanics and Working Men" met "to concentrate the efforts of the laboring classes, to regulate the hours of labor, by one uniform standard, to promote the cause of education and general information . . . and to maintain their rights, as American Freemen." From this gathering of more than eighty "delegates," the New England Association of Farmers, Mechanics, and other Working Men (NEA) emerged.[1]

At the NEA's birth, Boston was a port city of more than 60,000 inhabitants, dominated by wharves and warehouses, including the recently completed Faneuil Hall marketplace. In this closely settled community, wealth and poverty constantly intertwined and overlapped. Merchants' homes stood near the Marlborough Hotel, as well as along nearby Beacon Hill, the Statehouse, and Boston Common. But the Town Dock was also close by, where John Winthrop's intrepid band of Puritans had first settled two hundred years earlier, where narrow streets were now clogged daily with wagons, and where the city's sewer system emptied into stinking tidal mudflats. The city's economy reflected its commercial character. The port itself employed stevedores, haulers, draymen, and teamsters; while the construction of homes, warehouses, and shops kept carpenters, masons, plumbers, and painters busy. Within the city's workshops, butchers, bakers, tailors, and seamstresses plied their trades. Meanwhile, a growing cadre of urban professionals—bankers, lawyers, clergymen, and even college professors—also made Boston their home. Several manufacturing sites sprang up south of the central commercial district. Since waterpower was scarce, Bostonians invested in modest-sized industries such as glass furnaces, sugar refineries, iron foundries, leather tanneries, and of course shipyards.[2]

The city's waterfront teemed not only with goods from across the globe but also with newly arrived migrants and immigrants as well. Young men and women from hard-pressed rural New England families frequently came to the city looking for work. Farmers, craftsmen, and millworkers from England and Scotland—squeezed by the British industrial economy—made up many of the new foreign arrivals. Most shared a common language and Protestant faith with the majority of native-born Bostonians. Yet, some 7,000 Irish Catholics also now called Boston their home, as did hundreds of recent arrivals from France, Germany, and Italy. The occasional seaman (or perhaps deserter) from the Azores, Armenia, Poland, Spain, Sweden, Russia, or China added to the polyglot character of the boardinghouses in the city's North End.[3]

The NEA convened in a city that was also well known for its vibrant and variegated community of reformers. Drawing on a deep historical taproot of Puritan ideas about communal obligation, as well as more recently coined Unitarian beliefs in rationality and improvement, many Bostonians put a high premium on education and social welfare. The city's elite often contributed to voluntary societies promoting poor relief, prison reform, care for the mentally ill, temperance, and sometimes even women's rights and universal peace. Though many of these reforms and reformers were driven by conservative notions of moral stewardship and noblesse oblige, the myriad organizations also created a climate of conscience and debate that sometimes stimulated more radical concepts of social change and more venturesome activists. Perhaps most provocative of all, Boston was now home to William Lloyd Garrison, the outspoken abolitionist who had recently launched his newspaper *The Liberator* on Washington Street, blocks from the Marlborough Hotel.[4]

The NEA was indeed an organization of farmers, mechanics, and other workingmen from all over the region, but the association's leaders also included men who earned their living through "mental labor." Universalist minister Jacob Frieze served as the organization's founding secretary; Charles Douglas, a physician, was elected president and editor of its newspaper (*New England Artisan*). The association addressed issues of immediate import to workers such as the demand for a ten-hour workday, and broader questions such as the morality of child labor and the need for wider access to public education. The NEA was distinct from—though certainly cognizant of—the trade unions and workingmen's political parties of the early 1830s. Reaching deliberately across occupational categories and class lines to build a coalition

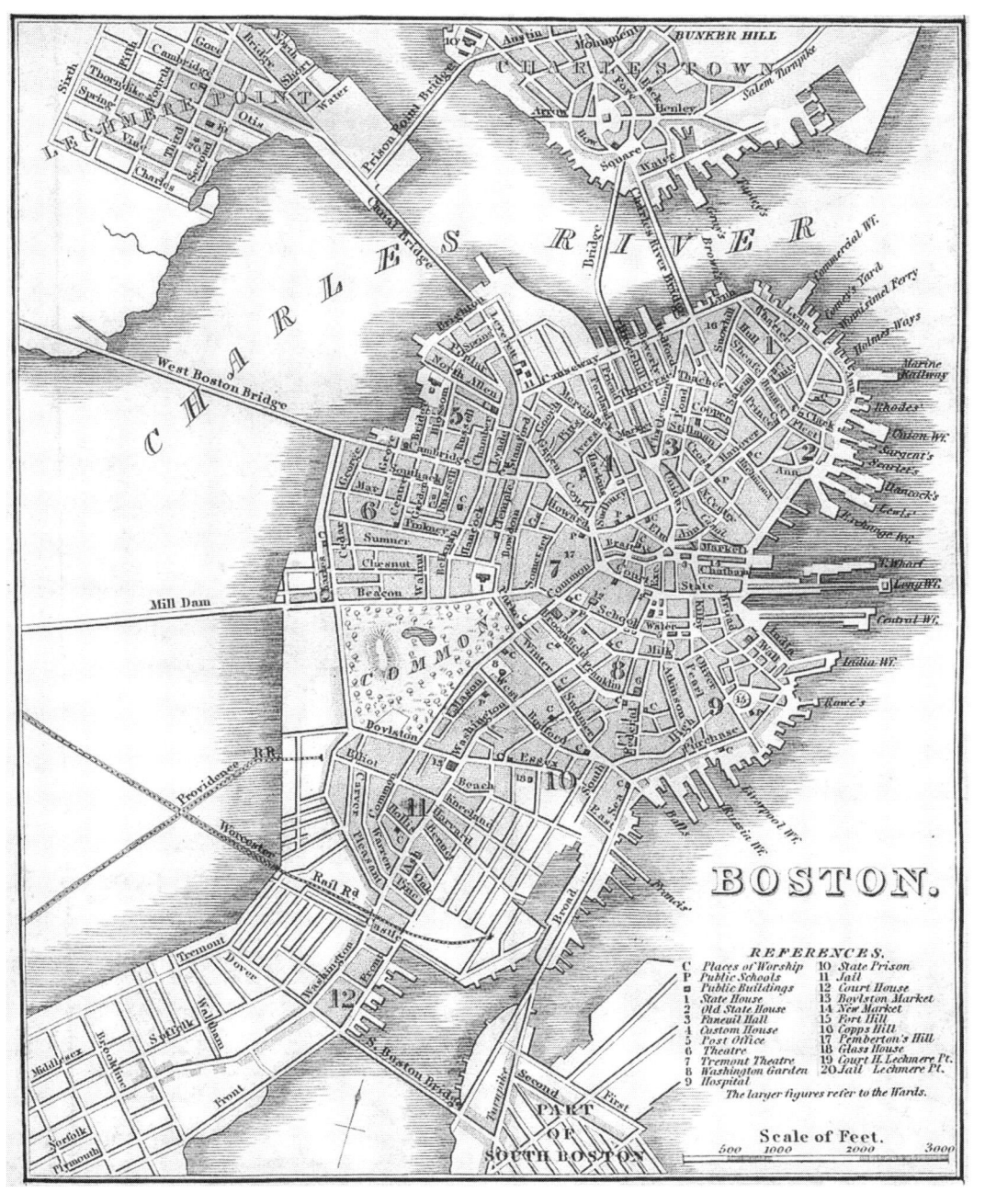

Map of Boston, 1842, from H. S. Tanner, *The American Traveller,* 8th ed. (New York, 1842). Courtesy University of Texas Libraries.

to reform working conditions and improve workers' status, the organization saw political action as an essential component of its struggle but tried to avoid plunging into the hurly-burly of political parties. The association believed that labor reform was a goal beyond any narrow class interests; it was a campaign to restore the producers of wealth to their proper place of respect in society and thereby redeem the nation's ideals of equality.

The association was the first of many cross-class labor reform groups that strove to secure justice for workers in nineteenth-century Boston. The NEA, and other organizational pioneers of the 1830s and 1840s, established the basic framework for bringing together working-class activists and middle-class reformers. Yet within these groups, debates soon emerged as to what exactly constituted labor reform: should the emphasis be on immediate workplace demands (wages, hours) or on a broader vision of social change? Could ideological and organizational bridges be built between these short-term needs and long-term goals? Would these bridges be strong enough to hold together a coalition of men and women, workers and their middle-class supporters? And where and how exactly would these alliances fight their battle for labor reform: through protest at the workplace, proclamations published in the press, petitions presented to the legislature?

The first cross-class labor reform groups began to answer these questions by linking their organizations with the growing demand for a ten-hour workday, as well as with other broader movements such as land reform and utopian socialism. With rhetoric steeped in abolitionist images of freedom and slavery, as well as memories of the American Revolution, antebellum activists and reformers tried to argue for both immediate improvements in working conditions and ideals of long-term social change. They rooted their demands for the ten-hour workday (and even an occasional plea for eight hours) in appeals to a popular sense of justice and fairness, and sought to secure their rights through mass political mobilization and legislative enactments where necessary. Yet political action, especially when it veered toward the male realm of electioneering and party politicians, ran the risk of alienating the growing number of wage-earning women who wanted to assert some control over the terms of their labor.

Striving to hold together cross-class and cross-gender coalitions, reformers and activists tried to sustain broad-based leadership structures and organizational platforms. But such diverse groups and constituencies often pulled in different directions, leading to shifting goals and tactics. Workers and reformers both expressed frustration with organizations that seemed unable to do more than pass resolutions at periodic conventions. Yet each side blamed the other for the failure to take more decisive action to forward their ostensibly shared agenda. The devil was in the details or, more precisely, in the process for prioritizing which particular reforms would be pursued in which order. Workers often insisted that addressing immediate needs—especially shorter working hours—would be the first step on the road leading to the broader vision of social transformation they shared with reformers. Middle-class reformers countered that bold structural changes would necessarily entail an improvement in working conditions. Emerging class conflicts began to be played out in the very organizations struggling to build bridges across differences in education and wealth. Yet despite the toll exacted on both workers and reformers by years of shared struggle—for and against each other—the desire for cross-class labor reform organizing did not burn out with this pioneering generation. Rather, many individuals remained committed decade after decade to the fight for justice for working men and women.

I

The NEA made it clear in the preamble to its constitution, ratified at the first meeting in 1832, that the association intended to tackle pressing matters of working hours and wages. The issue was not whether labor would be measured in hours and wages but whether workers would have any say in how many hours they worked and how much they would be paid. With language steeped in images of masculinity and the battle of free men against the specter of slavery, frequent motifs for this time period, the association declared:

> When the capitalist, the merchant, and the manufacturer assume to themselves the absolute and unconditional right of stipulating the prices of labor, ... when they assume to themselves the right to extend the hours of labor at pleasure, and compel their workmen to submit to those regulations, ... we can anticipate nothing short of a complete subjection of the working classes to a state of servile dependence on their employers, for a bare and scanty subsistence; and a deprivation of the means of education for their children, ... and we feel fully assured, that without some speedy and efficient check, the poor must eventually become the slaves of the rich. ... We deem it a duty we owe to ourselves, to our country, and to posterity to take a firm, manly, and decided stand in defense of our rights—to claim the privileges of freemen. ... We disclaim all hostility to the interest of the employer. Our only object is ... to re-establish the usage by which our labor may be offered and disposed of as any other article in the market—to be allowed, in our own behalf to be consulted as to the prices and hours of labor—that so we may be enabled to obtain a comfortable livelihood, by the reasonable exercise of industrious habits, and our children be afforded

the necessary means and opportunity to acquire that education and intelligence absolutely necessary to American freemen.[5]

This preamble called for organization and action, for changes in workplaces throughout New England, and for workers to exercise some power over the conditions of their employment. But this document also asserted that the association's demands were not radical, that they contained no assaults on employers' interests or pleas to rearrange the distribution of property and wealth. The constitution avoided any mention of organizing by wards or trades, or any explicit endorsement of strikes or party politics. Instead, the association urged its members to organize auxiliaries "in each town and manufacturing village, where there may be fifteen members of this Association." Each auxiliary should hold an annual meeting to elect delegates to a "General Convention" of the association, to be held "annually on the first Thursday in September." The NEA also directed auxiliaries to "collect a tax of fifty five cents, annually" per member to be paid into a "general Treasury." Individual affiliates could then draw on this treasury "for the relief of distressed members ... who may have been thrown out of employ, by having conformed to the provisions of this constitution."[6]

Thus, the NEA wanted to be ready financially to aid any workers who stood by the organization's principles and lost their jobs. And, indeed, there were risks involved in sticking by the association—or in betraying its principles. For this organization also stated:

> ARTICLE 3. Each and every person that shall sign this constitution, except practical farmers, shall, so long as he may remain a member of the Association stand pledged on his honor, to labor no more than ten hours for one day, unless on the condition of receiving an extra compensation, at the rate of one tenth part of a day's wages, for each extra hour he may labor, over and above the said ten hours per day. And any member offending against the said provisions of this article shall forthwith be expelled.

The association thereby insisted that the questions of hours and wages center on the ten-hour day and the principle of overtime pay. The group backed up these demands not with a direct call for work stoppages but with each member's pledge (similar to a temperance pledge) to work no more than ten hours a day or risk expulsion from the organization. (The association exempted mill workers, who had to pay dues but did not have to sign the pledge. Association leaders knew that any factory operatives who refused to work more than ten hours per day would be dismissed immediately from their jobs.) Those who honored the pledge—regardless of their status or craft—were individuals of high moral character worthy of belonging to the association. Thus, the NEA considered personal obligations, and collective shaming, powerful weapons in the battle for the ten-hour day.[7]

The NEA went beyond proclaiming this ten-hour pledge. The first convention also passed a resolution "that the 20th of March next should be the day when the system of ten hours for a day's labor should go into operation." This proposal initially triggered "an animated debate" on the convention floor, with September 20 and the highly symbolic July 4 put forth as alternative dates. But the majority argued for setting the time for action as soon as possible, in little more than a month. No one mentioned the word "strike," so workers were left to ponder whether they had any other device available beyond their personal promises to secure their rights to a ten-hour workday. Workingmen in Boston decided to put the association's principles into action on the appointed day, and strike if they had to. On March 20, 1832, ship caulkers, carpenters, painters, masons and other tradesmen in Boston all protested, walked off their jobs, and demanded a ten-hour workday. Employer associations quickly countered with denunciations and even lockouts; soon each of the strikes collapsed. The NEA did not play a prominent role in leading those protests, but the organization never denied that its call to action helped to inspire the walkouts.[8]

The association also issued a report on education focusing on the long hours of labor for children in textile factories, extended workdays that undermined the youngsters' opportunities for schooling. The association's investigating committee further discovered that no children could be taken from the mills to attend school without losing their jobs. Even if parents had more than one child at work, mothers and fathers were often told to either keep all the youngsters on the job or remove them all. And, "as such children are generally the offspring of parents whose poverty has made them entirely dependent on the will of their employers, [the children] are very seldom taken from the mills to be placed at school." The committee concluded that "the only opportunities allowed to children generally, employed in manufactories, to obtain an education, are on the Sabbath, and half past eight o'clock of the evening of other days." The report painted a disturbing scene of young workers being exploited and kept in ignorance, of children growing up with stunted bodies and minds unprepared to assume the duties incumbent upon them as citizens in a republic. Therefore, the authors recommended that a "committee of vigilance be appointed in each State" to collect and publish details on "the condition of laboring men, women, and children, and abuses practiced on them by their employers." Furthermore, the report urged each vigilance committee to petition state legislatures for the ten-hour day and the mandatory education of children employed in factories.[9]

Thus, the NEA was one of the first labor reform organizations to insist that government had the right and the duty to regulate the conditions of labor, especially by legally limiting the length of the workday for those who could not secure such limits for themselves. Skilled craftsmen preferred to guarantee such rights through voluntary agreements with their employers—they looked to the state as a last resort. But many of these workers also knew that unskilled laborers and the growing ranks of textile operatives had less leverage with capital and needed a ten-hour law as soon as possible. The ten-hour petition campaign, in conjunction with the ten-hour pledge, combined collective political lobbying (rather than party politics) with individual workers' pressure at the point of production to accelerate the adoption of a shorter workday for all labor throughout the region. Here again, the association called for a petition drive yet never pursued this campaign with much consistency or vigor; but labor reform groups in the 1840s picked up on this strategy and often made legislation for the ten-hour day a centerpiece of their public pronouncements.

Workers in the NEA believed that factory operatives were especially vulnerable to exploitation and overwork because of their poverty and the corporate wealth arrayed against them, (not to mention that so many of these workers were women and children, and hence defined as dependents by legal and social conventions). Therefore, the industrial workforce stood in need of legal protection more than any other group of workers. Moreover, the association linked education not necessarily with broad schemes of school reform but to the basic demands that all children have minimal schooling and all workers have legal limits on their hours of labor. Put simply, the shorter workday would give everyone more time for the education needed to become properly informed and responsible citizens.[10]

The association continued to press for a ten-hour workday and the education of factory children at its next convention in the Representatives' Chamber of the Massachusetts State House on September 6, 1832. (The meeting's location may indicate that this organization had some influence among the state's political leaders.) Charles Douglas was reelected president at this session. The meeting's "consideration of the ten hour system" prompted a debate as to whether the organization wanted to continue "to make its adoption by their associates indispensable, or to leave it to the discretion of the various associations in New England." Since the recent wave of ten-hour strikes in Boston had failed and workers were often back to toiling sunup to sundown, the organization retracted its plans to expel any member or local affiliate who worked more than a ten-hour day. It seemed unfair to punish workers who had fought and lost a valiant battle, and whose long days of labor were no fault of their own.

The convention also welcomed Seth Luther, a thirty-seven-year-old itinerant Rhode Island carpenter, mill worker, and tireless campaigner for factory operatives' legal rights. Luther was a well-known—even infamous—figure in mill towns across the region, and would be a regular fixture at labor reform conventions for years to come. He had spent much of 1832 traveling across New England delivering an address on the exploitation of factory workers and the need for education (similar to the NEA's own report at its previous convention). The association thanked Luther for his efforts in collecting facts about the poor conditions of workers throughout the region and his outspoken defense of their rights to organize.[11]

The association returned to the Marlborough Hotel for its annual convention on October 2, 1833, with about twenty-five delegates in attendance. This meeting considered other strategies, beside political petitions, for spreading the idea of labor reform organizing and agitation. A Boston delegate suggested that corresponding "societies" be set up in every town "with a view to the establishment of *Trades Unions*," but the assembly never specifically discussed any actual alliances with unions. Charles Douglas also urged that the association's new president—William Thompson, a farmer from the western Massachusetts town of Northampton—"have the authority whenever applications may be made by suitable persons, to appoint *Lecturers* for the purpose of disseminating the principles" of the organization. Douglas believed that these traveling lecturers, in combination with the association's newspaper (*New England Artisan*), the 1,000 copies of the convention proceedings to be printed and distributed, and the lyceums discussed at the last convention would all enlighten workers throughout the region as to the benefits of the association and its reform program.[12]

Throughout the winter of 1833–34, the *New England Artisan* published numerous reports on women's working conditions. Douglas proposed a new newspaper written especially for these women, to be called "The Female Advocate and Factory Girl's Friend," and he condemned the practice of paying women less than men for the same jobs. He lashed out at attempts to cut female operatives' wages and "the disposition to treat them as hirelings and dependents, entitled to no respect on account of their sex, of their usefulness, or of their general character . . . [as] high-handed attacks upon justice and decency." Douglas concluded that such wage cuts "show the necessity of a firm union among females to resist oppression, and make a common cause in defense of their natural rights."

When he addressed a gathering of textile workers at Jefferson Hall in Lowell, Massachusetts, Douglas shifted his emphasis back to the hours of labor, even though many women had recently walked off their job to protest wage cuts.

He urged the women to take "immediate measures to diminish their hours of labor so as to afford them ample time for mental improvement and healthful recreation in the open air." Douglas even proposed that *eight* hours a day was "enough to devote to regular productive labor" and "that all beyond this was bodily destroying toil, which should never be performed merely to satisfy the unjust and unreasonable demands of avaricious employers." Douglas closed his report on the meeting in surprisingly masculine tones when he remarked: "The able bodies, the brawny arms, the hard hands, the stout hearts, and the power of numbers belong to the working class. This class now begins to know their rights . . . and they will not as heretofore, passively submit to every species of indignity, heaped upon them by a purse proud aristocracy."[13]

Despite Douglas's speeches to women workers, and the association's sympathetic reports on the plight of factory operatives, mill workers—especially the large numbers of young women in the growing textile industry—remained conspicuously absent from the NEA's meetings. Facing strong social pressures against speaking at public gatherings, many women workers probably felt reluctant to attend the conventions and testify to their working conditions. At the same time, those women who did protest wage cuts in the mill towns of New England may have resented the association's discussing their problems in the same context as that of dependent children. Representatives from New Haven at the 1833 convention noted "the absence of delegates from the factory villages" and feared that all such operatives—women, children, and even men—were "already subdued to the bidding of the employers—that they are already sold to the oppressor, that they have felt the chains riveted upon themselves and their children, and despair of redemption."[14]

Without many women in attendance, the NEA lacked essential components of the emerging antebellum working class: textile operatives, and urban workers such as seamstresses and domestics. A crucial tactical gap opened between women workers, who were more likely to protest wage cuts in the 1830s, and the association's many urban male artisan leaders, who emphasized the ten-hour day. The discussion of women workers took place in a kind of organizational vacuum, and this vacuum sucked out some of the association's potential vitality and relevance. In fact, its failure to bring women into the fold may have been a key reason why the association veered toward the male-dominated realm of party politics, and disintegrated after one final, lackluster fall 1834 meeting in President Thompson's hometown of Northampton. The NEA—now trying to recruit more members from rural areas—published an address that never mentioned the ten-hour workday but focused instead on financial problems facing farmers. The association demanded the repeal of what it saw as unfair laws regulating mortgages, debt, banks and "other incorporated monopolies," public education, and criminal courts. The "remedy for these abuses" lay in "the wooden scepter of the sovereignty of the people, ... the ballot box." The NEA insisted that it was still distinct from political parties; but its new emphasis on agrarian politics now made it a close adjunct of the Massachusetts Workingmen's Party. And its descent into the electoral maelstrom may well have helped to seal the association's fate as it was subsumed by bigger players in Jacksonian politics.[15]

As the NEA dissipated, workers in Boston channeled their organizational energies into the newly formed (March 1834) Boston Trades Union (BTU). Despite its name, and unlike general trades unions in other cities, this group opened its ranks to Charles Douglas and other middle-class sympathizers. Douglas called the first meeting to order and sat on the committee to draft the union's constitution. The BTU also made a conscious effort to bring masters and journeymen together in common cause against merchant capitalists. A "Boston Mechanic" justified this organizational structure by stating that "the interest of all who obtain their living by honest labour is substantially the same, since the boss is often brought back to journeywork by hard luck, and the journeyman may expect in his turn to become an employer, while both of them are invariably imposed upon and treated as if belonging to an inferior grade of society by those who live without labour." This mechanic articulated both a preindustrial ideal of an economy where all craftsmen could rise through the ranks and own a modest shop, and a more contemporary fear that the competitive market could drive a small shop owner back to the journeyman's workbench. Both scenarios underscored the need to build alliances across emerging—yet still fluid—class lines to prevent powerful elites from exploiting all honest hardworking producers—journeymen and masters alike.[16]

On May 8, 1835, as tradesmen throughout Boston walked off their jobs and renewed their struggle for the ten-hour workday, the union published its stirring "Ten Hour Circular." Written by Seth Luther and two others, the circular was a ringing endorsement of the workers' "Natural Right to dispose of their own time." The authors stated simply that "the work in which we are now engaged is neither more nor less than a contest between Money and Labor: Capital, which can only be made productive by labor, is endeavoring to crush labor the only source of all wealth. . . . We cannot, we will not, longer be mere slaves to inhuman, insatiable and unpitying avarice." Luther and his coauthors took pains to say that they were not asking for a wage increase but were "willing that demand and supply should govern the price as it does that of all other disposable property." They also warned workers that "to induce you to assist them to form shackles and fetters for your limbs and your own minds," employers would promise higher wages to those who defied the strike. The authors cautioned the tradesmen not to be "deceived by this old and shallow artifice."

The circular specifically defended workers from the charge that a decrease in working hours would lead to an increase in drunkenness and debauchery. The authors responded that overwork and exhaustion were the more likely causes for any worker's excessive drinking. "We are friends to temperance 'in all things,'" they asserted, "but any man who requires of us excessive labor is intemperate; and if he is not actuated by ardent spirits, he is controlled by a spirit of inhumanity equally fatal to human happiness."

Even as the circular lashed out at those who opposed the workers, the authors added a conciliatory note for masters and shopowners still in the union. "We would not be too severe on our employers, they are slaves to the Capitalists, as we are to them." But sympathy went only so far in this struggle. Luther and his cowriters warned: "We cannot bear to be the servant of servants and slaves to oppression, let the source be where it may. . . . Further, they threaten to starve us into submission to their will. Starve us to prevent us from getting drunk! Wonderful Wisdom! Refined Benevolence! Exalted Philanthropy!" The document closed with another clarion call to action rooted in the workers' revolutionary patrimony:

> We claim by the blood of our fathers, shed on our battle-fields in the War of the Revolution, the rights of American Freemen, and no earthly power shall resist our righteous claims with impunity; . . . the public mind is with us. The glorious work goes nobly on. Many employers have acceded to our reasonable demands. . . . Mechanics of Boston—stand firm—Be true to yourselves. Now is the time to enroll your names on the scroll of history as the undaunted enemies of oppression, as the enemies of mental, moral and physical degradation. [17]

Less than two weeks after the publication of the Ten Hour Circular, on the evening of Wednesday, May 20, 1835, a thirty-four-year-old ex-Universalist minister—Theophilus Fisk—addressed the "Mechanics of Boston" in Julien Hall at the corner of Milk and Congress Streets in heart of the city's financial district. Fisk's presentation was titled simply "Capital against Labor," but it was a bold defense of the workers' campaign for a shorter workday. Fisk was so outspoken in his advocacy that he made one of the first extended arguments for the eight-hour day. He stated forthrightly that "eight hours for work, eight hours for sleep, and eight hours for amusement and instruction, is the equitable allotment of the twenty four." (Similar slogans about an even tripartite division of the day started to appear with great frequency and forcefulness during the Civil War, and soon thereafter became a mainstay of the American labor movement. Fisk was just a generation or two ahead of his time.) "We demand not mere justice to the animal body," Fisk argued, "but time to do justice to the heart and mind—time to grow in knowledge, and the practice of equity and virtue." Fisk once again quickly dismissed the assertion that workers would become unruly with more time away from the job; capital's exploitation of labor was far more sinful than workers' desire for a respite from toil. Fisk also believed that laborers who worked shorter hours became physically healthier and stronger, and could produce as much as (if not more than) those worn down under the present "barbarous 'all day' bondage."

Fisk concluded his speech with a call for workers' political ambitions to reach far beyond legislation on the ten-hour day. He believed that many employers feared the campaign less for what it would mean at the workplace than for its potential to reorder Boston's entire political economy and social structure. Fisk insisted that workers who had the time away from work to read and study politics would quickly learn just how many laws were stacked against them. They would demand more legislative action in their own interests, and form their own parties to secure economic justice. The ten-hour day was thus the first step to genuine political power for workers. The owners knew and feared this prospect, which was why they fought so tenaciously.

> So long as you allow Capital to make laws for Labor, standing out for higher wages, or reducing the hours of toil, will only be doing the work by halves. There must be a radical reform—and this can only be accomplished at the ballot boxes. Allow the Capitalists to make a compromise with you—allow them to play the lawgiver, and they will not care a brass farthing how few hours you work, or what prices you receive. They will take good care how to strike the balance when they come to pay you for your labor. For every hour you subtract from toil, they will levy an indirect tax upon you that shall treble its value. No. There is not a nabob in Boston that would raise a finger to prevent the "ten hour system" if he thought the great work of reform would stop there, for all that could be remedied in a hundred ways by partial legislation next Winter. But the great fear of those who grow rich upon your industry, is, that if you get time to improve your minds, you will get your eyes open to the monstrous frauds that have been perpetrated upon you by the heathen idolaters—the worshippers of Mammon.... Throw away all party names—ALL PARTIES are, and ever have been, opposed to your interests. Form a party of your own.... Your opposers will seek to divide you by some petty jealousy—because they know that divide and ruin is the only policy that will overthrow you. Bind yourselves together by the strongest of all bonds—that of self interest. You have all one common

cause—one common name—one common interest—the interest of Labor—the interest of honest industry.

Despite the impassioned rhetoric of Fisk and Luther, and the efforts of tradesmen to hold out through the summer of 1835 for the ten-hour day, the Boston Trades Union and its supporters were no match for the merchant capitalists' economic and political power. The strike and the organization both collapsed before the year had ended. The bonds between journeymen and small masters ripped apart, never to be rebuilt; cross-class alliances for labor reform in Boston would take new forms in the future.[18]

In a July 4, 1836, oration to the mechanics of Brooklyn, Seth Luther reflected on the Ten Hour Circular's impact on workingmen in Boston and beyond, and the toll exacted on his mind and body by his own struggles for labor reform. Luther expressed deep concern "that Workingmen are sometimes ungrateful to those who are devoting the energies of their minds, and wearing out their physical powers in their service. Frequently he that labors hardest in their cause is not treated with that kindness he deserves. . . . False friends to the cause, endeavor to injure the old veterans and reduce them in the estimation of the army of Workingmen." Luther may have spoken for many supporters of labor reform who now, in the wake of another defeat, felt shunned by the very people who had so recently "hovered round him in the days of his triumph over oppression . . . [and] cheered [him] as the champion of equal rights." Luther wanted his audience to remember that if they were "crying out against *injustice,* let them not be so inconsiderate as to be unjust to those who have sacrificed all for them." Luther hoped that cross-class bonds forged in adversity would endure, even though the struggle itself seemed to drag on with few if any victories. His plea for the forgotten reformer—dismissed, perhaps, as a crank because he was physically and financially broken in the service of labor—would become a painfully common refrain as the century progressed, but it was an appeal more often honored in the breach.[19]

Yet the labor reform alliances of the 1830s did try to transcend boundaries of skill and social status, and offer a vision of a more equitable political economy where working men and women would not be relegated to the permanent status of wage laborer or factory hand. Ministers and doctors became editors and pamphleteers in fighting for workers' rights; especially for the ten-hour workday. At the same time, tension and frustration between working-class activists and middle-class reformers may have been especially acute in Boston, because workers still did not have what laborers in other cities often took for granted—that ten-hour day. This city seemed to be an especially tough nut to crack: despite dedicated workers and a substantial population of sympathetic reformers, the merchants of Boston mobilized effectively and turned back every campaign for a shorter workday in the 1830s. Repeated failures eroded the goodwill between activists and reformers as they tried to explain to each other (and sometimes blame each other for) why they could not reach their goals. But the ideal of building a successful cross-class coalition never faded away completely, no matter how dim the prospects for social change seemed to be.

II

Cross-class labor reform organizing in Boston reemerged nearly a decade after the demise of the NEA and the Boston Trades Union. This long hiatus may have been due in part to a deep depression that gripped the nation from 1837 until 1843. The following spring (May 1844), with the economy rebounding and workers again laboring longer hours, the Fall River Mechanics' Association published a series of resolutions calling on "the Mechanics of the different Towns in New England to form themselves into Associations for the purpose of . . . holding . . . a general convention of the Mechanics and Laborers of New England." The convention would consider strategies for securing the ten-hour workday throughout the region, as well as broader questions relating to labor reform. Two months later, the editor of *The Mechanic*, Fall River's labor newspaper, suggested a meeting in Boston in September at the time of the annual "Mechanics' Fair." The paper also announced that it intended to send a "Lecturer into the field" to rally support for the proposed convention.[20]

Shortly thereafter, the Mechanics' Association did send a traveling lecturer throughout southeastern Massachusetts, Rhode Island, and eastern Connecticut. Simon C. Hewitt—a self-described mechanic and Universalist preacher, as well as a utopian socialist and ten-hour advocate, from Dighton, Massachusetts—journeyed to mill towns and commercial cities from late July to the end of August 1844. He tried to organize local labor reform associations wherever he went, and encourage these associations to send delegates to the convention in Boston. Hewitt also noted that veterans of the earlier New England Association, such as Charles Douglas, joined in the renewed movement and helped him to organize meetings. Copies of Seth Luther's *Address to the Workingmen of New England* (1832) were circulated to workers' committees in various towns as part of the concerted effort to generate enthusiasm for the proposed meeting.[21]

By early August, labor papers across the region—such as the *Boston Laborer* and the *Manchester Operative*—endorsed the idea of a convention in Boston around the time of the Mechanics' Fair. But other papers—such as the *New England Operative*—asked that the first convention be delayed a few months so as to give labor groups in isolated towns a chance to organize. Finally, a meeting of Boston workingmen proposed Wednesday, October 16, as the convention date; other groups across the region quickly agreed to that idea. Some organizers remained concerned that workers, especially from northern New England, might not show up in large numbers. But others believed that enough local associations had been formed to supply delegates, and that this initial meeting would promote future assemblies which would attract even more participants.[22]

Once again, the time and place seemed propitious for such a gathering. Boston swirled with renewed currents of reform sweeping through its churches and meeting halls, and reverberating beyond the city's boundaries. Ralph Waldo Emerson, surveying the scene at the dawn of the decade, remarked to the English author Thomas Carlyle: "We are all a little wild here with numberless projects of social reform. Not a reading man but has a draft of a new Community in his waistcoat pocket." Examining the economic and human costs of the recently concluded depression on the city's more than 100,000 inhabitants, many Bostonians seemed anxious to discuss a range of possible options to prevent such social disasters from reoccurring. A new generation of reformers pressed to go beyond their predecessors' humanitarian reforms—as generous as they may have seemed. There was a new call to challenge the underlying assumptions of the American economy and society at midcentury in the search for a more just and equitable distribution of wealth and power. It was not enough anymore to help the poor; in the eyes of these new reformers, the root causes of poverty had to be interrogated. And the questions raised often went right into the heart of the new industrial workplace—the hours and wages and conditions of labor.[23]

The stage was set, and the New England Workingmen's Association (NEWA) convened on Wednesday, October 16, 1844 at 10:30 a.m. in Boston's Faneuil Hall—a favorite locale for Revolutionary era orators and antebellum abolitionists, and thus a site of great symbolic value which the organizers deliberately secured for their first meeting. The outline of a new cross-class organization was clearly visible at this initial gathering. Workers from across New England answered the call for this convention, and so did many middle-class reformers. Several hundred delegates filled the hall, with large contingents from the industrial cities of Fall River, Lowell, and Lynn. Nearly a dozen representatives from the Brook Farm utopian community in Boston, which had just adopted a new constitution based on the principles of the French social theorist Charles Fourier, and land reformers from New York led by George Henry Evans of the National Reform Association also took seats at the convention.[24]

The NEWA spent the first several days debating a series of resolutions, including a call for state legislatures "to pass a law that shall prohibit any corporation from employing any person more than ten hours per day." This ringing demand for the ten-hour workday was based on the belief "that the time now devoted to manual labor is unreasonable and unjust, is equally destructive to physical health and mental vigor, and requiring long continued and excessive physical exertion, amounts to a denial of the invaluable right every man should possess to an opportunity for recreation [and] social enjoyment." The NEWA's key justification for the ten-hour workday, therefore, was to prevent workers' physical and mental overexertion. Shorter hours were simply a fundamental human need and a matter of fairness. Many female factory operatives, increasingly active in the ten-hour movement, emphasized these same straightforward reasons; moreover, shorter hours would preserve and protect their dignity—as people, workers, and women. Arguments about the ten-hour day leading to more jobs, or to increased productivity, profit, and wages, would emerge more in later decades. The resolutions also called on "brother mechanics and laborers throughout the country . . . to organize . . . to vindicate labor from reproach—to secure to the laborer a more just equivalent for his toil . . . [and] to inquire why . . . the workingmen in society, by whose wealth all labor is produced, on whose industry rests the arts of civilized life, are condemned to occupy the meanest position in that society, [and] are stigmatized as ignorant and inferior."[25]

The resolution advocating ten-hour petitions to the legislature sparked an intense debate among many who attended the meeting. Some dismissed petitions as useless; others thought of them as unnecessarily submissive political gestures for men who already had the right to vote and hold office. Advocates, however, pointed out that the petition campaign was a way to demand legal protection for poor women and children who were being exploited by legislatively created manufacturing corporations. In fact, the act of petitioning itself was a way for disenfranchised women to make a public political statement in defense of their rights at the workplace. Some women already had experience in antislavery petition campaigns and knew the political benefits that could accrue from such activism. Still others argued that skilled workers and craft unions had secured the ten-hour day in other cities, but since Boston employers remained recalcitrant, less skilled workers faced even bleaker prospects without some legal intervention.

Supporters hoped that the process of petitioning would bring together men and women from various backgrounds to exercise their rights as citizens, rather than pulling them apart by gender or class differences. Politicizing the ten-hour movement, insisting that workers press their demands beyond the shopfloor and into the hall of the legislature, necessitated building the largest coalition possible to transform worker activism into concrete reforms through state action. The arguments supporting the petition campaign as an expression of power in the political arena eventually carried the day. But advocates constantly emphasized that petition drives should be promoted through broad-based labor reform associations—including men and women—rather than partisan politics. This strategy kept female labor in the coalition, gave women a potential political voice, and avoided the factionalism that had plagued earlier workingmen's parties.[26]

Other resolutions went beyond the campaign for the ten-hour day. One supported the "formation of practical associations in which working men can use their own capital, work their own stock, establish their own hours, and have their own price." This initial call for producers' cooperatives hinted at an alternative to workplace legislation. If new laws were not enacted to protect workers, then workers would have to protect their own interests by becoming their own employers. In their own workshops they could establish reasonable hours and wages, and provide steady employment under safe working conditions—simple demands that owners had never granted and legislators would not enforce. Yet this alternative generated relatively little interest at the convention, and the NEWA by the fall of 1845 began to talk much more about consumer cooperative stores. But the idea of cooperative workplaces did appeal to the Brook Farm Associationists. And the convention did endorse the Fourierists' concept of "attractive industry, a system in which every laborer has a direct personal interest in the fruits of his labor" through an elaborate hierarchy of "groups and series" designed to match each worker with his or her particular abilities. Thus, the Associationists pressed for labor reform that would change the nature of work itself into something more pleasant and meaningful. Ten-hour advocates might also dream of such a system but chose to focus on limiting the hours of labor in a real world where work was becoming increasingly onerous for many men and women.[27]

The NEWA's first convention set the rhetorical and organizational tone for many of its subsequent meetings. The NEWA brought together a variety of working people and middle-class reformers to discuss the issue of labor reform in the broadest sense possible. The resolutions they passed displayed no hostile cleavage between workers' organizing at the point of production and agitating for a reduction in working hours, and some reformers' grander schemes for national land reform and Fourierist-attractive industry. The convention's emphasis was on debate and petitioning, not overt protest and strikes. Both workers and reformers supported immediate action for improving working conditions and long-term plans for broader social change, though they might disagree on how to prioritize this growing list of labor reform schemes.

But it was that very disagreement over priorities—over the roadmap for social change, not the necessity for it—that would eventually pull apart the association.

Word spread throughout New England about this new labor reform organization, and when the NEWA met for the second time, in March 1845 in Lowell, over 2,000 delegates were reported to be in attendance. The meeting ratified the organization's constitution which provided for an annual convention every May; for local associations to affiliate with the regional body and send delegates to conventions whenever called; and for the "Female Labor Reform Associations" springing up in industrial cities such as Lowell and Fall River to become full members of the NEWA. The association also reaffirmed its commitment to a variety of reforms, such as free settlement on public lands, and urged affiliated associations to pursue the ten-hour workday on their own if the legislature refused to pass the necessary laws.

New and unusual ideas also emerged at this meeting. Lewis Ryckman introduced a resolution that the NEWA organize "a permanent Industrial Revolutionary Government, upon the model of the confederation of the States in 1776, which shall be pledged, to direct the legal political action of the workingmen so as to destroy the hostile relations that at present prevail between capital and labor ... and the practical enjoyment of the only inherent and inalienable right of man—the right of labor." Ryckman was a forty-seven-year-old shoemaker, formerly from New York City and now residing at Brook Farm. He was living proof that not all Associationists were middle-class utopians, and that workers could also be enthusiastic supporters of broad social reform schemes. Horace Greeley, one of the nation's leading journalists, who knew Ryckman back in New York City, described the shoemaker as "a strong, robust, intelligent man, ... a man of ideas, who knows the world, ... a whole man—not a dreamer, nor a fanatic, but one who knows life, and has large, practical, benevolent, cheerful views of it." Ryckman, as both an idealist and a practical workingman, encouraged workers to blend the Associationist concepts of attractive industry with the nation's Revolutionary heritage to gain labor's rightful share of wealth and power in the emerging industrial order. Clearly, Fourierist rhetoric about radically changing the capitalist division of labor and the nature of work itself was being heard throughout the meeting hall. At the same time, the ten-hour legislative petition campaign had already secured thousands of signatures across Massachusetts and New Hampshire. By not zeroing in on that campaign, the NEWA missed an opportunity to devote more of its influence—whatever that may have been—to the petition drive. Yet the Fourierists cannot be accused of being hostile to other labor reform ideas; they never spoke against the ten-hour law. Rather, they saw the law as a stopgap measure that some workers felt strongly about, and they tried to encompass these more specific reforms within their broader vision of a new economy and new ways of working.[28]

Attendance plummeted when the NEWA convened again on Wednesday, May 28, 1845, at the Baptist Tremont Temple across from the Boston Common—only thirty people showed up. The meager turnout may have been due to rumors circulating that the Associationists were trying to take over the organization, or to the simple fact that this meeting took place just two months after the last gathering. Despite the small numbers, those in the hall welcomed a significant new addition to the group. The Lowell Female Labor Reform Association (LFLRA)—an organization of female textile mill operatives—came to Boston and presented a banner to the NEWA bearing the message "UNION FOR POWER, POWER TO BLESS HUMANITY." It hung over the podium throughout the convention. The LFLRA opened the door for other women workers and their organizations to join the NEWA and subsequent labor reform groups. Over time, more middle-class women would follow their wage-earning sisters into these alliances.

The LFLRA's president, Sarah Bagley, gave a lengthy speech to the assembled delegates, the first public address by a woman to the NEWA. Bagley was the thirty-nine-year-old daughter of a struggling New Hampshire farm family; she had worked for nearly a decade in the Lowell textile mills, longer than many other female factory operatives in previous decades. She had seen firsthand the operatives' increasing workload and growing economic insecurity during the depression years of the late 1830s and early 1840s. Bagley announced that factory women had come to participate as active members in the growing labor reform alliance. After all, female operatives had direct knowledge of how the long hours within factories threatened their physical health and social status; therefore, they had a significant stake in the outcome of both the ten-hour campaign and the broader labor reform effort. But Bagley also tried to reassure the predominantly male audience that activist working women did not threaten the men's sphere of power and politics. She linked the crusade for working women's rights with more traditional concepts of female nurturing and morality. Thus, Bagley's speech about women and protest took public political acts and reconfigured them as gestures of personal benevolence.

> For the last half a century, it has been deemed a violation of woman's sphere to appear before the public as a speaker, but when our rights are trampled upon and we appeal in vain to legislators, what shall we do but appeal to the people? Shall not our voice be heard, and our rights acknowledged here; shall it be said again to the daughters of New England, that they have no political rights and are not subject to legislative action? It is

for the working men of this country to answer these questions—what shall we expect from your hands in the future? . . . We do not expect to enter the field as soldiers in this great warfare; but we would, like the heroines of the Revolution, be permitted to furnish the soldiers with a blanket or replenish their knapsacks from our pantries.[29]

Bagley saw the fight for reform—whether women acted on their own or in support of men—as essential to women's health and dignity. Those women who spoke up and agitated did not violate the ideal of female modesty; they defended working women's virtue from avaricious capital. Women best fulfilled their duty as guardians of morality, not in isolation from the outside world but by helping each other and their male coworkers do battle for labor reform. Bagley saw women's participation in organizations such as the NEWA as an expression of their natural maternal and benevolent instincts. Women had an obligation to organize and fight against the factory system's injustices and for workplace justice.[30]

Bagley also wanted to assure male workers, outside observers, and even female factory operatives themselves that public agitation would not destroy women's femininity or the basic gender divisions in society. Bagley argued that working women had to come together, for themselves and as part of the broader movement for all working people, and speak out in the factories, the press, the legislature, and even the streets if necessary, but always in the name of preserving women's decency and dignity. Bagley never envisioned a revolution of fire and blood; she wanted a reassertion of workers' fundamental economic and political rights. Public protest and the labor reform campaign did not compromise morality; it preserved workers' status and respect.[31]

The NEWA responded favorably to Bagley's call for women to join men in a united labor reform campaign and chose her as corresponding secretary for the coming year. Lewis Ryckman, again embodying the hopes that Associationism would reach more workers like himself, was elected president. George Ripley, the leader of the Brook Farm community, sat on the executive committee. The association also selected a committee to attend the national reform convention (sponsored by George Henry Evans's land reformers) in New York in October. The delegation included the abolitionists Wendell Phillips and William Lloyd Garrison; Lewis Ryckman and Charles Dana, another resident of Brook Farm; and Sarah Bagley and Huldah Stone, another officer in the LFLRA. The strong presence of both Associationists and women at this meeting, and in the contingent scheduled to travel to New York, may have been linked. Since Fourierism emphasized the emancipation of women as a key step toward total social regeneration, the Brook Farmers were probably especially strong advocates for including women workers in the NEWA.

Ryckman also delivered a speech to the convention, in his capacity as the new NEWA president. He urged support for the grand meeting in New York and its capacious political and legislative agenda. He argued that although the primary impetus for labor reform originated with workers, "the position to which the laws condemn the working class, forbids the hope that, alone and unassisted, [workers] should achieve [their] own emancipation." Thus organizations like the NEWA, which brought together workers and reformers, would build the broad activist cross-class alliances necessary for alleviating working-class suffering and pursuing a larger vision of social reform.[32]

By the close of the May 1845 meeting, the NEWA's organizational and rhetorical contours had emerged more clearly. The group's leaders included land reformers and Associationists, male artisans and female factory operatives. Both women and men served on the key committees drafting convention resolutions (often the major activity at each meeting) and setting goals for the organization's future. It is true that women were only a small minority of the officers and that those who did hold these official posts, such as Bagley, usually had to couch their public pronouncements in terms that did not upset their male comrades. Yet compared with many other labor and reform groups of the antebellum period—a time when custom continued to frown on the idea of women speaking in public (especially working women)—the NEWA displayed a growing commitment to cross-gender as well as cross-class organizing. And with an eclectic membership encompassing both workers and reformers, the NEWA continued to define labor reform as an expansive program that included the ten-hour movement, national land reform, and Associationism. Everyone agreed that the goal was to end exploitation and guarantee justice for workers; but they did not always concur on exactly which path would lead them all to the good society.

Yet even as the NEWA endorsed a reform agenda with something for almost everyone, reports began to circulate that the alliance was undergoing internal strain. An article in the region's leading labor reform newspaper *Voice of Industry* (*VOI*), written just weeks after the May meeting, spoke of "apparent conflicts and differences" in the association. The disagreements centered on some proposals coming from the Brook Farm Fourierist contingent. Some members of the NEWA could accept Associationist principles as individuals, but not as an organization. They feared that these utopian schemes, if adopted by the NEWA as a whole, would cut the organization "loose from many good and honest workingmen" who did not fully understand Associationism and feared some of its more arcane theories. These workers were not necessarily "conservatives" or "pragmatists" opposed to broader social reform, but they were skeptical about the specific Fourierist models being promoted by the Brook Farmers. Meanwhile, many Associationists continued to insist that unless there was a radical change in the social relations of production and the nature of work itself, workers' demands for shorter hours and higher wages would do little to alter their exploitation in the capitalist marketplace. The *VOI* urged the NEWA to renew its commitment to unity on the basis of a two-pronged strategy: first, "agitating [for] speedy and partial ameliorations; beginning at the incipient stages of our glorious reform, taking servitude's victims, and pointing them on to a brighter day" (that is, continuing to back basic workplace demands such as the ten-hour day), and then encouraging the "friends of social science and philosophy" (that is, the Associationists) to continue their long-term project of perfecting "their system of human elevation, and receive all who are prepared for so high a stand."[33]

Despite the reports of internal friction, the NEWA reconvened at the Berean Temple in Fall River on Thursday, September 11, 1845. But if those assembled thought they would have a reunited convention, they were sadly mistaken. Conflicts emerged quickly when the committee on resolutions—which included Ryckman and William F. Young, a twenty-three-year-old harnessmaker from Fitchburg who was then editor of the *VOI*—nearly dismissed some of the more visionary schemes proposed at previous NEWA meetings. The committee proposed that the association now endorse the political proposition that "a resort to the polls is the only practical and effectual measure which the Workingmen can at present adopt for the defense of their rights." The committee may not have appreciated that this new emphasis on voting threatened to displace the female members who were increasingly involved in the organization, and made many utopian reformers suspect that Ryckman was abandoning his commitment to Associationist principles.[34]

The committee followed up on its recommendation for political action with another resolution urging workers to pursue consumer cooperatives as the solution to their precarious economic existence (so this committee also seemed confused as to whether voting or cooperative stores was the key to solving workers' problems):

> WHEREAS, All means of Reform heretofore offered by the friends of Social Reform, have failed to unite the producing classes, much less attract their attention, Therefore, RESOLVED, That Protective Charity and concert of action in the purchase of the necessaries of life, are the only means to the end, to obtain that union which will end in their amelioration.

For the first time, the NEWA debated such a proposal for cooperative stores, but it certainly would not be the last discussion. What became known as the protective store movement quickly attracted a great deal of interest among workers in cities and towns across New England. And the NEWA, throughout the rest of its existence, continually reaffirmed its commitment to these consumer cooperatives. Many individual members, however (and many subsequent labor reform groups) doubted that such commercial ventures could alleviate the broader economic exploitation of workers.[35]

The September 1845 resolutions were unlike any the NEWA had discussed previously. These proposals were quite narrow and sharply critical of other reform schemes, compared with most previous NEWA pronouncements, which emphasized tolerance and a deliberate rhetorical vagueness. Not surprisingly, then, these motions prompted intense and sometimes heated debate. John G. Kaulback—a Boston tailor who later became a leading figure in the New England Protective Union cooperative stores movement—spoke in favor of "some united system to protect the workingmen against the cupidity of mercenary speculation and grasping monopolization and unite them into a charitable business organization." But Lewis Ryckman opposed his own committee's resolution on protective stores, "as the N. E. Association was organized upon a broader and nobler basis." More than ameliorate harsh conditions among the working classes, he argued that the NEWA needed to "disenthrall the laborer from the power of misused capital.... He wished to see some united, moral, intelligent action through the ballot box." (His continued insistence on voting was an unusual argument for someone who lived in a Fourierist utopian socialist commune.) "He thought the sentiments embodied in the Resolution tended to retrograde rather than progress." William F. Young responded that cooperative stores did not conflict with any of the NEWA's basic principles:

> It merely recommended a united, mutual and charitable action, whereby the producers might secure the necessaries of life without having them enhanced by passing through the speculators' and useless exchangers' hands. It is a point of no small importance to provide the half starved women and children of Boston and New York with the means of daily subsistence, without being dependent upon the mercenary insanity and heartless capital of the day. The resolution suggested the importance of some *mutual pecuniary organization* among the mechanics and laborers ... furnishing a stepping-stone and providing some means for their future progress and preparing the way for their final elevation.[36]

When the delegates reconvened in the evening, they took up a more familiar series of resolutions on the "reduction of the hours of Labor [as] an important step towards the elevation and advancement of the laboring classes," and the demand that labor receive a greater share of all profits. The debate continued the next morning when a Mr. March from Lowell linked the proposal for a ten-hour day with the previous ideas about political action. March "urged political action as the best means to gain a reduction of the hours of labor, in our manufactories, and the final redemption of the working classes from the power of combined, incorporated, protected capital." He insisted on the "necessity of resorting to the ballot box to ameliorate the condition of the working people."

Mr. Douglass of Bridgewater, Massachusetts, challenged March's remarks. Douglass believed "that a resort to the ballot box would fail to accomplish any immediate good, or unite the mechanics and laborers into any efficient organization.—He thought . . . the Press should be invoked, and public opinion set at work." Mr. Allen added that he had "attended a convention held in Boston in 1824 when political action was introduced and adopted, and the result was a signal failure and death to the movement of that time. He had no confidence in such a course as it would, in case of a political triumph, merely transfer the evils instead of exterminating them. He wished to see . . . more talking and more *thinking* among the working classes." The arguments continued to rage about the very nature and necessity of political action—was it voting itself, party politics, or some other forms of political activism that were essential means or goals for the NEWA? Eventually, the association's officers had to adjourn the convention and postpone discussion of many other resolutions; in light of the heated debate, they would call another meeting in one month.[37]

The NEWA reconvened at Lowell City Hall on the morning of October 29, 1845. At the afternoon session, a committee brought forward several resolutions from the previous meeting, including those controversial statements on political action, protective stores, and the hours and profits of labor. The committee also introduced a number of new motions, including an appeal for workers to organize themselves:

> In the judgment of this Convention, the greatest obstacle in the way of ameliorating the conditions of the laboring classes, is the apparent indifference and apathy among the workingmen and women themselves, and the want of union, harmony, and united action. . . . We earnestly call upon the producing portion of New England, and all friendly to their moral, mental and physical prosperity . . . to organize themselves into associations . . . as Associations, and workingmen in *particular*, are the ones most interested in this movement; it is our bounden duty as workingmen to sustain them by our presence.

This resolution echoed the NEWA's earliest calls for organizing local associations to support regional conventions, but it also took aim at the workers themselves for their failure to organize. The text implied that workers' lack of commitment to agitation could very well be the key cause of their continuing oppression. Yet the resolution offered no specific way for workers to break a cycle of exploitation and pessimism except to repeat the call for labor to organize. It was one thing not to encourage strikes, which had often failed throughout the previous decade; it was quite another to hold out to workers no concrete strategies for mobilization and agitation.

The resolution on political action again stirred up a long debate lasting into the evening session. Many speakers remained troubled by the motion's all-or-nothing tone, which implied that political action should be the driving force behind all labor reform. William F. Young offered an amendment "that a resort to the polls *is one* of the effectual measures which workingmen can adopt for the defense of their rights," and the convention accepted the modification. The convention later amended the resolution on consumer cooperatives in a similar manner. These carefully phrased amendments returned the NEWA to its previous position—no single reform scheme would be privileged above others as the key to social change, and therefore no single ideological stance undermined the broad coalition of reformers and workers.

After the delegates defused the heated arguments over politics and protective stores, Joel Hatch of Roxbury then rose and implored the association to design some immediate course of direct action, political or otherwise. "He was tired of passing resolution after resolution, the influence of which [is] lost as the Conventions adjourn—he wanted some standard around which the workingmen and women of New England can rally, some measure that shall unite the producing sons and daughters into one permanent phalanx." When the convention reassembled the next morning at Dickerson's Hall, Hatch went on to argue that the first step in his plan of action was for the NEWA to publish its own independent newspaper. The convention enthusiastically adopted Hatch's suggestion and soon established formal links between the NEWA and the *Voice of Industry* as the organization's official publication. At the beginning of November, the *VOI* moved to Lowell; and Hatch, William F. Young, and Sarah Bagley formed a publishing committee to oversee the newspaper's daily operations. The *VOI* provided the NEWA with a reliable forum for publicizing convention proceedings. But the association still showed little inclination to develop any other strategies—such as setting up an office or organizing public protests—for turning resolutions into action at the workplace, the legislature, or anywhere else.

Shortly after the October meeting, another flurry of criticism concerning organizational priorities and policies again threatened to disrupt the NEWA's fragile coalition. Within two weeks of the newspaper's move to Lowell, the *VOI*'s editors had to vigorously defend the NEWA against complaints from the national land reformers' recent convention in New York. The National

Reformers, followers of George Henry Evan's federal homestead schemes, castigated the NEWA for not being politically active enough in labor reform issues beyond New England. This charge was actually a thinly veiled critique of the NEWA for not agreeing to make land reform the organization's first priority, and for not supporting renewed interest in a workingmen's political party.

The *VOI* countered that "the [October] convention acted the part of wisdom in their decision . . . that political supremacy is not the *primary* object of the workingmen's Reform." The paper cautioned the National Reformers not to "look upon all efforts in behalf of the working classes, which do not tend *directly*" to further the cause of land reform, as "*inferior* and unavailing." "There is a moral power in the workingmen's Reform of N. England," the *VOI* concluded, "that looks beyond a mere political triumph." The NEWA did not oppose political activism, particularly when lobbying state legislatures for a ten-hour bill. But the organization remained concerned that, having just concluded a lengthy debate about the primacy of politics, a turn toward a labor party would risk fracturing their cross-class and cross-gender alliances along electoral fault lines.[38]

The NEWA celebrated the New Year 1846 by meeting on Friday, January 16, at the Town Hall in Lynn with delegates from all over eastern Massachusetts and "quite a number of the Ladies Association being present." This gathering considered a new strategy to secure the ten-hour workday, even as land reformers and cooperative store advocates also continued to jockey for the convention's support. David Bryant, a land reformer from Boston, was chosen president, and William F. Young was among the other officers elected. This meeting heard and endorsed John Cluer's proposal for a conference of manufacturers and factory operatives to discuss the ten-hour day. (Cluer, a forty-year-old former weaver and veteran of the Chartist petition campaigns to the British Parliament for expanded workingmen's voting rights, had recently emigrated from Scotland.) Several committees assembled to promote this idea of a labor-management conference by issuing a circular and securing a hall in Boston. In the final day's sessions, the NEWA also passed resolution endorsing the Workingmen's Protective Union as "an Institution well adapted to serve as a complete organization of the working men into Associations . . . and create a Brotherhood among the workingmen at large." President Bryant closed his report by stating that the "resolutions adopted . . . if carried into action by the laboring classes of New England, will strike an effective blow at the very root of slavery, black and white, foreign and domestic."[39]

Two months later, when the NEWA reconvened on Wednesday morning, March 25, 1846, at "Temple Hall" in Manchester, New Hampshire, an old familiar face appeared on the platform. Seth Luther, now more than fifty years old, weakened in body and mind by four years of imprisonment for his role in Rhode Island's Dorr Rebellion (a failed protest against the state's narrow suffrage laws), yet still capable of inspiring workers with his impassioned arguments for labor reform, urged the convention to "go unitedly, in one great phalanx for a reduction of the hours of labor." Luther's plea found a receptive audience throughout the hall. Several other delegates also rose and offered various motions to declare that the ten-hour campaign should be the association's primary objective.

On the following day, the convention unanimously adopted the ten-hour resolutions. A committee including Luther and Cluer then recommended promoting even more discussion of the issue through the press and the lecture circuit, distributing published tracts throughout New England, and communicating with workers outside of the region who had already gained the ten-hour day. William F. Young also joined a Committee of Correspondence on Ways and Means to promote writing in support of reduced working hours. So the ten-hour movement continued to dominate the NEWA's agenda in the spring of 1846, perhaps because of the growing presence of women workers who were often active in the legislative petition campaign to regulate the workday. These women activists—especially textile workers such as Sarah Bagley—increasingly embraced the ten-hour campaign because many of them now toiled long hours tending more machines (the "stretch-out") running at faster speeds (the "speed-up"). And many of them also now believed that laboring in a mill was no longer just a brief sojourn before marriage but was more likely to be a long-term necessity for years to come. Faced with the prospect of remaining factory hands under continuing stress and strain, many of these women now advocated openly for some legal regulation of their working hours. Land reformers, meanwhile, also stayed with the coalition and asked that their campaign continue to receive the convention's endorsement. The delegates, still not wanting to drive away any allies by putting all their efforts behind any one crusade, agreed to another resolution supporting land reform.[40]

By the fall of 1846, the organization had reached the obvious conclusion that the name New England Workingmen's Association was inappropriate for an alliance that now regularly included women at its conventions and in its leadership. At a meeting in Union Hall in Nashua, New Hampshire, on September 17, the association approved a new constitution changing it's name to the Labor Reform League of New England (LRLNE). Under the new constitution, David Bryant was again elected president, Huldah Stone recording secretary, William F. Young corresponding secretary; John Allen (a former Universalist minister and current Fourierist lecturer from Brook Farm) and

Mary Emerson (from the LFLRA) became directors. The delegates present also witnessed a strike by local machinists and a mass rally of female factory operatives in support of the ten-hour movement and against the textile corporations' practice of using lamplight to keep the mills open after dark in the fall and winter months.[41]

The newly christened LRLNE returned to Boston four months later for a meeting at Chapman Hall. Whereas the past year's conventions had reemphasized agitation for the ten-hour day, continuing legislative inaction on this issue left many workers frustrated and searching once again in 1847 for alternative reform strategies outside the statehouses. (League leaders never explained whether they now downplayed the ten-hour movement because the regionwide petition campaign had yielded few results and dissipated. Nor did they ever admit that the petition campaign may have fizzled because, despite all the talk of new strategies, the league still never stepped up to take an active ongoing role in directing the agitation.) Meanwhile, Fourierists in the winter of 1847 saw their Brook Farm experiment collapsing, and returned to the LRLNE with renewed arguments that their plans for a new system of labor should extend beyond the fragile utopian communes. Charles Hosmer, a former Brook Farmer, proposed a series of Associationist resolutions that the convention eventually tabled. Hosmer, anxious that his ideas not be forgotten, published a lengthy pamphlet shortly after the meeting concluded. (The pamphlet was probably the text of a speech he gave to the convention in support of his resolutions.) He argued that the root of all social reform lay in the "equitable Distribution of the Profits of Labor . . . [and] that for this we do not look to political action, but to the Organization of Labor, and Association of Laborers, whereby they shall work for themselves . . . and receive the Profits of their own Labor."

Hosmer described in detail how the imbalance of power and wealth between labor and capital forced workers to live and toil in miserable conditions every day of their lives. Labor remained dependent on a system of private competitive capital for its meager daily wages. He also argued that abolitionism, pacifism, land reform, and free trade were all worthwhile causes but did not address the root of the workers' problems, which lay in the inherent inequities of the current socioeconomic system. A fundamental reorganization of society, under the auspices of such farsighted groups as the LRLNE, would benefit labor far more than all the philanthropic societies' partial ameliorative remedies combined. "Poverty, the prime source of vice, indulgence and crime, would be removed. . . . Let us have justice rather than generosity." And justice lay in workers' associating together in productive enterprises—be they cooperatives or Fourierist phalanxes—"to labor for ourselves, and to reap ourselves, the fruit of our own labor . . . [and to] secure a wider, a more general distribution of the wealth of the country." Hosmer added that "it undoubtedly belongs to New England, to take the lead in the onward, the progressive, movements of the age; in the movements for the emancipation, the enfranchisement, the elevation of the race."[42]

Shortly after the January 1847 meeting, the league finally did something it had urged everyone else to do since its inception more than two years before: send a ten-hour petition to the government—in this case, the Massachusetts legislature's Joint Committee on Manufactures. (Ironically, the league's officers finally took some form of direct action—albeit a rather modest gesture—months after the petition campaign had begun to ebb and the Associationists had begun to reassert their ideas at the quarterly meetings.) The petition was signed by Stone, Bryant, and other league officers, and asked for the committee's aid

> in relieving the Laboring Classes of N. E. from the ruinous system of long hours of toil, which is now crushing the very life-blood and vital energies from the great mass of the people, . . . believing this system of tedious protracted toil to exist, in great degree by virtue of legislative enactments, in opposition to the great principles of Justice, equality and republicanism laid down in the Declaration of Rights, . . . therefore this *League* anxiously and hopefully invokes your aid and assistance in removing this oppressive burden by enacting such a law as will constitute ten hours a day's work . . . the present hours of labor are too long, and tend to aggrandize the capitalist and depress the laborer . . . and this League trusts by every consideration of *duty* to your highly revered state and the prosperity of her industrious population, as just and righteous legislators, you will be induced to grant this reasonable petition; thereby saving our country from many of the calamities which have visited other people who have suffered *wealth* and *monopoly* to feed upon and destroy the *natural rights* of the working classes.

This petition summed up many of the arguments heard at almost every league gathering. It appealed to the ideal of a state that should not offer special protection to monopolies or the elites but rather protect the rights of all its citizens, resolve economic conflicts, and promote social harmony. But why the league's officers chose to send the petition when they did remains an open question—was it the last gasp of ten-hour advocates trying to keep their campaign on the organization's front burner, or was the league making a relatively empty gesture, knowing that the petition campaign was already waning?[43]

Brook Farmers and their allies continued to press their cases throughout 1847. When the league met at Smith's Hall in Dover, New Hampshire, on July 14, the Boston Union of Associationists offered a resolution stating that "the one sure means" of achieving true labor reform was "to substitute Combination for Isolation, Co-operation for Competition, United Interests for Antagonistic Interests, and Attraction for Compulsion throughout all arrangement of social life." Not everyone in attendance, however, was prepared to hand over the league to the Associationists. As the day's discussions progressed, one female factory worker from Manchester cautioned the league "not to get too many subjects mixed up with the great object which must be kept in view." This woman argued that the great objective was a labor reform program that kept its focus on working people's crucial needs—shorter hours, better wages, safer working conditions—and always considered those demands as the essential first steps toward any broader reform scheme. For this worker and others like her, the return of Associationist arguments to center stage at the league's conventions was a source of unease and concern for the organization's future. The league's spirit of tolerance, and the grand vision of a multifaceted labor reform movement, again showed signs of strain.

The *VOI*'s editors—William F. Young, and Mehitabel Eastman from the Manchester Female Labor Reform Association—also expressed concern with the league's continuing inability to do anything but discuss the issue of labor reform. "Although many noble sentiments were uttered during the meeting," the editors lamented, "yet we regret to see that no effectual measures were taken, no plans proposed or *work* laid out for the progress of the Labor Reform cause. The people want *light* upon the rights of Labor, and the League should take some measures to give it to them." But, despite these urgings, the LRLNE still did little to help workers translate resolutions into concrete programs for labor reform. The league had no regional presence between meetings, and made no efforts to organize or agitate continually on any issues. In its efforts to avoid direct confrontation and fragmentation, the league erred on the side of organizational caution and near paralysis.[44]

By early 1848, the *VOI*'s new editors—Daniel H. Jaques, a former medical student and schoolteacher in Lowell, and John Orvis, a Vermont Quaker who had left Oberlin College and traveled as one of Brook Farm's leading lecturers on Associationism—were worrying that the league might soon cease to exist. They expressed their sadness and frustration with the labor reform movement's current predicament, and their newspaper's precarious existence. But these editors, more middle-class in outlook than their predecessors Young and Eastman, lashed out at workers as the primary cause of the league's and the *VOI*'s deteriorating condition. They castigated labor for its continuing loyalty to the party system and went so far as to declare that workers deserved their exploited status because they did not seize each opportunity offered by the labor reform campaign.

We are at times strongly made to feel that the Working Men never will do anything for themselves. They are so half-hearted in what ever they attempt, so servile under capital, and so inconsistent in their course, that we cannot hope for much. If a meeting is called to promote objects dear to their interests, it is sparsely attended, is without a sustained enthusiasm, and comes so lonely off, that the whole affair is a matter of ridicule and contempt on the part of their oppressor, and the working men themselves go home in shame-facedness and despair. If a paper devotes itself to their cause they are almost sure to desert or neglect it.... Thus they are doing today, in regard to the only paper in New England, which is devoted to their cause—aye, is the one which they professedly regard as the organ of their movement.... Certain we are, their paper will not be much longer in existence, unless they are more true and faithful in its support;—and without an efficient organ in this day of newspaper reign, the Working Men's Movement would not be worth a snap of one's finger.

If you speak of the movement of the Labor Reform League they will bravely tell you how strong the laboring classes are—how they might control Legislation ... but when you look for the fruit of that bravery in deeds, you find the cowards have fled.... We do not speak thus in anger. Our words are but too evidently just; and so long as the laboring classes will desert the cause of Labor Reform in its broad and comprehensive scope—so long as they will cling blindly and fanatically to but one idea, or the fragment of an idea, ... so long as they ... [sustain] the shamefully corrupt parties, and party presses, so long as they allow the important movement of a Free Soil, the Homestead Exemption, Lein Law and Ten Hour System to be spit upon by indifferent and contemptuous partizans, so long, will they deserve the miseries and oppressions under which they suffer....

Friends, we know [that] the Laboring men of New England by true and loyal combinations, by fearless and independent action may command the respect and obedience of the very interest which now treats them as slaves. Come together then, in hundreds to the approaching meeting ... but come still more for the purpose of *doing,* and sustaining your cause, with a deathless determination.[45]

Shortly after this plaintive article was published, the LRLNE met in Boston's Washingtonian Hall on Wednesday, January 19, 1848 (the Washingtonians were a fast-growing temperance organization run by reformed working-class alcoholics). Here again, another new year brought another shift in priorities for the league, and a further drift away from what many workers thought were their most pressing problems. The league followed its standard procedure of naming a committee to prepare resolutions; this committee included Orvis and Jaques (perhaps because of their recent concern for the LRLNE's fate and their call for action), and Mehitabel Eastman. Surprisingly, the resolution on the ten-hour day—a mainstay of virtually every convention and a necessity in the eyes of so many workers—was relegated to a minor spot at the meeting's conclusion. Instead, the convention focused its attention this time on land reform; and directed the league's officers not only to promote a resolution on homestead exemption laws but also to send a signed petition to the Massachusetts legislature supporting such laws (just as the league had sent a petition on the ten-hour day during the previous year).

Jaques and Orvis—as the *VOI*'s editors—had the last word on this LRLNE meeting, and they remained unimpressed and troubled by what they saw. Their frustration, and a whiff of middle-class snobbery (something that reformers usually tried to avoid), filled the newspaper's columns. Once again, the editors blamed labor for the failure of the league and its convention; and they heaped particular scorn on what they believed to be workers' boorish behavior. Somehow, bad manners could now explain the league's inability to address fundamental economic and social problems.

> We confess that our opinion of the importance of the *League*, as now constituted, was not at all strengthened by our observation.... Self-respect, order, decorum, a sincere and generous earnestness were but too much needed.... If some of the working men, whom we have heard make large claim to intelligence and high sense of honor, can give no better evidence of their possession than they displayed at that meeting, we humbly think they will do as well to leave the work of reforming public abuses.... We are not *less* than ever convinced of the importance of a Labor Reform Movement, but on the contrary, *more* since attending that meeting; but we are sure it must summon a higher character to its aid.

The editors closed their remarks by revealing their allegiance to land reform as the key to social progress. Their anger with the Labor Reform League was based not only on some convention delegates' bad behavior but also on the meeting's failure to embrace the National Reform platform over all other labor reform schemes (even though land reform seemed to dominate much of the proceedings). The editors' pique seems curious, to say the least, since two weeks earlier these same men had criticized workers for undermining labor reform efforts by clinging "blindly and fanatically to but one idea."[46]

The LRLNE's final gathering was its annual meeting at Humanity Hall in Lowell on the afternoon of March 22, 1848. The convention unanimously elected a slate of officers that included many men active in the protective union movement, as well as Huldah Stone as recording secretary, and John Orvis and Mary Emerson as directors. The delegates adopted only two motions, one of which started out by decrying the long hours of labor in factories and ended by pledging the league's members to the cause of land reform. The second rather grandiosely reaffirmed that "the question of the 'Rights of Labor' is not one of a faction, seeking personal gratification or political supremacy— nor is it one of mere crusade between the poor and the rich, the employed and the employer ... but one of *universal* interest, one of political economy, ... one of domestic and political peace—of *human safety*" for workers across the globe as well as the United States. James Campbell, the new president of the league, spoke that evening almost exclusively on the issue of land reform. The convention then adjourned indefinitely, and the league ceased to exist. The LRLNE's passing caused little consternation among many workers. After all, the league had drifted in recent meetings from Associationism into an almost undivided focus on land reform, and further away from more immediate workplace issues such as the ten-hour day. Thus, many working-class members concluded that the group was actually now quite skewed in its conception of labor reform and irrelevant to workers' most pressing needs. Most of these workers were not set against ideas such as land reform; but they still believed that genuine labor reform began in the workplace, especially with a reduction in the hours of labor.[47]

Why did the LRLNE disappear in the early months of 1848? No one has left behind any definitive postmortem on the organization. But there are several reasonable explanations for its demise. The final *VOI* editorials about the league indicate that at least some middle-class reformers were becoming exasperated with the group's lack of action, which they interpreted as a lack of total commitment to Associationism and land reform. Reformers such as Jaques and Orvis blamed this inaction on the apathy and bad manners of workers in the organization. As for workers in the league, they too were growing impatient with an organization that did little more than hold quarterly meetings, with an occasional petition or holiday rally thrown into the mix. The league never established an active executive committee or a permanent office to direct lobbying campaigns or organizing drives. Thus, the group could not sustain enthusiasm and momentum when conventions were not in session. Recall that in the summer of 1847, William Young (harnessmaker) and Mehitabel Eastman (factory operative), who were then editing the *VOI,* wrote specifically about the league's failure to turn talk into a clear plan of direct action to organize workers and press for reforms at the workplace. These editors argued that the problem lay with those reformers who spoke about radical change but counseled moderation in actual tactics. Any discussion of public protest, let alone strikes, had usually been off the table at NEWA conventions. Meanwhile, workers wanted to build cross-class coalitions that would actively participate in the political and economic arena— working directly at the point of production and in the legislature first for shorter hours, higher wages, and better working conditions, and then perhaps moving on to other issues such as land reform.

The league constantly tried to take deliberate steps to prevent tactical or ideological rifts between the wage workers and the middle-class reformers in its ranks. It fashioned an open organizational structure and offered leadership positions to men and women from varying occupational backgrounds. The league worked hard at being inclusive and cooperative; leaders often changed ranks without acrimony. Most gatherings ran like town meetings and adopted a veritable smorgasbord of resolutions endorsing a constantly shifting array of immediate and long-range reform schemes. The league also went to great lengths to arrange its conventions throughout eastern Massachusetts and southern New Hampshire so as to spread its message over a wide area encompassing mill towns and commercial cities.

In the midst of these efforts to build and maintain broad alliances, specific issues often competed for attention on the convention floor. The Associationists assumed an influential role in the NEWA's early meetings; the ten-hour advocates then gained the spotlight a year later, only to see the utopians and then land reformers reemerge in 1847 and early 1848. But these transitions were not pitched battles for complete domination of the organization. The debates usually centered on ordering priorities and trying to find the right combination of reform schemes to balance the various constituencies' many interests. The goal was not to subdue and expel those who had a different plan; rather, most league members tried to find points of inclusion and compromise without abandoning convictions, hoping to persuade others eventually to adopt their key reform demands. Of course, persuasion did not always work, and frustration grew between supporters of competing schemes, but no one faction held the league hostage.

Another reason for the league's dissolution may have been that so many of its major initiatives met with failure. To be sure, most of these efforts were not the league's alone; they were regional and even national movements. Nevertheless, the constant litany of defeats within and beyond the league may have undermined the membership's willingness to continue to fight what appeared to be a series of losing battles. Among the key planks in the league's platform, that of the protective unionists achieved some modest success as many stores sprang up around New England, and a few of these firms did outlast the league. But most such stores eventually succumbed to competition from private merchants, and these consumer cooperatives never fundamentally altered the course of capitalist commerce. Land reformers pressed their cause for many years, but Congress never passed the legislation necessary to reserve all lands for settlers, though Abraham Lincoln signed a modified federal

Homestead Act in 1862. The Associationist movement fell on particularly hard times in New England when Brook Farm suffered a disastrous fire in 1846 and closed its operations in 1847. And the ten-hour campaign faced continual rebuffs throughout the 1840s from a Massachusetts legislature dominated by conservative Whigs representing commercial and manufacturing interests. Even the New Hampshire ten-hour law, which seemed to promise legal regulation of the workday, was riddled with loopholes that corporations quickly exploited.[48]

Given this record of eventual defeat on virtually every issue that the league had considered important at some point in its existence, it is not surprising that these dismal results combined with growing internal tensions to finish off the organization. The conjunction of failure and frustration eventually revealed the league's organizational and ideological fractures. These fault lines were based on a growing consciousness of wage workers' and reformers' divergent priorities—an emerging sense of class differences. These were the very differences that the league had tried to eliminate in its own internal structure and to reject in its public platforms. But when its efforts failed to stem the tide of exploitation in the wage labor market, growing social and economic conflicts began to be played out inside the organization. In the end, an alliance premised on the ideal that different classes could come together and fashion both a structure and a vision that transcended class conflict foundered on precisely those emerging, opposing worldviews.

Thus, the traditional view of labor reform organizations being plagued by differences between utopian reformers and pragmatic workers has some merit, but that explanation is not completely satisfactory.[49] The conflicts in the league were often quite complex and dynamic; they were not always framed as simple dichotomies of dreamy idealists versus bread-and-butter trade unionists, and they were not inherently intractable from the first convention onward. Reformers and workers often shared a commitment to both basic workplace issues and broader reform goals; but they disagreed over the political and economic means to reach those goals, and the order in which they should be attained. Workers argued that higher wages and shorter working hours constituted a crucial first step on the road to further social and economic change. Reformers countered that changing the arrangement and meaning of work itself in the economy as a whole would, of necessity, change working conditions for the better. The league eventually collapsed because these tactical disagreements, when combined with political stalemates and economic hardships, built up over time and led frustrated workers and reformers finally to blame each other for the organization's lack of concrete achievements.

With all the different constituencies and schemes clamoring for attention, fashioning a program to meet everyone's needs in the order they wanted them to be fulfilled was simply an impossible task. Workers and reformers discovered, in practice, that broadly defining the labor reform agenda and labor reform organizations eventually produced many tensions and few direct results. And yet these men and women did not give up on their ideals of waging a struggle for social justice that remained all encompassing in its vision of fairness and equality. Many early reformers and activists reappeared for decades in a constantly shifting array of labor reform groups.

The dual struggle to hold together a cross-class alliance and to campaign against an increasingly stratified society lay at the heart of many labor reform organizations that followed the NEA and the NEWA into the field of economic and political conflict. Indeed, what makes the early groups so important is that they organized in the first place, and worked hard to stay together through years of internal debates and external opposition. Moreover, these pioneers prepared the ground for literally dozens of labor reform organizations in Boston throughout the remainder of the nineteenth century. The cycle of collective conjoining, creating, arguing, dissolving, and reconstituting went on for decades—with activists and reformers learning lessons from their predecessors' successes and failures.

Labor reform organizations reemerged soon after the LRLNE's demise and remained active in the years of sectional crisis and civil war—proof that the reform impulse was not lost in the growing political tensions of that period. Producer cooperatives briefly attracted more attention from craftsmen and Associationists; and the ten-hour movement reappeared in the 1850s with new political and economic arguments for a legal limit on the workday. All of these efforts testify to the enduring vision and power of the labor reform ideal in mid-nineteenth-century Boston.

2
KEEPING THE FLAME ALIVE
The Enduring Vision of Antebellum Labor Reform,
1848–1865

THE YEAR 1848 did not begin auspiciously for Boston labor reformers and activists. The Labor Reform League of New England (LRLNE), successor to the New England Workingmen's Association (NEWA), ceased meeting after March. The Massachusetts legislature continued to turn back massive petition drives for a legal limit on the workday, and no other issue offered much hope of unifying an increasingly fragmented labor reform community.

All was not lost for these determined campaigners, however. Reports of revolutionary activity in the capitals of Europe prompted sympathetic Bostonians to hold rallies supporting their compatriots across the Atlantic. Workers at one such meeting used the opportunity to connect agitation in Paris with the need for labor reform at home. On Tuesday evening, May 9, 1848, workers from Boston and surrounding towns gathered in Faneuil Hall "to congratulate each other on the late auspicious event in Europe"—the overthrow of the French monarchy—"and to express their views in relation to reform in our own country." Those assembled heard speeches from both working-class orators such as John Cluer, the recent Chartist immigrant from Scotland, and middle-class sympathizers such as John Orvis, a recent resident of the Brook Farm utopian community. The meeting also adopted a series of resolutions condemning the "*monied Oligarchy* in the North as . . . hostile to the interest of *Labor*" and demanded that workers, as the "great majority of the nation," use their latent political power to "purge the halls of legislation of the hirelings who basely pander to the interests of capital." In order to accomplish this goal of political purification, the resolutions urged "the laboring classes to try for once the experiment of trusting the management of their political affairs to men of their own class, who know their interests."

The assembly also renewed the demand for reducing the hours of labor, a measure requiring "immediate action," and addressed the problems of wage-working women by resolving to protect traditional ideals of female morality through better pay and healthier working conditions. This resolution blended moral concern and sympathy for the particular plight of poor working women with a clear demand that they be paid a living wage as a matter of basic fairness to all who labor: "*Resolved,* That the oppressed condition of female labor is a reproach to the age in which we live—that it is hypocritical to deplore the prevalence of immorality while no efficient efforts are made to protect the honor of womanhood by securing to female industry a just and adequate reward. And we earnestly call upon the friends of Humanity and Justice to assist in surrounding the industrious poor of the sex with those circumstances of decency and comfort which are the surest guarantee of virtue." The resolutions closed with a ringing declaration that "the glory and perpetuity of the American Republic . . . depend upon . . . the political and social equality of the *whole people,* their prosperity, contentment and morality—enjoying all the rights of men—industrious, intelligent, and happy."[1]

If labor reformers and activists in Boston were going to try once more to put words into action, they would have to rebuild organizations in a city that was on the verge of profound shifts in its social and economic structure. Responding to new sources of power (such as steam), new technology, and new consumer demands, Boston became home in the 1850s to emerging manufacturers of locomotives, sewing machines, watches, and even pianos. And, reflecting the concerns voiced by the gathering at Faneuil Hall, perhaps as much as 40 percent of all Boston women engaged in paid labor—much of it poorly remunerated. Though women made up nearly half of several skilled trades, such as bookbinding and upholstering, they often were paid far less than half a man's weekly wage. Many other women found themselves consigned to work as seamstresses in the burgeoning ready-made clothing trade, laboring seven days a week in their cramped garret rooms for a dollar, at a time when a wage of three dollars a week was needed to maintain a decent standard of living for a single adult. Of course, the circumstances for an abandoned wife or widow with children could be even grimmer. For these sewing women in particular, as opposed to the "factory girls" in cities such as Lowell, the core of labor reform was literally a wage (or piece rate) they could live on—a basic demand even more essential than a legislative limit to the workday.[2]

In the midst of economic transformation, the fires of labor reform, which had burned so brightly earlier in the 1840s along with many other social crusades, still glowed as the nation entered an era of growing political crisis and eventually civil war. A close examination of labor reform in Boston at the end of the 1840s, and for fifteen years thereafter, reveals an enduring vision of social change and activism that survived the increasingly intense conflict over slavery, abolition, and sectionalism. Producer cooperatives, drawing enthusiastic support from Associationists still anxious to change the nature of work itself, enjoyed a brief burst of success as an alternative model for labor reform. Reformers and activists also reconstituted the campaign for the ten-hour workday in the 1850s, even as they shifted its emphasis from mass petitions to openly supporting pro-labor candidates. This tactical move toward independent politics reflected a desire to change the head count in the statehouse, as an increasing number of lawmakers began to show some sympathy for decreasing working hours. In order to win this new battle for legislators' allegiances, leaders of the ten-hour campaign insisted on a more tightly focused initiative with a clear definition of what the law should be and new arguments connecting fewer hours, higher wages, and economic expansion. At the height of the Civil War, the struggle for shorter working hours began to revolve around the first sustained demand for an eight-hour workday—presented as an essential first step toward a larger labor reform vision, a crucial link with middle-class supporters, and a foundation for new concepts of working-class consumption. The advocates of the eight-hour day saw in their campaign, and in the imminent destruction of slavery and the restoration of the Union, a conjunction of forces opening the door to a profound social transformation. A new generation of activists began to emerge who saw in workers' control of their labor time the road to a genuinely reconstructed nation with social justice for all.[3]

I

As the 1840s drew to a close, producer cooperatives attracted increasing attention from labor reformers and activists in Boston. More than just a way for workers to make more money, cooperatives contained the seeds of fundamental economic change. Worker-owned shops and factories provided an opportunity to restructure the industrial economy and shift the balance of bargaining power toward labor, without depending on partisan politics or waiting for legislation that was never enacted. Producer cooperatives also could be especially attractive to urban artisans looking for worksites where they could preserve their skills, status, and independence in the face of growing pressure from industrial capitalism, new technology, and immigrant labor.

In September 1849, after a bitter fourteen-week strike, seventy journeymen tailors pooled their meager resources and created the Boston Tailors' Associative Union. The preamble to their charter—written by B. S. Treanon, an exiled

Irish Chartist leader and an active Associationist—stated boldly that "competitive society must be re-organized upon the principle of co-operation, before Labor can be protected against the despotic weight of capital." The tailors now concluded that they would not improve their conditions through strikes or trade unions. These past efforts to raise wages had been unsuccessful because they did not address the fundamental inequities of the wage system: the increasing concentration of capital in the hands "of a few individuals or corporations" was "depreciating, oppressing and degrading the laborers." Workers had to become "their own employers" and divide "the profits of their labors among themselves" if they were ever to break free of their status as wage slaves. A worker who joined others in a cooperative shop or factory could achieve economic independence, freedom from unemployment, and control over his labor time. Cooperating workers could reclaim the ideal of the artisan toiling in his own craft shop doing work that was creative and satisfying—a goal increasingly difficult to achieve or maintain in a competitive capitalist marketplace increasingly filled with exploited labor.[4]

The tailors opened a shop in the garment district of antebellum Boston on 88 Ann Street near Faneuil Hall and the city's wholesale markets; reformers and sympathizers from across the city quickly flocked to the store. The tailors made a conscious effort to transform not only the structure of ownership and the distribution of profits but also the work process and working conditions. All clothing sold in their store was made by members of the Tailors' Associative Union in well-lighted and ventilated workshops operating on a ten-hour workday. During the slack seasons in production, the workers pledged to reduce their hours so that all would have an equal share of the work available.[5]

On January 1, 1850, the tailors' efforts received a public endorsement from the Boston Union of Associationists. The Fourierists saw these cooperatives as welcome extensions of their own ideas for transforming labor beyond the physical and political confines of their rapidly disappearing utopian communities. Local Associationists provided capital for the tailors' workshop and others in the city; they also offered organizational models based on similar enterprises in France. The Associationists proclaimed that the cooperative tailor shop proved "the practicability of a system . . . where the man who works receives the full value of what he creates; . . . where the whole profits of industry are secured to those who do the work; where the *Capital* is considered of less consequence than the Labor; where Man is deemed of more importance than Money." The Associationists went on to praise the tailors for placing "Human Brotherhood" over "monopoly" by offering every member of their craft the chance to buy a share in their enterprise. The published address closed by noting that "other craftsmen are preparing for similar organizations.

A deeper feeling of fraternity is springing up in the great heart of the workingmen, who have become conscious of the identity of their interests in this righteous idea of Labor Reform."[6]

Printers in Boston followed close on the tailors' heels. They too set up a cooperative association and shop—the Boston Printers' Protective Union—after a protracted strike. In that shop they published the *Protective Union*, which became the principal newspaper for producer and consumer cooperatives throughout New England. The newspaper reported on a growing chorus of support for cooperative workshops throughout the spring and summer of 1850. There was a mass meeting at Faneuil Hall in early April. The next month, another gathering of trade unionists, protective unionists, and labor reformers met at the Boston Union of Associationists' office (22 Bromfield Street, near the Boston Common) to endorse "the establishment of a labor state in which there shall be no half-fed, half-clad, badly-housed worker, or fat, well-dressed, well-housed idler."[7]

By the end of May, the New England Industrial League emerged from continuing discussions among labor activists and reformers about support for cooperatives. The league brought together trade union leaders, organizers of cooperatives, and Associationists for monthly meetings to discuss mutual interests in labor reform, to organize new trade societies and cooperative associations, and to provide financial support if necessary for striking workers. Quite deliberately, as was often the case with labor organizations, this new league chose July 4 as the day to elect its first slate of officers.[8]

In early September, the league's president Henry Trask (harnessmaker) and secretary Edward Coddington (printer) called for a workingmen's convention in October to consider candidates for governor and lieutenant governor. The *Protective Union* encouraged these efforts at independent labor politics: "We have already a powerful organization throughout the State, in our 'Protective Union' 'Co-operative Associations' and 'Trades Societies,' and if the influence which these possess is brought to bear on the forthcoming election, the victory is ours." Yet producer cooperatives had been established as an alternative means of labor reform removed from the arena of partisan politics. And several cooperatives seemed to be succeeding with encouragement from the league. So why was the league urging a return to the electoral fray? Wouldn't that strategy drain money and support from the cooperatives into party coffers, just when the workshops needed capital and customers?[9]

Perhaps all was not well with the cooperative workshops. After all, many of them were formed in the wake of strikes by workers whose meager resources were nearly exhausted; and all were surrounded by privately owned competitors in a capitalist marketplace that dwarfed these modest enterprises.

Thus, most workers remained far removed from the benefits of cooperative labor. Perhaps the cooperatives' supporters felt they had to take a calculated risk, reenter the political arena, and secure legal protection (through incorporation) for their fledgling enterprises. By encouraging a renewed interest in nominations and electoral politics, the Industrial League's leaders admitted what some reformers may have realized all along—these new workshops could not stand alone as the sole answer to the deterioration of working conditions and labor's declining status. Partisan politicking, as distasteful and frustrating as it may have been, could not be avoided entirely; electioneering and petitioning still seemed to be necessary parts of the labor reform process.

In answer to the league's convention call, a small group of delegates gathered at Hancock Hall on the morning of October 10. Veteran reformers and activists, such as Charles Douglas and William F. Young, quickly expanded the agenda beyond cooperatives; they urged those assembled to take political action on issues ranging from the ten-hour workday to land reform to resistance against the recently enacted Fugitive Slave Law. The convention decided not to nominate candidates for state offices or to form an independent labor party. But the delegates did pass a series of stinging resolutions declaring the existing two-party system antithetical to workers' interests:

> Whereas, the present condition of labor and the laboring interests of the country clearly indicate the imperative necessity of some thorough and radical change in our State and National legislation, to save the people from Industrial, Political and Social degradation; and whereas the history of the two great political parties of the land, for at least the last twenty-five years, is one of assumption, usurpation, and treachery, whereby they have forfeited all claim to the confidence and support of the honest working classes, rendered their long supremacy, a disgrace to the Union....
> 1. Resolved, That we call upon our fellow workingmen, throughout Massachusetts and the Union, to absolve themselves from all connection with these parties....
> 2. Resolved, That our object is not so much the political triumph of parties and men, as the practical recognition of *rights,* through which we become *men,* and which form the basis of all righteous civil governments.

The meeting concluded by urging workingmen to vote for whichever candidates they believed would support a labor reform legislative agenda, regardless of party affiliation—a message that was clearly pro–political action and anti–partisan politics. Despite this ringing rhetoric, the Industrial League disappeared early the following year. Along with its demise, the brief flowering of producer cooperatives soon withered; and the influence of Associationism in labor reform circles also waned. The stage was cleared for the ten-hour campaign to reassert itself in new political forms.[10]

The Industrial League existed for only a short time. Yet its arguments for working-class political activism and voting, without necessarily creating an independent labor party or formally allying with an existing party, set the strategic tone for the ten-hour movement in the 1850s. The political struggle for shorter working hours moved away from its nearly exclusive reliance on mass petitions, a tactic that had attracted many working women (especially textile operatives) in the mid-1840s. By 1850, ten-hour advocates shifted toward politics at the ward and district levels, where men would wield much more leverage as voters and candidates. Shorter-hour rallies and meetings tended to become male-only affairs. Women, being legally disenfranchised, found their participation in such organizations and in local campaigning to be muted or marginalized (even though it was female factory workers who often remained vulnerable to overwork and in need of legislation regulating the hours of labor). The goal now was not just to persuade those already sitting in the statehouse to support a ten-hour law but to elect men who did not have to be convinced about the justice of this cause. The change in tactics evolved over time, but it was a significant turn. Workers would continue to send petitions to the legislature urging that a ten-hour law be passed, and the legislators would continue to draft reports and bills on the subject. But labor reform organizations now vowed to keep a closer eye on who voted which way on this issue and to do everything in their power to elect pro-labor candidates to the statehouse, regardless of which party they belonged to. Yet even as many workers tried to keep the movement above mere partisan politicking, once they plunged into the contest for votes they often found that it was party politicians who emerged as the leading mouthpieces for the ten-hour law.[11]

The ten-hour movement's political strategy shifted because the legislative climate also changed. The campaign for the shorter workday in the mid-1840s had usually run into a legislative stonewall, and organizations such as the NEWA decided not to put much effort into leading petition or lobbying campaigns. What went on in the statehouse was, in some ways, tangential to what the NEWA said and did. But the ten-hour campaign started to make some modest progress by 1850 in the Massachusetts legislature, because a coalition of Democrats, Free Soilers, and dissident Whigs now outvoted the powerful commercial-manufacturing bloc, which had long controlled the statehouse. This new coalition, which dominated state elections for two years, at least paid lip service to ten-hour legislation. An 1850 House committee minority report offered extensive arguments, including medical testimony on the adverse effects of overwork, in favor of legally limiting the hours of labor. One of the bill's coauthors was James Stone, a printer from Charlestown whose district included numerous machine shops and shipyards where mechanics had long been agitating for the ten-hour day. Ten-hour advocates also thought that, as the state's textile mill population began to shift from Yankee farmers' daughters to Irish immigrant families, the legislature might be more willing to consider government regulation of working hours. This is not to say that a ten-hour law was proposed because of any direct sympathy with the plight of the famine Irish. Rather, the old argument that the independent daughters of free men needed no legislative protection started to ring hollow. The ten-hour bill even had the support of Governor George S. Boutwell, but it failed to gather a majority on the House floor. In fact, the bill's defeat in the spring of 1850 may have been one of the reasons why some workers answered the Industrial League's call for a political convention in the fall. These workers were convinced that a targeted campaign to elect more pro-labor legislators could eventually tip the balance at the statehouse.[12]

In April 1852, another House committee filed two minority reports in support of proposed ten-hour legislation. The strongest proposal was drafted by William Robinson—a thirty-three-year-old journalist and recently elected Free Soil representative from Lowell. Robinson specified a one-year period for phasing in a legally enforceable ten-hour workday. Robinson said he was motivated by the appeals of more than 500 male petitioners. These men signed proclamations asserting that long hours of labor prevented them from spending time with their families or educating themselves about important public issues. The hours required to meet their economic responsibilities—earning money to feed their wives and children—overwhelmed all attempts to meet their domestic obligations as fathers and to represent their families' interests as voting citizens.

> While we recognize and acknowledge ... our obligations to render a full equivalent in labor for our wages, at the same time GOD has imposed other obligations upon us, as MEN, HEADS OF FAMILIES, AND MEMBERS OF SOCIETY; that *now* our working hours are so far claimed by the present system of labor, as to leave *little or no time* to devote to the great and holy duties of our common humanity. To secure a small portion of time in which to perform these sacred social and domestic duties, and to work out, to live out our mission, not simply as machines of labor, but as *living, thinking, breathing Men*, we pray that the legislature will establish by law the number of hours of labor which shall be held and taken as the legal measure of a day's work. And in view of our responsibilities, to ourselves as well as our employers; of their rights and of ours; of the value of LIFE, HEALTH, and INTELLIGENCE, as well as the profits of labor; of the greatest good, both to the employer and the employed, we would respectfully ask that the measure may be ten hours.[13]

The legislature once again declined to enact any ten-hour legislation, probably because the old Whig power bloc had regained control of key state offices. But continued legislative inaction did not stop the ten-hour movement in Boston. A "Ten-Hour State Convention" assembled at the end of September 1852 with nearly 200 delegates from across the commonwealth. This gathering followed the mass meeting model of earlier labor reform groups but also advocated what would become an increasingly common strategy—focus on one issue rooted in the workplace: securing a shorter workday. The presiding officials included Representatives Stone and Robinson, and William F. Young. The convention published a pamphlet that summarized numerous arguments for legal regulation of the workday and reprinted Robinson's minority report.[14]

Those assembled declared that they would "take the field, by organized political action, for the purpose of securing an enactment effective to reduce the hours of labor." They quickly added that they did "not propose to form a distinct political party; but . . . to present this question distinctly at the polls, in the election of State Senators and Representatives" who would unequivocally support a strong ten-hour law. (This strategy was similar to that of their predecessors in the Industrial League.)[15]

The convention then called on citizens to "protest against ineffective Ten Hours Laws" that merely set a legal standard for a day's work, without any enforcement mechanism or provision for those occupations already working less than ten hours a day. Instead, the pamphlet delineated carefully the convention's definition of a "genuine law" to compel shorter working hours in the corporations dominating the state's manufacturing sector. Such a law would be enforced by the legal authority of the commonwealth. Since the legislature created corporations to give capital certain rights and privileges, the government also had the duty to regulate those corporations when they used their consolidated powers to oppress workers. "We seek the abridgement of the hours of labor—not a new method of measuring the present hours. . . . Our whole purpose, is, the enactment of a law which shall *prohibit, in stringent and unmistakable terms, and under adequate penalties, the corporations, chartered by the laws of the State, from employing any person in laboring more than ten hours in any one day.* This is just the law—and all the law—we want on this subject; and we shall not relax our organization or efforts, until this be accomplished!" The proposed legislation was precise and unambiguous, and applicable to "any person" in the labor force. The convention had no interest in halfway measures designed to protect only women or children. These arguments for a ten-hour day were based not on workingmen's paternalism or altruism but on every worker's right to be free from overwork and exploitation.[16]

Thus, the convention spelled out a clear legislative agenda so that its campaign would not be fragmented or distracted by politicians promising support for some vague "Ten Hours System," or manufacturers offering skilled workmen an eleven-hour day. This convention, like the NEWA of the preceding decade, wanted to build a broad coalition for labor reform. But unlike some past organizations, this group tried to hold itself together not by offering a different reform to each constituency but by focusing everyone's attention on a precisely defined ten-hour law and a carefully orchestrated campaign to pass that law. There might be more labor reform initiatives down the road; but for the moment, the Ten-Hour State Convention would focus its efforts on securing the shorter workday.

The convention insisted on a precisely defined ten-hour law, but the pamphlet also laid out broad justifications for this legislation—offering economic rationales for shorter working hours far more complex than those seen in past decades. The convention argued for investment in human capital and asserted that there was ultimately a harmony of interests between labor and capital on the issue of shorter hours. A reduction in working hours would allow laborers to spend more time on their education and training, and a more intelligent working population would be more productive and generate more profits.

The pamphlet also asserted "*that a* REDUCTION *of the hours will* INCREASE *the wages of labor,*" an argument in direct opposition to the prevailing antebellum economic wisdom that a decrease in the workday would lead to an equivalent decline in workers' earnings. The convention insisted that if each worker labored fewer hours each day, more workers would be hired, the supply of surplus labor would decrease, and wages paid to increasingly scarce labor would increase. Furthermore, "the reduction of the hours of labor, by improving the moral, social and physical condition of the laboring people, and by increasing their wages, will tend to increase their consumption of the products of labor.... If the production of machinery now running be diminished under the Ten Hours System, more mills and more machines will be required. These new demands for things produced by labor, will increase the demand for laborers, and tend to enhance wages still more." This economic model linking decreased working hours, increased consumption, and higher wages—first articulated by the Ten-Hour State Convention (written by an unnamed committee)—was something previously unheard of in Boston labor reform circles. The theory seemed counterintuitive and even revolutionary. But working-class intellectuals such as Ira Steward, the leading theorist of the eight-hour movement, would refine these consumption-based arguments for shorter working hours in the decades following the Civil War. By the late nineteenth century, Steward's theories—rooted in that ten-hour convention of 1852—became a fundamental economic touchstone for legal limitations on the workday.[17]

The antebellum legislative campaign for a ten-hour day reached its political peak in 1855 and 1856 with the meteoric rise and fall of the Know-Nothing Party. Labor reform and an insurgent party found common ground. The Know-Nothings pledged to break once and for all the old Whig establishment's stranglehold on state politics and attracted thousands of working-class voters who were tired of seeing commercial interests vote down economic reforms. Surging into a political vacuum, following the Whigs' disintegration and preceding the Republicans' ascendancy, the party elected more than 100 sympathetic legislators in the fall of 1854. One-quarter of the new legislature was made up of working men; statehouse leaders included a shoemaker and a machinist. Once in office, the Know-Nothings promised to reform the legislative process itself and pass reform legislation for workers, in addition to pursuing their own nativist, anti-immigrant agenda. In fact, Know-Nothing legislators and their working-class supporters saw shorter hours and immigration restrictions as two sides of the same labor reform coin. They believed that controlling the influx of foreign workers, and circumscribing the rights of recent arrivals already in the United States, would protect the status of native-born American labor from further competition and degradation.[18]

The Know-Nothings' nativism was a direct response to the recent surge in Irish immigration through the port of Boston. By 1850, approximately 35,000 Irish lived in a city of about 135,000 inhabitants; five years later that figure stood at more than 50,000 Irish—nearly one-third of the population at that time. Most of these newcomers were poor peasants from the southern and western counties of Clare, Cork, Galway, and Kerry; fleeing famine, they arrived with no money and few skills outside of small-scale subsistence farming. Previous waves of immigrants to Boston had been much smaller in number, and many had left the city quickly for agricultural or industrial opportunities farther west. But most of the famine Irish stayed where they disembarked because they had no resources to travel into the American heartland. They crowded into cheap flats in the North End and Fort Hill neighborhoods near the wharves. Fathers and sons often tried to scratch out meager wages as day laborers on the docks or streets or construction sites; daughters frequently went into domestic service; mothers took in sewing or boarders. These recent immigrants sometimes found themselves in competition, and conflict, with new arrivals from the New England countryside also looking for jobs and housing. And this growing tension increased the Know-Nothings' appeal to native-born American workers that immigration restriction would protect their livelihoods and status just as much as any other labor reform.[19]

Many Protestant workers and reformers also probably felt comfortable with the Know-Nothings' anti-Catholic sentiments. Recent Irish immigrants flooding into Boston's labor market and the textile industry outside the city displaced outspoken, independent-minded Yankee workers with a more easily intimidated foreign labor force. To oppose immigration was to oppose newly arrived workers who seemed to threaten established jobs and wages, and who often did not support the labor reform agenda. Thus, both the democratic-reformist and nativist-reactionary elements of the Know-Nothing phenomenon had a certain appeal to some labor reformers and activists. Native-born workers often blamed immigrants who were the victims of nativist prejudice; these reformers and activists seemed to be blind at this time to the possibility of broader multi-ethnic coalitions.

The ten-hour day sat high on the Know-Nothing Party's legislative calendar. For the first time, both House and Senate committees of the state legislature filed *majority* reports advocating legal limitations on the workday. In 1855, the ten-hour bill carried the House by a large margin. But the Senate again balked at passage, leading to rumors that corporate lobbyists had bought key votes in the smaller upper chamber (including, perhaps, some previous supporters of the law).[20] This bitter defeat led many workers to defect from the Know-Nothings, hastening the party's rapid decline. Without any other third-party alternative, and with established parties disintegrating or reforming amid the growing sectional controversy over slavery, no new legislative coalition emerged to press the case for a ten-hour workday. Moreover, as some manufacturers made modest voluntary reductions in the workday, and as a severe economic downturn struck the nation in 1857, workers seemed to have less leverage on the issue. Thus, little more was heard from the ten-hour movement in Boston for the remainder of the decade.[21]

II

Boston's labor reform efforts remained dormant from 1857 to 1862 as the nation lurched toward civil war and fighting eventually engulfed the country. But in the fall of 1863, just months after the battle of Gettysburg and well before the war's conclusion, Boston labor reformers and activists renewed their efforts for a shorter workday. The city's population now approached 200,000; and the economy boomed with wartime orders for uniforms, cannons, and iron-clad ships. The foundries of South Boston and garret workrooms in the heart of the city hummed with activity; jobs were plentiful for new immigrants and war widows alike. Many workers decided to take advantage of their increased bargaining power in a wartime economy where labor was in great demand.

Instead of listening to pseudopatriotic appeals to toil unceasingly for the war effort, working men and women often pressed for higher wages to keep pace with rapidly rising wartime prices on food and fuel. Some activists and reformers framed a renewed call for legal regulation of the workday as a necessary and just reward for labor's efforts in meeting the intense wartime demands for military production.[22]

This new push for a shorter workday in late 1863 also brought to the fore a man who would become the eight-hour movement's leading theorist and the Boston labor reform community's leading agitator—Ira Steward. A thirty-two-year-old machinist, Steward was the son of a day laborer. Born in Connecticut, he had been raised in Boston and apprenticed as a teenager in Rhode Island, working twelve-hour days. Steward first urged his own union, the Machinists and Blacksmiths, to make the eight-hour day their top priority and to allocate funds so he could lobby the legislature. On November 17, 1863, the Trades Assembly of Boston responded to Steward and his fellow union members' request for cooperation in this new campaign. The Assembly declared that

> a reduction of the number of hours for a day's work, be the cardinal point to which our movement ought to be directed; that we make this point with the understanding that it is not antagonistic with capital, while at the same time it invests our cause with the dignity and power of a great Moral and Social reform, and that it is every way worthy of the sympathy and co-operation of the most progressive and liberal thinkers of the age, and that the time has fully arrived in which to commence a thorough and systematic agitation of this, the leading point in the great problem of Labor Reform.

In the midst of the Civil War, workers in Boston once again declared that the question of working hours was central to their larger vision of social and labor reform, and a crucial link with their middle-class supporters. Many skilled male workers—such as machinists and blacksmiths—were bold enough to say that now they would not settle for anything but the eight-hour day.[23]

In 1864, Steward and other activists created the Boston Labor Reform Association (BLRA)—an organization dedicated to securing eight-hour legislation for all workers, and promoting cooperative consumer purchasing. The BLRA set up an office at 221 Washington Street in Boston's commercial district and appointed another member of the machinists' union, Charles Livermore, as its agent to recruit members and distribute publications. Opening an office may not seem like a momentous event, but the BLRA was the first labor reform organization in the city to set up such quarters—and thereby established a precedent that other groups would follow in the postwar decades. Steward seemed acutely aware that labor reform agitation required something more than periodic conventions and resolutions. If labor reform were to succeed in its quest for social justice, reformers and activists needed a place to meet and organize on an ongoing basis. From its office, the association enrolled individual workers and reformers interested in the campaign for the eight-hour day, rather than delegates from established organizations. Steward and his supporters hoped that this association would complement the efforts of existing labor unions. But they also specifically criticized strikes as "expensive, unsuccessful and incompatible with a moral movement invoking legislation and public sympathy, and as tending to discourage, rather than encourage, the investment of capital in productive labor." Several unions, meanwhile, had organized the Boston Workingmen's Assembly, and its leaders suspected Steward of trying to form a rival group that he could control. Discussions about merging the two organizations broke off by year's end.[24]

In December 1864, the BLRA issued its first report and argued that the impending destruction of southern chattel slavery would have a profound impact on northern industry and labor. "How clearly will Northern Capital comprehend the idea," the report asked, "that 'the rapid accumulation of wealth' is not a matter of muscular endurance simply, but of thought; that we think the better for working, we work the better for thinking." The association also asserted that if capital reduced the workday, there would be "opportunities for the fair exercise of all our faculties, while the present long hour system means, mostly, the fair exercise of our muscles." The report implied that the North could secure a long-term competitive advantage over any new southern free labor system if northern workers were well educated, rested, and trained to be productive at their jobs. "*Real comforts and proper leisure for the people* is the controlling idea of this movement," the report proclaimed, "and if it can be shown that a reduction of hours will result in a more rapid accumulation of wealth and of comfort, it must prevail."[25]

Steward summed up his initial vision of labor reform in a letter to the abolitionist leader Wendell Phillips (who would soon emerge as another influential figure in the postwar campaign for the eight-hour day). Drawing on their shared commitment to the destruction of slavery, and his interest in both consumer cooperation and the shorter workday, Steward stated that the "Labor Reform Movement means *the Discharge of all useless Middle Men and the Abolition of all Useless Working Hours*." In subsequent correspondence, Steward started to articulate his consumption-based economic model for the shorter workday—picking up ideas first proposed by the Ten-Hour State Convention of 1852, and eventually developing them into an argument heard across the nation. "All who live must *consume!*" he wrote. "All who *consume* must *produce*! . . . *Productive* Capital and *Labor* are Natural Allies." Given these early optimistic views of possible harmony on the shopfloor, Steward again insisted on "the necessity of *clearing* our movement altogether of strikes."[26]

While Steward was pressing forward with the BLRA, striking printers in Boston decided to publish their own newspaper (as they had fifteen years earlier). The *Daily Evening Voice* (*DEV*) first appeared on December 2, 1864, and remained in business for nearly three years. The *DEV* quickly became the de facto "paper of record" for labor reform arguments circulating throughout Boston at the end of the Civil War. Workers and reformers contributed constantly to its pages in an effort to stake out crucial political and organizational high ground as the nation's fratricidal conflict concluded. Operating out of offices in the city's newspaper district at 77 Washington Street (near the BLRA headquarters), where printers also produced pamphlets and proceedings for various local unions and labor reform groups, the *DEV* published a string of articles and editorials supporting trade unions, higher wages, the eight-hour workday, the right to strike when necessary, and the need for workers to become politically active and demand specific labor legislation without depending on the existing parties for support.[27]

Throughout 1865, at the very moment when the nation began to confront the implications of slavery's destruction, the *DEV*'s columns practically burst with arguments for the eight-hour day. Some assertions were familiar to veterans of the previous decade's ten-hour movement, such as the need to regulate corporations and the insistence that reducing the hours of labor would actually lead to an increase in wages. Other advocates tested new ideas for the postwar era: for example, the eight-hour day would open up job opportunities for returning soldiers, since no workers would be forced to work ten and twelve hours anymore. One correspondent prophesied that new machinery might even "reduce the hours of labor to four or six hours a day with full pay" and leave ample time to "give exercise every day for the normal development of man's physical, mental, moral, and religious nature."[28]

The newspaper's editors insisted that workers already had the innate ability for higher thought and culture; but labor lacked the opportunity to cultivate those inherent intellectual faculties. Thus, the system of overwork robbed individuals and society of talent and innovative skills that might advance the human race. The editors further argued for a balanced day with "eight hours for labor, eight for recreation, and eight for rest—the eight for recreation being as indispensable to health and happiness as the eight for labor and the eight for rest." This division of each day into three equal parts echoed Theophilus Fisk's speech thirty years earlier and became a cardinal tenet of the eight-hour movement for the remainder of the nineteenth century.[29]

The *DEV* made specific appeals to both women and men in support of the eight-hour day. The paper urged workingmen's wives to attend meetings and rallies for the shorter workday "to fire their souls with the grand thought of this movement, and to exalt and strengthen" the cause "with the inspiration of [their] presence." The editors also recognized that "woman herself is a toiler; and as a workingwoman the prevailing system of long hours is even more oppressive upon her than upon men. The thousands of women in our factories work eleven, twelve and thirteen hours, in close and unwholesome atmospheres, to the serious detriment of their health." As for men, the newspaper issued a call to action—both within and beyond the political arena, if necessary—replete with the republican and masculine rhetoric of fundamental rights, duties, and respect often seen in past campaigns. Workingmen had to seize the initiative in the immediate postwar era and set the terms of their own labor; self-rule in the workplace would be the foundation of workers' rights in a reconstructed nation.

> It is the right of American workingmen to rule this country, and it is their solemn duty to themselves, to posterity, to the memory of their patriot fathers, and to God, to maintain that right—to be men—self-reliant, self-respecting, intelligent men;—not to wait the sanction of public sentiment and the tardy action of legislatures, but to *take* the Eight-Hour system, and to claim and have a fair share of the product of their labor. If more labor is wanted, there are non-producing hands enough, and society would be better for setting them to work.[30]

The *DEV*'s editors further argued, as did many other reformers and activists, that the eight-hour day was but one step (though a necessary first step) in a grander project—the "ELEVATION OF LABOR." The eight-hour system was not only a "public blessing, but . . . a moral and social NECESSITY" for the nation's future stability and orderly growth. Workers had to convince capitalists "that labor is honorable; that social distinction does not properly arise from occupation, but from manly and womanly merit; and that human happiness is not to be sought in out-doing one's neighbor in costliness of style; but in useful employment, intelligent minds and loving hearts." Thus, labor had to take the lead in transforming the nation's fundamental social and economic priorities and values at the very moment when the country was reuniting its political structure and setting its course for the postwar years.[31]

With slavery's downfall, the next battle would be for the rights of free labor in a modern industrial economy. The *DEV* did not advocate a new war across class lines but demanded equality of opportunity in the marketplace and a chance for workers' children to pursue intellectual advancement. Intelligent labor would not subjugate capital but would strive to end the system of antagonistic economic institutions and promote the ultimate harmony of employees' and employers' interests in a prosperous nation. On the other hand, the editors warned, labor left in a state of ignorance and oppression would become a breeding ground for crime, depravity, and violent upheaval. The *DEV* looked especially to the rising generation of young workers to carry forward this broad vision of labor and social reform; to create a movement that would ultimately transcend any narrow sense of class interests and represent the nation's vast majority of working people and their families.

> Do not think you can find a theatre of action more promising, a work more enobling? It has been the fashion to despise labor, but it is a false idea. There is really nothing so noble and dignified as labor; and this true idea the world is about to receive.... You will see... upon what broad ground our reform rests. You will see that as labor is the source of all wealth, so it is the source of all power and virtue. It is the foundation upon which everything rests. If labor is servile, whatever grows out of it will be selfish and depraved. If labor is broadly enlightened, cultivated and independent, as it should be, we have the most wholesome conditions for a high-toned morality and the best scientific, literary and religious culture. If you wish to rise, or would be useful, you can find no opening so eligible as the labor reform. As labor is honorable, resolve that you will honor it. Embark your fortunes in its cause without fear.[32]

In the first week of April 1865, just days before Robert E. Lee's surrender at Appomattox, Anna Dickinson—a twenty-two-year-old Quaker abolitionist and women's rights orator with a rapidly growing national reputation on the lecture circuit—arrived from New York to give a speech at the Tremont Temple. Dickinson's address placed the subject of working women back on center stage for labor reformers and activists in Boston. After a warm and laudatory introduction from Wendell Phillips, Dickinson launched into an extensive analysis of women's work and wages. She clearly linked the low status of female labor with the low pay received in factories and "slop shops" where women sewed cheap clothing. Women faced restricted opportunities for wage work and hence crowded into lower skilled occupations under constantly deteriorating pay and working conditions. Dickinson even broached the delicate and controversial subject of low wages driving some women into the depths of degradation and prostitution. She "asked simply for woman that she should have an equal chance with man. Not teach the boy that industry and ambition is honorable, and teach the girl that work is a disgrace. Take the impediments out of her way and give her the same pay for the same work; and then, if she shall fall by the way-side, let her fall." Dickinson concluded that women should have opportunities for education and meaningful work, not to displace men from their roles in society but to fulfill women's own potential for achievement and advancement.

Both the *DEV* and organizations such as the Workingmen's Assembly praised Dickinson's speech. The *DEV* encouraged women to reject popular conceptions of female dependence and inferiority and to form their own labor organizations. Editors urged legislators to make the problem of working women's wages and health a top priority in the postwar era. Ending the exploitation of female labor was no mere exercise in paternalistic sympathy or charity; it was part and parcel of the struggle to secure justice for all workers. Once again, labor reformers and activists envisioned their efforts as reaching beyond any one demand or any one constituency of workers—no working man's rights could be secure until working women's interests were also recognized and protected. This forceful political and ideological connection between working women's interests and the broader conception of labor reform echoed the ten-hour petition campaigns of the 1840s and the public rally at Faneuil Hall back in May of 1848.[33]

Thus, labor reform's fundamental arguments about justice and fairness for all who toiled had indeed survived the fires of sectional conflict and civil war, and remained a vibrant ideal for men and women poised to fight new economic struggles as the cannons fell silent. Legislative defeats and organizational dissolution did not lead to the disintegration of the labor reform impulse. Rather, new groups and leaders with new arguments picked up the banner, decade after decade. Sometimes earlier campaigns—especially the ten-hour movement—returned to the fray with new strategies. Sometimes new projects—such as workers' cooperatives—sprang up around the city. This resilient labor reform effort, with all its transformations and limitations, provided a legacy of people and ideas for generations to come. The era of sectionalism and civil war was not a gap but a bridge that connected pre- and postwar labor reform activism. Many labor reformers and activists in Boston saw in the very struggle to destroy chattel slavery an inspiration and an opening for their arguments to resolve all the questions surrounding the rights of free labor and capital. The passion for social change survived, even in the harshest political and social conditions, and served as a catalyst for a near-explosion of activity in the immediate postwar era.

3

ACTS OF COMMISSION
Labor Reformers, Activists, and the Levers of Political Power, 1865–1870

THE YEARS 1865 to 1870 were a time of political reconstruction for the nation and of strategic reconstitution for labor reform organizations in Boston. As one observer noted: with "the breaking up of the rebellion and the return of the Grand Army of the Republic to the grand army of labor, from the process of destruction to the process of Production ... the full force" of the labor reform campaign could be realized. The very concept of Reconstruction, as defined by labor reformers and activists, extended beyond legal reunification and embraced a restructuring of the nation's economy and workplaces. With chattel slavery abolished and the Union restored, labor reformers and activists urged that the rights of free workers now be placed at the top of the nation's postwar agenda. Timing was everything: the months and years following the war's conclusion would involve the crucial moment when national goals could be molded for the future, and labor deserved to be rewarded for its contributions to preserving the nation.[1]

Within months of the war's conclusion, the Boston labor reform community—building on its antebellum organizational and ideological foundations—swelled its ranks with new supporters and renewed demands for working people's rights. A new generation of labor reformers and activists emerged to join veterans from the previous decades' campaigns—young men often born in the small towns outside of Boston and nurtured in a world of antislavery activism, republican ideology, and Protestant reform efforts. Some had served in the army while others fought to organize labor against wartime inflation, but they all brought a crusading spirit back home to their workplaces and meeting halls.

The demand for the eight-hour workday quickly emerged as a central rallying cry for the early postwar labor reform effort. New appeals to regulate the hours of labor came not only from citizen petitioners but also from legislators themselves, who began to see political advantages in at least paying lip service to the issue. In less than two years, as politicians scrambled to respond to the increasing public pressure and party maneuvering, without necessarily enacting any new laws, three Massachusetts legislative committees and special commissions issued extensive reports on the hours of labor in the commonwealth. These governmental bodies were not always cross-class in composition, nor were they necessarily sympathetic to labor reform arguments. Nevertheless, their public inquiries into working conditions brought reformers and activists deeper into the political process than ever before. Eight-hour advocates had to hone their appeals for legislation. And the extensive hearings, testimony, and reports still extant are all barometers of the shifting political storms surrounding the labor reform struggle in the year immediately following the Civil War.

Ira Steward, through his testimony before the various committees and commissions, as well as his numerous speeches at public rallies and his published pamphlets, emerged as the leading thinker and organizer for the eight-hour campaign in Boston. Steward, in the months and years following the war's conclusion, further developed his consumption-based arguments for the shorter workday—always insisting that a decrease in the hours of labor was the essential first step in a broader process of social change. He believed that an unwavering focus on the eight-hour workday, framed as the foundation for far-reaching economic transformation, would be the ideological glue to hold together a broad cross-class labor reform coalition.

Through committee appearances, and political leverage built in meeting halls and street rallies, labor activists and reformers drew closer to the mechanisms of electioneering and governing. And their initial reception in the statehouse corridors and hearing rooms was sometimes warmer than that of their antebellum predecessors. But as the decade closed, the labor reform community still found itself stymied in the legislative process. Politicians continued just to smile, pass the eight-hour hot potato from committee to commission, and pen increasingly hostile reports, but never to enact restrictions on the hours of labor for working men and women. Activists and reformers had to look again beyond the legislative process for new organizations and strategies to press the campaign for labor reform, even if many still believed that at some point they had to get the law on their side. Several leaders insisted that building a stable organization with a central office—a labor reform headquarters for the entire city—would accomplish more than all the past quarterly meetings and outdoor rallies. But efforts to establish a Labor Reform Institute soon foundered because of persistent financial problems—rented office space had to be paid for—and recurrent debates about answering the siren call of the political arena.

I

In January of 1865, before the final Union offensive in the South began, the *Daily Evening Voice* (*DEV*) reported on a petition to regulate wages and hours, submitted to the Massachusetts legislature. Written by Rufus Wyman, an abolitionist minister and labor reformer from Roxbury (a nearby community that Boston would annex in 1868), the document revealed a keen sense of the economic issues at stake for working men and women as the nation neared the conclusion of its long and bloody civil war.

> The "cruel war" now in progress, begun by the slaveholders and those in their interest, is in danger of being changed into a war between capitalists and laborers, to determine which shall rule.... We may not hope for peace until all the useful industries are esteemed by law and by public opinion as worthy of equal respect and reward.... God has made some men to be hewers of wood and drawers of water, but it is not all plain that He intended that they should eat poorer or less bread than those of the learned professions or the speculators; nor that He intended that they should be made to work so many hours in their vocation that they cannot have a chance to become learned.... The undersigned therefore prays that a law may be enacted establishing a rate of wages, somewhat above the average (say ten dollars) and the time (say six hours) for a day of work.... It is not expected that the legislation prayed for will remove all the wrongs and affronts to which labor is subjected, but it is believed that it will help to remove it.

Though Wyman thought that his request for a law regulating hours and wages was a modest proposal, and only one stop along the road to justice for workers, the legislature thought otherwise. The petition was read in the House, referred to the Judiciary Committee, and quickly died there. Wyman's appeal, however, made him one of the first reformers in Boston to state publicly what many others would say for years to come—that the war would settle the fundamental question of chattel slavery but would not resolve the essential debates about the rights of free labor in postwar America.[2]

Two months later, with the final Union spring offensive unfolding and the war's end clearly in sight, the hours-of-labor question came up again; and this time the Massachusetts legislature placed the matter squarely on its calendar.

Why? After all, in early spring of 1865, the issue was not the subject of a statewide petition campaign, as in the 1840s, or promoted by a convention writing a model law and questioning prospective candidates about their stand on the proposal, as in the 1850s. Rather, one of the few Democratic legislators in the overwhelmingly Republican body, Representative John Mahan of Boston (a veteran of the Ninth Massachusetts Regiment), went to the House floor on March 8, 1865, and moved that the Judiciary Committee consider a law to regulate the hours of labor. Mahan's colleagues quickly honored his request, partly because the resolution came from a member of the legislative body rather than from an outside petitioner. And, perhaps more significantly, Mahan made his motion before a legislature increasingly dominated by reform-minded Republicans who believed that state power could be used to address social problems in the emerging postwar era. These same Republicans also thought they now saw an issue that could be seized from Mahan and the Democrats and offered to returning soldiers and workers as a reward for their contributions to the Union victory.[3]

On the following Monday morning, March 13, the Judiciary Committee convened a hearing to consider both working hours and the apprenticeship system. Realizing that both issues were complex, and of great interest to a labor movement grown in size and power during the war years, the committee reported back to the House that a special committee should be appointed to consider the proposed legislation. So these representatives did not confront the question of labor laws; they played pass the political football, an evasive tactic that would be repeated several more times before the decade ended. Yet, they did recommend a thorough investigation into the conditions of labor in postwar Massachusetts. This call for a government inquiry into the workplace would have important implications for labor reformers and activists in Boston. In testimony before the special committee, and subsequent commissions, workers and their allies sharpened their critiques of the emerging industrial economy and extended their demands for labor legislation.[4]

The House and Senate quickly empaneled a Joint Special Committee. Many in the Boston labor reform community hoped they would get a sympathetic hearing from the panel, which included several legislators with working-class backgrounds. Edward H. Rogers, a forty-one-year-old ship's carpenter from Chelsea, selected the House members for the joint committee. Rogers supported the eight-hour movement; however, he had closer ties with trade unionists in the Workingmen's Assembly than with Ira Steward's Labor Reform Association. In addition to Rogers, the committee included Charles McLean, a millwright from East Boston; and State Senator Martin Griffin, a journeyman printer from Boston, who wrote the committee's final report.[5]

In early April, the Joint Special Committee held a series of evening meetings so that working men and women could come and give testimony without losing a day's wages. Edward Rogers recalled that "it was the first result of the incoming of workingmen into the halls of Legislation, in our own rights and on equal terms with the representatives of cultured society." The *Daily Evening Voice* reported, alongside the latest dispatches announcing Richmond's fall and Lee's surrender, that literally dozens of wage workers, union leaders, and even sympathetic employers testified to the physical, mental, and moral advantages of an eight-hour workday. Witnesses often spoke of factory women as being especially overworked and underpaid. Mechanics declared that they wanted more time to spend at the library and lyceum—not at the grogshops, as their critics charged. C. J. Spenceley, a Boston carpenter, echoed earlier political arguments from the prewar ten-hour movement when he said: "Nine out of ten mechanics in Boston . . . [are] deficient in ability to look after their own interests as mechanics and to understand the political questions of the day. . . . They were simply 'bamboozled' by politicians when they were lauded by them for their intelligence and independence."[6]

Ira Steward, representing the Boston Labor Reform Association, argued that "the ten-hour system was never intended to give sufficient time for self-improvement. The questions with employers were how many hours can I keep my machinery running? how many can the men endure?" Steward added that "he did not want to obtain legislation for a class. The questions to be considered were, will the wealth of the State be increased, and will the intelligence and happiness of the people be increased? . . . The old standard was the endurance of the laborer, the new must be the skill of the laborer." Steward concluded his remarks by asserting his belief that the labor movement was unified in endorsing shorter hours as a crucial first step—but just that, a first step—in "the elevation of the working classes." Though Steward may have overstated the movement's ideological unity, his argument for the primacy of the eight-hour day was one he would repeat with growing frequency and urgency for nearly two decades.[7]

Steward elaborated on what he saw as the vital link between the eight-hour day and a broader vision of labor reform in an article for *Fincher's Trade Review*, a pro-labor newspaper published in Philadelphia. Workers who labored fewer hours had more time to consider other improvements in their working conditions, and eventually they would ponder even deeper questions of social justice and economic change.

> The Labor Reform movement embraces more than will be solved by this generation or perhaps in centuries. The question of reducing the number

of hours for a day's labor is a *single point* in the movement, which may and will be settled in a very short time.... The idea of making the number of hours for a day's labor the first point in the Labor Reform movement, is from this fact; that *with more leisure,* workingmen are in a very much better situation to discuss the general subject for themselves.... The appeal of workingmen and women to employers and to the State to reduce the hours of labor may be put thus: "Get out of our sunshine and we will settle for ourselves questions and problems in production and consumption, wages ... [and] improved ventilation of workshops."

Steward went on to insist that if employers and employees actually talked to each other, they would learn that both of their biggest fears about the eight-hour day—that it would lead to lower wages for labor, and lower profits for capital—were unfounded. Labor could say what it knew, that workers were often more productive when they had more time for rest; and employers could tell what they saw, that wages go up when hours are decreased.[8]

On April 28, 1865, just two weeks after concluding its hearings, the Joint Special Committee submitted its report to the House. The committee noted that, in the prewar period, workers had often demanded a legally enforceable ten-hour day, but their efforts never succeeded in the legislature. (In fact, the report mentioned only one of the many failed ten-hour bills—the one from 1850.) Despite this legislative inaction, the ten-hour workday had become standard in many industries. Textile mills remained the glaring exception to this trend toward shorter hours. Many mills still ran eleven hours each day; and the report condemned them as "a disgrace ... to Massachusetts, and an outrage on humanity." The committee went on to acknowledge that many postwar labor reformers and activists now insisted on an eight-hour day. Drawing on the working-class background of several members, the committee hastened to add that it endorsed this bold call for an even shorter workday. The report argued that the eight-hour workday would actually prove to be an economic boon to the state, not a threat to industry's competitive position. The commonwealth would gain a more productive and inventive workforce, and spend less time and money trying to control social problems generated by an overworked and undereducated laboring population.

Despite its ringing endorsement of workers' testimony about the eight-hour day's many benefits, however, the committee refused to write a bill on the subject. The members pleaded that since they had been appointed late in the legislative session, they did not have time to work out details for drafting such a law. Instead, they proposed that this potentially explosive issue be passed on to another political body. The Joint Special Committee resolved and the legislature approved a resolution "that a commission to consist of five, be appointed by the governor—without compensation—to collect information and statistics, in regard to the hours of labor; the condition and prospects of the industrial classes . . . and report the result of such investigation, to the next legislature for its action."[9]

The Joint Special Committee tried to write a sympathetic report that acknowledged workers' and reformers' reasonable demands for an eight-hour workday. At the same time, this committee tried not to antagonize business interests and therefore refused to recommend specific legislation restricting the hours of labor, instead passing the political hot potato to an unpaid, appointed fact-finding commission. Because those commissioners would perform their duties without compensation, workers probably would not serve on the new panel, since wage laborers could rarely afford to take any extended time away from their jobs. Thus, whatever report this new commission wrote might prove to be far less sympathetic to workers' demands for the eight-hour day.

During the summer of 1865, while the governor labored to assemble all the members of the Special Commission, labor activists urged their followers to keep public attention focused on the issue of working hours. The long delay in organizing the new body and holding new hearings led some to suspect that politicians were trying to sidetrack the demand for a shorter workday. Their suspicions were probably warranted. Ira Steward thought it imperative to address the question of working hours in the months immediately following the Civil War's conclusion; and he made just such an appeal when he wrote to William Lloyd Garrison's newspaper, *The Liberator*. Steward believed that the abolitionist movement's postwar mission was to join the wage workers' struggle for justice. "Aside from the question of [Southern] reconstruction," Steward asserted, "there is no American question which presents stronger claims for immediate attention and adjustment than that of the claims of Labor:. . . since there is no evil in America which affects so directly and generally the health, morals, intelligence, wealth and happiness of the masses, as that of excessive toil: And further, that there is no moral or social reform claiming our attention that is not interested—directly or indirectly—in reducing the hours of labor."[10]

Martin Griffin, author of the Joint Special Committee's report recommending the appointment of a Special Commission, admonished the Workingmen's Assembly in June to strike if necessary to secure the eight-hour day. He even told his listeners to take a pay cut, if they had to. And "if it should be offered on condition of a reduction of wages, welcome it at that, for they need not fear. Get the eight hours at any rate. . . . If it robs you of half your pay, be men, and have some time for reflection!" Echoing the Ten-Hour State Convention resolutions from the previous decade, Griffin also counseled the assembled workers to "organize in every town in the Commonwealth. This is the way wealth carries its purpose. . . . In every single town in the State have it clearly understood among workingmen that their votes are to be given to no man who is not in favor of this great reform." The assembled trade unionists loudly applauded Griffin's remarks—his bold call for walkouts, his appeal for political action, even his warning about pay cuts.[11]

In the fall of 1865, Ira Steward wrote a lecture and published it as a pamphlet under the no-nonsense title *The Eight Hour Movement. A Reduction of Hours Is an Increase of Wages*. In this essay, Steward presented the first sustained discussion of his economic theory underlying the eight-hour movement: decreasing the hours of labor meant increasing the hours of leisure; increased leisure would lead workers to "cultivate tastes and create wants in addition to mere physical comforts"; these tastes and wants would stimulate more consumer spending, which would create more jobs, more profits, and the demand for higher wages to meet these new wants; and since the demand for higher wages would be nearly universal, no one employer would have the power or the motivation to resist such a demand. The connections between shorter hours, more leisure time for consumer spending, and higher wages had first been made more than a decade previously by the Ten-Hour State Convention of 1852. Steward's pamphlet, however, offered a much more extensive and sophisticated argument for this consumption-based model of work and wages.[12]

Steward did not argue that shorter working hours meant more productive and profitable workers, as other reformers often did. Rather, he stressed the idea that laborers deserved more leisure to be more effective consumers. Instead of an iron law of low wages in a world of limited capital, Steward saw a golden mean of shorter working hours stimulating a higher economic and intellectual standard of living. Human intelligence and new technology would lead to more goods and more leisure time in which to consume those goods, not a fearful future of mass unemployment and declining wages. Consumption itself was not a frivolous exercise but a way for workers to reclaim some value from their labor and their earnings. Thus, unlike many other labor leaders, Steward did not believe that wage labor per se led to social and economic inequality. It was low wages and long hours on the job that created the growing gap between poor laborers and wealthy capitalists.[13]

Steward's consumptionist arguments for the eight-hour day revolved around the basic premise that decreasing the most elemental standard of labor—the length of the workday—increases the standard of living, which in turn promotes higher wages and further economic growth. Steward encouraged workers to embrace the emerging industrial order as a potential source of abundance, and to use the wage labor system and the market to their immediate advantage. But he also held out a long-term vision of a radically altered economy in which workers would someday own and thereby control all that they produced. Steward saw the logical conclusion of his economic model to be that "the simple increase of Wages is the first step on that long road which ends at last in a more equal distribution of the fruits of toil. For Wages will continue to increase until the Capitalist and Laborer are One." In the short term, Steward insisted, workers should be educated about how their immediate physical and pecuniary conditions would improve if they worked fewer hours, and how to agitate for an eight-hour law in their own interest. Then, further down that long road which he sketched out, the eight-hour day would open up opportunities to consider broader social reforms leading to a progressive, modern, technological economy centered on equity and justice for all who labored.

Steward also believed that the labor movement had to be united in demanding both short-term and long-term reforms. Labor could not allow caste differences within the working class to be exploited by capitalists. Steward warned "mechanics, who affect a social distinction between the uncultivated laborer and yourself;—on election day the Capitalist and the common laborer unite and vote you down, and the rest of the year you and the shrewder Capitalist unite and keep down and away from you the 'common and unclean' laborer. Hasten the day when we shall hear no more of any honorable industry being 'common and unclean.' . . . The Eight Hour system will make a coalition between ignorant labor and selfish Capital on election day, impossible." Steward insisted not only that working-class equity and unity were moral imperatives and political necessities but also that "by the inexorable law of *self-interest,* we are bound to lift up the lowest and most degraded laborer. . . . *We* shall never occupy comfortable and healthy dwellings until *they* are well out of their hovels, tenement-houses and cellars, and they will never come out of them until leisure has opened their eyes to their own shame and filth." All workers, regardless of skill or status, could rally around their common need for an eight-hour workday. And, in turn, a united labor reform effort could press the case for shorter working hours.

Steward attached an addendum to his pamphlet—"The Eight Hour Movement Brought to a 'Yes' or 'No' Point"—containing a series of questions addressed to all political candidates in city, state, or federal elections. Did congressional candidates support the eight-hour day at all federal government installations? Did those running for governor or the state legislature endorse "a law making Eight Hours a legal day's labor in the absence of a written agreement . . . a law forbidding the employment of minors, under eighteen years of age, more than Eight Hours a day . . . [and] a law prohibiting any company incorporated by the laws of this State from employing Laborers, or Operatives, more than Eight Hours a day?" Did municipal contestants want "to secure the adoption of the Eight Hour System for the Laborers and Mechanics employed by the City Government?"[14]

Steward wrote up these specific interrogatories for particular legislation at all levels of government, including several different forms of eight-hour laws for workers in a variety of jobs and workplaces, because he wanted to emphasize that activists and reformers had to formulate their own precise legislative objectives and electoral standards without outside interference from so-called practical politicians. Reformers and workers had to hold politicians accountable for taking an unequivocal public stand on these specific demands. This technique of openly vetting candidates had been endorsed by the ten-hour conventions of the 1850s, and Steward urged eight-hour campaigners in 1865 to pin down slippery politicians as well. Like labor reformers and activists before him, Steward was trying to build cross-class political coalitions, and mobilize voters to elect pro-labor candidates, without letting party politicians dominate the campaign for shorter working hours.

With the publication of his pamphlet, Ira Steward emerged as a leading theorist, organizer, and political activist for the eight-hour day and for the entire labor reform community in Boston. He took the increasingly familiar assertion that shorter working hours were a crucial first step toward broader social transformation and gave that argument more depth, sophistication, and urgency. Steward was truly a working-class intellectual, a machinist self-schooled in a vast literature concerning mid-nineteenth-century political economy, and a man convinced that his ideas for labor reform would succeed because they arose from his own working experiences. He believed that workers who read his writings would learn both innovative theory and useful insights into the emerging American industrial economy. Activists and reformers would need this knowledge to develop a coherent reform program and a plan of political action to accomplish their goals. His arguments for the eight-hour day blended pragmatic considerations for improving working conditions with a larger conception of economic transformation through workers' increased leisure and consumption.

In terms of organizational leadership, Steward and the Boston Labor Reform Association tried to steer a middle course between trade union demands concerning wages and hours and contracts, and more radical schemes for social change which often left many workers puzzled and intimidated. Steward stood apart from those reformers who advocated broad organizational platforms with a multitude of causes to keep every potential ally in the fold. He believed that a diverse coalition could be held together by focusing on one issue, and that one issue was the eight-hour day. But Steward always also insisted that his demand for shorter hours was no narrow appeal; eight hours would create a foundation for a social vision that extended beyond immediate self-interest. He believed that to be successful, the struggle for labor reform had to continue drawing support from both working-class activists and middle-class sympathizers, and putting the eight-hour day at the forefront of its political agenda. Steward also argued, however, that a shorter workday was not an end in itself but the first step in improving working people's status throughout American society.

II

Governor John H. Andrews established the Special Commission on the Hours of Labor immediately following the legislature's vote in April 1865. But the commission did not hold hearings until six months later—having to muddle first through the resignation and replacement of several original members. The commissioners eventually included as chair Rev. William P. Tilden, minister of the New South Congregational Society in Boston and a one-time ship's carpenter; Dr. Henry Ingersoll Bowditch, Harvard Medical School professor, ardent abolitionist, and former State Sanitary Commissioner; Franklin B. Sanborn, another outspoken abolitionist and secretary of the State Board of Charities; George H. Snelling, translator and political reformer active in Boston municipal affairs; and Elizur Wright, yet another abolitionist leader and State Insurance Commissioner. These men all had connections to the state's political elite, organized charity work, and the wealthier wing of the Boston reform community, but none of them had close ties with any labor reform organizations. Thus, they could be presented to the public as men sympathetic to reform in general, without being predisposed to any particular position on the controversial issue of labor legislation.[15]

Following the precedent established by the Joint Special Committee, the Special Commission responded to requests from workers eager to testify and held several evening sessions. Starting in late October and all through November, dozens of witnesses from farms, factories, and workshops across the commonwealth appeared before the five-man body to speak on both sides of the eight-hour question. Those who could not make the trip to Boston submitted detailed responses to printed questionnaires distributed by the commission. Many farmers and rural mechanics firmly opposed any eight-hour law; shoeworkers, hatters, and many men in the building trades made strong pleas in favor of legislatively regulating the workday.[16]

Ira Steward, in his testimony at the end of November, offered several intriguing arguments in support of the eight-hour day. He drew a parallel between federal efforts to protect the freedom and improve the material conditions of former southern slaves and the positive impact that local and state eight-hour legislation would have on Irish immigrant day laborers in Boston. Later in his remarks, he asserted that "with the bettering of every man's condition, you will find that fathers having now no object[ion], will begin to take children from the labor market and put them into schools. That will reform the juvenile vagrancy." Steward also urged the commissioners to see that "we have got to make it a cardinal point in politics, that such things as extreme ignorance and extreme poverty shall not prevail, we can only do it by taking that course which shall bring up the habits of the people and bring up their wages." He insisted that charting such a course for the future, like the final struggle to abolish slavery, would have to include state action to stop the exploitation of workers in the labor market.

Steward, as he went forward with his statement, became impassioned about his vision for the future under the eight-hour system. And he declared that his vision was not utopian but based on a reconstructed American economy where wealth belonged to those who produced it and where everyone who worked had a fair share of the nation's material and cultural resources.

> I believe it was testified here that there was too much done [for labor reform]. There is not 1/20 enough done. When every family lives in a palace; when every man, woman and child has enough to eat, wear and drink; when the earth is turned into a flower garden; when the implements of war have been beaten into pruning hooks, you may talk about too much work being done. What I want is a system of things that will produce wealth a great deal faster; that the man shall have the wealth he produces himself instead of giving it to another. . . . How much does a man need? Pure air to breathe, good food to eat, plenty of rooms to live in, education for his children, comforts for his wife, those things which belong to refinement and industry. He needs all this. Why does he not have them? It is simply because we are not producing wealth fast enough.

Steward then used his final moments of testimony to launch a critique of those who still pressed for a popular reform scheme from the previous decade—producer cooperatives. Steward actively promoted cooperative consumer purchasing through the Boston Labor Reform Association, but he also insisted that his eight-hour system was the most pragmatic first step along the road to permanent and profound social change. That road would eventually lead to workers' cooperative ownership of the means of production, but Steward saw before him a long journey with no easy shortcuts. "Remember that [Horace] Greeley and other men in the country are perfectly willing to talk of 'co-operation.' Co-operation is the millennium.... I, who mark the line am called 'visionary,' while they who jump to the goal are called 'practical.' Co-operation is the end so far as labor goes.... Before we can have co-operation every man must have all that he earns."[17]

While the Special Commission met in session, labor reformers and activists continued to agitate for their cause beyond the hearing room. On the first Thursday evening in November, just days before state legislative elections, a mass rally gathered at Faneuil Hall in support of the eight-hour day. (The crowd also heard speeches endorsing independent political action, and even independent workingmen's candidates.) Hundreds of workers came from all over Boston and surrounding towns, filling the "cradle of liberty" and spilling out into the streets. Workers cheered and applauded Steward as he presented a series of resolutions. He reiterated his call for eight-hour legislation at all levels of government, and "the appointment of commissioners with full power to investigate and prosecute all violations" of these laws. Steward closed his resolutions with a direct reference to labor's role in winning the war and rebuilding the Union. He insisted that the nation honor workers' sacrifices, on and off the battlefields, and that the government recognize labor's demands for equality. "We rejoice that the rebel aristocracy of the South has been crushed, ... that beneath the glorious shadow of our victorious flag men of every clime, lineage and color are recognized as free. But ... we yet want it to be known that the workingmen of America will in future claim a more equal share in the wealth their industry creates in peace and a more equal participation in the privileges and blessings of those free institutions defended by their manhood on many a bloody field of battle."

Representative John Mahan—the man who, earlier in the spring, had prompted the first legislative investigation into the hours of labor—also cut right to the heart of the postwar labor reform argument. He spoke of "the readiness with which workingmen responded to the call of the country in the hour of danger. They had by their devotion and bravery preserved the Union in all its integrity and broken the shackles from off the slave. Now that they had emancipated the black man, the workingmen intended to ask for recognition of their own rights, and furthermore, were determined to have them." Mahan concurred with Steward that the workers' reward for loyal service to the Union cause should include a legislatively guaranteed eight-hour workday as the first step toward securing justice for all labor.[18]

The audience, however, had not come out that night to hear either Steward or Mahan. They were there for Wendell Phillips, the internationally renowned abolitionist orator. Phillips had always been careful not to endorse labor reform openly before the Civil War. He feared that critics and allies alike might perceive his support for wage workers' demands as somehow equating injustice to free labor with the abomination of chattel slavery. But with the war over and the slaves emancipated, Phillips felt free to speak out on other issues, especially labor reform. Since Steward, Rogers, and other labor activists had participated in the abolitionist movement, they welcomed Phillips into their ranks. And Phillips went further than many other former abolitionists in promoting the labor reform campaign. He not only gave money and encouragement; he also became a leader in several emerging cross-class organizations during the Reconstruction era.

Tall, slender, and graceful, even in his mid-fifties, Phillips looked every bit the patrician Boston Brahmin, scion of a well-to-do and politically well-connected family. But he was also a man who had deliberately turned his back on a lucrative legal career, and a chance to succeed in mainstream electoral politics, because he frequently put his wealth and reputation at risk championing unpopular causes. When Phillips ascended the Faneuil Hall podium, where he had often declaimed for the abolitionist cause, thunderous applause filled the chamber. The *DEV* reported that "the workingmen present seemed to view him in the light of a prophet who had appeared among them to instruct and guide them.... His address ... was truly a splendid effort; ... [it was] a candid, clear and logical argument in support of an Eight Hour law."[19]

Phillips spoke for over an hour, and he too took careful note of the historic opportunities presented at the end of 1865. The "accursed form of human bondage seems drawing to its end, at least so far as the right of one man to sell another goes. Therefore ... we commence ... the struggle to discover, define and arrange the true and lasting relations between capital and labor in society." Echoing the Republican Party's free labor rhetoric, as well as some of Steward's vision, Phillips asserted: "My principle is that every child born in America shall have, as far as possible, an equal chance with each other.... There shall be no separate laborer and separate capitalist as such; but that in the final arrangement every man shall combine in his own person laborer and capitalist."

Phillips emphatically stated his belief that there was no inherent antagonism between labor and capital and that the eight-hour day would be a great benefit to employers. "Capital, for its own security, seeing that labor holds the majority at the ballot-box, is bound, moved only by its own selfishness, to see that labor has leisure to look calmly into and patiently comprehends the great questions of politics. Therefore I say it is a fair division of man's day—eight hours for sleep, eight hours for work, and eight hours for his soul." Phillips also unequivocally defended workers' rights to manage their own time. Labor did not have to prove how it would use its hours away from work, any more than capital had to show how it used its time or money. Phillips expressed his confidence that the vast majority of workers would spend their extra leisure hours on education and personal improvement. The experiment in shorter working hours was clearly worth any risk that a few bad apples might waste their time in dissipation.

Phillips also offered his audience some lessons in activism drawn from his years as an abolitionist. He urged that the labor reform campaign be united, outspoken, persistent, and politically engaged. Reformers and activists had to get their demands on the front page of every newspaper and on the agenda of every legislative session, put consistent pressure on politicians and parties to make those demands a priority, and peacefully persuade the public that the demands were morally righteous rather than frighten people into submission. "Once do you plant in men's minds the conviction that it is right to give you eight hours rest, and the conviction will become *custom* and soon firmly fixed like the saving of every seventh day from labor. . . . When you have convinced the thinking man that it is right, and the humane man that it is just, it will go into the statute book." Phillips also told his listeners that they "had a much easier battle" than the abolitionists before them. "You have no prejudice of race to wipe out—you have no Constitution to change." Nevertheless, the task would not be accomplished only by conventions and resolutions; that belief was a clear weakness of many antebellum labor reform groups. "A mass meeting is a flaming meteor—seen today and gone tomorrow; but a political movement behind which stand ten thousand men, saying, 'This is our right: we will have it, if we grow gray in fighting for it'; that never adjourns. It is in everlasting session."[20]

Like Steward, Phillips insisted that the eight-hour campaign had to enter the political arena and stay there for the long haul in order to secure legislation to regulate the workday. Also like Steward, Phillips believed that this effort should not bind itself to any established parties but stake out its own political turf and endorse whichever candidate pledged himself to support specific labor reforms. Thus, Phillips encouraged labor reformers and activists to be fiercely independent in their political allegiances and to find allies, whatever their party label. But he never called for the formation of a labor reform party in the closing days of 1865. (Phillips probably realized that creating a rival party could complicate Republican efforts with southern Reconstruction, an issue that he considered absolutely essential to the nation's future.) A statewide labor reform party would not emerge until the end of the decade.[21]

Three months after the election rally, on February 7, 1866, the Special Commission issued its seventy-page report—filled with excerpts from testimony, written responses to published circulars distributed throughout the state, and "especially ... reliable *statistics* rather than individual opinion." The commission did support stronger state laws regulating child labor, and strict enforcement of those regulations so that youngsters would spend less time at work and more time in school. The report backed up those recommendations with frequent references to a better-educated workforce being a more reasonable, responsible, and efficient one. The commissioners concluded that "whatever differences of opinion there may be as to the propriety of legislating upon the hours of labor for *adults,* all believe it is perfectly legitimate for the State to legislate for the protection and welfare of its children."

Turning to the question of regulating the workday for men and women, the report gave a thoughtful summary of the arguments for shorter hours. The commissioners saw that long hours of labor were particularly onerous for those performing hard physical work and monotonous machine tending. "Not only the interest of the laborer but of labor, demands a reduction of hours. You must make labor tolerable before you can make it honorable. It is degraded by ignorance, it is elevated by intelligence. To dignify work, you must dignify the workman." The commissioners also understood the larger political stakes in the debate. They noted that the fundamental rights of citizenship, which labor reformers had struggled to protect for decades, seemed particularly important in the aftermath of a civil war fought to sustain republican principles. "This is the workingman's country. The welfare of the State and nation demand that time be given him to fit himself for worthy citizenship. A free country demands an intelligent as well as a free people. Now, while the nation is being reconstructed, is the time to reconstruct our labor system."

Despite acknowledging this broad conception of reconstruction shared by many in the labor reform community, the commissioners also cited legal, economic, political, and moral arguments against legislation to regulate the workday. They dismissed the idea of a strict law that would punish those who worked more than eight hours a day. The commissioners seemed to have deliberately misunderstood the intent of that law as penalizing individuals who wanted to set their own hours, rather than restraining employers who demanded longer workdays. The commissioners also claimed, erroneously, that the vast majority of eight-hour advocates wanted merely a symbolic law proclaiming eight hours to be a legal day's work. Actually, many labor reformers and activists had argued for decades (going all the way back to debates over language in the ten-hour petitions of the 1840s) that such vague legal pronouncements were worthless, and the commission came to the same conclusion. In the end, the commissioners took a step backward from the Joint Special Committee's enthusiastic support of the eight-hour workday and concluded that they were "opposed to the adoption of an eight-hour law" for four reasons:

1. Because they deemed it unsound in principle to apply one measure of time to all kinds of labor.
2. Because, if adopted as a general law, in the way proposed, it would be rendered void by special contracts, and so add another to the dead laws that cumber the statutes.
3. Because a very large proportion of the industrial interests of the country *could not* observe it.
4. Because if restricted, as some proposed, to the employees of the State, it would be manifestly *partial,* and therefore unjust.

The Special Commission did see much to praise in the arguments for shorter hours and predicted that modern industrial society was evolving toward fewer working hours, which would indeed improve workers' lives. Yet the commissioners also insisted that there was an inherent harmony between capital and labor, an essential freedom of markets and contracts, and an imperative need for government to let workers and employers hash out their own agreements on the hours of labor. The commissioners believed that the legislature would make better use of its time and authority by promoting more investment in manufacturing corporations to create more jobs, encouraging healthy public leisure facilities, discouraging monopolies, and providing "for the annual collection of reliable statistics, in regard to the condition, prospects, and wants of the industrial classes."[22]

This commission concluded its report by piously passing the labor reform buck back into the hands of workers seeking legislative support for their efforts. "Let the great body of working men prove," they counseled,

> by temperate and industrious habits, by ambition in work and workmanship, by the practice of that economy that will help them to become their own capitalists, by co-operative labor securing to each workman a share in the profits of his work, by associations for mutual *good* as well as mutual gain,—let them prove thus, by logic that no sophistry can refute or evade, that working men are bent on elevating labor by the elevation of themselves, and the wide-spread distrust of the proper use of leisure hours will speedily disappear.... They will have no need to ask of any one how many or how few hours they shall labor; for they will be masters of their own time and their own terms, and increase or reduce hours as the real interests of each and all may require—convincing capitalists by ... *intelligent and high-minded workmen* ... that capital is as dependent on labor, as labor upon capital; and, that it is only as both work together in harmony, that the

industrial interests of the country are most truly promoted, and the greatest good of all secured.... The cause of the working man was advocated, not only by professional men friendly to the movement, but by some of the working men themselves.... It is plain, that the industrial interests of the country are vital interests; that the cause of the laborer is the cause of all. We shall rise or sink, in national prosperity and true greatness, as labor is elevated or depressed. The great problem given us to solve is, the elevation of work to its rightful place of power, by the elevation of the workmen to intelligent and Christian manhood. In this solution the State may aid, but only the working men themselves can *demonstrate* the problem.

In the end, even though the commissioners wanted their study and its recommendations to carry the imprimatur of the emerging social sciences—with their emphasis on statistics, rational arguments, and seemingly objective conclusions—traditional notions of middle-class morality, Christian character, and individual uplift also suffused the report and its admonitions to workers.[23]

The *Daily Evening Voice* reprinted the commission's report and endorsed its call for new child labor laws. But the newspaper clearly was not satisfied with the document as a whole, for the editors also urged the appointment of yet another fact-finding body. A new commission, the editors wrote, should be paid, be authorized to go beyond conducting hearings at the statehouse, and travel throughout the commonwealth investigating working conditions. (Edward Rogers had made similar suggestions in his correspondence with the Special Commission, well before their report was issued.) In the end, the *DEV* remained frustrated with the commission's underlying arguments against government intervention in the labor market. "We must remind the Commission, the Legislature, and the public that the doctrine set forth in this report[,] that the law is impotent to defend the laborer against the encroachments of the capitalist[,] is not only ridiculous but dangerous. We have more hope of our institutions than to doubt for a moment not only that law can defend the rights of labor, but that it will."[24]

Despite the Special Commission's refusal to recommend an eight-hour law, supporters of the measure testified before a state legislative committee one month later, in March 1866. Rufus Wyman and Edward Rogers continued to argue that there was broad public support for a strong law, in contradiction to what the commission claimed to have found in its hearings. Wendell Phillips asked why government clerks, whose tasks seemed far less strenuous than those of many mechanics, worked two or three hours less per day. Why did the legislature reduce their own employees' working hours and then ignore the demands of those people working ten and twelve hours each day in mills and factories? When the committee reported favorably to the House on a bill to declare eight hours as a day's work but to leave the option for individual contracts to be based on longer hours, the DEV supported this weaker law as the best that workers could hope for during that legislative session. Like the recent commission, the editors argued that a stronger law would probably restrain workers' freedom more than employers' rapacity, though other reformers and activists continued to disagree with that conclusion. Moreover, the editors believed that any legislation, no matter how limited, would encourage workers to push their own demands for a shorter workday. A law would bring the eight-hour movement "into notice and give it force. It will especially encourage those trades which are debating and halting; and, when a few trades have led the way, under sanction of a law, others will follow. Some employers, also shrewd enough to see their own interest in a liberal and progressive policy, will, of their own account, adopt the system."[25]

Later in the spring of 1866, another organization—the Grand Eight Hour League of Massachusetts—launched a statewide fund-raising and publicity campaign to secure the shorter workday. That league, formed the previous July, quickly spun off local affiliates in cities and towns throughout the commonwealth. These associations often linked up with local trade unions, but leading reformers and activists such as Ira Steward, Edward Rogers, Rufus Wyman, and Martin Griffin also spoke at rallies around the Boston area. In early 1866, Steward became president of the statewide league and brought his distinctive economic theories and his passionate activism to the organization. He coauthored a long letter to the workers of Massachusetts "and their Friends," seeking to raise thousands of dollars to support speakers, rallies, and publications on the shorter-hours movement. Steward wanted to make this league a statewide extension of the cross-class alliances he had developed in the Boston Labor Reform Association, rather than just a political lobbying effort led by trade unions.[26]

The fund-raising appeal marshaled a series of arguments in support of a shorter workday, all of them echoing Steward's earlier writing on the subject.

> It is precisely *because* the Wealth necessary to make *all* comfortable and happy *is not produced* in the present long hour system; ... Because the present unequal periods of Labor and Rest tempt the toilers to misspend their scanty leisure, and *less* Hours of Labor, and more Thought will *reduce* that Temptation; Because the wages of the Producer will be *increased,* and *without* increasing the price of the article produced; and Because the number of Idlers and useless Middle-men will be reduced, that we insist upon a reduction of the Hours for mere muscular Labor. We do not assume that *simply* reducing the Hours of Labor will *accomplish* all this, but if they are

not reduced *these things are not possible.* In short, a reduction of hours is the first remedy to be applied to the very difficulties so vehemently urged as the great objection to reducing them.

Steward and his coauthors continued to distill the central themes of his pamphlet on the eight-hour day for working-class readers and their supporters around the state.

> The great central idea of the Short time movement is, that a proper amount of *leisure* or *time* for the working classes, will *Revolutionize* their *Habits, Manners, Customs, Feelings,* and *Ways of Living,* since people who have more TIME are more deliberate, ... *Deliberation* tends to *thought,* and thoughtful people grow wiser, and wise people soon learn *what* belongs to them and *how* to get it! This central idea is the pivot, upon which turns the *vast moral and material* consequences flowing from a reduction in the Hours of Labor. ... The same circumstances which teach them *how to increase their wages,* teach them at the same time *how* to spend them to better advantage; ... the *increase* and *wiser* expenditure of Wages—results [in] a gradual improvement in their *material* conditions; and this means an improvement in their *morals;* for the great material cause of their *immorality* is *low* wages, *foolishly* expended! ... Upon this road we are to travel, gradually, but surely and naturally, up to [the] millennium of Universal Labor Reform—Co-operative Industry—in which the producer and the capitalist *are one*!

The appeal then announced, in dramatic rhetoric clearly attuned to the themes of abolitionist struggle and postwar victory, that "the Emancipation of American Industry from Excessive physical Labor stands *Number One* in the problems of Social Science to be discussed and accomplished." As such, the authors believed that a broad cross section of American society should give financial support to labor reform speakers and pamphleteers. "We appeal to all classes—ministers, statesmen, physicians, lawyers, merchants, and leading men generally, as well as to workingmen. ... All who are underpaid have a *pecuniary* interest in the success of our cause, and those who are overpaid have a *moral* interest." James Stone, who had endorsed ten-hour laws in the 1850s and was now Speaker of the Massachusetts House of Representatives, served as treasurer for all funds raised through the circular. Wendell Phillips and some of his colleagues in the abolitionist movement, such as William Lloyd Garrison and Gerrit Smith, contributed to this cause. Even some readers who did not agree with all of the league's pronouncements sent money because they believed in public discussion and debate on the eight-hour workday.[27]

III

Boston labor reformers and activists, faced with an unfavorable commission report and a vacillating legislature, continued to speak out against the long hours of labor and the lack of political will to confront the problem of overwork. In fact, criticism of the failure to enact an eight-hour law was so widespread that the legislature felt compelled on May 28, 1866, to pass yet another resolution for the governor to appoint yet another commission "to investigate the subject of the hours of labor, especially in its relation to the social, educational and sanitary condition of the industrial classes, and to the permanent prosperity of the productive interests of the state."[28]

The new commission would be a three-member paid body. Governor Alexander Bullock appointed Edward Rogers, who had been defeated for reelection to the House; Amasa Walker, another former state legislator, college professor, member of Congress, and author of several well-known books on banking and currency; and William Hyde, a cottonmill owner from the western town of Ware. Rogers recalled that the class differences between him and the two other commissioners emerged right from the start of deliberations. "I was treated with as much consideration in the conduct of the commission as could have been expected from men who had passed all their lives in the control of laborers under such low principles as the so-called law of 'supply and demand' admits. They were intense individualists, both of them, this meant that they were incompetent from the first to deal with ... the whole world-wide movement of Labor."[29]

While this new commission held another series of hearings and sent its own surveys across the commonwealth, leaders such as Ira Steward renewed their public efforts on behalf of the eight-hour day. Many labor reformers and activists now argued that mass political meetings, if they mobilized votes for pro-labor-reform candidates, could be more important than whatever legislative commission was currently in session. If enough friends of labor were elected, the legislature might actually pass an eight-hour law instead of creating more committees. On a Thursday evening in mid-October 1866, another Faneuil Hall rally endorsed Patrick Guiney—Irish immigrant machinist, lawyer, and war hero—for Congress from the Third District around Boston. A local Workingmen's Party nominated Guiney after Wendell Phillips declined to run. Steward, never one to let an audience get away without a healthy dose of eight-hour agitation, proposed a series of resolutions on what he called—in yet another obvious reference to the recently concluded war against slavery—"the abolition of excessive toil."

Steward perceptively noted that "the great obstacle which stands most in the way of the immediate success of the Eight-Hour movement, is the hesitation of the mass of workingmen, and the positive opposition of employers, for reasons which exactly contradict each other,—that the hesitation of workingmen is caused by their fear that reducing the hours of labor will reduce wages, while the opposition of employers is caused by the fact that wages *cannot* be reduced." Steward asserted that if employers could simply reduce wages in proportion to shorter hours, as so many workers feared, then capital would quickly cut their labor costs to cover any loss of production and would not fight so ferociously against the eight-hour movement. But the reality was, Steward argued, "that employers are correct in supposing that wages cannot be reduced by merely reducing the hours of labor, for wages are where they are through moral, social and material causes which are beyond the immediate control of either party." Moreover, to "the charge made by employers that as much wealth cannot be produced in eight as in ten or more hours of daily labor," Steward responded confidently that such an assertion "raises a question of *production,* which, in the present unparalleled progress of labor-saving and wealth-producing inventions, has been placed beyond all cause for doubt or question." Finally, Steward insisted that "the great idea of the Eight Hour movement" was focused not solely on the workday but also on "a more equal DISTRIBUTION of wealth, . . . and we therefore write upon our banners, and stamp upon our platform, the sentiment, 'Eight Hours—a better Distribution of Wealth!'"[30]

Less than two months after the fall elections, the new commission on the hours of labor issued its report on New Year's Day, 1867. The commissioners expanded on many recommendations from the previous bodies. They unanimously endorsed legislation to ban employment of children between the ages of ten and fourteen and require their attendance at school; to prohibit youth under age eighteen from working more than ten hours a day, or sixty hours a week in factories; to appoint a special inspector of labor to enforce all labor laws; and to establish a state bureau of statistics. But on the crucial question of legislating the eight-hour workday for all employees, the commission split: two of its members, constituting a majority, voted against such a law. Edward Rogers went on to file an extensive minority report endorsing the proposal.

Amasa Walker and William Hyde, in their majority opinion, reaffirmed many of the familiar arguments against an eight-hour law. In fact, Walker and Hyde seemed intent on beating back any further demands for a shorter workday (or for yet another commission). Their report's tone was less sympathetic to labor and more adamant in opposing pleas for legislation than the previous commission's had been. Walker had recently published a major work on political economy, *The Science of Wealth,* in which he opposed legislation to regulate the hours of labor but recognized the legitimacy of labor unions. He probably also wrote the majority report, which echoed his other writings, and asserted that an eight-hour day would decrease wages and place the commonwealth's industries at a competitive disadvantage with respect to those of other states. Moreover, these commissioners remained convinced that working people would not use their increased leisure time in a wise fashion, that there was no real public outcry for such a law, and that the hours of labor would be reduced gradually over time "by the natural progress of industry, not by governmental action." Therefore, they argued, the legislature should not interfere in contractual matters between free men and women, or in the natural functioning of an economic system governed by forces far beyond any state laws. To enact such a law, the majority concluded, would insult workers by implying that they were incapable of managing their own affairs and were akin to wards of the state.[31]

Rogers's minority report was a rather rambling and disjointed defense of the eight-hour movement. But, beneath the numerous digressions, he publicly endorsed the basic principle that the legislature should regulate the hours of labor for all workers. Rogers may have been appointed to this commission because, as a former state legislator and a wage worker himself, he was familiar with both the art of political compromise in Massachusetts and labor's postwar demands. But he chose not to follow the path trod by all the previous commissioners who, with their connections to the state's political elite, failed to endorse legislation for the eight-hour day. He had also been on the legislative Joint Special Committee in 1865, which had tried to steer a middle course by praising the eight-hour movement and then turning the question of legal remedies over to the first commission. But he was not going to let the second commission pass into history without putting on the record a full justification for the eight-hour law. Thus, in writing his minority report, Rogers drew more on his experience as an activist in the local ship carpenters' union than on his years in the legislature to support the eight-hour day.

Despite abrupt shifts in logic, Rogers's writing did reveal some real insights into the agricultural labor market, housing conditions among the working poor, and the growing links between industrialization and urbanization in mid-nineteenth-century Massachusetts. He noted: "Bound by no tie of business interest to any particular locality, workmen and operatives, as classes, are unwilling to purchase a home, or even to settle in any small place, where they are limited in their choice of employers. They understand instinctively, that permanency in this respect, means reduced wages, and . . . a limitation of the liberty of action." On the other hand, Rogers saw that "any successful system of co-operation in manufactures; of partnerships of labor and capital, or any means by which the industrial classes can be made sharers in the profits of labor, will operate to fix the residence of the workman, and, in connection with the local expression of reduced hours, to decide its healthfulness, and counteract the tendencies to centralization."

Rogers disagreed emphatically with the assertion that a reduction in hours meant a reduction in wages. Citing evidence from English sources, rather than making a broader theoretical analysis like Steward, Rogers concluded: "So far as a standard of labor has been established, either by executive authority, by legislation for minors, or by the good sense of adults in connection with such rules, it has proved to be a barrier to the evils of overtime and the consequent reduction of wages. The working classes, without a standard of time for a day's labor, are at the mercy of the employing interest." Rogers also argued forcefully that

> the decision of a length of time which shall be held to constitute a day's work, is not simply a commercial question. Viewed by this light alone, the condition of the masses is hopeless, because pure commerce is pure selfishness. The interest . . . arises from the relation which those measures bore to the liberation of great populations of adults from the absolute control of pecuniary influences; thus making the length of a day's labor a "brain question," to be decided in the interest of intelligence and morals, and tending by its influence to restrain within reasonable limits, the natural rise and fall of wages, in obedience to commercial laws.

Yet, in the end, Rogers did not prove to be quite as bold as he appeared when proclaiming the hours of labor to be a fundamental moral question rather than a matter of money and commerce. He concluded his dissent by recommending specifically a ten-hour day for "factory and farm work" and an eight-hour day for "mechanical labor." (Rogers had first proposed this bifurcated standard in his letter to the previous commission.) Thus, he showed his continued willingness to compromise on the principle of the eight-hour day—and his compromise would have permitted longer working days for women and children in factories than for male mechanics. He also favored legislative language to establish the standard for a legal day's work as one would measure any other commodity fairly in the market, and to permit contractual exceptions to the standard. Thus, Rogers found himself in agreement with the minimalist wing of the eight-hour movement, like the editors of the *Daily Evening Voice,* rather than with those who advocated a more stringent law that would compel employers' adherence to the eight-hour workday.[32]

After nearly two years of committee hearings and reports, labor reformers and activists had gained more direct access to the legislative decision-making process than ever before. But the statute books still contained precious little law to protect the interests of adult workers, despite all their testimony and correspondence with lawmakers and commissioners. The Republican majority in the Massachusetts statehouse made a great display of its sympathy for working people with this steady stream of committees and commissions all devoted to the labor question. In reality, though, each august body deflected labor's growing political pressure away from the legislature, even as workers' frustration built up with each successive hearing. The reports added up to hundreds of pages, sometimes filled with revealing testimony and insightful analysis. Yet as the proposal for an eight-hour law passed from one investigative body to the next, the tone of each successive document grew increasingly hostile to any law limiting the hours of labor for working men and women. Faced with yet another political stonewall, labor reformers and activists had to look once again beyond the statehouse, no matter how much they thought that legislative action was essential to changing working conditions.

IV

In the weeks before Christmas 1866, a small group of men "interested in the reform of the present social, moral, and pecuniary conditions of the laboring people, and desirous of promoting unity of sentiment and action among that class relative to the best methods of accomplishing that reform," began to meet at the *Daily Evening Voice* office on Washington Street. On the day after Christmas, eleven men—including William Falls, former president of the Grand Eight Hour League, and Henry L. Saxton, printer of the *DEV*—became charter members of a new Workingmen's Institute. These founders believed (even before the last commission had issued its report) that legislators and commissions offered little of tangible value to the labor reform cause; therefore, some alternative course of action had to be considered. Within a month, one of Ira Steward's closest allies, George McNeill, joined the organization and helped prepare its constitution for publication. By March 1867, McNeill was elected a trustee and vice president of the new institute.[33]

McNeill, nearly thirty years old, was originally from the northeastern Massachusetts town of Amesbury, where his father, John, had been an early supporter of William Lloyd Garrison. George worked as a young boy in a woolen mill, until a bitter strike in 1851 shut down the factory for six months. Though only fourteen at the time, he organized other youthful protesters into a union of doffers (who replaced full bobbins of yarn with empty ones), backboys (who helped piece together broken yarn), and other machine tenders. He subsequently learned the shoemaker's trade, and then moved to Boston in 1854 at the age of seventeen. There he worked at a series of jobs until finding steady employment in newspaper offices. By the late 1850s, he was trying to organize an independent labor party. He returned to Amesbury in 1860 to care for his dying father. After his father's death, he went to secure a position that had been promised him in the countingroom of a large textile corporation but was told that no such job existed. The superintendent offered him the chance to become a woolsorter, but when required to sign a book containing the corporation's regulations, McNeill refused and was said to have declared: "My father was an abolitionist, and I do not intend to sell myself into slavery; and more than that, as he fought slavery so will I, and, so help me God, I will fight the corporation till I die."

In 1864, back in Boston, McNeill combined his publishing experience with his passion for labor activism through his work at the *Daily Evening Voice*. He sold subscriptions, solicited advertisements, and formed local Voice clubs to support the labor paper. He probably linked up with Steward and other eight-hour advocates through his efforts with the *DEV*. McNeill developed a reputation for his ability to bring the campaign for eight hours into the heart of the trade union movement, as well as into the halls of business and finance. Steward characterized his close associate as

> not the orator, nor essayist, though he can do well enough in either to give an ordinary man a reputation. He is the prince of *organizers!* A good reader of men. Always keeps his eye on the essential point. Is harmonizing if possible, but can show his teeth if absolutely necessary. Gets along splendidly with ignorant men, and is equally at home with the highest.... He deals best with situations where so many people are ready to express different opinions.... And add[ed] to his powers to deal with a difficult situation is his absolute integrity and devotion to the cause.[34]

McNeill and other institute leaders wanted their new organization to be a forum for public speeches and debates on the labor question. Officers wrote to well-known speakers—such as Ralph Waldo Emerson, Wendell Phillips, Frederick Douglass, and Anna Dickinson—asking them to address the institute. A Committee on Subscription solicited donations from supporters across the city, including Governor Bullock, who gave five dollars, and Mayor Otis Norcross of Boston, who contributed ten dollars. In the summer of 1867, the organization rented rooms on Tremont Row near the recently built City Hall and Court Square—rooms quickly christened Institute Hall—for weekly meetings and monthly socials. Institute Hall provided the Boston labor reform community with a base of operations—a physical location from which to coordinate organizational activities and public agitation beyond periodic rallies and annual conventions. The hall became a combination lyceum, library, and social center where kindred spirits in the cause of labor reform could reaffirm their existing bonds of solidarity and recruit new supporters. Reformers and activists knew that maintaining a vibrant intellectual community and a constant public presence in the city was essential if they were to promote their cause beyond the legislature's hearings.[35]

Before year's end, the institute's ranks began to expand. By Thanksgiving Day of 1867, Ira Steward had been elected to membership. (Steward may have delayed joining for nearly a year because he saw the institute as a rival to his own labor reform schemes.) On the day before New Year's, McNeill assumed the presidency for 1868. In early February 1868, "the Subject of admitting Ladies to our Meetings was discussed at some length," and those in attendance passed a motion permitting women to come to the next session. At the end of June, members unanimously amended the constitution to allow women to join the institute. McNeill nominated his wife to be the first female member; those assembled approved the nomination without dissent. Ira Steward's wife, Mary, became a member one week later. Thus, the first families of labor reform in Boston all joined an organization where husbands and wives could both assume active roles.[36]

In March 1868, the institute made its first foray into political lobbying. For more than a year, the group had avoided this strategy; probably because members had seen other organizations struggle mightily and usually futilely to secure labor legislation. The institute began its political activity tentatively with a petition to Boston's mayor and aldermen for free reading rooms in each of the city's wards. By July, Steward pushed the organization to speak out on national labor issues. He proposed "a resolution of Approval and Disapproval of the course of our Senators in Congress touching the passage of the Eight Hour Bill [for federal workers] with approval of Senator [Henry] Wilson and disapproval of Senator [Charles] Sumner." In late August, the institute again looked at local politics and adopted Steward's strongly worded resolution on the fall elections. "We will take no action whatsoever so far as the choice of Mayor and Alderman is concerned," the resolution read, "but will confine our efforts exclusively to securing a majority of the Common Council, so radically in favor of the 'eight hour system,' that in case an Aristocratic Mayor and Board of Alderman shall refuse the municipal legislation necessary, that all supplies of money shall stop, and the wheels of the city government be brought to a dead lock." Thus, the institute boldly called for a new strategy in local labor politics focused on the power of the purse and annual appropriations bills as the pressure points to move forward on an eight-hour law. Like a moth to a flame, Steward kept returning to the political arena—in this case, pressing the Workingmen's Institute into municipal affairs—no matter how many times he may have been burned by recalcitrant politicians.[37]

In early September 1868, Steward was elected to fill a vacancy as trustee, and activist lawyer Edwin Chamberlin joined the institute. Herbert and Elizabeth L. Daniels, well known in labor and women's rights circles, enrolled at year's end; other activists and reformers such as Edward Place, Charles McLean, Edward Linton, and William Greene also became members. The institute looked more and more like a who's who in the Boston labor reform community at the close of the 1860s. Steward became president for 1869; Elizabeth Daniels was one of the vice presidents; her husband and Steward's wife served as secretaries; and George McNeill continued as one of the trustees. Not since the 1840s had a labor reform organization brought so many women and men into its leadership ranks.[38]

Ira Steward proved to be not only an outspoken activist but also an able administrator. He tackled the institute's chronic financial problems (members' dues were constantly in arrears) by raising money in his own Cambridgeport neighborhood as well as securing contributions from Wendell Phillips and other wealthy reformers. Steward renamed the organization's meeting hall the Labor Reform Headquarters, and backed women members' efforts to rename the organization the Labor Reform Institute to better reflect its cross-gender and cross-class constituency. Under his leadership, the institute's meetings generated lively discussions on crucial labor reform issues such as shorter hours and higher wages. The organization also renewed efforts to petition the city of Boston for a public hearing on the eight-hour workday.[39]

Despite Steward's fund-raising efforts, the institute continued to be strapped for cash. The group suspended several members in August 1869 for nonpayment of dues, including founder William Falls. At the same time, the organization tried to raise additional funds so it could publicize the Boston aldermen's public hearing in September on the eight-hour workday for city employees, and it voted to send Steward and Charles McLean as representatives to the meeting. Steward reported favorably on the hearing, and urged members to fan out across the greater Boston area to round up support for another public meeting. He believed that political pressure exerted this time at the municipal level might yield more benefits than taking another run at the seemingly impregnable state legislature. Yet in the same fall season, George McNeill resigned his trusteeship and Steward stepped down as president because the institute signed over its property to one of its more conservative members, the machinist George Randall, who then assumed responsibility for all debts and rentals on the headquarters.[40]

Steward's resignation threw the institute into confusion. At one meeting in early October a shadowy figure named S. N. Bryant was both elected to membership and chosen president! William Greene resigned, and Edward Linton and Edith L. Daniels became trustees. George McNeill, having previously stepped down as a trustee, left the organization altogether, along with his wife, at the end of November, apparently in protest over the decision to give financial control to Randall instead of to him. By the end of December 1869, Linton insisted that the institute should abandon politics completely. He offered a resolution: "The Labor Reform Institute has distinctly for its objects the intellectual, moral, and pecuniary improvement of the laboring people and is not a political organization and is not responsible for the political action of any of its members, or for the action of any political party." Steward and McNeill now saw their efforts to prod the institute into the political arena, especially in local affairs, foundering on the rocks of financial instability, and their colleagues' persistent skepticism about lobbying offering any real hope for achieving substantive changes in working conditions.[41]

The institute's final months proved to be rather desultory. No one stepped up to assume responsibility as the debts kept accumulating. In early 1870, the group approached the State Labor Union about taking over the rented hall and all its furnishings. Officers continued to resign on a weekly basis. Ira and Mary Steward left the organization, as did S. N. Bryant, and even George Randall gave up his efforts to manage the group's financial affairs. But on February 1, a committee reviewing the institute's books reported that seventy members remained on the rolls. And two weeks later, Edward Place gave a lecture emphatically arguing for renewed agitation to reduce working hours. The secretary reported that "it was an admirable lecture and commanded from beginning to end the profound attention of all present." But in March, yet another president resigned, and the trustees looked to transfer "the property of this Institute into the hands of any whom [sic] they may think are responsible parties."[42]

Edward Linton, in his lecture to the group on May 31, 1870, tried to lift the organization's spirit, though his efforts seemed to be a rather defiant grasping at straws to justify the group's declining membership, money, leadership, and influence in labor reform circles. Speaking on the topic "The Present Aspect of the Labor Cause," Linton "took the ground that the success of the cause did not depend upon numbers but rather upon the earnestness of a few devotees." Despite the institute's shift back to lectures rather than lobbying, Linton insisted that "the cause [was] far too sacred a one to be trusted with or to be made the means of mere displays of eloquence." Linton's talk then drifted into currency reform and concluded rather dramatically that "a few persons honestly determined to die for the truth would be certain to triumph in the end."

Linton's heated rhetoric set off an extended discussion among the audience, some of the remarks becoming quite polemical and even spiritual in nature. A few commentators, however, insisted that politics and labor reform could never be separated in the real world. A Mrs. Albertson said: "It was not alone the working men who would or could affect the reform,—it could only be done by the combination of the really enlightened men and women of all classes. It was the few noble and valiant souls devoted to principle who would do the work." Another working man remarked "that every effort was being made by both the Republican and Democratic parties to divide and sub-divide the labor movement, and therefore it behooves the labor reformers to keep their eyes open.... The labor party who united on a single or central idea would succeed." Charles McLean said plainly that "the only way to make the scoundrels at Washington afraid was through the ballot box, and the ballot box must be purified. The present Republican party was the most corrupt on God's earth. The Democratic party was dead."[43]

Three weeks later, at the institute's final recorded meeting, those in attendance admitted how difficult it was to get people to show up on a weekly basis, no matter what the lecture topic. The assembly adopted a motion to adjourn for a month "and that exertions be made to get a full meeting in order that the Institute might not lose its prestige." Given the dwindling membership, disappearing leadership, and beleaguered finances, however, the institute had already lost most of its standing in the Boston labor reform community. And there is no record of any further meetings—one month later, or beyond.[44]

While the Labor Reform Institute waxed and waned, Ira Steward always continued searching for new allies and promising strategies in his labor reform campaign. Steward sometimes took to the hustings even to support demands that seemed at odds with his efforts for the eight-hour workday. For example, throughout the winter of 1867, he publicly endorsed the ten-hour day for factory workers in northern New England mills. Though clearly aware that this effort was a compromise with his demand for a universal eight-hour law, Steward also understood the political obstacles facing poor and unskilled operatives fighting against the power and wealth of large corporations. Small gains for these workers might eventually translate into bigger victories for labor reform as a whole. (Steward apparently did not consider the alternative possibility that factory workers, if they achieved the legislatively guaranteed ten-hour day, might then abandon any further agitation to regulate the hours of labor.)

Steward argued that the mill owners would "refuse the Ten Hour system until the public opinion of the State is exasperated up to the point where it is willing to sanction legislation upon the hours of labor, and just before the Senate and House finally agree upon a law, they expect to grant the operatives just enough to prevent legislative interference." Exactly this scenario had played out in the mid-1850s, when many mills reduced their workdays to eleven hours as a response to growing legislative interest in a ten-hour law. Steward went on to warn about the dangers of giving in to the textile magnates' apparent generosity. "Having yielded at this point the Ten Hour system," he thundered, "they will then say to the timid and stupid in our ranks, 'you have got all you asked for, what is the use of legislation?'" But Steward claimed that "the reason *why* those adroit capitalists will yield just before we succeed in passing a Ten Hour Law, is because they know what will follow if they do not. They know that a *real* Ten Hour Law upon the statutes of Massachusetts will simplify the contest between them and the people." Steward saw that a ten-hour law established the precedent for "Legislative interference" in the entire debate over working hours; and an eight-hour law would then become "a question of expediency simply" by changing a number in the statute books. He concluded that "the *right* to legislate for Ten Hours, is the right to legislate for Eight." Therefore, Steward believed that the ten-hour movement for factory workers did not necessarily undermine the eight-hour campaign's long-term goals. Rather, a ten-hour law would immediately improve the operatives' lives, and set a legal/political precedent for more progressive legislation in the future.[45]

In the winter of 1868, as he coaxed the Labor Reform Institute into a more activist stance on politics, Steward also published his second major work—*The Meaning of the Eight Hour Movement*. This pamphlet reiterated many of his basic arguments from previous speeches and writings. Reasserting his theory that a healthy economy was based on high wages and growing consumer purchasing power, Steward wrote that "Capitalists remember us as *Producers,* to be paid as little as possible; but not as *Consumers, to be paid enough* to enable us to *buy* their commodities. . . . When will they learn that their immediate and special interest in *Cheap Labor* has blinded their eyes to their final and general interest in Labor sufficiently well paid to buy all that *they* desire to manufacture?" To the workers, Steward stated boldly: "We have decided that THEY are making too much money! *They* cut down OUR *Prices! We shall cut down* THEIR *Hours!*"

Steward also emphasized how important it was to have a practical demonstration of the eight-hour day. He suggested a legislative provision to put public workers on such a system, which he hoped would prove that shorter hours did indeed lead to higher, not lower, wages. He also proposed other specific legislative remedies, such as awarding state contracts to businesses that worked shorter hours, new patent laws to prevent so-called labor-saving machinery from driving any workers more than eight hours a day, and a law that stated, *"The Corporations of the State* MUST ADOPT THE EIGHT HOUR SYSTEM OR BE FORCED TO SURRENDER THEIR CHARTERS." Moreover, Steward urged his supporters in city halls and statehouses to play political hardball and freeze every appropriations bill until legislators enacted labor reform.[46]

Steward's bold words reflected his continuing experimentation to find just the right combination of arguments, actions, and allies to press his demands for a legal eight-hour workday. His occasional triumphs, and more often his frustrations, also frequently paralleled the larger labor reform campaign in Boston during those crucial years following the Civil War. The second half of the 1860s saw new working-class leaders such as Steward and McNeill, backed by wealthier supporters such as Wendell Phillips, assume central roles in the struggle for labor reform. New organizations, such as the Labor Reform Institute, tried to build venues for sustained activism that stretched beyond the antebellum models of quarterly meetings and published resolutions.

Thus, the labor reform campaign was more organized, more energized, and more politicized than ever before. Yet for all its hard work, it still achieved few significant legal or economic victories for working men and women. The nearly endless stream of legislative committees and commissions produced no new statutes to protect the rights of adults who labored long hours in workshops, fields, and factories. And the Labor Reform Institute's attempts to create a headquarters for activists and their supporters collapsed after a few years. But, as usual, all was not lost for this intrepid band of dreamers and doers. To the contrary, before the decade closed—in 1869, to be precise—four new labor reform organizations emerged in one year! Each of these alliances would, in turn, shape the Boston labor reform community and its agenda well into the following decade.

4

THE GENERATION OF 1869

Two Leagues, a Bureau, and a Party

In 1869, as the nation continued to wrestle with fundamental legal and political questions surrounding Reconstruction, the Boston labor reform community exploded in a frenzy of organizing. Four new institutions formed, all in the closing year of that tumultuous decade. It was as if reformers and activists feared that the dawn of a new decade might push the emotional intensity of the Civil War years into a rapidly receding past, and diminish the enthusiasm for social change.

Two of these new organizations—the New England Labor Reform League (NELRL) and the Boston Eight Hour League—stood on opposite sides in an increasingly bitter struggle over strategies to build and sustain cross-class alliances. Each of these rival groups provided an organizational and intellectual home for one of two competing visions of social transformation; and neither side saw any compelling reason to compromise or change its tactics so as to welcome back those who disagreed. Ironically, with two disparate organizations each claiming to be the central locus for labor reform agitation, neither could or would build a coalition broad enough to speak for the community as a whole.

The NELRL, led by Ezra Heywood, echoed its namesake of the 1840s. The league deliberately courted reformers and activists of all persuasions, and held a series of regular public meetings where the podium remained wide open to a broad array of schemes, many of them far removed from workplace concerns. Heywood and the league's leaders often insisted that financial reform contained the real core of labor reform, and that an uncompromising antimonopoly libertarianism would free workers from the thrall of all exploitation. Heywood's strident individualistic rhetoric quickly made him suspicious of all government legislation and regulation—including any laws concerning the eight-hour day.

Heywood's idiosyncratic definition of labor reform, and his insistence that the NELRL stood for the principle of open continuous debate above all possible direct action, put him on a collision course with many others—especially Ira Steward. Most working men and women did not want to return to an earlier time in which organizations passed countless resolutions on a host of disparate issues but offered no specific plans for tackling the pressing problems of long hours, low wages, child labor, and dangerous shopfloor conditions. Financial reform benefited only those who already had money, Steward and his allies argued; true labor reform had to begin where workers lived and toiled for meager rewards.

Steward's Eight Hour League embodied his fundamental principles that the shorter workday was the first step on the road to meaningful social change, and that the entire labor reform effort had to focus on that issue as its top priority. Steward combined the familiar practice of annual conventions with an effort to reestablish a headquarters building as the base for a campaign of continuous labor reform agitation and lobbying. He offered creative legislative options—such as the eight-hour day for public employees—and new economic arguments for shorter working hours as a cure for chronic unemployment.

In a curious way, Steward's and Heywood's rival organizations mirrored each other: both claimed to have the solution for the crisis of industrial capitalism, but each group offered distinctly different courses of treatment for what ailed the nation. The Eight Hour League argued that wealth could not be legislatively redistributed through changes in banking and currency laws. The economic system that created such stark inequities in resources and power would begin to change only when laborers worked fewer hours and had more time to become active agents for social and political justice.

Steward not only broke sharply with Heywood's league; he also eventually had an acrimonious falling-out with his longtime ally Wendell Phillips. The Steward-Phillips schism—a complex amalgam of personality clashes, leadership rivalries, and deep philosophical disagreements—sundered many other links in the Boston labor reform community. Here again, competing visions of the nature of reform came into play: Phillips's all-encompassing ideal of a veritable social change smorgasbord clashed with Steward's laserlike focus on the eight-hour day as the fount of all future progress. The more Steward insisted on his unitary model, the more he alienated potential allies and undercut the very organizational unity he so wanted to inspire.

The Massachusetts Bureau of the Statistics of Labor (BSL) and the Massachusetts Labor Reform Party reflected reformers' and activists' efforts to go beyond organization-building within their own community and to explore the possibilities of shaping the regulatory authority of a new state agency and of creating a third-party alternative in the cauldron of Reconstruction-era politics. The BSL was, for all intents and purposes, a cross-class labor reform organization—at least in its first four years of existence. With strong links to eight-hour advocates in Boston, the bureau became an early example of an activist state regulatory agency providing data to back up its own legislative agenda for labor reform. The bureau's rapid transformation from an ostensibly neutral investigative body into an outspoken advocate for working-class interests in the halls of the statehouse soon generated growing opposition from startled legislators, enraged businessmen, and jealous rival reformers. With the labor reformers and activists pitted against each other—eight-hour advocates facing off against cooperators and trade unionists over the bureau's future—the agency's pro-labor chief (Henry Oliver) and deputy (George McNeill) found themselves out of their jobs by 1873, and the bureau moved steadily away from its activist stance and its connections with the Boston labor reform community.

The Massachusetts Labor Reform Party strove to mobilize activists and reformers to go beyond petitions and lobbying and to move boldly into the political arena through their own party. The party, seeing divisions in other alliances and hoping to cobble together a viable electoral coalition, promulgated a platform of what might be called labor reform's greatest hits: shorter working hours, cooperative factories, and even currency reform. The initial success of this cross-class political alliance tapped into years of frustration with mainstream parties and legislative lethargy, and reaffirmed the ideal that the government could be reshaped into a force for social justice.

Soon, however, the party faced internecine fights over more radical platform planks and contested gubernatorial nominations. Meanwhile, Republicans tried to pull voters back into their party with vague appeals to rebuild past reform alliances. Even a productive coalition with the ten-hour movement in textile towns could not save the Labor Reform Party. Leaders reverted to an old strategy of endorsing local candidates rather than fielding a slate of statewide officers. Within five years, the party that had held such early promise for unifying the labor reform community, and bringing it into the legislative process as a coherent political movement, succeeded only in driving wedges deeper between increasingly bitter factions.

Examining the birth of all four organizations in 1869 and tracing their trajectories into the following decade offers many vantage points for analyzing how these groups grappled with the constant challenges of creating coalitions and deploying arguments for social change into the public arena. Grand visions of universal reform soured many working-class skeptics, whereas a narrow focus on the hours of labor disillusioned some middle-class enthusiasts. Legislative lobbying on the eight-hour workday continued to meet a stony response from many lawmakers; meanwhile, a new state bureau and third-party politics offered brief moments of triumph followed by painful retrenchments. The generation of 1869 was indeed a contentious lot, both among themselves and with the powers of corporate capital in Boston.

I

Shortly after New Year's Day, 1869, a notice appeared in several labor and reform papers announcing yet another convention in Boston at the end of January to establish yet another reform organization—a New England Labor Reform League. The "Committee on Arrangements" drew extensively from the recently rechristened Labor Reform Institute's leadership, including Ira Steward, George McNeill, Edward Linton, and Edith L. Daniels. The committee also included William S. Goss, publisher of the *American Workman*, a Boston labor paper with close ties to the shoeworkers' union (Knights of St. Crispin). The cochairs were Henry L. Saxton, a charter member of the institute and printer of the *Daily Evening Voice* (*DEV*), and Ezra Heywood. Heywood quickly became the league's leading organizer, and the author of literally hundreds of resolutions which the league debated over the course of nearly two decades. Almost single-handedly, he kept the organization going intellectually and practically from year to year—calling meetings, renting halls, writing announcements, and publishing pronouncements. Heywood and the league became virtually synonymous; to understand his emergence as a labor reformer is to understand the league's origins.[1]

Heywood was born on a farm in the central Massachusetts town of Westminster in 1829, graduated from Brown University in 1856, and stayed on for two years of additional study to prepare for the Congregational ministry. In 1858, instead a taking a pulpit, Heywood joined William Lloyd Garrison's antislavery organization as a traveling lecturer and pamphleteer. A committed pacifist, Heywood broke with abolitionists such as Wendell Phillips and did not openly support the North during the Civil War, but he remained an ardent critic of slavery in all forms. Shortly after the war, he moved from Boston to Worcester and reconciled with Phillips as both became active in the labor reform crusade. Benjamin Tucker, who met Heywood while a student at the Massachusetts Institute of Technology and later worked closely with him on several anarchist publications, recalled Heywood as a "tall and rather lank New Englander, with a fine profile and full blond beard and flowing hair. A little angular in his movements, his presence on the platform nevertheless... was almost graceful. His delivery was slow and measured, but without hesitancy, and his appearance was that of a scholar and a gentleman."[2]

In 1867 Heywood helped found the Worcester Labor Reform League, which served as a model for the New England league. One year later, he delivered a speech before the Worcester league that explained his emerging conception of labor reform in the Reconstruction era. Taking aim at the legal structure of capitalism, he declared that "the same spirit which made men slaves by law in South Carolina makes them criminals and paupers by legislation in Massachusetts." In such an inequitable and unjust society, "labor reform is a protest against these savage and needless conditions, it is a loud outcry of somebody hurt; it is a struggle for liberty, equality, fraternity; a revolt against class rule, against the sentence of degradation, which titled classes, in all ages, have affixed on the masses of mankind." Noting the campaign for a shorter workday, Heywood observed that especially in manufacturing communities, "the sway of capital is most oppressive and impoverishing, [and] the short-time banner naturally heads the column of resistance."

Since the title of Heywood's talk was "The Labor Party," he wholeheartedly supported a politically engaged labor reform campaign. For him, labor reform politics was neither a "class movement" nor a "vague disquietude of those employed at manual labor, usually termed the working classes, but an enterprise which deeply concerns the rights and interests of the whole people." In Heywood's worldview, the word "worker" encompassed nearly the entire nation, including (in a capacious definition that echoed Walt Whitman's poetry) "the capitalist whose genius and energy make him the natural head of a concern, the honest merchant serving both producer and consumer, the philosopher in his closet, the preacher of truth, . . . earthquake reformers, counselors in equity, statesmen enacting justice, girls adorning industry, [even] mothers in birth pangs." Looking at existing labor organizations, Heywood noted that although "trades' unions, eight-hour associations, and co-operative societies are necessary steps toward right . . . they are not organized victory, but recruiting agencies—a marshaling of forces for the impending conflict." Political action still held the key to real reform and social change. "Not that voting will bring the millennium," he hastened to add, "but the sooner we put good sense into the ballot-box, the sooner good Government will come out of it."

Heywood cautioned his listeners not to equate political action with the established parties. He urged "that every voter shall leave his old party creed outside the door when he enters this League, and henceforth make the interests of labor paramount to all other considerations in political action." Drawing on his ministerial training, Heywood argued that the commitment to labor reform politics must be like a religious conviction. When mainstream parties came looking for votes on Election Day, reformers and activists would have to avoid being seduced by politicians' failed promises. "Individually weak, united we are irresistible," Heywood counseled, "and may control almost any election by wise and firm use of the balance of power we already hold between the parties." In the future, labor would prove to be "too large a matter to be permanently corked up in any of the old political bottles; and since both parties are mainly inspired by capital, it will be impossible for either long to administer the advancing tendencies of this movement." Workers, therefore, had to go beyond the settled political order and seek new opportunities in the electoral arena.[3]

Examining the power of government, and revealing a streak of antimonopoly libertarianism that would suffuse many of his resolutions for the New England league in years to come, Heywood asserted that "Government helps reform chiefly by getting out of its way, we ask no special legislation for labor.... The issue is fair play against monopoly—the masses against the classes." Perhaps sensing that such a bold assertion of freedom from government might lead workers to question his support for the eight-hour day, which he had previously endorsed in his lecture, Heywood quickly explained why he thought a law regulating the workday was not class legislation: "Capital, asserting the right of the strong to oppress the weak, enforces long hours against the consent of operatives unable to resist. We reply by writing on the flag which floats over city hall and capitol, 'Eight hours a legal day's work.' Not as an arbitrary standard, but as a rule expressing the public sense of right, to be observed in the public service; as an enabling act to assist labor to make fair terms. And wherever a public servant does not face that music, workingmen should walk him out of office at the next election." Heywood's justification for the eight-hour day was fraught with tension. He advocated an active political campaign for labor reform and legislation for the shorter workday, yet he remained deeply suspicious of government power as a whole.

Heywood went on to argue that although the shorter workday was an important goal, something even more fundamental drove all labor and economic reform—"sound finance. If we make the basis of things honest, eight hours, co-operation, impartial suffrage, and other needed reforms, will follow easily and naturally; otherwise they will ultimately fail, for the present administration of affairs is drifting us rapidly toward a great industrial feudalism." Heywood's insistence that financial reform lay at the head of all real labor reform eventually put him on a collision course with eight-hour proponents such as

Steward and McNeill, and others who also argued that labor reform had to start with changes at the workplace.

Whether aware of these potential contradictions and conflicts or not, Heywood held high hopes for his ideal of labor reform. "We shall redeem labor," he told his listeners, "renovate society, and furnish an example of what the world has not yet seen—a Government without a sword; sinking race, sex, caste, nationality, in a common brotherhood, there shall be no foreigners, no natives, no masters, no slaves, no 'bosses,' no 'hands,' none to command and none to obey, but one law, one love, one interest, one destiny." Heywood presented a compelling vision of social change in Worcester, but would it be inspiring enough to hold together the fractious Boston labor reform community? Would Heywood's definition of labor reform, and the new organization he led, take command of the struggle?[4]

The New England Labor Reform League held its first convention January 27–29, 1869, in the Melodeon Theatre on Washington Street; Heywood chaired the meeting. He used his opening remarks to draw a strong parallel between his abolitionist background and his campaign for workers' rights in the postwar era. "We are all negroes," he analogized, "because wealth centralizes in a few, and the working classes are the poorer classes, and woman is reduced and held in wretched pecuniary servitude. We put our brand upon the denial that these are 'necessary evils.'" Steward soon followed Heywood's opening statement with a series of resolutions which, not surprisingly, revealed his strong desire to shape this league into another vehicle for promoting the eight-hour day. He warned that any organization that did not put the eight-hour day first would end up drifting away from labor's most compelling concerns. Workers, who had little time for reflection or to attend labor reform conventions, would see little reason to support resolutions made on their behalf but without regard for their needs.

> The whole power of the Labor Reform movement should be concentrated upon the single and simple idea of first reducing the hours of labor for the masses, and thus giving them more time to discuss for themselves other questions in Labor Reform; for, until the working classes have sufficient time, all deliberations in their behalf must be conducted almost entirely in their absence, without the advantage of their counsel, increasing our chances for mistakes, as well as the certainty of their voting down, on election day, under the leadership of demagogues and the ruling classes, the very measures which, if successful, would best serve their real progress and happiness.

Steward, as always, pulled no punches in his demands; but others in attendance did not see the organization as he defined it. Rather, this league—much like its namesake from the 1840s—preferred to follow the older strategy of holding public meetings where the podium and platform remained open to a series of speakers advocating a range of reforms. Veteran abolitionists, and Associationists such as John Orvis, addressed the meeting. The assembly debated taxes, tariffs, and currency, along with working hours and wages. The convention did declare (in language echoing Heywood's earlier speeches) that it regarded "the effort to reduce the hours of service as a struggle for liberty . . . and where officials refuse to obey the public sense of right thus expressed, or continue to side with the money oligarchy which keeps labor down, it is both the privilege and duty of the working men to walk them out of office, at the next election." But the new organization consciously fashioned itself as something broader in its leadership and platform than just an eight-hour league, it did not let any one issue define its conception of reform. When the convention concluded, the league kept up the appearance of harmony among competing reformers and activists by electing Heywood president; Steward, McNeill, and Edith Daniels all became vice presidents; and Herbert Daniels served as recording secretary.[5]

Edith Daniels, in her glowing convention report to the women's rights newspaper *The Revolution,* stressed the league's potential for encouraging what she saw as genuine intellectual exchange across class lines. "The great feature of the convention," she wrote—in terms that veered close to middle-class condescension, "was the mingling together and sympathy of . . . genius, scholarly talent, beauty, wealth, wit, and wisdom . . . with the hosts of men and women who labor with their hands. The living ideas, the real talent and genius displayed by these bees, these workers, direct from the shop and the factory, . . . who have worked all their lives for just enough to keep soul and body together—these so long oppressed and enslaved by long hours, hard labor, poor pay, poverty and misery, are in themselves a living evidence that the spirit cannot be enslaved." A correspondent from South Boston, writing to the *Workingmen's Advocate,* was far less sanguine in his appraisal. He dismissed the gathering as "the most windy Convention I ever had the honor to look in upon . . . worse than useless." This worker voiced a deep skepticism that would follow the league from meeting to meeting: the convocation was quite simply all talk and no action.[6]

Despite early signs of workers' skepticism, the league reconvened in Boston at the end of May 1869, in the Meionaon hall under the Tremont Temple, with a large contingent of shoemakers, carpenters, factory operatives, and working women in attendance. Heywood opened the meeting by declaring that the organization was a "union to liberate, not to coerce; no class movement; it . . . hastens the day when men will have neither the power nor the wish to own more than they earn." Heywood's conception of the league continued to be shaped by his uncompromising antimonopoly sentiment. He believed that all class-based efforts were monopolistic—even those that were supposed to benefit poor workers. He wanted the league to embody his vision of a truly classless movement, dissolving differences between working people and middle-class reformers, and restructuring relations between labor and capital.[7]

Once again, many workers in the audience did not share Heywood's vision. For them, labor reform was more pragmatic and programmatic. Efforts to improve their working conditions had nothing to do with condemning monopoly power in the abstract, and everything to do with restraining corporate power at the point of production. No sooner had Heywood concluded his remarks, and was about to read a series of resolutions prepared in advance by the executive committee, than McNeill and Steward both tried to seize the floor to challenge Heywood's authority. Joined by several other labor activists—such as Thomas Webb from Fall River and S. P. Cummings from the Knights of St. Crispin—they demanded that a committee drawn from the convention prepare the resolutions. Their assumption was that such a committee would include some of the workers in attendance and would thus be more likely to draft proposals on specific workplace issues such as the eight-hour day, rather than just the series of more theoretical pronouncements on money and monopolies favored by Heywood's allies. When Heywood tried to rule his challengers out of order, cries of protest filled the hall, and brewing class tensions erupted when the proceedings had scarcely begun. "This is no workingman's convention," someone shouted. Others chimed in: "It is your convention, not ours, and it is nothing but an assumption of power on your part."[8]

Heywood defused the revolt, at least temporarily, by promising that "freedom of speech was to be obtained there in the fullest extent, and that the resolutions were to be open to the freest discussion." Heywood tried to defend his leadership of the organization, and his definition of the league as a place where many visions of labor reform could be discussed (including his own preference for currency reform), by reassuring Steward and his supporters that they would be heard as the convention proceeded. The eight-hour advocates, perhaps fearing that they and their demands could still be squelched through some sort of parliamentary procedure, remained suspicious of Heywood's motives.

When order was restored, Heywood read the nine resolutions prepared in advance. Not surprisingly, given so many of his previous statements, the first four pronouncements all dealt with the money question and currency reform. Only one of Heywood's resolutions addressed directly what concerned workers most about money—their wages. Heywood took note of the especially low wages paid to working women, but his explanation for their exploitation offered little in the way of constructive alternatives. "The extreme penury of working-women is not so much the fault of individual employers implicated in the crime as the natural result of a system which makes cheating lucrative and honorable, most of all to rob the weak and defenseless.... [P]ermanent relief will come only through utter abolition of the power to take one's earnings without equitable return."

Steward immediately proposed a series of counterresolutions: five proposals which—also not surprisingly, given his years of agitation on the issue—all revolved around the campaign for the shorter workday. Reiterating his previous pamphlets and speeches, Steward insisted that the eight-hour movement should be the first priority of any labor reform organization, that manufacturing corporations should be targeted for legislation, and that an eight-hour day for public employees (as a test of the law's benefits) could be compatible with a ten-hour law for factory workers.[9]

Steward's resolutions triggered an intense debate over the eight-hour day, and revealed that the workers in attendance were themselves divided in their particular priorities for labor reform. S. P. Cummings, though critical of Heywood's control of the convention, remained skeptical of legislative efforts to limit working hours unless lawmakers also passed a statute to regulate wages. Moreover, he stated from his personal experience (probably working in a small cobbler's shop and not in one of the massive shoe factories engulfing cities such as Lynn) that ten hours' labor per day was not excessive, and that he always had "two hours a day to devote to recreation and culture." He admitted that such a law "might be beneficial ... in factories, but that branch is only one of a hundred in Massachusetts." Then, taking a page from Heywood's proposals on currency reform, Cummings concluded: "The first thing to be done is to break up the hold that the money-power of the country has upon its industry. When that is done, you can fix the hours of labor by common consent without any special act of legislation."

George McNeill responded that, contrary to Heywood's model of financial questions preceding all labor reform, "the reduction of the hours of labor underlies all other questions." To Cummings's claims of how he managed his time, McNeill remarked sarcastically: "I was surprised as well as pleased to hear that a man working ten hours a day can get two out of them for recreation. He must be favored above all others." In contrast, McNeill asserted, many factory operatives from Lowell and Lawrence could not attend the meeting to speak about their own needs because they simply had no time. Thomas Webb, representing Fall River millworkers, emphatically agreed that his constituents wanted shorter hours far more than financial reforms. Although "it was a ticklish thing to meddle with the labor question by law," Webb observed, "the importance of the question demanded some legislative enactment."[10]

When the convention reconvened for its afternoon session, it heard from Jennie Andrews, representing the Working-people's Industrial Order, which had organized a meeting of working women the week before. Andrews appealed to the league for guidance and support. Previous overtures to "reformatory ladies" had brought offers of temporary charity, and warnings "that men are our enemies," but little in the way of concrete proposals for improving working conditions. Addressing the many working men in attendance (as Sarah Bagley had done more than two decades earlier), Andrews appealed to these "solid men of Boston, not to pedantic political economists, who hold that man was made for money and not money for man, but to . . . mechanics . . . who have human hearts." The meeting listened attentively to Andrews's remarks, which emphasized urban working women's shockingly low wages and frequently cramped living conditions. Yet this assemblage approved no specific measures for aiding these women—even the proposal to help rent a meeting hall met with only a tepid response.

The remaining sessions included addresses by familiar figures such as Wendell Phillips, John Cluer, John Orvis, and Edward Rogers, who all spoke on familiar issues such as eight hours, producer cooperatives, and woman suffrage. Ira Steward tried to have the last word when he argued, at the closing of the convention, "that the corporations of the State must adopt the eight-hour system or be forced to surrender their charters, in spite of the cowardice, stupidity, and selfishness of the legislators. All he hoped for, and more, would be yielded, sooner or later, because the friends of labor reform were right." Steward's bold, angry words expressed frustration with both the legislature and the league, and confidence that his vision of labor reform would prevail eventually.[11]

The league's second meeting ended on an ironic note. Heywood sought to control the agenda, and his resolutions revolved around his belief that financial reform was the true source of labor reform. Yet Steward and the eight-hour men, and Andrews and the urban working women, dominated the convention's debates. The convocation adjourned, however, without offering any plan of action to meet workers' demands for a shorter day and better conditions on the job. Those who held the floor the longest still could not move the league away from its focus on debate itself. Heywood and the majority of the executive committee still wanted the organization to remain essentially an instrument for public instruction, rather than an agent for protest at the legislature or at the point of production. Labor activists became even more impatient with just talk when they wanted action.

Reflecting on the convention one month later, John Orvis captured the core of the league's tension when he wrote to the *American Workman* that there was a "great deal of diversity of thought, not as to the need of labor reform, but as to what should be the nature of that reform and the methods of accomplishing it." Yet Orvis did not dwell on these internal debates concerning the league's basic strategies, tactics, and goals, because he believed "it is always the first work of any reform ... to effect a permanent good, to get firmly grounded as to principles and methods." He also thought it healthy for the organization "that any difference on these points should appear now, rather than at a later period." Eventually, however, Orvis knew that "unity upon these points is indispensable to solid and compact action [because] genuine reform admits of no palliative, apologies, or ameliorations. It demands immediate, unconditional extirpation of the evil it assails."

Orvis proceeded to ask fundamental questions about labor reform's first principles: "Does the labor reform movement attack an evil? ... Is it that the laboring people are overworked? ... Is it the land monopoly ... [or] a vicious monetary system?" All of these problems had been raised at the recent gathering, but Orvis insisted that none of them was "the root itself, of our social miseries. We might abolish any one or all of these evils tomorrow; but if we did nothing more they would return upon us the next day." Drawing on his earlier experiences in the Fourierist movement, Orvis had his own opinion as to the central problem the league had to confront. He declared that "the structure of society is itself vicious, resting as it does upon incoherent, antagonistical, and competitive, instead of coherent, unitary and co-operative relations. The fact is that each man is the enemy of every other man in community, not from desire, but from the mechanism of society." In such a cruel world, "the chief aim of each is no longer beneficent use of production, but selfish strife to appropriate to himself without labor the most he can of the goods produced by the labor of others."

Echoing other writers in the postwar period, Orvis stated emphatically that "the labor question ... is the question of Reconstruction come North, but it is not that petty reconstruction talked of by fanatical politicians. ... It means the deliverance, exaltation, and ennobling of labor and the laboring classes." Real freedom, Orvis asserted, came from real knowledge of the nation's economic system—a system of exploitation based not on mere overwork but on the reality of class conflict which many other reformers tried to deny.

It is not worth debating as to how many hours shall make a day's work under the wages system itself. There can be no help for the working class, so long as the relation of master and man, employer and employed, exists. The relation is one of antagonism, and one in which the laborer always goes to the bottom. It is sheer nonsense to talk about there being no conflict between labor and capital. There is a fierce, satanic and deadly feud between capitalist and laborer, and this feud will continue inevitably, so long as a wages slave and a wages slave driver remains the curse and scourge of society.

For Orvis, then, the wage system lay at the heart of America's distorted social structure. He did not share Steward's confidence that the eight-hour day would allow labor to bend that system to workers' advantage and eventually displace it. Labor reformers could make no compromise with that system, Orvis insisted, if they were true to their principles.

The wages system must be attacked as being a scheme of organized robbery and oppression, without a parallel in infamy and meanness. So long as it exists, let us not make ourselves ridiculous by laying any stress upon a reduction of the hours of labor. Our true work it to make the wages system odious and infamous; and to stamp with infamy everybody who upholds it. . . . If lessening the hours of labor is to have the influence to render the working class satisfied with, or even tolerant towards, the system of wages, then for one I would oppose the shortening of the number of hours of labor, and would rather go for their increase. The working-people have got to achieve their own emancipation, and it is not impossible that their burdens will have to be increased many-fold, before they will get the courage, perhaps the desperation, to make their attack upon the citadel of their woes, instead of a weak cowardly skirmish with a mere picket line.

Whether Orvis intended the last remark as a pun on the idea of a Civil War or a labor picket line is not known, but he closed his long letter with the assertion that

the real question is, whether the laboring classes shall work as freemen or slaves; whether they shall work by right or by permission; whether they shall be self-employed or beg of a master "to give them leave to toil"; . . . whether they shall have all they earn, or whether a third or a quarter, or even a tittle of their earning shall go into the hands of some thief or pickpocket, called employer, banker, landlord . . . or speculator. When the laborer works from choice and not from necessity, when he is self-employed, when intelligent industry becomes honorable . . . it will be no matter whether he works four hours or fourteen per day. Such labor will be ennobling, healthful, attractive, and enriching—one hour of any other labor is too much.

Orvis made a passionate appeal for workers' cooperatives as the primary goal for labor reform. He believed a cooperatively based economy, where workers owned all the shops and factories, would make the eight-hour day irrelevant and superfluous. (Steward and his allies may have agreed with that ultimate destination, but always insisted that the eight-hour day had to be the first step toward creating such a cooperative economy.) But for all his powerful rhetoric and vision, Orvis provided no practical plan for building cooperative workshops and creating an entirely self-employed labor force. In encouraging the league, Orvis ended up merely articulating yet another broad conception of labor reform, one at odds with both Heywood's financial schemes and Steward's demands for the eight-hour day.[12]

In late August 1869, with fall elections looming, Heywood wrote an essay for the *American Workman* defending the league's stance toward political action. Heywood insisted that, contrary to what his critics said, the league did engage in politics (reflecting his original conception of labor reform). He believed that "one of the most cheering signs of the times, is the dawning purpose of working-men to abandon old party swindles and make the interests of labor paramount to all other consideration in political action." Looking at his own organization, Heywood observed: "Our object being educational, holding relations to the voting masses, similar to those which the old anti-slavery society bore to republican politics, the Labor Reform League does not officially identify itself with any political party. . . . [W]e shall endeavor, in the coming elections, to concentrate votes on the most practicable measures to advance the interests of labor."

Heywood went on to endorse several reforms including "the recognition of ten hours as a legal day's work," and "the right of voluntary associations of working-men, whether Crispins or other trade-unionists, to the same incorporated privileges which are accorded to associations of capitalists." Echoing early advocates of labor reform politics, Heywood added that "a definite committal of a candidate or party to one issue is better than general expressions of sympathy with labor measures to be forgotten afterwards." But Heywood remained very chary of third-party politics. He cautioned that "independent political nominations, like strikes, should be avoided if possible" because they risked alienating potential allies. In the end, he urged his readers "to stay and fight," and give party politicians "their first lesson in labor reform at the coming election." But, endorsing only a weak ten-hour law and eschewing independent candidates, Heywood did not stake out issues or strategies that would give him much political leverage or many supporters in the fall campaigns.[13]

The NELRL executive committee published its Declaration of Sentiments and Constitution in this same issue of the *American Workman*. Drawing extensively on Heywood's past speeches and convention resolutions, the document broadly condemned the existing society, and offered a grab bag of reforms with an emphasis on antimonopoly rhetoric. But the constitution contained virtually no discussion of specific workplace issues except for one sentence which ended in vague allusions to freedom. "Fair pay, reduced hours of service, and co-operative industry, can be permanently secured only by abolishment of those chronic usurpations which make property a many-headed master, empowered to increase illimitably, at labor's expense; and by guaranteeing to all parties a free contract." Thus, in its founding documents, the league again enunciated a definition of labor reform far removed from most workers' problems on the job.[14]

When the league next met, in early October at Horticultural Hall on the corner of Tremont Street and Montgomery Place near the Boston Common, the sparsely attended gathering bristled with hostility toward workers and their interests. Steward and McNeill were conspicuously absent, having left the group to form the Boston Eight Hour League. Heywood, addressing the first session, declared the NELRL "entirely independent of the ten-hour movers" (even though he had recently endorsed a ten-hour law). Another speaker stated that the "labor of the muscle got its support from brain labor; the thinking workers supplied the inventions, by which the world was kept moving and muscular labor fed. In regard to trade unions, he said that they were not an American institution.... They had agitated reform and done good incidentally, but were, on the whole, a failure." The handful of workers in the audience found those remarks difficult enough to swallow. But when this speaker then praised "republicans as the friends of labor, the democrats the enemies, ... many rose from their seats and left the hall, saying they did not come to hear politics discussed." The following day John Orvis tried to mount some defense of the working class. Sitting as president of this convention, Orvis criticized those remarks which "constantly alluded to brain power, without recognizing the thinking powers of the workingmen. He said that inventions and improvements all come from the real, actual mechanics; that professional men, lawyers, clergymen, &c., were parasites, who got their living off the working class." But Orvis's remarks were too little too late; few working-class activists had even bothered to return for the second day's proceedings.[15]

Thus, within less than a year of its inception, the league had lost much of its initial support from working-class men and women in the Boston labor reform community. Steward and McNeill left the organization, never to return. Despite its name, many other workers also concluded that the league simply had no idea what labor reform meant to people on the shopfloor. In fact, the league's resolutions continually subordinated basic workplace demands to vague schemes for financial transformations that were supposed to cure all social ills. Working-class critics now saw the league as little more than an open debating society for anyone who wanted to vent about any scheme for solving what they saw as the labor problem, no matter how outlandish or ill conceived or far removed from working people's real needs. Most workers were not opposed to conventions or resolutions, but they wanted their organizations' public statements to contain specific plans for economic and political action to benefit labor. And they wanted their organizations to follow through on their resolutions with sustained collective activity—something more than quarterly meetings.

Heywood and his supporters countered that freewheeling debate was a necessary prelude to building a consensus for social transformation. But working men and women stated that labor reform was not an abstract set of propositions to be bandied about; reform had to be rooted in a clearly defined course of action to secure specific improvements in their working conditions. The league, in their views, was trying to reach a utopia constructed out of monetary theories without building a foundation of pragmatic reforms. Workers criticized the league's leaders not for their idealism but because these idealists provided no clear mechanisms for working logically and directly toward a better society. Many workers, too, had a vision for a world transformed, a belief that labor reform should be construed broadly in social ideals. But they believed just as fervently that labor reform would begin with improving the working lives of men and women, who then would take the lead in changing society as a whole.

Thus, the split in the league was not simply one of bread-and-butter workers versus dreamy reformers. The dispute revolved around two competing maps of social change: one started with theories about financial reform and their dissemination through public debate; the other began with improving conditions on the job as a way of liberating workers to become agents of broader economic and political transformation. This debate certainly echoed discussions in the earlier labor reform league of the 1840s, but this organizational split developed much more quickly, and became deeper and more acrimonious. Working-class leaders, such as Steward and McNeill, washed their hands of Heywood's group because they had a readily available alternative ideology and organization in their eight-hour leagues. They simply refused to consider any labor reform program that did not start with the workplace, and they knew that the NELRL was not the only game in town. Meanwhile, Heywood and his supporters clung to their own brand of labor reform, which remained quite distant from any real interest in wage laborers' working conditions. More than in the previous generation, the fight in this league was seen by many participants as an all-or-nothing contest for the ideological soul of labor reform itself.

As the league's leaders saw early supporters leaving and rival resolutions competing for attention on the convention floor, they tried to institute new procedures that they thought would promote freer debate and inquiry: resolutions would now be printed in advance and offered for discussion purposes only, not for a vote. Skeptics howled that Heywood deliberately steered the organization increasingly toward his own ideas of financial reform; and the critics dismissed the new rules for discussion as merely leading the league into a cul-de-sac of pointless debates.

Benjamin Tucker keenly observed the league's internal dynamics and operations, and he thought the new rules for discussion might serve the league well in the long term. In his manuscript autobiography, he left a detailed account of Heywood's struggles to get what he thought was a fair hearing for his ideas. Just eighteen when he attended his first league meeting, Tucker had been raised in a middle-class Unitarian family near the seacoast city of New Bedford, Massachusetts. Though he would emerge as a leading anarchist thinker in late nineteenth-century America, he always dressed the part of the well-bred New Englander from good stock. A slightly built man with a dark complexion, black eyes, neatly trimmed mustache, and a nervous laugh, Tucker recalled that the league's

> early meetings had been conducted on the usual democratic plan, any resolutions that were presented being submitted to the vote of the audience present, regardless of membership. The method was soon found to be incautious and disastrous. Eight-hour advocates and trade-unionists attended in force; and introduced and passed resolutions not at all in keeping with the purposes of the League's founders. It became necessary, therefore, to adopt a new plan. The League existing for propagandism rather than political action, it was decided that resolutions would be offered for discussion only, and that no questions should be put to vote. Resolutions were desirable for the reason that, being carefully considered in advance and presented in the form of printed proof-slips, they were generally given in full to the newspapers, while speeches suffered from condensation and misrepresentation. In the long run the new plan proved workable, but was very shocking at first to those accustomed to determining the truth or falsity of a proposition by a counting of noses.[26]

The new procedures were instituted at the league's first meeting in 1870. On the morning of January 24, at the Boston Opera House on Washington Street near the city's central commercial district, the executive committee presented preprinted resolutions for discussion purposes only. The resolutions contained little of interest to working people on the shopfloor. Only one statement made even a veiled reference to the eight-hour movement, declaring that although the organization endorsed "any honorable effort likely to afford even temporary aid to the victims of excessive and unremunerative toil, still we assure our friends, in the factory districts, that permanent relief will come only through the utter overthrow of the money despotism which keeps them down." One other resolution offered support to working women and the suffrage movement: "That those to whom the world owes the most, and without whom human society would cease to exist, the working-women, are the very class whom present laws and customs doom to the most abject poverty and degradation; that we will aid them in speedy and thorough organization for self-protection, and welcome them to rights, privileges, and duties equal with men, foremost among which is the right to vote."[17]

Even though the convention's resolutions endorsed working women's rights, discussion on the floor became misogynistic at times. Mr. Appleby received a round of applause when he stated that "nine-tenths of the women in this country produced nothing, and they got nothing for it." These remarks, and the crowd's enthusiastic approval, brought Jennie Collins "to her feet with a spring and a flashing eye." Collins, a former New Hampshire mill operative and well-known activist for working women in Boston, took great offense at Appleby's gross generalizations. Later on, she also urged the convention to support the eight-hour day. She said that eight hours was "to this Labor Reform what the State Militia was to the Grand Army of the Union." Though the league's resolutions continued to proclaim that a new monetary system would provide the key to labor reform, Collins insisted that financial reform mattered only to those who already had money and offered little to the struggling workers for whom the league professed so much sympathy.

The treasurer's report revealed that the league, whatever its ideological faults and fault lines, was financially robust compared with other reform groups. The organization had collected nearly $5,000 in its first year from book sales, membership dues, and donations. Most of those funds had been spent to distribute 30,000 books and pamphlets, sponsor lectures, and rent halls for meetings. True to its public declarations, the league expended a substantial amount of time and money agitating and debating the labor question in conventions, resolutions, and publications. But this league was not in the business of organizing workers or building strong alliances with other labor reform groups.

At the meeting's conclusion, the assembly elected a new slate of officers for the coming year. Surprisingly, despite its many critics, several veterans of the Boston labor reform community stepped forward to fill leadership positions in the league. John Orvis became president; Edith Daniels and J. G. Blanchard (former editor of the *Daily Evening Voice*) served as vice presidents; Heywood took over as corresponding secretary and Herbert Daniels as recording secretary; and the executive committee that prepared resolutions for each meeting included Heywood, Orvis, Edith Daniels, and Edward Linton.[18]

Four months later, at the spring convocation in Mercantile Hall near the intersection of Washington and Summer Streets (also in the city's commercial district), Heywood lashed out at his critics. Resolutions included a blunt condemnation of Wendell Phillips, eight-hour advocates, and trade union organizers—all of whom now dismissed the league as irrelevant to their campaigns for workers' rights. The league, in turn, rejected these individuals and groups as narrow-minded special interests who underestimated their own constituents' intelligence:

> To withhold truth, because some people are thought unready to receive it, is a new doctrine of reform in Boston, and we deny the right of Wendell Phillips, or any other man, or class of men, to postpone the claims of justice . . . to suppose that our purpose is expressed in special legislation to reduce the hours of service or, that the rights and true interest of labor are embodied in organizations which monopolize mechanical skill, and prevent those less fortunate from learning trades, shows either lack of intelligent comprehension or reprehensible trifling with the grave issues involved.

The league also warned that "ruling politicians are using the eight-hour law to strangle the labor movement." Rather than pursue single-issue campaigns, the league now offered laudatory yet still cautionary words to those pursuing independent labor parties. "Rejoicing in the tendency of workingmen to cut loose from old parties and make the interests of labor paramount to all other considerations in political action, we yet solemnly warn that, so long as they continue to side with Republican and Democratic transgressors . . . the success of the Labor Party will be both impossible and undesirable." The league wanted to encourage political action by workers but remained leery of endorsing any reputed independent labor party. For Heywood and other league leaders, party politics—even third-party politics—smacked of partisan infighting, alliances of mutual convenience rather than principle, and backroom maneuvering for offices—all rather unpalatable prospects for men and women who saw themselves committed to attaining higher ideals through free intellectual discussion.[19]

The following January (1871), in a meeting at Elliott Hall, Heywood mercilessly flayed labor reform politics in Massachusetts. Angered that his advice on platforms, candidates, and alliances had been spurned, he excoriated "the

Labor Reform party of Massachusetts" as a "party without an idea, whose ruling purpose is public plunder." Furthermore, he warned that "special and class legislation, should they succeed, which happily they cannot, would make the labor movement a common nuisance." Heywood insisted that the party had to return to his core vision of what labor reform was all about. "The beneficent tendency of voters to sever old party ties and side with right, will never achieve or deserve success until it stands squarely for impartial liberty . . . and demands free money, free transit, free trade and free land."[20]

In the spring of 1872, the league's executive committee issued a report tracing the intellectual history of the organization's guiding libertarian, antimonopoly philosophy. Certainly aware that many workers now dismissed the league as irrelevant to any substantive discussion of labor reform, the committee countered that its broader vision of social change grew out of more specific workplace problems. The report stated that when the league began, it regarded "a reduction of the hours of labor as at least one of [its] chief objects." But when it examined closely the conditions of overworked operatives, it concluded that "the causes of poverty" had to be "looked into." Not surprisingly, the league declared that "one does not desire to be poor, to be drunk, ignorant or dependent, but is pushed that way by adverse conditions." Furthermore, "those doomed to be always at work, but always poor, if they reason at all, will ask why the wealth which they create is enjoyed by the class whose business is to get a living without work." Such questions led the league to proclaim that it is a "universally admitted principle that labor is the source of wealth" but that the nation's wealth and property accumulated in the hands of a few rich and powerful monopolists who robbed the workers of what they produced. Thus, the executive committee concluded, smashing all forms of monopoly was the true solution to workers' exploitation at the point of production. The league believed in "opportunity and reciprocity, in the natural right of workers of all nations to create and exchange commodities, unrestricted by local class interests. Our purpose is to abolish utterly, the existing speculative tenure of property and put the wealth of the world into the hands of those who created it."[21]

The league also continued to show some interest in the especially heavy burdens of wage-earning women. At a meeting in late May 1873 at Nassau Hall, Heywood offered a resolution "that the stealthy and determined purpose of employers to discriminate against women, in the payment of wages, is an exhibition of depravity not agreeable to contemplate; that the revolt of working girls against this injustice is, on their part, a demand for opportunity and fair play; and we regard it as a part of our work to encourage and support this effort of human nature to relieve itself from still prevailing barbarism." Heywood's wife, Angela, who wrote extensively on women's rights, took up the cause of domestic servants in another resolution: "The labor of girls in housework is better performed than present compensation deserves it should be; if it is uneducated and unreliable, it is because it is underpaid and regarded as disreputable; when bread making and house cleaning are justly rewarded and honored as all true labor should be, and the idleness of so-called ladies is alone deemed vulgar, the vexed question of 'our help' will virtually be settled." Both of these resolutions reflected the Heywoods' shared conviction that equal pay for women workers was part of a much larger goal to grant full economic, social, political, and sexual equality to all women. They also believed that such equal rights should be extended to all people regardless of race, nationality, or religion; and that such universal equity and justice would build the foundation for a truly reformed society.

The Heywoods' outspoken support for women workers encouraged some observers; but most of the convention's resolutions still reflected an organization more interested in pronouncing grand schemes for radical change than in promoting pragmatic reforms at the workplace. One declaration stated: "While not undervaluing the short-time movement, co-operation, financial reform, or free trade, it is the essential object of this League to concentrate attention upon the fact that property not founded on a labor title is robbery; and we demand the entire abolition of profits, and the restoration of existing wealth to its rightful owners." Strong words perhaps, but since the league still preferred discussion to direct action, it offered no clear guidance on how it planned to accomplish this bold scheme to eliminate capitalism's central tenets. What would be the steps along the road to the new society, if not some of the individual reforms proposed by other activists?[22]

By 1874, Heywood's antimonopoly rhetoric had become so intense that his resolutions lacked even a veneer of sympathy for basic workplace reforms. At the February convention, he condemned the "Massachusetts Labor-Bureau" as a "successful effort to get money out of tax-cursed producers for the benefit of State-House-parasites and the republican party." He abandoned all previous support for limiting the workday: "The ten-hour-law scheme which denies the right of citizens to make their own contracts, and meanly discriminates against women, though a clever trick to catch votes, is chiefly useful in revealing the ignorant perversity of its authors." At the May meeting, Heywood jettisoned all interest in politics and announced that "working people are the natural sovereigns and benefactors of society, and have no favors to ask of government, except to be let alone." He now dismissed the entire movement for a shorter workday as "hostile to the best interests of the industrial classes" because he thought it was hopelessly enmeshed with the machinery of political parties and the state.[23]

At the league's fall 1875 convocation, Heywood stated boldly that "the labor question is essentially a property question; ... trade unions, short-time movement and co-operation are incidental and secondary" issues for reformers to consider. The ultimate success of any labor reform depended on a clear understanding of how property was created and distributed, or maldistributed. Any understanding of property, Heywood argued, had to be based on an analysis of currency and financial issues in the broadest terms possible, not just fair wages or an equitable return for labor. Furthermore, he concluded that recent ten-hour legislation was a failure: "Instead of the 'less hours—more wages' prophecy of eight hour philosophers proving true, the enforcement of the ten-hour law was attended by an unparalleled reduction of wages." He also fulminated "that laborers who expect pay without regard to the quality or quantity of work done are fit disciples of that gospel of shirks and sharpers which teaches capitalists to get the most possible money for the least possible service." In a final dig at other labor reformers, Heywood insisted "that employers, in all senses, are the equals of employees, and have our full sympathy in resisting legislative or trade-union interference."[24]

Heywood's aggressively individualistic, antistatist, and now avowedly antiunion rhetoric signaled his and the league's virtual divorce from other individuals and organizations in the labor reform community. Yet the group did continue to meet, at least on an annual basis, until at least 1886. And it often pointed to its own longevity as proof that its highly idiosyncratic definition of labor reform was actually the most accurate assessment of social conditions in Gilded Age America. In an editorial for *The Word,* in June 1877, Heywood redefined labor reform to mean refashioning working people's demands through his own conception of social change. "When ... we placed 'labor reform' on the banner of industrial progress, we were impelled to do it by a settled conviction that, whatever may be the sins of capitalists, working people themselves, compulsive eight-hour trade unionists, ... co-operators in profits, and all other 'labor' exponents of intrusion, *imperatively need reforming.*" At the conclusion of the league's 1880 meeting, Heywood thundered that "the League strikes death-blows at invasive, stealthy Collectivism, which with its illegitimate children,—compulsive eight-hourism, co-operation in profits, unsocial democracy and majority usurpation, must give way to Individual Liberty and Natural right." Such hostile rhetoric revealed that Heywood spoke for a hollow shell of an organization that had virtually no working-class members, opposed every popular labor reform initiative, and openly scorned any efforts to rebuild alliances with other reformers and activists. The league was now content to preach its own negative version of labor reform to a rapidly diminishing circle of adherents.[25]

For most of its nearly two-decade existence, the New England Labor Reform League sought to liberate all individuals from what the organization saw as unnatural legal, political, economic, and social constraints. Many workers embraced antimonopoly arguments—especially those criticisms directed at manufacturing corporations and financial institutions. But Heywood insisted that his philosophy of individual freedom also required that he condemn trade unions, producer cooperatives, and legislative limits on the workday— the very institutions and ideas that many other labor reformers promoted as essential building blocks for workers' emancipation. Heywood often spoke passionately and sympathetically about the injustices heaped on American workers, and the need for equity and fairness in American society. But the organization he led became a labor reform group antagonistic to virtually all popular ideas for labor reform. Thus, the league doomed itself to irrelevance for the cause it claimed to be championing.

II

Back in the summer of 1869, Ira Steward and George McNeill—already disillusioned with the New England Labor Reform League—gathered their supporters together and formed the Boston Eight Hour League. Steward became president, and McNeill one of the vice presidents. Both men also served on the executive committee along with their wives and Charles McLean, all of them veterans of the Labor Reform Institute. This new league would become the organizational embodiment of Steward's economic philosophy and his strategy for a political lobbying campaign focused on first achieving the eight-hour day. To accomplish this crucial first step, Steward combined the familiar format of annual meetings and resolutions with innovative legislative proposals and new efforts to establish a headquarters for labor reform agitation.

The organization adopted a constitution on September 2 in a room at 14 Bromfield Street—a narrow lane off Tremont Street, near the Boston Common, dominated by the city's First Methodist Church. The document stated forthrightly that this league's "object shall be to concentrate the whole power and strength of the Labor-Reform movement upon the single issue of first securing the Eight-Hour system for the mass of Wage Laborers." Yet even as the league insisted on the primacy of gaining the eight-hour workday, Steward never intended for this organization to make just a narrow argument about working hours. The campaign was rooted in the idea that a shorter workday was the essential first step down the road leading to an entirely new economy. The constitution's preamble, echoing Steward's writings on the subject, held out great hopes that shorter working hours, more than any convention resolutions or talk of revolution, would change the workers' world. "Wealth may be more equally distributed, as well as more rapidly produced, Poverty abolished, Human Life lengthened, getting a living made easy, and Cooperative labor become the general rule in the production of wealth." But that was not all—"profits upon labor, the Wages system, the wages and employing classes and interest on money may finally cease to exist; together with Idleness, Speculation, Class Legislation, Financial Convulsions, Intemperance, Prostitution and War." Such bold statements reveal that this organization was, in some ways, not much different from the NELRL. Both proclaimed their own vision of a world transformed through a unitary, all-encompassing solution to the crisis of industrial capitalism. But the Eight Hour League insisted that the new world began with something as simple, direct, and pragmatic as a shorter workday. Workers would benefit immediately (both physically and mentally) from shorter hours, and the ripple effects eventually would engulf the entire economy and society.[26]

The following May (1870), the Eight Hour League called for a convention at Horticultural Hall (practically around the corner from its rooms on Bromfield Street) to unify the labor reform effort around the campaign for an eight-hour day. Declaring that "Capital is an *army of occupation,* always on a war footing, against which the straggling bands of labor reform operate in vain," the executive committee insisted that "no other measure" besides the eight-hour day "is so generally acceptable to the mass of laborers, and to those who speak in their behalf." Despite the enthusiasm for monetary reform in some quarters, the eight-hour advocates argued that "on the subject of finances, the theories and measures proposed are in conflicting variety. Seeing all this, intelligent working-men, and their friends everywhere, are powerfully impressed that more leisure is required for investigation, and reflection upon the great themes involved, not only to attain sound conclusions, but to any conclusions at all." Here again, the Eight Hour League's leaders emphasized that the shorter workday was the foundation for building a nation where citizens had the time, knowledge, and material resources to both improve their immediate physical surroundings and intelligently evaluate potential solutions for larger economic and social problems.[27]

When the Eight Hour League assembled for its next annual convention on May 31, 1871, again at Horticultural Hall, Wendell Phillips read a series of resolutions reaffirming the shorter workday as a key solution for postwar labor problems. Reiterating Steward's arguments that a reduction in working hours would actually lead to an increase in wages, a more equitable distribution of wealth, and the beginnings of a genuine cooperative economy, Phillips also confronted the naysayers who scoffed at labor's demand for fewer working hours without a corresponding cut in pay. "Resolved, That the so-called injustice of expecting ten hours pay for eight hours work, unless as much can be done in the shorter as in the longer time, is grounded upon the mistaken assumption, that the wages paid under the ten hour rule represent the actual worth of the work done. While the increasing wealth of the wealthy proves that the laborer has never received an equivalent for even his ten hours toil, and with the aid of labor-saving machinery is actually doing twelve or fifteen hours work for ten hours pay." Phillips also noted that "bad as is the condition of the workingman under the present system, we are not unmindful of the fact" that the working woman labors under worse circumstances, "since she is doubly enslaved, first, as he is to an aristocracy of wealth; second, as he is not to an aristocracy of sex." Phillips agreed with a recent report from the state's Bureau of the Statistics of Labor "that not charity but justice is what the workingwoman wants, and a just share of the world's money for her share of the world's work . . . and the general prejudice which denies her admittance into many classes of employment be denounced and destroyed."

Turning to the organization's legislative priorities, Phillips stressed a new idea for experimenting with an eight-hour law, a strategy that Steward had proposed in his recent writings. Rather than pressing for a law to regulate all corporations, Phillips suggested "that the first legislation" should be "the adoption by the State, Counties, Cities and Towns, of the eight hour system for all labor employed at the public expense; and thus to prove by actual experiment, to the entire satisfaction of all, that wages cannot be reduced." A league committee had made the same proposal in a petition sent to the Massachusetts legislature several months earlier—again emphasizing Steward's argument about demonstrating the eight-hour day's practical benefits, and reminding legislators that the federal government had already passed just such a law for its employees. Such limited laws, written with few means of enforcement, might directly impact only a small number of workers. But if the experiment proved successful in improving public employees' lives without reducing services, this law could stimulate further eight-hour legislation. Moreover, the law could set a practical example for private sector employers to follow, without being compelled by legislation. In assessing the chances for passing such a law, however, Phillips frankly noted that the recent rejection of yet another ten-hour bill did not bode well for the eight-hour movement. There was a hostile political climate in the Massachusetts legislature that crossed party boundaries. "In this struggle between privileged capital and unfairly burdened labor," he observed, "there are no Republican and no Democratic lines; but that for us are all the just and fair-minded men, and against us are all the greedy and unscrupulous, who sacrifice justice to party and interest, and make haste to be rich by any means."[28]

In the fall of 1871, the Eight Hour League launched a fund-raising campaign to open a meeting hall under the league's management. Since many of this league's leaders were veterans of the recently defunct Labor Reform Institute, they certainly recognized how important Institute Hall had been as a meeting place for that and other labor organizations in the city. Securing a permanent headquarters location could help this new league evolve into something more than a vehicle for just another series of annual conventions. A league hall would provide a base for ongoing organizational and political efforts that could sustain and extend the enthusiasm generated at public gatherings. The initial fund-raising circular emphasized the need for a place where labor reform could be discussed in an open manner, so that workers throughout the city could be educated about a range of options for activism beyond trade unions and strikes. Though the Eight Hour League clearly had its own ideas about the centrality of shorter working hours to labor reform as a whole, and kept its annual meetings focused closely on that one issue, the leaders seemed willing to consider more free-ranging debate in planning for their new hall so as to rally the widest possible network of potential contributors.

The fund-raising committee, led by McNeill, Steward, and others, admitted that "the Trade Union, is in most cases, the only school where the workingman learns what he knows of Social Science or Political Economy. The discussion of Wages, Hours of Labor, Laws of Trade and Commerce, etc., must and does have an educating influence." But labor reform organizations with members from beyond one trade and even one class, devoted to both immediate workplace issues and broader social change, could open up a world of new arguments and allies for hard-pressed workers if all the parties could gather in one place to discuss possible future directions for collective action.[29]

When the fund-raising committee laid out a "plan and estimates" for the hall, they specified the range of organizations and issues to be discussed within its "anti-rooms." The hall would be rented out three nights per week "to societies of Working-men and Working-women." One evening every week would be devoted to "a free public discussion upon Labor Questions, including that of Woman's Work and Wages," and one evening would be given over to free public temperance meetings. Sunday evenings were set aside for lectures by clergymen or others who wished to raise any other reform topic, but "no societies of a partisan or sectarian nature" could use the hall.

By the spring of 1873, Sylvis Hall—named in memory of William Sylvis, late president of the National Labor Union (founded in 1866)—became the new generally recognized headquarters for labor reform in Boston. The hall was located at 144 Hanover Street, near the city's mercantile exchanges and financial district—that is, close to the center of so much powerful opposition to the eight-hour day. Almost twenty leading reformers and activists (not all of whom were close allies of Steward) supported the project, including Edwin Chamberlin, Edward Linton, John Orvis, Wendell Phillips, Edward Rogers, and Benjamin Tucker. Once established, the hall did open its doors to wide-ranging debate; eight-hour men were no longer the sole proprietors. It is unclear whether Steward willingly ceded control to get the project off the ground, or other reformers took over the reins on their own accord.[30]

Even as the Eight Hour League struggled to raise money for renting rooms in Boston, it also petitioned the U.S. Congress in the spring of 1872 to keep hands off the existing eight-hour law for federal laborers and manual workers (passed in 1868). The league saw that law as precisely the kind of experiment, national in scope, which would ultimately prove their consumer-based theory "that wages are not regulated by the amount of work performed, but by the habits and customs, and consequent cost of living of the workers." Furthermore, the eight-hour law would bring the wages and working conditions of manual laborers on government projects closer to those of salaried federal clerks, thus reinforcing the ideal that there should be no moral distinction between hand and brain work. The league's petition also stressed that "Republicanism . . . means that a person shall receive what he earns; and [since] in the present ignorance of economic laws, no certain data for such payments can be fixed, constant approaches to it must be made in the direction of shorter working days, and more pay, until that point is reached where no profit can be made upon labor." With so many crucial economic gains at stake, the league concluded that "the repeal of the Eight Hour Law would be a denial of the right of labor to better pay, and the consequent postponement of the solution of the Labor Problem."[31]

As its annual meeting drew closer in May 1872, the Eight Hour League became caught up in a bitter dispute that would sunder the Boston labor reform community. In the middle of the conflict stood Wendell Phillips and Ira Steward, the two men who for nearly a decade had worked side by side to advance the eight-hour day through political agitation and cross-class organizing. But in the spring of 1872, these two central figures stood at odds with each other; and their fellow activists quickly took sides and fractured whatever unity had existed in the campaign for shorter hours. Personal grudges became commingled with growing differences over specific reforms and strategies for achieving those reforms, and the combination proved to be highly combustible.

The conflict may have been rooted in personalities, since both men saw themselves as leading thinkers and spokesmen for labor reform. Steward, though younger and far less formally educated than Phillips, remained fiercely proud of his self-taught expertise in political economy, his position as the foremost theorist for the eight-hour day, and his blunt rhetoric at conventions and rallies. One contributor to the *American Workman* described Steward (in the summer of 1869) as nearly monomaniacal in his pursuit of the shorter workday. He could be seen

> steam[ing] along the street (like most enthusiasts, he is always in a hurry), and, although he will apologize and excuse himself, if you talk to him of other affairs, and say that he is sorry, that he must rush back to his shop, if you only introduce the pet topic of "hours of labor," and show a willingness to listen, he will stop and plead with you till night-fall.... Every ready writer for the press and every able speaker whom he can approach, he pleads with earnest arguments on behalf of his class.... He has called out Wendell Phillips more than once to argue for his clients before legislative committees.[32]

As for Steward's erstwhile ally, Phillips, though he displayed a willingness to cooperate across class lines far beyond that of most of his fellow patrician reformers, he was still quite cognizant of his stature as a nationally prominent writer and orator lending his influence to the cause of labor reform. Needless to say, the rift cannot be explained away merely by pitting Phillips as some rich dilettante dabbling in reform against Steward as the genuine hardhanded man of toil struggling to liberate his oppressed working-class brethren. But personalities, egos, leadership positions, oratorical skills, and rhetorical arguments all did figure in the growing conflict.

Personal tensions may have been exacerbated by Phillips's expansive reform rhetoric and vision. Although he recognized the importance of the eight-hour day to workers, he also began to speak out in support of cooperatives and other labor reform schemes. He endorsed graduated taxes, and showed growing interest in the arguments for financial and currency reform voiced by Ezra Heywood and the New England Labor Reform League. Meanwhile, Steward publicly condemned virtually all of those individuals, organizations, and ideas as unnecessary distractions from his vision of labor reform based on achieving the eight-hour workday first. Steward seemed most distressed not by the possibility that the Greenbackers or any other rival reform movement had captured Phillips but that Phillips simply refused to devote himself to any one reform above all else, especially Steward's nearly sacred cause of the eight-hour workday. Phillips's ever expanding universe of reform ideas could be inspiring in its breadth and ambitious reach, but maddeningly unfocused to those who wanted a clear path toward social justice. Meanwhile, moderate politicians and newspaper editors increasingly looked to the well-known Phillips as the de facto spokesman for the labor reform community, and his pronouncements often became the generally accepted definition of labor reform. Steward found himself in a losing battle to gain a broader popular audience for his views, which he considered to be more relevant to working people. The two men had always been aware of their differences, but Steward now concluded that he would never persuade Phillips to embrace completely the primacy of the eight-hour doctrine. In fact, Phillips seemed to acquire new reform projects nearly every week, and his catholic view of social change now enraged Steward.

Phillips, knowing that he was not invited to the eight-hour convention (where he had always been welcome in the past), and hearing that the assembly would censure him, encouraged another group—the Massachusetts Labor Union—to convene on May 29, the night before the Eight Hour League's meeting. Phillips's gathering drew many local trade union leaders, but despite subsequent claims that Phillips was in the Greenbacker camp and returning to the New England Labor Reform League, Ezra Heywood did not attend. The statewide union drafted a resolution thanking Henry Oliver, head of the Bureau of the Statistics of Labor (even though Phillips himself had been critical of the bureau); however, the resolution made no mention of Oliver's deputy George McNeill, Steward's closest ally and the Boston Eight Hour League's current president. Steward and his supporters, who made a point of being in the audience that evening, took exception to what they perceived as a deliberate slight of McNeill. Phillips responded angrily and ripped down a poster advertising the next day's meeting of the Eight Hour League—a highly uncharacteristic physical display of temper which shocked the crowd and brought inadvertent attention to the rival convention.[33]

As predicted, the next day's meeting of the Eight Hour League did censure Phillips. The league charged that Phillips had undermined the factory operatives' campaign for ten-hour legislation by distracting public and political attention with his attacks on corporate dividends and the Bureau of the Statistics of Labor. In a subsequent letter to *The Commonwealth,* Steward declared: "We reiterate the charge that upon him, more than upon any other man, rests the responsibility for the fact that in this commonwealth thousands of women and children are still toiling in our factories eleven and twelve hours a day." The split between Phillips and Steward had come into the open, codified in rival resolutions, which touched only the surface of the complex personal and ideological conflicts between these men. The divisions would reverberate for years thereafter in the organizational structures and politics of the Boston labor reform community.

Steward, reflecting on the competing conventions, insisted that Phillips and his supporters had placed their grand vision of political and social reform ahead of workers' basic needs. Steward had raised similar objections to

Ezra Heywood and the New England Labor Reform League. (Steward's concerns also paralleled those voiced about the Associationists in the 1840s.) He wrote that in his league, "Eight hours is never put as an IDEA, or a panacea, but as a *first measure*. We discuss the dangers threatening the republic and the laborer, and we have our visions of the ideal future, but take excellent care to make the duty of the hour the most conspicuous.... The answer of the League is, first reduce the hours of labor, and then you will see what next. This is a reply adapted to those who cannot understand more." Furthermore, Steward argued that Phillips was abandoning their shared commitment to the primacy of the eight-hour day. In 1866, Phillips had said at Faneuil Hall, "Don't meddle with ethics, don't discuss debts, keep clear of finance, talk only eight hours." In 1869, Phillips played a crucial role in organizing and funding the Boston Eight Hour League. But three years later, Steward concluded, "the differences fomented in our ranks—always great enough at best—are now more angry and unmanageable than ever." He believed that Phillips had strayed from the right path and wandered into a wilderness of unrelated reform ideas.[34]

Steward tried to temper his anger, and he admitted that his "reflections are written without forgetting for one moment the untold obligations mankind are under for [Phillips's] great services in the past." But Steward could not get over his sense of indignation, and his deep feelings of pride and near proprietary ownership in the eight-hour campaign. He warned that "the laurels of the past can never be substituted for the duties of the present, neither by the Republican party nor by Wendell Phillips." In the end, Steward had no time to pay homage to the past achievements of those individuals or institutions that would not join him in moving his agenda forward. Venting his sense of frustration and betrayal by a former ally, he judged Phillips quite harshly. Moreover, in making his condemnations public, Steward failed to see that his own judgmental attitude was splitting the campaign he so desperately wanted to unite and lead to victory.[35]

The 1872 convention not only censured Wendell Phillips; it also revealed Steward and his followers' growing anger at the entire financial reform movement. They worried more about monetary and banking schemes masquerading as labor reform than about whether or not Phillips himself was a Greenbacker. Steward had always been skeptical of such financial ideas, going back to his brief foray in the New England Labor Reform League and perhaps even earlier. Now, his resolutions stated unambiguously (if not entirely accurately, in the eyes of many modern economists): "Whether National Banks are abolished or bonds are taxed, or whether taxes or tariffs are high or low, or whether greenbacks or gold, or any system of finance proposed is adopted ... are not *laborers'* questions, because they have no appreciable relation to the *wage system* through which the wage classes secure all they can ever obtain of the world's wealth, until they become sufficiently wealthy and intelligent to cooperate in its production." Put simply, Steward insisted that most money questions mattered only to people who already had wealth. Workers had to worry about long days on the job, feeding their families on meager weekly wages, and dangerous conditions on the shopfloor. Steward restated this emphatic, nearly exasperated, plea—to keep money matters and workplace issues separate—with increasing vigor and venom at subsequent conventions.[36]

Steward elaborated on his concerns about what he termed "financial reform" in his 1873 essay, *Poverty*. He used the label of financial reform to criticize not only greenbacks, banking legislation, repudiation of public debts, progressive taxation, and the abolition of interest but also the nationalization of land and manufacturing, and even loans to workingmen's cooperatives and public works projects in times of high unemployment. Steward insisted that all these schemes, some of them endorsed by other labor reformers, tried to redistribute existing wealth by legislative fiat. He believed all these plans would fail because of popular opposition to radical redistribution, and because most of them did nothing to change the fundamental structure of the economic system which led to such maldistribution of wages and wealth in the first place.[37]

At the Eight Hour League's annual convention in 1874, held as usual during the last week in May, at Horticultural Hall, Steward presented another series of resolutions that reiterated his "emphatic protest against the discussion or the consideration of financial theories, in the name of Labor Reform." Steward dismissed "financial reform" as being "interesting and important chiefly, to that small per cent of our fellow citizens who belong to the capitalist classes... and believe that upon their financial success must depend all who work with their hands." Currency and tax reform, Steward asserted, "still leaves the laborer a laborer, and the capitalist a capitalist, between whom there is an irrepressible conflict which must continue until all are laborers and all are capitalists." Furthermore, "as long as the wage system prevails... any re-distribution of wealth, through a supplementary financial system, can never occur."

Without explicitly naming any other organizations, Steward distinguished between the Eight Hour League and others that claimed to speak on labor's behalf (such as the New England Labor Reform League). He dismissed "the so-called 'Labor Reform' conventions that assemble and discuss almost everything else but labor, and confuse and disgust those who stop to listen, by the impracticable nature of their claims." Such groups merely "furnish a theatre or a platform for a crowd of adventurers who are without a purpose, and without a constituency among those who labor." These psuedo–labor reformers, cut off from any working-class base, "flippantly denounce as narrow and unimportant . . . the uprising of labor everywhere for less hours." In the end, Steward argued, the formless conventions offered "no theory . . . of the labor and poverty problem, and no measures that could be enacted or repealed with profit to labor . . . and our interest in them begins and ends with the wish, that as often as they call the public to discuss financial theories, they will call in the name of Capital and not in the precious name of Labor."

Steward was troubled by the conflation of financial reform with labor reform, in part because all the talk of money and interest distracted the movement from what he thought workers wanted most—immediate improvements in their working lives and straightforward schemes for broader social change. Financial reformers also often spoke about radically redistributing the nation's existing wealth, whereas eight-hour advocates saw no practical benefits in idly threatening to summarily expropriate private fortunes. Unrealistic schemes for financial revolution only stirred up public opposition and undermined potential political alliances for new labor legislation. Steward was convinced that the rearrangement of economic power would happen not through financial markets but through his ideas for a new political economy beginning with the eight-hour workday. He closed his convention remarks by reasserting the central tenet of his faith: "The reduction of the hours of labor is not a panacea . . . but it is *the* first step for the elevation of the masses, and that is why we press it so steadfastly." In the end, Steward condemned financial reformers not necessarily because they were utopians—for he also had high hopes that the eight-hour workday would provide the initial key to unlocking a future free from industrial crisis and poverty—but because these Greenbackers and antimonopolists, as Steward saw them, peddled a monetary cure-all for what ailed the nation, a nostrum that had to be swallowed whole with no questions asked by workers who usually had little money of their own.[38]

By the Eight Hour League's seventh annual convention, held this time at the Meionaon hall under Tremont Temple on May 31, 1876, the delegates focused their attention on the lingering effects of a long and deep depression that began back in 1873. Unlike the New England Labor Reform League, which rarely addressed directly the hard times faced by those out of work and those still working for falling wages, the eight-hour advocates devoted much of their meeting to grappling with the causes of the nation's prolonged downturn. One banner summed up many of the reformers' concerns, and their conviction that the eight-hour day was needed more than ever in times of economic trouble. "Machinery is discharging *labor,* faster than new employments are provided. The machinery cannot be stopped, and *tramps* must not be increased. New employments will come from new wants; and new wants will follow *Eight Hours!*"

Steward delivered a litany of resolutions containing his own diagnosis of the nation's economic ills, and his growing fear that the depression might prove to be a harbinger of increasing permanent inequities in wealth and power which would steadily undermine the nation's political institutions. Unlike those of many past conventions, these proposals had a fragmented quality to them. Steward—ever the experimental alchemist of the eight-hour movement—presented snippets of thoughts as he tried to throw every explanation he could think of against the growing economic crisis around him.

> *Resolved,* That the existence of a Laboring *class,* and a Capitalist *class,* in the United States of America, is the great fact that most endangers our Republic! That those who are *merely* Laborers are increasing while the Capitalist class is decreasing in number—though increasing in wealth—as fast as large enterprises are absorbing small ones!
>
> *Resolved,* That the Laborer is *nothing but a Laborer,* if he can *sell* nothing but his Labor.
>
> That he can sell nothing but his Labor, if he cannot sell the *products* of his Labor.
>
> That he cannot sell the "products" of his Labor, if they can be *undersold,* through the machinery and capital of the Capitalist.
>
> And the essential difference between the Laborer and the Capitalist of 1876, is, that the Capitalist classes buy the products of *other* men's Labor, *as Labor,* and sell them *as commodities,* leaving the Laborer nothing of his own that he can sell, but his Labor,—which is his *personality or himself,* for the time during which his services are bought.

Steward was especially troubled by this growing commodification of labor, which left workers more vulnerable than ever to their employers' power and the economy's fluctuations. He also utterly dismissed the standard economic explanation that the depression was caused by overproduction due to new technology and larger corporations. "The machinery that saves labor, and creates a tramp, has wasted infinitely more than it has saved," he observed. And, insisting that his own consumer-based economic model made more sense in pointing a way out of the economic mire, he argued that "wants, opportunities, wages, new employments, must be increased. The cry of overproduction must be changed to *under-consumption!*" Other speakers echoed Steward's skepticism about surplus production being a problem in a nation where literally millions of families remained underfed and poorly housed. As Steward himself had said for more than a decade, the economy's problems revolved around the distribution of resources to sustain the nation's standard of living. And that question of distribution boiled down to who controlled the wealth that workers produced.

At the close of the convention, the league discussed expanding its field of operations in the face of the national crisis. Recalling their antebellum predecessors in the labor reform community, the convocation unanimously endorsed a resolution to organize a shorter-hour movement throughout New England, and to raise money for printing tracts and sending speakers across the region. The assembly also recommended reviving the practice of questioning legislative candidates about their stand on labor legislation.

State legislator John Carruthers delivered the convention's final address. He returned to earlier concerns about "how much the labor movement is disgraced and discredited among the more thoughtful, by a certain class of dreamers and adventurers that parade themselves frequently in the name of labor reform." Carruthers perceptively noted that the conservative press often used these false reformers to deflect attention from more cogent critiques of the labor problem. "Labor *de*formers," as Carruthers acidly termed them, "were sufficiently sensational in their absurdities and crudities to be published by an unfriendly daily press; while rational labor literature was consigned to comparative obscurity or oblivion."[39]

Ira Steward noted this same problem of financial reformers garnering all the newspaper copy, for all the wrong reasons, when he wrote to the New York Marxist leader Friedrich Sorge before the league's eighth annual convention on Wednesday, May 31, 1877. Steward described the mood among the Boston eight-hour advocates as "the forlorn hope of a besieged fort.... The most of our few are dispirited in a measure." Steward urged Sorge to send word "of the few here & there over the country, and in Europe, if there are any, who are sympathizing with *our side* of the reform. And make our friends all feel that in opposing *financial* reform, with *Labor* reform, we are by no means alone." In closing his letter, Steward pointed out that the rival reform wings held their conventions only days apart, which tended to blur crucial distinctions and muddle the reform message in the mainstream press. "The dailys report... the lunatics or financials, under Heywood's leadership... fully," Steward observed. But the Eight Hour League's convention was "not sufficiently sensational" to warrant more than a brief notice in most newspapers.[40]

By 1878, the economy had rebounded from the depths of the mid-decade depression. But the Eight Hour League, still sensitive to the problem of unemployment, argued that a reduction in the workday would mean in practice "a demand for more days work and more workers." Advocates insisted that the eight-hour day would ensure a more equitable distribution of labor and eliminate an economy where overwork and idleness coexisted. The shorter workday could then serve as a fulcrum, raising workers' standard of living and expectations for social change as it lowered unemployment. With the economy improving, the league also appealed for "a complete *Factory Act*" that would not only grant the eight-hour day to public employees but also "prohibit the employment of children under fourteen years of age." Furthermore, the league wanted this act to include the "effectual protection from accidents from fire and machinery" and to establish "an efficient corps of factory Inspectors." But, here again, the league clearly saw that the political climate of the late 1870s was not conducive to passing such ambitious labor legislation. In fact, the convention "publicly censured" Governor Alexander Rice for his failure to enforce the laws already on the statute books regarding the ten-hour day and the employment of children.

The annual resolutions concluded by noting the death of Mary Steward, the league's longtime secretary. Virtually everyone in the Boston labor reform community knew Mary Steward as not only a supporter of her husband's campaigns, but also an activist and theorist in her own right. She penned the little couplet that distilled so much of her husband's voluminous writings on the political economy of the eight-hour workday: "Whether you work by the piece, or work by the day, Decreasing the hours increases the pay." Those assembled in 1878 remembered: "She loved the Eight Hour movement and the League for her sex sake and for humanity. This was her church." Mary Steward's death dealt a profound blow to both her husband and the league with which they so closely identified. The organization continued to meet, at least until 1880, but made little effort to publicize or promote its activities any further. Steward left his job as a customs house inspector, a post he had held since early in the decade. He then moved to Plano, Illinois, where he married a wealthy cousin in 1880. He died there three years later, estranged from even his closest allies such as George McNeill. With Steward's departure, Boston's labor reform community lost its most passionate advocate for the primacy of the eight-hour day. Without Steward's constant insistence on placing that issue front and center, other labor reform ideas and institutions would intersect increasingly and compete with the arguments for shorter working days.[41]

Mary Steward, like many others active in the Eight Hour League, had dedicated herself to the organization through nearly a decade of agitation and struggle which did not yield any easy victories. In resolutions, petitions, and fund-raising appeals, the eight-hour advocates always insisted that labor reform had to start with improving working people's lives on the job and in their homes. The Stewards and their allies also never wavered from their fundamental belief that the eight-hour workday was the crucial initial step toward an entirely transformed economy—where the wage system would eventually evaporate as workers received the full value of their labor, and genuine cooperation based first on equity and justice would be the standard in all workplaces.

Other cross-class labor reform organizations might drift away from workplace issues and try to articulate a more amorphous universal ideal of reform to please everyone within their ranks. But the Boston Eight Hour League demonstrated that many workers, and at least some middle-class reformers, could rally around a platform based on shorter hours and better wages and then on the future promise of broader economic and social transformation. Ira Steward knew that keeping a tight rein on the shorter-hours campaign might cost the Eight Hour League some less-committed members looking for a place to push their pet projects. And, at times, his desire for control was so strong and his patience so thin that he alienated even some of his admirers with his nearly obsessive focus on the eight-hour workday. But Steward was always willing to trade numbers for an ideologically consistent appeal. Writing to Friedrich Sorge, and once again renewing the links between labor reform and the abolitionist heritage, Steward insisted that other larger groups anxious to secure their membership base "must have some *flummery!* We had and have none of this in the Boston Eight Hour League. But ours is not a popular or large organization. It works much after the methods of the American Anti-Slavery Society. We never cater or trim for any thing." Steward and the Boston Eight Hour League understood the trade-offs between maintaining their focus on one issue and losing potential allies who might also dilute the organization's ideological principles and rhetorical messages. They concluded that most compromises exacted too high a price, even in a public arena where coalitions often practiced the art of making the right deal.[42]

III

In the summer of 1869, the Commonwealth of Massachusetts created, rather reluctantly, a new state agency that was for all intents and purposes a cross-class labor reform organization—at least for its first four years of operation. Activists and reformers had lobbied over several years for a state labor statistics office to provide accurate information about wages, hours, working conditions, and living standards. The two Commissions on the Hours of Labor also endorsed such an agency so that legislators and government officials could make well-informed decisions about proposed labor laws. What finally persuaded the Massachusetts legislature to create the Bureau of the Statistics of Labor (BSL), however, was not the reformers' past appeals, or any particular petition campaigns, or even the commissioners' recommendations; rather, the lawmakers hastily approved the bureau as a token gesture of political appeasement toward an aggrieved trade union.

Back in the spring of 1869, as the House considered appointing yet another commission to examine the hours of labor, both legislative chambers rejected a request from the Knights of St. Crispin to incorporate their planned cooperative factories and stores. Soon, legislators realized that they had alienated an organization claiming to have 40,000 members (though that number was probably inflated). Something had to be done to placate a growing chorus of angry workers. So, on June 22, two days before adjournment and after several previous rejections, the legislature quickly approved the BSL. The bureau, with headquarters in the statehouse, would "collect, assort, systematize and present in annual Reports . . . statistical details relating to . . . the commercial, industrial, social, educational and sanitary condition of the laboring classes, and to the permanent prosperity of the productive industry of the Commonwealth." Most legislators saw the bureau as a data-collecting mechanism, a harmless gesture of general concern for workers without any strong commitment to new labor laws or their enforcement. Though it was a more permanent bureaucratic institution than the previous progression of commissions; the bureau was supposed to focus on assembling statistical information, not on making policy recommendations.

Labor activists and reformers greeted this new agency, grudgingly approved by the legislature, with mixed reviews of their own. The Crispins saw the bureau as a consolation prize—"a mere quietus," one of them termed it; they resented the agency and wanted nothing to do with it. Millworkers pushing for a ten-hour law continued to petition the legislature for relief from long hours in the factories; they too saw little immediate benefit in statistical studies supervised by the bureau, which they expected would tell them what they already knew about their arduous working conditions. But leaders of the eight-hour movement had previously supported the creation of just such an agency. They believed that a careful statistical study of working conditions across the commonwealth would support their models of political economy and their arguments for the eight-hour workday. Thus, they made every effort to help the bureau succeed as both an investigative agency and a potential advocate for specific labor reforms. (The divisions between Crispins and eight-hour advocates over the bureau may also have reflected the heated exchanges between these two groups at the recently concluded NELRL convention.)

Despite the labor movement's divided response, Governor William Claflin—a former boot and shoe manufacturer who had supported such an agency before his election and even expressed his willingness to appoint staff drawn from the reform community—acted quickly to name a chief for the BSL. Edward Rogers subsequently claimed that Governor Claflin initially intended to appoint Martin Griffin as head of the bureau and Rogers as his deputy. But this proposal was vetoed by Wendell Phillips, who supposedly had the governor's ear as spokesman for the Boston labor reform community (much to Ira Steward's later chagrin). Claflin then selected Henry K. Oliver—who, like many of the earlier commissioners, had close ties with the state's political elite, and with its textile industry.[43]

Oliver, a seventy-year-old alumnus of both Dartmouth and Harvard, had previously worked as a teacher, as superintendent of the Atlantic Cotton Mills in Lawrence, and as state treasurer. Combining his many areas of expertise, he also served as a special state constable to enforce recently enacted laws (1866 and 1867) regulating the hours of labor and schooling for children employed in incorporated factories, and had written two official reports on the subject of child labor. These reports revealed Oliver's growing sympathy with the plight of factory workers and their children, as well as his frustration with the business community and the legal system for their failure to enforce the laws protecting child workers. Massachusetts politicians may have thought that Oliver would be a safe choice to head the bureau, given his advanced age and high social standing. But Oliver proved to be an energetic senior citizen, and he devoted his energies to righting the industrial wrongs he had seen with his own eyes. He also made a bold choice for his assistants: he selected George McNeill as his deputy, who, in turn, chose Mary Steward to be his secretary—clearly linking the bureau closely with the Boston labor reform community, especially advocates for the eight-hour workday.[44]

The bureau's first years were certainly not easy ones. Many companies balked at providing even the most rudimentary data on their employment practices, and the agency had little power to compel them to divulge such information. Workers often feared for their jobs if they spoke to bureau investigators. Meanwhile, some in the reform community accused the bureau of focusing on only skilled workers' wages and working conditions, thus skewing the reports and painting a relatively rosy picture of the labor market. Before the first report was even issued, Charles McLean—a fellow officer in the Eight Hour League with McNeill—turned on his colleague and condemned the bureau for selling out to the Republican Party.

When Oliver went to the legislature in 1870 for additional funds to hire more staff—including female assistants to interview working women—in order to conduct thorough surveys across the state, lawmakers cut his request by one-third. Already, several legislators and a number of powerful manufacturing interests were growing wary of the bureau's investigations into working hours and wages. They saw in the agency's findings not an optimistic portrait of the state's working population but statistical ammunition for the advocates of shorter workdays. These legislators wanted to cut off this exercise in political appeasement as quickly as possible, since the bureau was proving to be quite efficient and sympathetic to labor reform—more trouble than it was worth to these cautious politicians.[45]

Despite criticism from employers, legislators, and even some reformers, the bureau presented reports that were more than just a compendium of statistics and tables generated by a neutral investigative body. Oliver and McNeill defined their roles as advocates for the working class; they staked out a clear reform agenda to be achieved through both new legislative initiatives and strict enforcement of existing regulations. In their first annual report, published in March 1870, they called for a ten-hour law in factories, stricter regulation of child labor, legal protection for labor "associations," safety codes governing machinery, ventilation, and fire escapes, and a factory inspection system. The chief and his deputy reiterated these demands in every annual report they authored through 1873. The first report also included the bold assertion that "the wage system, . . . which has been to the present day, the accepted method of distribution of the proceeds of labor, has proved to be adverse in its influence to the general good, and . . . ought to yield to the system of cooperation." The bureau's second report contained an extensive discussion of how the ten-hour day would neither decrease factory workers' productivity nor lead to wasted hours spent in dissipation. In Oliver and McNeill's final report, the bureau's fourth, they continued to defend unions, manufacturing cooperatives, and shorter workdays. To no one's surprise, given McNeill's close association with Ira Steward, the report also included statements such as this one: "The opponents to a reduction of working time always forget that the producers, to whom they pay wages, are at the same time consumers, and consumers to the full amount of their earnings, and that to make them better consumers, is to stimulate production."[46]

In the summer of 1872, the bureau became caught up in the growing rift between supporters of Wendell Phillips and allies of Ira Steward within the Boston labor reform community. Phillips and eleven others sent a letter to the BSL requesting "a hearing in reference to the selection of employees of the Bureau." The authors specifically asked Oliver to hire staff that could represent the ten-hour movement, trade unions, and cooperatives. Many advocates of these particular causes had initially greeted the bureau with skepticism. But now that the agency was producing widely noticed pro-labor-reform reports, every group wanted to get more attention for its particular demands.

Moreover, Phillips, already publicly chastised at the Boston Eight Hour League's May 1872 convention for his previous criticisms of the bureau, saw an opportunity to put opponents like McNeill and Steward on the defensive. Oliver and McNeill, however, replied that they did not have the money to hire three new assistants to represent specific reform interests, and that they and the rest of the bureau staff were quite familiar with all the issues raised by their critics.

Governor William Washburn received a similar letter and decided to give the petitioners a hearing in late September. S. P. Cummings opened the meeting by proclaiming his support for the bureau and its senior staff. But he also concurred with Phillips that eight-hour advocates dominated the agency, "and that more attention should be given to co-operation." Phillips testified that the bureau's investigations revealed a bias toward arguments for the eight-hour day, "that the Bureau had used its power and influence against the Labor Party . . . and that nearly every phase of the Labor movement had publicly expressed its opposition to the Bureau."

The governor took no action on the requests to diversify the bureau's staff, but Oliver and McNeill still felt the need to defend their leadership. They insisted that most of their employees had been recommended by Phillips and others active in labor reform, and many of them had no connection to the eight-hour leagues. They pointed out that the annual reports contained far more discussion of the ten-hour movement than of the eight-hour campaign. They also explained that the bureau tried to steer clear of party politics, including labor parties, and electioneering. (McNeill was active in the Labor Reform Party, however, even as he served as a government official under several Republican administrations.) Finally, Oliver and McNeill expressed surprise and sadness that this attack had come from some people who had warmly endorsed the agency's creation, as well as from some early skeptics within the labor reform community who now hoped to turn the bureau to their own advantage.[47]

By 1873, matters came to a head between the bureau, the legislature, and the governor. Oliver and McNeill argued that the correct response to the critics' charges of bias was not to disband the agency; rather, the bureau needed to increase its budget and staff, and compel local officials to submit more detailed economic and employment statistics so that the agency's reports would be more accurate and thorough. Governor Washburn claimed that he also wanted to protect the bureau, but he planned to remove Oliver and McNeill, since they now drew so much fire from across the political spectrum. Some trade union leaders complained that eight-hour men ran the office to the exclusion of other activists; manufacturers grumbled that Oliver's staff shaded the bureau's reports from statistical analysis into campaign literature for a shorter workday; and many legislators declared that they wanted to get rid of a mistake and a nuisance. To save the agency, the governor and his supporters argued, the bureau's leadership had to be shaken up.

Oliver and McNeill's supporters tried to rally around the beleaguered bureau chief and his deputy as rumors swirled about their impending dismissal. As early as January, 1873, Edwin Chamberlin urged his fellow labor reformers, trade unionists, and political supporters to come together and defend the agency's leadership. Now was not the time to pick fights over which wing of the labor reform campaign had the most jobs in the BSL. Rather, all labor reformers and activists had to demand that the agency be protected from repeated legislative assaults, and from corporate lackeys who would reduce it to "an unobjectionable mediocrity" and "emasculate ... its more vigorous qualities." The labor reform community had to ensure that the bureau remained under the leadership of people who were sympathetic to the working men and women they surveyed.[48]

Labor reformers and activists knew the open secret: the early BSL was not a scientific data-gathering operation; it was an advocate for the laboring classes. This pro-labor stance was not what the legislature had intended, and precisely what angered the business community. But activists and reformers insisted that a labor bureau was needed to represent working-class interests in state government. The challenge in 1873 was to secure the bureau's position as a permanent state agency. Otherwise, the BSL would end up as little more than another commission disbanded after yet another series of inconclusive hearings and reports. By the end of February, more than 100 men had signed a public call "To the Friends of Labor Investigation in Massachusetts," demanding that the bureau and its present leadership be retained. To refute the governor's assertion that much of the labor movement opposed the bureau's methods, activists from across the state signed the proclamation. The list included a diverse collection of labor advocates, many of whom disagreed with one another on most other issues. Steward, Heywood, Orvis, and Chamberlin were among those who affixed their names; however, recent critics of the bureau—such as Phillips and Cummings—remained conspicuously absent from the list.[49]

In early March 1873, the bureau's defenders could claim a partial victory when the legislature declined to dismantle the agency. But a House committee report, issued on May 1, contained a mixed message: it recommended better salaries and more office space but also criticized the current leadership and implied that a new chief would be named soon. Later that month, the governor proved the rumors true when he selected Carroll Wright as the bureau's new head. Wright, a thirty-three-year-old patent attorney and former state senator from Reading, had no training in statistics and few connections to the labor reform campaign. In fact, he had recently voted against the latest proposed ten-hour law for factory workers. Yet he remained bureau chief for fifteen years, becoming a self-taught pioneer in the emerging field of social surveys and statistical analysis. During those years, Wright also steadily dismantled the links between the agency and local labor reformers. And, after a brief burst of experimentation in his first years on the job, which provoked more threats from some legislators to abolish the bureau, he wrote annual reports that deliberately avoided bold policy recommendations.[50]

Wright always believed that he was committed, both personally and professionally, to improving working people's lives. But he also insisted that the bureau could not cure, and should not even attempt to solve, the labor problem. True labor reform would more likely arise from workers' self-discipline and self-improvement, Wright proclaimed, than from legislative mandates. Moreover, he stated that the bureau should not become the enforcement mechanism for recently enacted school attendance laws or any proposed factory inspection programs. He asserted that Oliver's activist stance had put the bureau in hot water; therefore, a sense of scholarly detachment was a more professional and politically prudent bureaucratic posture. Wright tried to reclaim what he saw as the bureau's original legislative mandate to collect data objectively and scientifically. He hoped to secure the agency's legitimacy and long-term stability by emphasizing technical standards, not labor advocacy. Wright believed that he was following the advice offered by Francis Amasa Walker—son of Amasa Walker, who had served on the second Special Commission on the Hours of Labor—and a noted statistician in his own regard. The younger Walker wrote to Wright when he assumed control of the BSL, urging the new chief to "distinctly and decisively disconnect" the bureau "from politics" and "from dependence on organizations, whether of workingmen or of employers, and from the support of economical theories, individual views or class interests."[51]

The bureau's data, Wright argued, would give legislators the statistical information they needed to draft intelligent laws whenever necessary for the good of the commonwealth. Political leaders could also draw upon the work of clinical experts, who were above partisan and class interests, to promote a scientific approach to solving social problems. Though these assertions of professionalism and objective social science eventually would stir up controversy and new critics, Wright's policies as bureau chief clearly moved the agency far away from the center of Boston labor reform circles. Subsequent activists and reformers would often use the bureau's reports to buttress their own arguments for workplace change. But the longer Wright stayed at the helm, the more the agency refrained from drawing critical conclusions from or basing legislative recommendations on its own findings, even when the data continued to paint an often stark portrait of working-class life in Massachusetts.[52]

IV

In the fall of 1869, labor reformers and activists in Boston and across Massachusetts decided to do something they had talked about for years but had never done before—form a cross-class labor reform political party. Since many reformers and activists continually insisted that government intervention was essential to protect workers from exploitation, and since the established parties sidetracked so many legislative initiatives, these labor reform leaders now concluded that they had to take the plunge into third-party politics. The founders strove to blend the traditional notion of political loyalty with support for an outspoken labor reform agenda—supporters would vote along party lines, but for a new party as a distinct alternative to the mainstream candidates. An independent labor reform party, they hoped, could draw on the electoral system's power without being drawn into the established parties' corrupt practices.

On September 28, at a convention in Worcester, the Massachusetts Labor Reform Party was born. Factory operatives and shoeworkers filled the meeting hall—men and women skeptical about both eight-hour leagues and the new Bureau of the Statistics of Labor, and consequently still searching for yet another alternative labor reform organization. But more familiar reformers and activists also came to Worcester to join this nascent political party. Ira Steward and George McNeill represented the eight-hour movement. (McNeill, though having recently been appointed deputy chief of the BSL under a Republican governor, did not give up his own interest in independent labor politics.) Several leaders from the New England Labor Reform League, including John Orvis, also attended the founding convention.[53]

The newly formed party nominated veteran reformer and Yale-educated lawyer Edwin Chamberlin for governor. The party also built a platform around both shorter hours and currency reform—a deliberate effort to avoid the internal friction that had plagued so many other recently created labor reform groups. The Labor Reform Party urged its supporters to go beyond petitioning and lobbying, abandon old electoral allegiances, and actively embrace third-party politics in the upcoming state elections. The goal was no longer to find sympathetic individual candidates or create coalitions with established parties; those earlier marriages of political convenience had usually produced few viable legislative offspring for labor reform. Rather, the Labor Reform Party wanted to be the political extension of emerging coalitions built between workplace activists and their middle-class supporters—an expression of the abiding faith that government, led by an enlightened new political party, could be an active agent protecting workers' rights. The emphasis was on independent political action for all labor activists and reformers regardless of their class background, not the creation of a workingmen's party only for trade unionists. The party would not foment class conflict and violence, as the critics charged, but provide a potential antidote to increasing political polarization and antagonism.[54]

The Republican Party took this upstart political movement quite seriously. Republicans paid for the widespread circulation of a pamphlet, written by Edward Rogers, which criticized the labor reformers' political prospects. Rogers—an experienced man regarding labor and politics in postwar Massachusetts—doubted that the Labor Reform Party could raise the necessary funds for a statewide campaign. He also argued that the new party did not have a sufficiently mobilized political base among either workers or their middle-class supporters. Despite his own frustrations with the legislature's repeated failures on the eight-hour law, Rogers still believed that an independent labor party would succeed only in antagonizing the Republican Party's reform wing (his political home), which had sided with labor on many issues. Rather than breaking political bonds forged through years of legislative struggle, and injecting class tensions into the electoral arena, activists, Rogers urged, should rally support for sympathetic Republicans. Rogers's pamphlet also implied that labor activists who remained loyal Republicans, like himself, might gain some personal political patronage along with favorable consideration of their legislative proposals.[55]

Just six weeks after its first convention, the Labor Reform Party proved to be far more than a hastily assembled vehicle for a protest vote. The party evolved quickly into a statewide manifestation of reform politics, tapping into years of exasperation with a government that had continually stonewalled most labor legislation. Many activists and reformers spurned Rogers's advice, turned their backs on the Republican Party, and embraced the idea of an independent political movement devoted to labor reform. The new party amassed over 13,000 votes in the governor's race (10 percent of the total) and elected more than twenty legislative candidates, filling about one-quarter of all seats in the House. Some reports indicated that as many as fifty or more state representatives and senators in the new legislature supported the Labor Reform Party's platform, even if they did not all belong to the party. Party leaders knew that they were not yet the dominant player at the statehouse, but their strong showing certainly put Republicans and Democrats, and voters throughout the state, on notice that this new party was a force to be reckoned with in the legislature and in future elections.[56]

The Labor Reform Party followed its 1869 electoral successes with a second annual convention, again in Worcester, on September 8, 1870. Over 400 delegates attended, representing nearly fifty towns and cities across the commonwealth. S. P. Cummings, chairman of the party's central committee, declared that the "movement is no class movement, organized to war on any interest or class; but an earnest, honest protest at the ballot-box against the corrupt subserviency of both the old parties to the exaction of aggressive capital." He conceded that "there are good men in both parties, but their voice is unheeded; and for us there is no alternative but to turn our backs on them, and rally at the ballot with those who believe that democracy in this land means something more than dividend.... No matter how lavish the promises of old parties, no matter how profound their professions of sympathy, we know by bitter experience how insincere their professions, how utterly unkept their promises, and can rely only on ourselves and the justice of our cause." Cummings also alluded to a growing debate in the party over who would lead the ticket in 1870. He cautioned his listeners that "whatever differences of opinion may prevail here today as to who shall be our standard-bearer, or what shall be the character of our platform, there is one sentiment animating us, one and all, that the integrity and honor of the Labor party shall be preserved at every cost and every hazard."

During the afternoon session, a committee—headed by Cummings and including, among others, George McNeill—presented a series of resolutions. Once again aware that the party was trying to hold together a broad reform coalition in the electoral arena, the committee crafted a set of resolves that reflected the interests of Crispins, textile operatives, eight-hour leagues, and even currency and land reformers. The convention enthusiastically endorsed corporate charters for labor organizations, and the eight-hour workday for all public employees to "establish the preliminary claim necessary to prove finally that they mean a better paid and better educated labor." The party also required that every labor reform candidate "make a faithful pledge and guarantee that if elected he will vote for the enactment of a law prohibiting all incorporated and other manufacturing establishments in this Commonwealth from employing females and minors more than ten hours per day, and we pledge ourselves to use all honorable means to defeat every candidate for office who will not pledge himself unreservedly to the enactment of such a law." After assembling its platform, the party then nominated Wendell Phillips to lead the ticket as governor. Both Cummings and the previous year's standard-bearer, Edwin Chamberlin, delivered enthusiastic speeches in support of Phillips.[57]

Phillips abandoned his well-known distaste for party politics and accepted the Labor Reform Party's gubernatorial nomination, as well as a nod from the Prohibition Party. In his letter of acceptance, Phillips asserted "that the readiest way to turn public thought and effort . . . is for the workingmen to organize a political party. No social question ever gets fearlessly treated here till we make politics turn on it. . . . [A] political party is the surest and readiest, if not the only, way to stir discussion, and secure improvement." Mindful of both the party's potential and its limitations, Phillips added that "though we work for a large vote, we should not be discouraged by a small one. Last year's experience shows your strength, and the anti-slavery movement proves how quickly a correct principle wins assent if earnest men will work for it."[58]

Phillips launched his campaign by claiming that "the great value in our party movement this year is to educate the people in regard" to labor reform. "Nothing educates the people like a political canvass," he wrote to the *American Workman* in late October 1870. "It is more efficient than schools, colleges, lyceums or books." Phillips went on a two-week tour of the state, pledging that he would discuss difficult reform issues in the public arena rather than mouth just the right words and make the political deals necessary to be elected governor. Phillips may have constantly downplayed the need to win the election so as not to disappoint his supporters with false hopes for victory. In fact, had he thought that he had a real chance to win the race and sit in the governor's chair, and thereby give up his cherished position as Boston's most prominent political gadfly, he might never have accepted the nomination in the first place![59]

Phillips's modest predictions proved accurate—he garnered 13 percent of the vote, a slight increase over Chamberlin's efforts the previous year. But the number of labor reform candidates elected to the legislature was cut in half. With 1870 being a national election year for Congress, the Republican Party made great efforts to bring out its votes in Massachusetts for both federal and state offices. Though some might have hoped that Phillips's appeal would reach beyond labor reformers and activists, given both his broad sympathy for all kinds of social activism and his family roots among the Boston elite, most mainstream politicians and middle-class voters regarded him with deep suspicion. Moreover, since Phillips also ran on the Prohibition Party ticket, some workers hesitated to support a candidate pledged to a platform of social control and the policing of private life and leisure time. Even Phillips's old allies in the abolitionist movement worried that he was diverting votes from the Republicans and giving a backhanded advantage to their Democratic nemesis.[60]

Despite his failure to win office, and the scorn heaped on him by the Republican establishment, Phillips remained committed to political activism in the cause of labor reform. In a letter to the *American Workman,* written several months after the election, Phillips stated frankly that he did not

> believe in the wages system. It never got out of a man more than half the work he could really do; and it demoralized his nature, at the same time, by tempting him to skulk and cheat. It never resulted in any fair division of the joint profits of labor and capital.... It is the lion dividing the spoil and taking three-quarters for his share without asking advice or consent to the division.... Cooperation will cure that evil.... Leisure, books, travel, quiet enjoyment of nature, a fair share of the world's comforts will be considered the due of every man of average abilities who puts his best energies honestly into his work.

In the closing paragraph, Phillips launched one of his famous caustic critiques. Taking aim especially at many of his fellow elite reformers, whom he surmised would never contemplate independent labor reform party politics, Phillips showed no mercy for their timidity or their ethereal ideologies. He knew that his support for cooperatives and other reforms was beyond the pale of cautious, mainstream politicians. But he also realized that many so-called radicals were so busy theorizing that they never considered any substantive economic alternatives, nor would they fight the legislative battles necessary to achieve meaningful social reform. And it was the impracticality of this intelligentsia, their refusal to consider questions of practical politics, which drew Phillips's particular scorn:

> Still, very important aid can legitimately be rendered by political machinery. Indeed we shall not, for a long while, get any beginning made unless it is undertaken by the hard common sense and practical ability of politics. If we leave the matter wholly to the hair-splitters and word-weighers, the conservatives playing at radicalism, the Latin and Greek pedants, the self-complacent system-mongers, the dainty triflers and extractors of "sunbeams from cucumbers," who make the majority of our Social Science meetings, we shall possibly see a beginning made about the time when owls decide to fly in daytime and monkeys export cocoanuts instead of pelting travelers with them.[61]

The Labor Reform Party's third convention, held in early October 1871 at the railroad junction town of South Framingham, twenty miles west of Boston, took on a decidedly more radical cast. The platform committee proposed a preamble based on the "fundamental principle, that Labor, the creator of wealth, is entitled to all it creates." The committee went on to argue that the party should be "willing to accept the final results of the operation of a principle so radical such as the overthrow of the whole profit-making system, the extinction of all monopolies, the abolition of privileged classes, an extended rather than a restricted franchise, universal education and fraternity, perfect freedom of exchange, and best and grandest of all, the final obliteration of that foul stigma upon our Christian civilization—the poverty of the masses." The committee then laid out specific steps to reach this profound transformation of the social order. Under the heading "POINTS OF AGGRESSIVE CONTACT," it declared "war with the wages system, which demoralizes alike the hirer and the hired, cheats both, and enslaves the working man; War with the present system of Finance, which robs Labor and gorges Capital, makes the rich richer and the poor poorer, and turns a Republic into an Aristocracy of Capital." The platform writers also demanded that "all encouragement should be given by law to co-operation in all branches of industry and trade . . . a ten-hour day for factory work as a first step; and that eight hours be the working day of all persons employed at the public expense. . . . We [also] demand that women who do the same kind and same amount of work as men shall receive the same wages."[62]

Wendell Phillips said he strongly supported the new bold platform, but he also reaffirmed his conviction that meaningful social change could come through political agitation. Referring to the recent upheaval in France, Phillips remarked: "I, for one, honor Paris: but in the name of Heaven, and with the ballot in our right hands, we shall not need to write our record in fire and blood; we write it in the orderly majorities at the ballot-box." Phillips also insisted that there was "no war between labor and capital,—that they are partners, not enemies, . . . and this movement of ballot-bearing millions is to avoid the unnecessary waste of capital." Yet he concluded his speech with some strong fighting words for the assembled delegates.

> You don't kill a hundred millions of corporate capital, you don't destroy the virus of incorporate wealth, by any one election. The capitalists of Massachusetts are neither fools nor cowards; and you will have to whip them three times, and bury them under a monument weightier than Bunker Hill, before they will believe they are whipped. Now, gentlemen, the inference from this statement is this: The first duty resting on this convention, which rises above all candidates and platforms, is, that it should keep the labor-party religiously together.[63]

Phillips had scarcely finished his remarks about party unity when, ironically, he found himself in the middle of a nomination fight that fractured the convention. The platform committee nominated Edwin Chamberlin again for governor, but on the first ballot a large number of delegates supported the former general and congressman Benjamin Butler. Phillips himself had already given speeches endorsing Butler's candidacy and hoped that his pleas for party unity would bring other conventioneers in line behind Butler. As for Butler's credentials, he had always professed sympathy for the workers' cause, and endorsed some labor legislation. But he was a Republican Party dissident who never took an active leadership role in any Boston labor reform organization. Butler was also challenging the state's Republican leaders for that party's 1871 gubernatorial nomination, and Phillips believed that Butler could win on a joint Labor-Republican platform. However, other delegates doubted that Butler would accept the Labor Reform Party's nomination, since he might think such an endorsement would weaken his challenge to the Republican hierarchy. Amid these growing questions about Butler's nomination, Chamberlin handily won on the second ballot. But many of Butler's supporters—Phillips included, despite his rhetoric about party harmony—continued to back their man all the way to the Republican Party convention at the end of October.[64]

The November election returns were a mixed bag for the Labor Reform Party. In the plus column, the party was on the ballot in more locales then ever before. But, on the down side, the total statewide vote for the Chamberlin ticket was lower than in the previous two years. The labor press offered several astute reasons for the reform party's declining numbers: constant opposition from mainstream newspapers, presidential politics pushing many voters back into the major parties in advance of 1872, and the Butler campaign distracting potential supporters. Several party activists also acknowledged that their outspoken platform probably scared away undecided voters (some of whom might have voted for a more moderate reform agenda), even as it inspired the faithful with its fire-breathing rhetoric.[65]

By 1872, internal dissent wracked the Labor Reform Party. Phillips's active support of Butler may have contributed to the acrimonious feud with Steward which spilled over into reform conventions, the BSL, and independent party politics. The party nominated its statewide slate early in the spring to give the candidates sufficient time to drum up support. But by late fall the campaign seemed to be losing steam. Edwin Chamberlin's major address, as chair of the state committee, consisted of a lengthy appeal for workers to refrain from voting in the presidential election, since neither Republicans nor Democrats had any pro-labor record to stand on.[66]

The party's 1873 convention moved to Lowell and closely allied itself with the factory operatives' struggle for a ten-hour law. Chamberlin, Linton, Steward, and McNeill all attended the meeting and backed a series of resolutions aimed specifically at electing state senators who would pledge publicly (regardless of party) to move their recalcitrant body into the pro-labor column. This strategy recalled a similar tactic used by the ten-hour leagues of the 1850s. The convention also delivered a scathing condemnation of past supporters, such as Martin Griffin, whom it accused of using "influence, treachery, and double dealing" to defeat the latest legislative proposal on the ten-hour day. And the meeting censured Governor Washburn for "yielding to the demands of cotton lords, banking capitalists, [and] tenement house owners," removing the original BSL leadership, and replacing Henry Oliver with Carroll Wright—who had just voted against the ten-hour law! The convention's emphasis on recruiting specific pro-ten-hour state senatorial candidates, rather than following the past practice of nominating an independent slate for statewide offices, weakened the party's political coherence but succeeded in sending sympathetic senators to the statehouse.[67]

In 1874, a ten-hour bill for factory women and children finally made it through both legislative chambers and was signed into law by the new governor, Thomas Talbot. Thus, Boston eight-hour leaders helped secure a legally mandated ten-hour workday for factory operatives; even as their own efforts to promote a more ambitious eight-hour law for all workers—through petitions and third-party politics—continued to languish in the legislature. The successful halfway measure granted desperately needed relief to overworked industrial labor but may have also succeeded in removing a large population of mill workers from further struggles for the shorter workday. Ironically, Steward and his allies achieved a pyrrhic victory for their own cause, and encouraged alternative ideas about labor reform to intersect increasingly with an eight-hour campaign no longer seen as legislatively monolithic. What Steward had hoped would be a political opening for pressing further on the shorter workday may have actually served to take pressure off the legislature.[68]

The party also failed to capitalize on past electoral achievements or recent legislative victories. Old tensions remained, and the 1874 meeting once again did not nominate a slate of candidates, this time prompting a minority wing to break away and publish its own list of office seekers. This rump faction, calling itself the People's Reform Party of Massachusetts, was guided by veteran activist Charles McLean. The group's platform reaffirmed many of the previous party's stands on shorter hours, cooperatives, and currency and land reform. Party leaders approached several men to head the ticket, including Henry K. Oliver. But many leading reformers and activists declined nominations because they worried that leading such a splintered party faction would become an exercise in futility. Just five years earlier, the Labor Reform Party had burst onto the political scene with a surprisingly strong showing after less than two months of active campaigning, and seemed poised to become a key player in Massachusetts politics. Now, the party was irrevocably split, never again to reunite and mount a challenge to Republicans or Democrats.[69]

Wendell Phillips commented on labor reform politics in a letter written to the English cooperative leader George Holyoake during the summer of 1874. Phillips's correspondence revealed that his old skepticism about electioneering had returned, and he now thought that he might have been right all along to avoid the arena of parties and nominations. As a veteran of the bitter feuds within Boston labor reform circles, Phillips believed that he had been mistreated by many workers (echoing Seth Luther's sentiments from nearly forty years earlier). In turn, he blamed workers for many of the labor reform campaign's failures. "Neither shall I live long enough to see any marked result of our labor-movement here," he concluded glumly, "though it is true that our masses ripen marvelously quick; but, as you've said, the cliques, jealousies, distrust, and ignorance of workingmen are our chief obstacles. Indeed, we sometimes get better help from open-hearted capitalists." Though Phillips still championed many different causes, he admitted to Holyoake that "your ranks are infinitely better trained than ours to stand together on some one demand just long enough to be counted, and so insure that respect which numbers always command in politics where universal suffrage obtains."[70]

Yet despite Phillips's renewed doubts about being a political candidate, he consented to head another labor reform ticket in 1875. But the campaign started slowly with a sparsely attended nominating convention, and Phillips garnered only a few hundred votes running on a platform that emphasized greenbacks and currency reform (echoing the New England Labor Reform League). Many of his fellow activists—especially those who worked closely with Ira Steward in the eight-hour movement—now wrote off Phillips (much like Heywood) as hopelessly divorced from their conception of labor reform. Though Phillips would continue to lecture about labor and capital on the lyceum circuit almost until his death in 1884, he spent his last decade removed from the center of labor reform organizing and activism in Boston. Labor reform politics had not succeeded in bringing unity and power to the movement. Rather, the Labor Reform Party had driven even deeper fissures between various factions and their leaders.[71]

V

Looking back over the postwar years, when the Boston labor reform community grappled with a near-explosion of organizational activity, Ira Steward was (as usual) brutally frank in assessing what all this activism meant to him in terms of finding reliable allies and building lasting coalitions. He and George McNeill had participated at some point in all the different groups within the generation of 1869. Always insisting that the eight-hour workday had to be at the core of the labor reform struggle, Steward and McNeill nonetheless willingly plunged into these disparate organizations to try to spread their message to anyone who would listen. The results, even in their own Eight Hour League, were not always encouraging.

In the midst of internal dissension and economic depression, Steward believed that a small contingent of devoted men and women kept the heart of labor reform beating. Writing to Friedrich Sorge in late 1876, Steward divided Boston's labor reformers and activists into a range of categories, from unquestioning supporters to "some very vicious specimens of Labor Reform." He reserved his highest praise for just two men—George McNeill and George Gunton, a recent immigrant from England, who had organized weavers in Fall River, moved briefly near Steward in Cambridge, then later settled in New York City. "The fire of these two men *never goes out!*" Steward explained. "You can call them up day or night; they will stop eating if necessary to attend to a Labor cause. And they are shrewd, wise, good, unselfish, devoted." In a subsequent letter, Steward detailed how much his closest allies sacrificed for their (his) particular vision of labor reform: "Gunton is so poor that he sometimes goes for weeks without one cent in his pocket. . . . I have known him several times to be without the oil necessary to write his . . . letters, and the postage necessary to send those letters. McNeill has his brother's family with sickness on his hands besides his own family of seven. He is out of employment, earning very little. Gunton has six children bright but Oh! It makes my heart ache to see them sometimes. As long as my employment held out I could keep them somewhat."

Steward then considered activists and reformers such as Edwin Chamberlin, Henry Delano, Jesse Jones, and Edward Rogers—men who might deviate from the strict eight-hour line and consider labor reform in a broader context of politics and religion. Steward labeled them "the '*goodies*' who are simple, honest, pure, but useless in emergencies. . . . These are the men who never appreciate positive convictions enough to help the Eight Hours wing to fight." Steward further asserted that "these are the men who without realizing the fact . . . allowed the Massachusetts Bureau of Statistics of Labor to be turned over to the enemy; when it was too late for much service, . . . most of them made a feeble rally; and this effort was through our . . . arguing and planning." Not everyone in the Boston labor reform community agreed with Steward's assignment of blame for the bureau's political purge, but his harsh words clearly highlighted the deep rifts in that community as it reflected on its recent organizational struggles and failures.[72]

At least one member of Boston's labor reform network took issue with Steward's recollections of a hopelessly fragmented alliance. W. G. H. Smart remembered that a Boston Labor Council was formed in the fall of 1873, at the Sherman House in Court Square. Edward Linton served as president. Regular attendees at the council's biweekly meetings included Steward and McNeill from the Boston Eight Hour League, Rogers and Jones from the Christian Labor Union, Chamberlin, and Jennie Collins. The council represented yet another effort to hold together the fractious, and recently deeply fractured, labor reform campaign. The plan was a simple one: have this diverse group of people, with all their divergent opinions and causes, talk with each other on a regular basis in an informal setting without all the public posturing of a large annual convention or a political campaign.

The council supported the BSL as it fought continuing legislative efforts to disband the agency, championed a ten-hour law for factory workers, protested to the U.S. Congress against violations of the federal eight-hour law, and claimed to have many Labor Reform Party activists in its ranks. But even these attempts at private reconciliation and public advocacy ended up rehashing past arguments and producing more divisions. Smart recalled that "there were conflicting views . . . in regard to the terms of the petition for a continuance of the labor bureau, both as to its proper functions and as to whether it should be administered with strict impartiality or by labor advocates in the interest of labor, and this friction proved disastrous." Moreover, "an attempt by the Eight Hour League to commit the Council to the full endorsement of their theory that 'the entire efforts of the labor movement should be concentrated on the reduction of the hours of labor' . . . broke up the Labor Council at the zenith of its success and power" in 1875. So, in the end, Steward's uncompromising insistence on allegiance to the eight-hour day above all other labor reforms shattered another effort to promote dialogue across organizational and ideological boundaries, and reaffirmed his own gloomy appraisal of the labor reform community.[73]

The generation of 1869 traveled long and often difficult paths in the Boston labor reform community. The New England Labor Reform League endured for nearly two decades but found that its wide-open style of debate, growing passion for financial reform, and individualist antimonopoly rhetoric all combined to push it far from any constructive engagement with most other labor reformers and activists. The Boston Eight Hour League, under Ira Steward's firm—and sometimes nearly autocratic—control throughout the

1870s focused all its organizational energies on the legislative struggle for a shorter workday. The Eight Hour League stayed within the labor reform community, yet it too lost adherents through its lack of flexibility and tolerance. And when Steward left Boston at the end of the decade, he took with him the intellectual and agitational center of that eight-hour struggle, opening up the city to new currents of reform activism. The Massachusetts Bureau of the Statistics of Labor encompassed the potential benefits and pitfalls for labor reformers and activists who looked beyond their own cross-class organizations and embraced the emerging administrative powers of the state. With a sympathetic chief at the helm for the first four years, the bureau was a bold advocate for labor legislation based on detailed studies of working-class life in postwar Massachusetts. But when political pressure from employers, conservative legislators, and even rival reformers squeezed those outspoken leaders out of the agency, the BSL withdrew precipitously from any active engagement with the labor reform cause. Finally, the Labor Reform Party showed early potential as a potent expression of cross-class coalition-building in the political arena. But once the mainstream parties trained their sights on the young upstart, and once the labor reformers and activists brought their simmering squabbles into the party conventions, the combination of external pressure and internal strife crippled the third-party movement. The promise of unity through political victory devolved into deeper divisions between rival factions.

This outpouring of organizational energy, and frustration, does not tell the complete story of the postwar labor reform campaign in Boston. For while these leagues and the bureau and the party all struggled to press their agendas with and against each other, inside and outside the political arena, an emerging powerful amalgam of liberal Christianity with labor reform, and the growing intensity of labor conflicts in the decades following the Civil War, forced the Boston labor reform community to think harder about its ideological and moral underpinnings. Through the Gilded Age and into the early Progressive Era, Ira Steward and the eight-hour campaign eventually yielded much of the center stage to a more complex cast of activists and reformers fighting labor exploitation and creating alternative organizational forms such as labor churches, settlement houses, and consumer leagues.

Part II
1870s–1900

THE labor reform community in Boston confronted a rapidly changing city in the closing decades of the nineteenth century. Boston's population grew steadily and shifted in its ethnic composition from the Civil War to the end of the century. Fueled by ongoing inmigration from rural New England, the changing character of European immigration, and especially the annexation of surrounding towns, the city's population more than doubled from about a quarter of a million in 1870 to over 560,000 in 1900. New arrivals from Ireland and England continued to stream through the port of Boston—by 1875, 60,000 foreign-born Irish and their children constituted nearly 40 percent of the city's residents. Immigrants from the Canadian Maritime Provinces also entered the city in increasing numbers—25,000 by 1880. By the 1890s, newcomers from southern and eastern Europe, fleeing economic dislocation, political oppression, religious persecution, and military conscription—especially Italians, Poles, and Russian Jews—numbered in the tens of thousands. In 1900, 35 percent of Bostonians were foreign-born, and census enumerators classified nearly three-quarters of the city's inhabitants as either immigrants or children of immigrant parents.[1]

Boston expanded in physical size as well, filling in swamps and marshland on the Back Bay and South End. Between 1868 and 1873, the city annexed the previously independent towns of Roxbury, West Roxbury, Dorchester, Charlestown, and Brighton, which included manufacturing districts as well as tracts of open land for residential construction. Where it had once been almost an island of less than 800 acres, the city was now nearly thirty times its original size. Decade by decade, many wealthier Bostonians built homes farther from the core city (and some eventually moved to the suburbs). These new neighborhoods were distant from the tenements and sweatshops, yet close by the growing network of street railways that carried the men to their city offices in the morning and back to their living rooms at night. By the end of the century, an expansive web of gas, electric, and telephone lines serviced the homes of proper Bostonians (and their suburban counterparts). Ironically, the small army of workers who laid and strung these utilities often went home at night to cramped apartments in crowded neighborhoods lacking all these new urban conveniences.[2]

In the midst of this demographic and geographic expansion, Boston's labor reform community swirled with new organizations and new ideas, as Ira Steward and the eight-hour campaign had to share more of the public stage. (Steward himself had left Boston by 1880.) Many groups—such as labor churches, workingmen's institutes, consumer leagues, and settlement houses—often had overlapping memberships, leaders, and chronologies. These alliances sometimes supported familiar campaigns, such as that continuing crusade for the eight-hour workday; but they also pressed new demands, such as regulating tenement house labor and improving conditions in retail stores. New labor reform organizations, like some of their antebellum ancestors, agitated in the streets, meeting halls, and statehouse corridors as they strove to command the attention of the press, public, and politicians. Yet these new coalitions often extended their organizational activities by recruiting working women into trade unions and unemployed men into mass demonstrations for public works jobs. By the end of the nineteenth century, however, several of the newest labor reform groups displayed a more limited social vision and a more hierarchical organizational structure.

Organized religion, especially liberal Protestantism and its more radical offshoot Christian Socialism, intersected even more with the labor reform campaign than it had done in antebellum decades. Christian Socialists took Ira Steward's arguments for the eight-hour day and gave them a religious cast: shorter working days formed the foundation of moral regeneration as well as social transformation. At the same time, a series of sharp economic downturns and strike waves compelled sympathetic ministers and their allies to confront labor protest and consider its challenge to the ideals of Christian brotherhood and cross-class cooperation.

In the 1880s and 1890s, reformers and activists renewed their efforts to build stable labor reform headquarters. Central meeting places could provide organizational cohesion and continuity, and help sustain public agitation beyond the enthusiasm generated at periodic conventions and rallies. Four different institutions functioned as forums where cross-class dialogue could be promoted and coalitions built: the Wells Memorial Workingmen's Institute, the Wendell Phillips Union, and two settlement houses—Andover House and Denison House. Each of these organizations deliberately located in the city's South End, a neighborhood swelling rapidly with recently arrived immigrants.

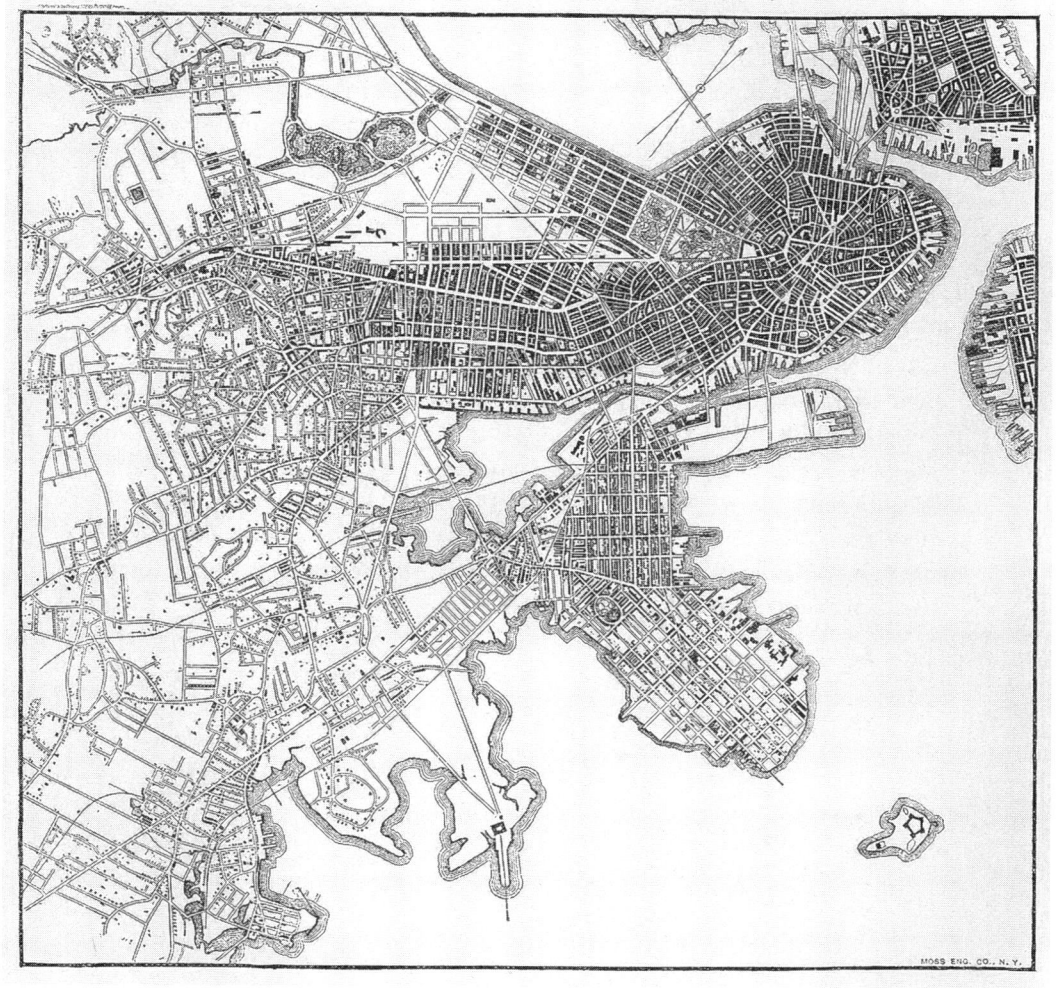

"Boston in 1880. Showing All Ground Occupied by Buildings," from *Report on the Social Statistics of Cities,* comp. George Waring (Washington, DC: United States Census Office, 1886). Courtesy University of Texas Libraries.

The labor reform campaign, thus, moved out of rented halls in Boston's central commercial sector and into the tenement districts where workers clamored for safer and healthier workplaces.

By the 1890s, two new organizations formed specifically to address the exploitation of immigrants and of young women and children in the urban economy. Both the Anti–Tenement House League and the Consumers' League of Massachusetts drew on more than half a century of labor reform activism and, at the same time, reshaped those earlier models to encompass new strategies of social investigation and social action from the emerging Progressive movement. The two leagues championed the rights of low-paid, low-skilled labor to better working conditions and higher wages, yet these organizations made little effort to bring downtrodden workers into genuine cross-class alliances. Faced with a growing population of Catholic and Jewish immigrants from southern and eastern Europe, the predominantly Protestant reformers in these leagues permitted religious and ethnic differences to erode the cross-class bridges they had labored so hard to build over so many decades. Immigrant communities seemed like increasingly foreign territory to those reformers who lived far away from tenement districts where residents spoke strange languages and practiced even stranger creeds. Religiously inspired campaigns for labor reform worked better when most workers and middle-class supporters shared a common denominator of Protestant denominations. By century's end, reformers increasingly saw foreign-born workers more as objects of reform than as partners in a shared quest for social justice.

5
PIETY AND PROTEST
Labor Reform, Religion, and Mass Demonstrations,
1872–1898

IN THE last quarter of the nineteenth century, religion—particularly liberal Protestantism and its more daring offshoot, Christian Socialism—assumed a more prominent role than ever before in Boston's labor reform community. In these same decades, deep economic downturns, open conflict between labor and capital, and spreading strike waves forced these new generations of sympathetic ministers and other religiously inspired activists to confront mass protest and its challenge to their ideals of Christian brotherhood and cross-class cooperation.

The growing links between organized religion and Boston's labor reform community were embodied first in the early 1870s by the young crusading minister Jesse Jones and his Christian Labor Union (CLU). These renewed ideals of brotherhood among reformers and activists were soon tested by the railroad strikes of 1877 and the eight-hour walkouts in 1886. Ministers and other religiously motivated individuals had to ask themselves if the increasingly intense forms of labor protest could be reconciled with their visions of cross-class harmony and shared struggle for social justice. By the early 1890s, veteran activists such as George McNeill had embraced the city's Christian Socialist movement, then championed by W. D. P. Bliss and his Church of the Carpenter. Bliss's appeal for an avowedly socialist congregation that would encompass labor reform emerged just before the city plunged into the depths of the 1893 depression, and Herbert Casson began to call for a labor church by and for workers alone. Thus, through good times and hard times, the effort to reconcile piety and protest, social conscience and class consciousness, continued to unfold in Boston's labor reform community right up to century's end.

I

In the summer of 1872, as the Boston labor reform community struggled with the public rifts between Wendell Phillips and Ira Steward, a printed circular invited a select group of men and women to "meet in council" on July 2 at 14 Bromfield Street (where the Boston Eight Hour League had formed in 1869). Labor reform veterans—including Ira Steward, George McNeill, Edwin Chamberlin, Edward Rogers, and Edward Linton—called the conference "to consider how we can best bring the Pulpit, the Rostrum, and the Press" together to discuss "the great subject of JUSTICE TO LABOR." The meeting was unusual in that it was by invitation only, and not a publicly advertised convention. Since so many recent labor reform conventions had devolved into open bickering and recriminations, these activists thought it better to hold this gathering in private.[1]

The conference participants, many of them activists and reformers well versed in lobbying and speechmaking, did not keep their deliberations private for very long. At the initial meeting, those assembled appointed a committee to write an address to "the three great classes" referenced in the original invitation—the clergy, the press, and the politicians. The conference reconvened on October 30 and unanimously adopted the address, which was then published under the title *Live to Help Live*. The authors included Chamberlin, Linton (president of the conference), McNeill, and Jennie Collins. *Live to Help Live* contained an amalgamation of arguments steeped in labor republicanism, antislavery activism, and the stark imagery of armed conflict from the recently concluded Civil War—a rhetorical combination similar to many other postwar labor reform pamphlets. The authors exclaimed: "The very existence of our free institutions is again imperiled, as truly as it was by slavery; and *the danger is greater and more to be dreaded*. . . . Like slavery, the wage system is in vital, eternal, and 'irrepressible conflict' with our political system." The "essential despotism" of the wage system and the "essential freedom" of the political system were on a collision course. "One of them must destroy the other. There is no other alternative, and no escape from this. The Wage System must die, or the Republic is doomed." The nation's fundamental values of justice, equality, and liberty hung in the balance. Therefore, the authors declared "the immediate abolition of the wage system is as truly our duty to-day as the immediate abolition of slavery was the duty of the South, when that doctrine was proclaimed in the land forty years ago."[2]

Although this forceful and articulate critique of wage slavery bore strong similarities to many other labor reform manifestos, the pamphlet's conclusion contained a particular twist on the familiar call to action. This document made a deliberate effort to bring "the pulpit"—the "heralds of the Glad Tidings of Jesus Christ"—into the labor reform campaign on an equal footing, if not an even higher plane, with more familiar allies in politics and the press. In addition to supporting labor newspapers and pro-labor candidates for public office, reformers and activists now increasingly sought out clergymen who would preach biblical principles and religious teachings to further the struggle for workplace reform. To be sure, the invocation of biblical justifications and religious rhetoric, and the participation of sympathetic ministers, was not an entirely new phenomenon in labor reform circles. Ever since cross-class alliances had begun to form in Boston four decades earlier, religious imagery and religious leaders had played significant supporting roles in some labor reform groups. In the early 1870s, however, several veteran reformers and clergymen formed new organizations that placed the word "Christian" front and center in the struggle. Perhaps this change was in name only, labeling a religious impulse that was already part of the campaign for labor reform. Yet there could be something more in a new moniker: a proclamation—more open and forceful than ever before—that Christian ideals of love and brotherhood, and labor reform itself, were one and the same thing.[3]

One reason why Christianity and labor reform became linked more explicitly was the emergence of Jesse Jones as a leader in the new conference. His name did not appear on the original invitation, but he became secretary of the conference and lead author for the address. Jones was born in Canada in 1836, educated at Hamilton and Williams Colleges, Harvard University, and Andover Theological Seminary, and ordained as a Congregational minister. After active service in Massachusetts and New York regiments during the Civil War, Jones held a pulpit in rural New York before moving on to Natick, Massachusetts—a town west of Boston. His social activism upset many congregants, and in 1871 he found a new position in Rockland—a small village southeast of Boston. Soon after helping to write the address on labor reform, and joining the Boston Eight Hour League, he took a pastorate in nearby North Abington (June 1873), where he served until 1880. The majority of his new congregation may not have openly endorsed his stand on labor reform, but they listened to his sermons and tolerated their minister's engagement with social problems.[4]

Jones approached labor reform from a perspective distinctly different from that of his contemporary Ezra Heywood. Heywood abandoned his ministerial career and linked his activism with withering condemnation of all organized religion for its hypocrisy and hostility to the poor. Jones also criticized most established churches and denominations, but he held out hope for transforming these institutions. Jones was one of the first young postwar ministers in Massachusetts who urged Protestant churches to go beyond questions of personal faith and salvation and give more attention to Christian teachings about social justice. He strove to merge his social reform work with his regular pastoral duties so as to create a truly engaged church that would confront worldly problems, and search for solutions both within the sanctuary and in the streets. Jones believed fervently that truly moral people had to express their Christian values through direct action for economic equity and the abolition of poverty—far better to give money to the needy than only to the church.

Jones wrote frequently on labor issues. He defended workers' rights to organize unions and bargain collectively with their employers. He saw trade unions as a key agent for achieving social justice. He was not averse to confrontation and standing up to the power of capital; but he also often cited Christian teachings about upholding the principle of nonviolence even in the face of injustice. In an early appeal for what might be called industrial democracy, Jones urged that workers "carry the town-meeting way into the management of ... all factories in the land ... and demand also that the principle of town meeting be applied here to establish industrial freedom." Jones insisted "that the application of the town-meeting idea was the Christian way, and the American way as well." He believed that over time the love of God and fellowmen, rather than the love of money and material goods, would control the world of business and industry. "Society will be so organized and managed that work adequate for a living will be provided for everyone who can work.... The managers of industry will be the servants of the people; and all business will be done so that an abundance of all that is needful for comfort and something also 'for glory and for beauty' will be provided to the hand of every human being."[5]

Merging labor reform with Christian millennialism and republican ideology, Jones argued that there was a coming "Kingdom-business system" embodying Jesus' teachings about land, money, equity, and justice. This system would save not only people's dignity and souls but also the nation itself. Christians had to pray for the coming of this "Kingdom-business system" in church on Sundays, but even more important, they had to work every day on the shopfloor for these egalitarian democratic principles.

> A nation can maintain itself as a free people only as its citizens, as a body, have complete legal control of the means of getting their living.... A man who would be free and his own master at the polls must be free and his own master in all that pertains to his living.... What is the supreme need

of the American nation? It is a business system which shall parallel our political system. As our government is "of the people, by the people, and for the people," so must our industrial system be made. As in our town governments the officials are elected by and are the servants of the people, so must the managers of industry be. The townshipization of all industries is what must come, if the American Republic is to abide. And it is to abide. God has decreed it. He is moving to achieve it; and He will not fail.[6]

Though his arguments contained a utopian streak, Jones was also pragmatic enough to realize that his ideals for a new Christian economy would not come to fruition in a single moment. Drawing on his membership in the Boston Eight Hour League, and giving a religious slant to Ira Steward's ideas, Jones asserted that the campaign to shorten the working day could launch a broader social and spiritual movement that would eventually lift up all wage workers. Enlightened employees would then claim their rightful ownership of workplaces and become truly independent freemen. The eight-hour movement was "the golden stairway up to the finest conditions of life." Following closely Steward's model of political economy, Jones showed all the steps on this staircase:

> Shortening the day raises the grade of the worker. Raising the grade of the worker increases his pay. Increasing his pay enables him to buy more goods, and raising his grade fits him to buy to better advantage for himself, and for the economic advantage of the community. Moreover, raising the grade of the worker enables him to use machinery better, by which he makes more product, and so deserves more pay, while the managers can well afford to give him more. Such are the steps by which every economic interest in the community is enhanced; and they all depend upon this one simple measure of shortening the working day.

Explaining the practical details of his plan, Jones laid out a scenario where labor and capital would mutually agree to reduce the workday gradually by fifteen minutes each year until they reached the eight-hour day. Jones was convinced that such a calibrated decrease would produce less conflict than Steward's demand for legislation requiring limitations on working hours.[7]

Jones found in Edward Rogers an ardent supporter for his ideals of a Christian economy. Rogers had always been a committed Methodist as well as a reform-minded Republican Party loyalist. By the early 1870s, Rogers's political career had stalled. He never regained the state representative's seat he held briefly after the war; and his efforts to keep workers in the Republican fold and away from the new Labor Reform Party in 1869 succeeded only in straining his relations with fellow activists and reformers. Whether from deep-seated spiritual convictions or the desire to steer clear of further political conflicts, Rogers shifted the locus of his labor activism from the electoral arena to the church. He began to preach (sometimes literally) a brand of labor reform unabashedly based on detailed scriptural arguments about work and property.[8]

Sometime before the end of 1872, Jones and Rogers (and Rogers's friend Henry T. Delano) fused their theological and social activism to create the Christian Labor Union. The CLU complemented the recently concluded conference and the published address encouraging churches and clergymen to embrace labor reform (even though other activists who attended that meeting—such as Steward and McNeill—remained uneasy about an open merger between religion and labor reform). Jones, Rogers, and their supporters quickly established the CLU as a pioneer in the emerging Christian Socialist movement—a movement which, being in its infancy, remained rather ill-defined. Some Christian Socialists wanted to link socialist arguments about property and the state with biblical laws and Christian teachings. Others wanted to prod organized Christianity into directly confronting social problems and reform. Thus, at the heart of the movement lay an open question: would this new school of thought Christianize socialism or socialize Christianity? The CLU, at times, tried to do both—it urged local churches to combat exploitation at the workplace, but it also proposed Bible-based schemes for sweeping social and economic change to fulfill Christ's kingdom on earth.[9]

The CLU held monthly meetings in Boston and sponsored two sparsely attended "Bible Labor Reform Conventions," one in conjunction with the Boston Eight Hour League. Jones soon saw that the CLU was becoming ensnared in on organizational no-mans-land: many churchgoers distrusted those labor reformers and activists whom they labeled critics and agitators; and some of those reformers and activists lacked confidence in professing Christians' commitment to social change. The organization, perhaps sensing it had only a tenuous hold on its members, devoted little time or energy to debating long lists of resolutions; it focused on sustaining itself as a bridge between advocates of religion and of labor. Nor did it put much effort into legislative lobbying, though it continued to share members and programs with the Eight Hour League.[10]

The CLU did, however, articulate a particular ideal of labor reform embedded in a renewed commitment to Christian spirituality and social activism. In fact, the CLU saw the foundation of labor reform built on both the American Revolutionary idea of resistance to tyranny (of capital, in this case) and the biblical injunction that every man is his brother's keeper. Jones, speaking as president of the organization, insisted that the "teachings, examples, and spirit of Jesus ... require the Church to establish Labor Partnerships, and other Industrial Co-operative organizations." Rather than focusing solely on individual salvation, churches had to use their organizational resources and moral authority to create this radical new vision of a cooperative industrial economy.[11]

Yet, like so many other labor reform groups, the CLU did not always speak with a unified voice, even among its leaders. Edward Rogers's conception of Christian labor reform was decidedly more fundamentalist and utopian than Jones's. Rogers argued that a literal interpretation of biblical law should form the blueprint for a new economy. The former state representative turned lay preacher challenged ordained ministers such as Jones to adopt strict Mosaic legal codes, not just the broader ethical teachings of Jesus, as the unalterable foundation for true labor reform. Rogers, speaking to the CLU in the vestry of the Park Street Church—a favorite pulpit for antebellum abolitionists, across the street from the Boston Common—during the spring of 1873, berated his fellow reformers and activists for squandering their faith on shorter working hours and producer cooperatives (not to mention land and financial reform). As long as the modern commercial rules of supply and demand were not replaced by Old Testament injunctions that "controlled ... Land, Labor and Capital ... in the interest of the masses," Rogers warned, the economy would continue to create vast inequities between rich and poor in the unending competition for jobs and markets. The true realization of Christ's kingdom on earth lay in recreating the collective, agrarian values of ancient Israelite society to stand in opposition to industrial capitalism's selfishness and materialism. Rogers proclaimed confidently, if vaguely, that "Faith in God, and in Humanity, constitute the appointed means for the overthrow of the existing mountains of poverty, vice and crime."[12]

In April 1874, Jones launched *Equity,* a new monthly "journal of Christian labor reform," in an effort to merge the power of the press with the moral authority of the pulpit. Jones gravely observed that the "house of the reformers is divided against itself, and its practical energies scattered." Some reformers focused on "extortion and hatred in the commercial life" and sought to "lay upon the sore a gigantic poultice of legislation, which would cure it once for all for the entire people." But Jones believed that legal remedies often had fatal loopholes, or inspired only lukewarm support even from their supposed advocates. In the end, he concluded, "to change a government is only to change the control of certain surpluses of wealth."

Jones wanted his new publication to promote a more ambitious agenda, beyond political action. Religious faith would provide the inspiration for a radical social transformation: "To revolutionize the work system of society is to change the control of the very processes themselves through which wealth is produced, and whereby men get a living." Reasserting his ideal of industrial equality as the necessary concomitant of political equality, Jones implored: "We have tried to put equal citizens in the place of noble and serf. Does not the very genius of our institutions require that we should strive to put equal artisans in the place of capitalist and wageman?" The only way to achieve this ideal of Christian equity was to mobilize and organize the faithful—those who saw injustice in the workplace but also saw flaws in labor legislation—into a coherent body of enlightened citizens pressing for religious and social reform. Religious reformers had to be more than isolated voices in the wilderness; they had to preach eight hours and cooperative workshops along with the gospel. They had to ensure that reformed hearts led to reformed actions, and that a just and equitable economic system allowed labor to earn the fair value of what it produced, so that legislative edicts would become unnecessary and charitable missions obsolete.[13]

Jones continued to publish his journal until the end of 1875, receiving constant support from Edward Rogers. Other activists and reformers—such as Ira Steward, George McNeill, Edwin Chamberlain, and Edward Linton—also helped Jones, even though many of these men did not share the editor's enthusiasm for a religiously inspired labor reform movement. As for his fellow clergymen, they often turned their backs on the enthusiastic minister and his paper. Nevertheless, Jones and his contributors insisted that scripture was on their side. They praised Jesus as the perfect prototype for the nineteenth-century labor reform leader, and asserted that the Bible contained all the justification necessary for a just workplace. They urged wealthy capitalists to point the way to a more equitable society by earning no more than senior ministers ($3,000 a year), and sharing all remaining business profits with their workers through industrial partnerships.[14]

In his final editorial remarks, however, Jones admitted that he had grown skeptical of journalism's power to effect social change. "No reform ought ever to be attempted through the press," he concluded in December 1875. "The only right way to originate a reform is by the living person face to face." Jones also noted, on the last page of his publication, that he had been elected recently to the state legislature, having been nominated by the local Republican caucus despite staunch opposition from party leaders. After feeling nearly alone in his struggle against entrenched capital and church leaders, Jones suddenly saw in his election to political office proof that his arguments had touched a responsive chord among workingmen in his district. The man who had always been skeptical of political activism and legislative remedies would now bring his ideals of religion and reform in person to the statehouse (even as Rogers, the former state legislator, was now preaching that Christian theology and strict biblical law had to be the foundation for all modern industrial reform). Jones returned to the editor's chair when the CLU launched its new publication, *Labor Balance,* in 1877. He and Rogers struggled to keep this journal financially solvent and focused on their ideals of Christian Socialism, but the publication and the CLU itself succumbed to a lack of funds and support in 1879.[15]

II

While the Christian Labor Union was striving to build new links between religion and labor reform in the mid-1870s, Boston plunged along with the rest of the nation into a deep economic depression. As wages fell and unemployment rose, workplace conflicts intensified. A growing number of strikes sent thousands of workers into the streets. Middle-class labor reformers soon realized that what was at stake was more than a question of whether to endorse a particular walkout. They had to consider whether mass protest could be an agent of social transformation. And they were forced to confront—more than ever before—the ramifications of labor protest: violence, destruction of property, and brutal government repression. These reformers struggled to understand the conflicts swirling around them, even as they continued to uphold the ideal of cross-class organizing for justice at the workplace. They walked a fine line between defending the rights of strikers and counseling their working-class brethren to avoid strikes whenever possible. They saw strikes as powerful but often dangerous instruments for social change—justified, perhaps, in self-defense but not always a constructive tool for promoting cross-class alliances. Many reformers eventually concluded that a stronger labor reform effort could emerge from the cauldron of violence and destruction, but that reformers and activists would have to work hard to rebuild coalitions, and rededicate themselves to the creation of a cooperative and equitable society.

Two years before a nationwide railroad strike virtually paralyzed portions of the United States in the summer of 1877, Edwin Chamberlin made a series of pointed and prescient remarks about labor protest in a book he wrote (ironically) about an emerging cooperative movement—the Sovereigns of Industry. Chamberlin insisted that the growing tide of labor conflict was an inevitable product of historical and economic change. Labor unrest was due far more to the harsh material conditions facing workers than to the machinations of any radical agitators. Quite simply, workers were now "demanding the ownership and control of their own productions, and like men who have been robbed, resort to force to obtain what they consider is wrongfully withheld from them. It is of no use to treat their associations as combinations of bad men to be put down by the strong hand. They are the result of the natural endeavors of men to prolong their lives."[16]

Looking closer at workers' protest, Chamberlin observed that strikes were usually "local and disconnected explosions"; strikers "content[ed] themselves, for the most part, with staying away from the field of employment, leaving the control of the workshops in the hands of their employers." But Chamberlin also raised the possibility that local labor protest might, "at a favorable moment, connect into a universal flame." He had in mind something akin to a general sit-down strike that would lead to radical social change—that is, "a general movement ... made by many laborers in many places at the same time to take and keep possession of the workshops wherein they worked, electing their own overseers, and disposing of their own products." If workers could physically seize and control the means of production, Chamberlin argued, "government might find it extremely difficult to put the legal proprietors into immediate possession of their property." And if workers wanted to maintain control of capital, "they would naturally form a government of their own, which would take the place of the old one, if it should be sloughed off."

Turning his attention to the labor reform campaign around him, in various states of activism or disrepair, Chamberlin insisted that groups such as eight-hour leagues could play a key role in channeling the burgeoning labor protest toward fundamental political and economic change. "They occupy a position midway between the Revolutionary but Unorganized Strike Movement, and the Legislative Labor Movement, which would appropriate to its ends the existing machinery of government." Though Chamberlin admitted that a "spirit of Conservatism seems to pervade [some groups] when their published declarations and purposes are examined"; at the same time, their "active expression of ... sympathies with those ... in trade disputes ... display what their opponents might call a dangerous Radicalism." Chamberlin predicted that, with support from labor reform organizations, "workingmen everywhere will be able to dethrone the present irresponsible lords of labor, and make themselves real, as they are rightful, Sovereigns of Industry." Thus, for Chamberlin, labor protest did not necessarily undermine the broader concept of cross-class reform activism. Rather, labor reform organizing, agitation, and politics enabled workers to go beyond immediate grievances and strive toward the ultimate goal of justice and equity within a political economy controlled by those who produced the nation's wealth.

Chamberlin believed that cooperative workshops and joint-stock companies where workers shared in the profits formed essential building blocks for this new economy. He insisted that the "Co-operative Movement is not ... a mere momentary expression of discontent on the part of the producing classes with the present method of conducting trade and industry, which may soon be forgotten, but rather a new ... contending force that is to exercise a permanent influence in the contest between Labor and Capital." Chamberlin clearly understood that class conflict existed in postwar America, but he also held out the cooperative ideal as an antidote to such social antagonism.

> As long as one class almost exclusively owns the surplus wealth that another class produced, their interests must necessarily be opposed. We can hope for no lasting reconciliation of these classes; or, rather, we can hope for no enduring peace till the classes themselves disappear; those producing the wealth receiving in return for their labor the full value ... of their productions. It may be expected that the Co-operative Movement will increase in importance, until the principle that underlies it, ... [that] it is of advantage to individual members of our societies to make no profit from one another, is recognized and acted upon by all members of society at large.

Chamberlin, in the midst of growing conflict at the workplace, and a gaping disparity between rich and poor which threatened the nation's political stability, still proclaimed an optimistic vision for a more just future society. "Though the Republic may crumble and decay," he reassured his readers, "the people will live to found a real democracy, whose corner-stone shall be Labor, and not Money."[17]

Chamberlin did not encourage physical confrontation on the job, but he warned that the ongoing exploitation of workers, grinding even deeper in the midst of a depression, would most assuredly create more conflict between labor and capital. He believed that the economy and labor relations could probably get worse before they got better. In the summer of 1877, Chamberlin's predictions of near-open warfare between workers and their employers came true as a mass railroad strike spread across the nation. Thousands of trains stood idle, and ten of thousands of workers took to the streets to protest near-starvation wages. General strikes engulfed several cities, as artisans put down their tools and factory operatives left their machines in support of the railroad employees. Some public protests turned violent: police and militias fired into crowds of strikers and their supporters. Eventually, federal troops broke the impasse at key railroad terminals in order to move mail trains along the tracks.

Boston had a preview of protest on the railroads in February 1877, when engineers struck the Boston and Maine lines. Sympathetic crowds supported the Brotherhood of Locomotive Engineers, but the strikers saw their jobs filled quickly from a large pool of unemployed railroad workers. In the wake of this unsuccessful walkout, railroad owners endorsed antistrike legislation and antiunion employer associations, both of which played crucial roles in the subsequent nationwide conflict. Ironically, the strikes in the summer of 1877 hardly affected rail lines around Boston; probably because most of the likely protesters had been fired back in February, and scabs now on the job refused to join the walkout. But local unions and activists held rallies to support workers in other cities, even amid reports that antistrike rowdies stalked the train stations in downtown Boston. Though the city experienced far less upheaval than locales such as Pittsburgh, Chicago, and St. Louis, Boston labor reformers still struggled to understand the enormous uprising that engulfed much of the nation.[18]

Just months after the summer strike, Ezra Heywood published an essay on the conflict in Benjamin Tucker's *Radical Review,* which Heywood then revised and reprinted as a pamphlet in 1878. It is true that Heywood and his New England Labor Reform League had distanced themselves ideologically from most of the Boston labor reform community by the late 1870s; thus his opinions on many issues no longer reflected the views of other labor reformers and activists. Nevertheless, in the midst of theorizing about his favorite topic of financial reform, Heywood also gave a thoroughgoing account of the mass protests and their lessons for industrial America—lessons not lost on others active in labor reform campaigns.

Heywood railed against the public's conclusion that it was "disorderly and revolutionary for working-people to have an opinion about their wages, and act on it associatively.... So long as it was capital *striking down* wages ... the action is accepted as orderly and proper. But if, obeying sterner necessities, to procure food and raiment for destitute ones at home ... labor objects to a cut-down," they are accused of a "riot" or "rebellion." Heywood insisted that the real threat to the nation lay not in the working masses' protests but in capital's immense wealth and power. If strikes were rebellions, they were justified collective resistance "against the unjust claims of capitalists to so control raw material and exchanges as to secure an income without work."

Like Chamberlin, Heywood did not praise labor conflict, but he did assert that such protest had legitimate roots in the fight against social inequality. Echoing his abolitionist heritage, he proclaimed that "between capital and labor there can be no truce and no compromise; the conflict is as inevitable and irrepressible as between Northern liberty and Southern slavery. Strikes are inevitable, liberty is assailed, and business prosperity, in a large, healthful, and permanent sense, is impossible, until the claim of capital to increase is utterly exterminated." Heywood added, in a footnote, that strikes should be understood as a symptom of, and not a cure for, the nation's distorted economic system. "It is needless to say that strikes, *per se,* are always objectionable; agreement and prosperous co-operation are natural and inevitable in the absence of disturbing elements of intrusion and fraud.... [A] great, general revolt, like the railway strike, could not have occurred except by the violation of rights and interests common to all." Heywood also tried to explain, with withering sarcasm similar to that of Wendell Phillips, that protesters were not the root cause of strikes. "To say it [the strike] was caused by 'agitators,' 'communists,' or 'doctrinaires,' is about as sensible as to say that the weather clerk produces storms, or that geologists are responsible for earthquakes."

Surveying the uprising as a whole, Heywood portrayed the railroad strikes as a simple and stark example of good versus evil—labor's righteous demands arrayed against a corporate tyranny backed by government authority.

> In asserting their natural right to live by their labor, and a just claim to ownership in, at least, a part of their earnings, the strikers fairly represented the claims of labor, and also the morally defensible rights of property. The officials, on the contrary, represented the existing financial, commercial, and political power of the strong to plunder the weak. In siding with capital against labor in such an issue, government reveals its own despotic, felonious character, and makes plain to all eyes the kind of "law and order" which good citizens are called upon to support.

Heywood believed that the battle's bitter ending held valuable lessons for labor reformers, in Boston and far beyond. No longer should reformers put their faith in simple "well-meant protests against present injustice"—such as "eight and ten hour laws," "the Greenback delusion," "government workshops," or "State and National labor bureaus"—which did not "discern clearly the spirit and scope of labor reform." Reformers now had an "imperative duty to recognize" the strikers "as lawful belligerents" in the fight against capital—even as the reformers also had to admit that violent confrontations "are unnatural and savage methods of progress."

In his conclusion, Heywood insisted "that no amount of violence" would lead to lasting social change. Rather, "*nothing short of the entire abolition of property in land and its kindred resources, and the removal of all restrictions on exchange,* will exterminate the invasive and murderous claim of capital to increase and secure to labor its natural right to opportunity and reciprocity." Thus, Heywood argued that the sheer intensity of the railroad strikes provided ample justification for his vision of a labor reform crusade that did not focus on the workplace but challenged the premise of private property and the legitimacy of government itself. Once again, Heywood found himself in sympathy with workers' struggles; but his ideology offered his readers little in the way of concrete measures to protect labor's rights on the job or in the streets.[19]

Jesse Jones also spoke out on the railroad strikes. He agreed with Heywood that the protesters had legitimate grievances, and that capital had deliberately condemned the strikers as a mob so that the state could demolish their ranks. He asserted that "the calling out of the military at the beck of the railroad czars to enforce their tyrannous edicts against their pinched and oppressed employees has done more to put in peril the liberties of the people and the safety of the American Republic than any strikes, or so-called 'mobs' have done." As for the explanation that the militia had to uphold law and order, Jones scoffed, "When law and order mean the cruel tyranny of ten men over ten hundred; taking the bread out of their mouths and the mouths of their families, . . . what then?" Jones answered his own rhetorical question by proclaiming, "The strikers stood for the liberties of the people against the money kings, just as the men on Lexington Green stood for those liberties against the political king."

Jones carefully dissected the state's use of force in putting down the strike, and the disturbing legal and political ramifications of the authorities' actions. "Shall the people's government shoot down men to enforce the will of a gigantic, tyrant corporation?" he implored his readers. Jones sadly concluded that the government had indeed gunned down men "to strengthen the hand of tyrants in grinding the faces of the poor." And by siding with powerful capital, the state "declared that property is of more importance than persons, and the legal rights of the rich than the bread of life of the poor,—a doctrine which the American Republic by its very nature abhors." The corrupt government now stood not for the people but "for the few rich against the many poor," and "to hold the industrious poor firmly down into the lower depths into which the money kings have trodden them." Jones feared that excessive use of government force would only stir more resentment and potential violence in the ranks of labor. Instead of looking to the state as a potential ally, through eight-hour laws and other legislation, more workers would now see government as openly hostile to labor's interests, and a force to be feared and opposed at every turn. In such a political and economic climate, labor reform was needed more than ever to restore republican ideals of justice and fairness for all who worked. But the campaign for such reform would be even more difficult in an atmosphere poisoned by capital's arrogance, government's hostility toward labor, and the conflict's widespread violence. The open class conflict—exacerbated by the often brutal intervention of local police, state militia, and even federal troops, all in the name of protecting capital—left open sores on the body politic that would take a long time to heal, if ever.[20]

Several years after the uprising of 1877, Jones sent a letter to the *Labor Standard* extending his thoughts on labor protest and arguing for the potential benefits of strikes. (Most other observers saw such clashes as painful necessities at best.) Commenting on the recently released annual report of the Massachusetts Bureau of the Statistics of Labor for 1880, Jones took issue with then bureau chief Carroll Wright's gloomy appraisal of walkouts. Jones conceded that workers could suffer enormous monetary losses during strikes "for which they never gain any indemnity in kind." He also agreed with Heywood that "strikes are not the best way to grow." And putting on his ministerial mien, he added that "the Christian way of patient endurance of wrong under peaceful protest is undoubtedly the best way; and if the church were doing its duty even approximately strikes would never or at most rarely be needed." But, drawing on his past criticism of established denominations from his days in the CLU, Jones declared that most organized religion neglected its obligation to protect the downtrodden: churches say nothing while their wealthy members "oppress and rob" poorer Christians; therefore, "there is no way left open to the poor and oppressed . . . only to combine together and strike." Once out on strike, Jones added, labor could actually gain far more than it lost in such conflicts—for "through them the courage, hardihood, patience, steadfastness, [and] skill . . . of those engaged in them are developed and strengthened." Workers who stood up to their bosses realized a sense of "their own manhood and self-respect," a feeling of self-worth that they would never lose. Even if in the end strikers had to "yield [when] crushed out by superior force," labor would remain in its heart "as resistful as ever." For Jones, this inextinguishable flame of resistance embodied "the incalculably great good in strikes, and should be fully declared in any adequate discussion of them."[21]

Veteran activist George McNeill joined middle-class reformers in reflecting on protest and labor reform when he gave an interview to the *Chicago Tribune* one year after the railroad strikes. McNeill labeled walkouts a "crude method and the result either of no organization, or of bad organization." But he hastened to add that "strikes are justifiable as a means just as wars are justifiable. We claim that there is a war between capital and labor. A war that we don't like, and which is the result of the separate and distinct interests of the two classes. I have said publicly 'Don't strike' but strikes are sometimes better than submission." Rather than emphasizing class conflict and violent confrontation, however, McNeill tried to steer his remarks toward more positive and peaceful visions of labor reform. He spoke of "the happy day . . . when profit upon labor shall cease and cooperation shall come in as a natural result. It will at first probably be cooperation of capital and labor in productive enterprise, and finally the elimination of the capitalists and working classes as classes."

McNeill, as he described the path toward this new cooperative society, emphatically refuted accusations about communism and violence in the labor movement. "We have no thought of force and we don't propose to disturb a cent of the past accumulations of wealth," he asserted. When asked by the *Tribune*'s reporter what was to be done "with the Scotts and Vanderbilts—the men who have hoarded millions and control so many thousand of the laboring classes," McNeill responded, "Let them alone. That class will die out just as did . . . the mastodons." As for the immediate future, in an economy where capital still ruled, McNeill turned the standard antilabor slogans on their head. The "railroad kings, merchant princes and cotton lords" posed the real threat to the nation; they were the dangerous and destabilizing radicals. "We believe that they today really represent the communists and are most to be feared. They are swallowing up the small capitalists. . . . They are crowding the middle classes down and they are a danger and a threat to republican institutions. . . . [They will] reduce workmen to the level of paupers and take from them the elective franchise." Meanwhile, labor activists and reformers, when they called the industrialists to account for their greed, assumed the role of true conservatives striving to uphold traditional values of work and fair play in the face of exploitation. What if the capitalists still insisted on calling the labor protesters communists? In that case, McNeill declared at a subsequent rally, workers would proclaim "a communism founded upon the Golden Rule, . . . dangerous only to those who are infidel to the interest of republican institutions, and infidel to the interests of humanity."[22]

III

In the spring and summer of 1886, thousands of workers in Boston took to the streets and joined another national strike wave—this time to press the demand for the eight-hour workday. With support from the Central Labor Union of Boston (a coalition of local trade unions), and unofficial encouragement from many in District Assembly 30 of the Knights of Labor, various local trade unions (especially in the construction industry) laid down their tools and demanded a shorter workday. In Boston as in many other cities, the eight-hour movement was no longer led primarily by local leagues with their focus on conventions and legislative lobbying for laws to protect all workers. Labor unions and trade federations now encouraged direct action at the workplace—strikes and boycotts—to get the eight-hour day written into contracts for their members.

On May 3, nearly 7,000 building trades workers—carpenters, painters, and plumbers—struck for the eight-hour day. (Workers at other jobs and worksites also walked out that spring and summer over wage issues.) Though the strikes were well organized, so was the employers' resistance. The plumbers stayed away from their jobs for more than six weeks but still could not secure the eight-hour day. Yet, despite these frustrations, the strikes in Boston generated less violence than in other cities such as Chicago.[23]

Although the eight-hour strikes of 1886 had a more direct impact on Boston than the railroad stoppages of the previous decade, few reformers wrote extensive comments on these walkouts. Perhaps the protests hit too close to home, and those who observed the events did not feel they had enough distance to reach any objective conclusions. Or perhaps most reformers had become inured to workplace conflict and were not as shocked by the violence (especially in other cities) as they had been a decade before.

But one exception is well worth noting. In the midst of the building trades strike, a new voice spoke up in Boston labor reform circles trying to understand the renewed surge in protest at the point of production. Philip Moxon, pastor of the First Baptist Church, published a sermon, "The Industrial Revolution," in the May 20 edition of *The Watchman*. Moxon stood on the leading edge of a second wave of liberal clergy confronting the labor question in late nineteenth-century Boston. Twelve years younger than Jesse Jones, who led the pioneering generation of postwar labor reform ministers, Moxon was also born in Canada (in 1848). He immigrated with his family to Illinois in 1857, and served in the Civil War while still a teenager. After the war, Moxon first studied law and then later succeeded his father in a Michigan Baptist pulpit. He did not complete his formal religious training, at the Rochester Theological Seminary, until he was thirty years old. After serving the First Baptist Church in Cleveland for six years, he took his position in Boston, where he remained for eight years, until 1893.

Moxon had been in Boston for less than a year when he witnessed the strikes of 1886 spread across the city. Leading one of the largest, wealthiest, and most socially prominent congregations in Boston, Moxon seemed an unlikely candidate to speak out publicly about the significance of these protests for the labor reform crusade. Yet he did not shy away from tackling such a controversial topic. A towering figure in the pulpit, standing six feet, four inches tall, Moxon had a reputation for physical grace and outspoken, eloquent homilies. "The Industrial Revolution" was no exception; Moxon's sermon pulled few punches in addressing both workers and employers.[24]

Echoing some of Jones's ideas about industrial democracy, Moxon stated: "Government passes steadily and surely into the hands of the many. Industrial organization, as well as political organization, is passing out of the control of the few into the control of the many.... [A]s government is to be *by* the many *for* the many, so industrial organization must be for the weal of the many—for the wage-earners as well as the wage-payers, for the operative as well as employer." On a pragmatic level, Moxon argued in defense of trade unions that "if merchants or manufacturers have a right to organize into corporations or 'pools,' to conserve and enlarge their gains, laboring men have an equal right to organize for the protection of their industry and the improvement of their condition." Moxon then reassured his congregants that workers through their unions would "increase their intelligence and acquire the discipline of self-control. Their mistakes and misdeeds do not destroy their right."

The core of Moxon's sermon, however, did not offer a ringing endorsement of labor organizing and protest. Rather, Moxon went to great lengths to assuage his well-to-do audience with statements such as "The industrial revolt ... as a whole, is not evil.... The great body of American workingmen is conservative and not anarchical. The present disturbance of industrial relations will result in good." In particular, he said that "the temporary check to commercial prosperity which the present labor troubles cause, may be a disguised blessing. We shall, perhaps, think less of mere cash and more of principles."

Moxon tried to mediate the conflict around him by distributing blame on all sides, and urging everyone to see the faults in themselves and in each other. He castigated employers for their selfishness and callous disregard of employees' physical and spiritual health. He took workers to task for being led astray by those who counseled violent resistance. (Moxon added that where both parties made mistakes and clashed, it was incumbent on those who possessed wealth and education—usually the owners—to uphold moral principles of charity and tolerance.) Both sides had to see the error of their ways and come to accept their common humanity. "The workman, or 'hand,' as he is called, is of the same flesh and blood as the employer. They are the children of the same God; they are under the same moral laws. The workman is not like coal and iron which the employer may burn up or wear out and then cast aside at his pleasure. On the other hand, the employer is not a legitimate subject of spoilation." With a sense of magnanimity, Moxon urged his listeners to remember that "the majority of capitalists in our country are honest, fair-minded men, who wish to do right, [and] the great body of workingmen are neither outlaws nor enemies of the social order."

Moxon wrote his sermon as an extended essay about searching for harmony between labor and capital through the principles of Christian love and understanding. He intoned that "Christ in the common life of men is dissolving the bondage of arbitrary and outgrown industrial relations.... The wild vagaries of communism will disappear with the selfish maxims and exclusive customs of a commercial aristocracy." Moxon insisted that social peace was possible, and would arise out of the class conflict surrounding his church. Peaceful labor relations would, in the end, become both the true harbinger of material prosperity and the highest expression of Christian faith. He stated emphatically: "Capital is permanently safe and fruitful only when labor is its free and willing ally, only when the man who has muscles and mechanical skill works in fraternal accord, and for common ends, with the man who has dollars."[25]

Moxon, like other Gilded Age Boston labor reformers, struggled to bring the power and energy of protest back into the arena of cross-class activism. But the scale and scope of strike waves had increased through the 1870s and 1880s, and faced with the growing intensity of this class conflict, Moxon chose not to offer a radical solution to the labor crisis. Instead, he proffered a cautious and restrained vision of reform; he proclaimed that the harmony of labor and capital was real, and could be reclaimed through Christian charity and forgiveness. Moxon hoped that his message of tolerance and understanding between employer and employee would calm the waters and bring the city together.

In 1877, reformers held out an ultimately optimistic ideal that conflict—though not always beneficial in itself—could catalyze constructive and far-reaching change in the nation's social structure. Edwin Chamberlin argued that strikes would lead to a cooperative commonwealth. Ezra Heywood believed that mass walkouts opened up the possibility of a radically anarchistic society. Jesse Jones saw protests building the fundamental moral character of labor. And George McNeill declared that labor stoppages served merely as emergency measures before the coming peaceful revolution in the nation's economy. A decade later, Philip Moxon preached a more moderate "social gospel" that harmony between labor and capital could emerge from rancor at the workplace if everyone agreed to temper the industrial revolution's excesses with Christian brotherhood. Yet this benevolent (and rather vague) hope for the future seemed perhaps as unattainable as more radical schemes in a city scarred by deepening class divisions, with labor activists and reformers embittered and frustrated by continuing defeats at the hands of recalcitrant capitalists. Even as both protest and peaceful change seemed to be stymied in the summer of 1886, however, the Boston labor reform community would soon see another wave of religiously inspired organizing and agitation.

IV

After the trade unions failed to secure the eight-hour workday in 1886 through massive walkouts, the Boston labor reform community reexamined past legislative models for the shorter workday. During the winter of 1889, several reformers and activists revived a dormant campaign to grant the eight-hour day to public employees throughout the state. (Ira Steward and various eight-hour leagues had proposed a similar law in the late 1860s and early 1870s.) Though only a relatively small number of workers would be covered by the proposed legislation, the demand for a law protecting all workers might gain momentum if the state (and cities and towns) accepted the eight-hour day for its own labor force.

Boston's premier labor newspaper of the period, the *Labor Leader,* surveyed dozens of reformers and activists and found widespread support for reviving this particular legislative strategy. Jesse Jones wrote that "Massachusetts led the nation in establishing the ten-hour law for the toiler.... And, as a law establishing the Eight Hour day for all public works would be greatly for human welfare, therefore, doubtless, the state has a right to pass such a law, and 'compel the cites and towns' to observe it." George McNeill asserted that the law was necessary because "the employment of labor more than eight hours per day by the State, or by a city, or by a corporation, is not for the 'common good,' and tends to the profit and interest of a class." McNeill also insisted that "Eight hours means a more perfect and rapid production under economic and social machinery that will not only bear the strain, but leave a residue of strength for safety. 'Eight hours means more workers thinking and more thinkers working.'... Eight hours is statesmanship lifted above party." McNeill believed that fewer working hours meant more time for labor to increase its skill level, raise its wages, and educate itself about the benefits of collective action. Finally, McNeill urged support for the eight-hour workday from all those who "believe in freedom of contract that makes men free to contract, by adding that true dignity to manhood and womanhood, that comes from moral stamina, intellectual attainment and common prosperity.... Eight hours cannot come too quick. The danger is that it may be too long delayed. Eight hours is the safety valve of our high pressure system." Despite the forceful arguments of McNeill, Jones, and others, the Massachusetts legislature again defeated the proposal on the grounds that state and municipal employees should not receive preferential treatment, and that individual municipalities should regulate their own public workers. (Meanwhile, in another game of political pass-the-buck, city leaders in Boston told reformers that state authority was required to reduce local public employees' working hours!)[26]

The following year (1890), McNeill and others once again appealed to the legislature to enact an eight-hour law for public employees. This time, McNeill's passionate arguments for the legislation rested on his conception of government itself. "The State is a co-operative corporation," McNeill asserted, "in which all men and women who comply with its laws should have one share.... The State is not the State House or the Government... and whenever any person is hired... to do any work, manual or otherwise, that person is a servant of the State as much as is the Governor.... The manual laborer who performs faithful service is as much entitled to respect as the Governor." McNeill then stated that "the demand for eight hours means the putting of this theory" of political equality and the dignity of all labor "into practice.... The State in its capacity as an employer has the right to fix the standard of the hours of labor, and of wages, of the manual laborer, as much as of the clerks in the departments." If Massachusetts were true to its ideals as a "free commonwealth," then its "standard of wages should be the highest, and hours of labor be the least, consistent with co-operative economy."[27]

Not all labor reformers shared McNeill's vision that the state could function as an exemplar of freedom and cooperation above the often sordid details of politics and legislation. Just one week after the *Labor Leader* published McNeill's remarks, Edwin Chamberlin wrote a rejoinder that offered a more skeptical opinion of Massachusetts government, and called for a return to the previous decade's public agitation and protest. Chamberlin stated baldly that "the wage-earners who are most desirous of securing the 8-hour day are practically shut out from every position and all influence in the government.... Ours is not a democratic but an aristocratic republic. It cannot be called a government of, for and by, the people, but rather one of, for and by, the richest men of the people." Since the government was stacked against the workers, and Chamberlin saw little to be gained in appealing to some higher notion of the state, he counseled labor to secure its demands "by a display or use of force" in the workplace and in the streets.

> The working class is so much larger and stronger, physically, than the money class, that when their efforts are concentrated and well directed they occasionally obtain a concession in their favor. Though the working class is very feebly represented in the government, it is overwhelmingly represented in the field of labor. It is out in the world that the contest for eight hours must for the greater part be carried on.... Custom is the origin of law.... The legislature, the government, the State, is of small importance in the solution of the 8-hour question.... It is not energy thrown

away by any manner of means in endeavoring to secure for state or city employees the 8-hour day. The example would be worth all it cost to secure it. The main work though must be done outside of State Houses.[28]

Two months after this exchange in the labor press, McNeill published an extensive essay, "Eight Hours" in the religious reform periodical *The Dawn*. McNeill took many familiar economic arguments for shorter working hours and wove them together with a renewed emphasis on the movement's moral benefits. Not surprisingly, given the journal's audience, McNeill's writing took on a spiritual cast. He began his presentation not in the workplace but in the domestic sphere. "The universal movement for the establishment of the eight-hour work day," he intoned, "is a movement for the home and home-life of all who toil.... It means a lessening of intemperance, prostitution, vice and crime, and their final elimination. It means less household drudgery for women." McNeill told his readers that a shorter workday would produce "manly men and womanly women" who would elevate the "standard of thought" and improve "habits and customs" in working-class homes across the nation. Turning to a future where workers labored less, McNeill waxed optimistic that the campaign for the eight-hour day was "the first ethical economic step in the pathway of the wage-worker toward equity, the abolition of poverty, and the heralding of the kingdom of heaven on earth." He concluded his essay by stating simply (though perhaps surprisingly) that "Christian Socialism stands for eight hours as the step toward equity, upon which the hopes of the wage-workers are centered."[29]

During this same spring of 1890, as McNeill campaigned to secure the eight-hour day for state employees and wrote his essay for *The Dawn,* he also delivered a long lecture on socialism at Horticultural Hall. He ended his talk with another set of striking religious images that reflected Christ's kingdom on earth more than a purely secular cooperative commonwealth. McNeill told his audience that "the influence of the teachings of the Carpenter's Son still tends to counteract the influence of Mammon." In the eight-hour movement, people "will find a new revelation of the Old Gospel, when the Golden Rule of Christ shall measure the relations of men in all their duties toward their fellows in factory and workshop, in the mine, in the field, in common room and in counting room. Everywhere the challenge will go forth as never before, 'Choose ye this day whom ye will serve—God or Mammon.' Though the Mammon-worshipers may cry, 'Crucify Him! Crucify Him!' the promise of the prophet and the poet shall be fulfilled." To McNeill, that promise of a better day both reflected his radical abolitionist roots by reaffirming the fundamental equality of all human beings, and embraced his more radical economic vision by giving workers the full value of their labor. First, there would have to be "the free acceptance of the Gospel that all men are of one blood. Then the new Pentecost will come, when every man shall have according to his needs."[30]

McNeill's open invocation of Christian Socialism, both in name and in its ideals, as a direct link to the eight-hour movement was something new in his rhetorical arsenal and revealed his own evolving beliefs, as well as the resurgent connections between religion and labor reform in the late 1880s and early 1890s. Though previously skeptical about mixing religious enthusiasm with labor activism in organizations such as the CLU, McNeill was now increasingly interested in and inspired by Christian Socialism. The radical religious doctrine touched something spiritual in his idealistic nature and intrigued him as a powerful moral and economic alternative to industrial capitalism. The ranks of pro-labor ministers also began to grow in Boston, and McNeill saw them as potential allies and soulmates in the cause of labor reform. In fact, McNeill had already formed a friendship with one young minister who embodied these growing links between religious activism and labor reform.

William Dwight Porter (W. D. P.) Bliss, rector of the Grace (Episcopal) Church in the working-class Irish immigrant neighborhood of South Boston (1887–1890), became the leading spokesman for a new generation of Christian Socialist ministers who forged strong bonds with Boston's labor reform community. The son of a Congregational minister and missionary, Bliss was born in Constantinople in 1856 and educated at Amherst College and Hartford Theological Seminary. Ordained a Congregational minister himself in 1882, Bliss served a congregation in South Natick, Massachusetts (perhaps the same church Jesse Jones had led more than a decade earlier). By 1884, Bliss had resigned his position and converted to Episcopalianism; he wanted what he believed would be a more unified church structure along with increased individual intellectual freedom. Bliss also admired the work of Christian Socialists in England, many of whom belonged to the Anglican or Episcopal Church. He grew even more interested in social reform questions while observing workers in nearby factory villages, and began to read books by leading political economists such as Henry George. In 1886, Bliss served as a lay reader and deacon of an Episcopal church in Lee, a paper mill town in western Massachusetts. There, Bliss helped organize a local assembly of the Knights of Labor. Within a year, he was ordained an Episcopal priest and sent to Boston to lead Grace Church. The son of a missionary to the Turks now felt called to be something more than just another Protestant pastor trying to reach out to his overwhelmingly Catholic neighbors. Bliss wanted his real mission to be social and economic change. He strove to become a new kind of messenger preaching an engaged gospel to the poor and unchurched, as well as to the wealthy who filled the pews on Sunday yet seemed deaf to the oppressed's cries.[31]

Shortly after arriving in Boston, Bliss began to write about the need for continuing agitation in the wake of the failed 1886 strikes. "Organization, agitation gives the workingman something to think over, something to strive for. A strike compels the dullest man to think," Bliss argued, and walkouts "have raised wages or shortened hours, or at least have compelled employers to be more careful in their treatment of their employees." But something more than strikes was needed to move the struggle forward. Bliss saw that "political action is the method now coming into vogue. As a method it is vastly better, vastly cheaper to the individual wage worker, vastly more effective, vastly more permanent in its results" than strikes. In late summer 1887, Bliss joined with veteran labor reformers such as Edwin Chamberlin and John Orvis to call for a convention of Knights of Labor assemblies, trade unions, labor reform societies, and others interested in building a new labor party. For Bliss, independent political action was "prophetic; . . . it means the overthrow of the wage system; it means the establishment in our land of an industrial federation, democracy applied to business and manufactures." Despite his high hopes for such political activism, Bliss declined this new labor party's nomination for lieutenant governor, preferring to remain an enthusiastic supporter in the pulpit.[32]

In 1889, Bliss shifted away from independent party politics and focused his energies on launching the Society of Christian Socialists. He also started publishing *The Dawn*, at 36 Bromfield Street (on the same block as other reform groups), to promote the new society and Christian Socialist ideals. Bliss used the publication to explain his conception of a broad-based reform movement that was to begin with popular education and debate and remain open to a wide variety of strategies for improving industrial society including eight hours, profit sharing, and work relief for the unemployed. He argued that Christian Socialists did not have to join every reform campaign. At the same time, all reformers and activists had to embrace their causes knowing that no one campaign would cure all that ailed mankind. In fact, Bliss dismissed single-minded reformers because they usually became "positively reactionary and hinder[ed] progress." "What we need now," he urged his readers, "is not small political action, wire-pulling on some one subject, but broad, deep, varied, and yet definite education of the public mind. This is why we like the name Socialism—because it is broad, deep, comprehensive. Socialists have ever stood for many reforms, or rather, Reform in many lines, but ever in one direction—Fraternity for the world."[33]

In subsequent articles, Bliss detailed what the new Christian Socialist economy would look like. A "federated industrial state" would democratically control all production and distribution; this state would prevent individual capitalists from making "industrial war" on each other. Workers would elect their own foremen and department heads—"good workmen would be known, and enterprise and diligence rewarded by higher office." Everyone would be obligated to work in some productive enterprise; no one would be idle and hungry, and no one would work more than a few hours each day. And, Bliss declared, "if by working a few hours a day, every man could earn an independent, honest income for himself and his family, as would be possible under Socialism, it would do more to develop free individuality than any possible amount of mere individualism. It would also solve the woman question, by making woman financially independent of man."[34]

Bliss's ideas about an industrial state and workers' electing their own foremen echoed not only some of Jesse Jones's earlier writing but also another reform movement sweeping through Boston in the late 1880s and early 1890s—Nationalism. Based on Edward Bellamy's popular utopian novel *Looking Backward*, the Nationalist movement organized clubs across the country to carry out Bellamy's blueprint for a new society. The first club formed in Boston in December 1888 and quickly attracted the attention of various middle-class reformers throughout the city; however, Nationalist clubs earned a reputation among working-class activists as elite debating societies long on grandiose theories about social change and short on support for specific workplace reforms. Some club leaders, in their eagerness to snare more prominent proper Bostonians, deliberately kept any controversial working-class issues or individuals off the agenda.

Bliss attended a monthly meeting of the Boston club in July 1889 and voiced his concerns with single-issue reform campaigns, and with reformers who lost sight of those who deserved justice and fairness at the workplace. Though Bliss's writings sometimes paralleled Bellamy's ideas, the good reverend was not a convert to the gospel of Nationalism. The *Labor Leader* reported that Bliss warned the gathering: "The crying need of the hour was work for the masses. In his own parish in South Boston, there were hundreds of men out of work. In the country a vast army was in the same condition." Taking aim at the Nationalists' interest in public ownership of utilities as a first step toward their ideal of a new industrial state, Bliss observed tartly that "it would not benefit [working] people if gas was municipalized. Many wage-earners used no gas. He would have municipality and state furnish work to the unemployed—build houses, for instance, and sell them at cost price." Bliss was not alone in his interest in but also skepticism of Nationalism, and the movement never forged strong links with working-class activists in late nineteenth-century Boston.[35]

Though he was critical of the Nationalists' strategies as being misdirected, Bliss knew that many labor activists saw his own ideals as ethereal and impractical. And it is true that his definition of socialism emphasized broad notions of brotherhood and the ideal of the cooperative commonwealth, rather than Marxist concepts of surplus value and class struggle. But Bliss believed firmly that Christian teachings of love provided ample inspiration and justification for working-class solidarity and protest against social injustice. He insisted that infusing socialist ideas of collective ownership with Christian teachings about the unity of mankind would lead to a profound transformation of American life—a change that would be gradual, evolutionary, and non-violent but nevertheless far-reaching and all-encompassing.

Bliss always returned to his belief that organized religion and religious leaders had to take charge of this struggle for industrial society's soul. No other individuals or institutions had the ethical and organizational potential to lead the way toward social change. Though many churches and ministers had strayed from their calling to seek justice, they still had the ability to bring themselves and the world around them back to its moral foundations. Bliss observed, with a mixture of sympathy and a hint of condescension:

> Working men will never solve their own labor problem. This may not be their fault. They have been too wronged, too overworked in hours and strength, to have time and ability for the requisite education. Scrambling over each other to get for themselves and their families the rich man's bread, they can not stand long together. Still less can the rich men of this land solve the problem. In order to be rich to-day one must forget the golden rule, and push and plot and combine for self. God's kingdom will not come thus. One can not make money in the world's method, and then turn round and think to fulfill the law of God by giving a small portion to the poor. It is not enough to build chapels and libraries where the poor we have wronged may live on patronage. God's kingdom is righteousness, not almsgiving.

Since men and their worldly institutions could not "bring in the divine kingdom," Bliss believed that people of faith and goodwill had to "depend on God and appeal to the Church, the organization of His children, as the only power that can to-day save the land." Ultimately, Bliss and his fellow Christian Socialists thought that their fundamental goal was not to win adherents to a narrow ideological doctrine but to reawaken Christians and their churches to their social obligations as followers of Jesus' moral teachings. If men and women's hearts and minds could be converted to Christian Socialism, they would create a truly just social order without violently overthrowing the state or suddenly seizing private property.[36]

What exactly did Bliss and his fellow Christian Socialists want the churches to do? Here again, Bliss tried hard to get beyond vague platitudes and offer specific suggestions for preparing to change the world, and for changing it once churchfolk were ready to make that commitment. He began with his previous call for education: "Christian Socialists say study, study, study; organize classes, institute lectures; read, think, write; appeal, above all, to the moral power of an enlightened conscience." After studying what had already been written on current economic problems, Bliss urged church members not to "be content to derive your knowledge merely from books." Every potential reformer had to go "and see the wrongs and conditions under which many of your fellow men are smarting. . . . Visit the tenements of the poor, . . . see them in the factories and workshops. . . . You will find much of ignorance, much of prejudice, but also much to honor, much to pity, much to move the heart at the wrong and injustice done the workingmen. Then," Bliss further urged on his readers, "when the conscience is aflame with God's law, and the head is clear with facts, and the heart sore with the sorrows of your brethren, go out and preach, and write and lecture; organize societies, churches, suppers to bring the rich and poor together, not for almsgiving, but as brothers."

Bliss always insisted that unity and cooperation among middle-class reformers, and between reformers and workers, would lay the foundation for a truly reformed society (though he also made it clear that such cooperation was not predicated on enforced ideological homogeneity). Thus, he too embraced the ideal of cross-class activism so important to Boston labor reformers. Bliss also specifically said that activist church members would be better off joining a union, such as the Knights of Labor, than a charity or a mission to the poor. Though the Knights had fallen on hard times when he wrote this advice (1892), Bliss still believed that they were fighting the good fight for justice at the workplace, and "one ounce of justice is worth ten pounds of charity." Justice, as Bliss saw it, demanded that the economic system be reformed to give workers their fair reward; whereas charity conceived of social problems as individual moral failure.

Once activist Christians became educated and organized, they could be encouraged to focus on "definite lines of work"—specific reform campaigns that would build on each other to create the kingdom of God on earth. Bliss again reminded his readers that no one Christian Socialist could embrace every reform program, but every reformer had to choose ideas that could lead to substantive social change as expeditiously as possible. Bliss gave first priority to "political action": eliminating corruption and promoting an honest, efficient government that could actively regulate the industrial economy. Committed Christians, especially Christian Socialists, would cleanse government by articulating the links between politics and religious values such as integrity, equity, and justice.

Turning to specific labor reform issues, Bliss proclaimed (as McNeill had done) a strong connection between the greater Christian Socialist ideal and the eight-hour movement. "Second only to political action," he wrote, "if second to that, Christian Socialists would put less hours in factories, mines, railroads, and all forms of industry. Other reforms may seem at first, perhaps, of greater importance; but this reform is the only way to give permanent education to the working classes, and without education no other reforms in democratic countries are possible permanently." Taking a page from Ira Steward's arguments, Bliss reasserted that "short hours in the factory develop wants, and wants are the measure of wages. Wages are higher in the United States than in China because American wants are more. Short hours go with high wages, higher character, better homes." As for the familiar opposition from manufacturers, Bliss agreed with most other eight-hour advocates that the shorter workday did not "decrease production. At every proposed legislation to reduce hours, manufacturers have declared that it would ruin their business; but when it has been accomplished, they have gone on, paid higher wages, and produced more goods." Therefore, Bliss concluded, "Christian Socialists should aid every effort to reduce hours. We need more heads working, and more 'hands' thinking." The eight-hour workday alone would not bring about the kingdom of God, but as Steward and others had argued for so long, shorter working hours were a necessary early stage in the gradual transformation of the American economy.[37]

Given Bliss's commitment not just to the church and the ministry but to a church and ministry committed to Christian Socialism, it is not surprising that he left his pulpit at Grace Church in 1890 and set about establishing an explicitly Christian Socialist congregation. Bliss wanted to embody the links between religious regeneration and social activism in a simple ecclesiastical form. Early in the year, the Protestant Episcopal Mission informed Bliss that he had to either give up his editorship of *The Dawn* or resign from the Grace Church pulpit; his superiors insisted that he did not have the time to serve both obligations. He promptly resigned and worked quickly to find a new flock that would follow his vision of religious reform and social activism.

Bliss wrote to the *Labor Leader* in April 1890 calling readers' attention to a new series of Sunday evening services and Christian Socialist sermons at Brunswick Hall near the corner of Tremont and Eliot streets just south of the

Boston Common. Three hundred people came to hear the first service, and twenty-five stayed afterward to help create a permanent organization. The new fellowship would be nondenominational, though Bliss planned to follow the Episcopal prayer book, since he was still an ordained minister in that church. Bliss said that he wanted to "especially invite those who do not believe in the church, be they rich or poor. Christianity knows no classes. We do not believe in the chapel for the poor and the church for the rich. We find true Socialism in the services and sacraments of the church.... Christian Socialists believe in order and not confusion; in unity and not division; we would start no Christian Socialist denomination or sect, but a Mission" to bring organized religion as a whole back to the fundamental truths of Jesus' teachings about brotherhood. Anyone who attended these services would not be expected to leave any other church or parish, nor would they be required to profess any creed or even formally join this new congregation. All they had to do was enter the sanctuary with an open mind and a willing heart to hear Bliss preach his version of a gospel for modern times. Bliss's open-door policy may have been, in part, a strategy to make Protestant-based Christian Socialism more acceptable to Boston's growing population of working-class Irish and Italian immigrant Catholics. Rather than follow the urban mission model at Grace Church, and seek professing converts, Bliss held out Christian Socialism as an ideal of social change and moral regeneration that could transcend denominations and confessions of faith.[38]

Bliss's new congregation—the Church of the Carpenter—was more than another struggling little church in the big city; it became a gathering place for young and old enthusiasts in the cause of religious and social reform. By the fall of 1890, the church was holding regular meetings at 98 Boylston Street across from the Common; the next fall the congregation moved to 812 Washington Street, home of the Wendell Phillips Union. In the spring of 1893, with the Phillips Union falling apart, the church flitted "from hall to hall in search of less rent." Bliss finally relocated to 3 Boylston Place, an alleyway near the intersection of the Common and the Public Gardens. Veteran activists George McNeill and Edward Rogers assisted Bliss as wardens of the congregation, which also included the carpenters' union leader, Harry Lloyd, and Robert Woods from the Andover House settlement. Rogers was still searching, after more than two decades, for a religious doctrine that would meld his deep spirituality with his commitment to the labor movement. McNeill had come more recently to see the beneficial links between religion and labor reform, partly through the eyes of his friend the Reverend Mr. Bliss. Bliss described McNeill, whom Bliss had known from his first days in the Knights of Labor, as "an earnest Churchman ... [and] one of the best speakers in the country on Social Christianity.... His only desire is to wake up the Church. He has no hobby unless it be the Eight Hour movement which is not very radical."[39]

The church, following Bliss's advice, also started to hold regular Sunday evening meals where local labor leaders would break bread with sympathetic clergy, lawyers, and young college women working in nearby settlement houses. Some of these "Brotherhood suppers" attracted upward of fifty diners, who shared food, sang Christian Socialist hymns, and heard presentations on various reform schemes. Vida Scudder, a Wellesley College professor and settlement house activist, remembered the meals as "wonderful suppers, true agape, when the altar at the back of the room was curtained off and we feasted on ham and pickles and hope of an imminent revolution." On one occasion, Scudder brought eighteen Wellesley College students to have a meal with an equal number of female pants finishers from the local garment workers' union.

Despite the enthusiastic dinners, still only twenty-five men and women were listed on the new church's membership rolls. Bliss, echoing the struggles of Christian Socialist minister Jesse Jones and some of the stubbornness of eight-hour campaigner Ira Steward two decades earlier, confessed in 1893: "We are too socialistic for most Christians, and too churchly for most Socialists, but our members are slowly gaining and ... believing in neither unsocial Christianity nor unchristian socialism, we cannot change to suit either class, but quietly stand for what we think the Catholic Truth. Our socialism is not a mechanical scheme, but a simple life of brotherhood." Though the church's membership remained small, Bliss refused to change his message just to please those who spurned his proffer of a more open communion with men and women from all classes. And so the hearty little band of followers soldiered on, doing what they saw as their Christian duty. Three years later, in 1896, the church voted to discontinue as an active parish when Bliss was called to become a traveling lecturer for the Episcopal Church Social Union. (*The Dawn* ceased publication at the same time.) Several church members tried to form a Guild of the Carpenter within the Episcopal Church to continue promoting Christian Socialism, but nothing came of their efforts.[40]

V

While W. D. P. Bliss struggled to find an affordable home for his Church of the Carpenter, the depression of 1893 forced thousands of workers out of their jobs and their dwellings. Boston's labor reform community felt compelled to respond to the nineteenth century's worst economic crisis. Two residents from the Andover House settlement, drawing on new statistical tools from the emerging social sciences, conducted a citywide unemployment survey. They consulted "the highest authorities in the different trades" and concluded that the city had a 37 percent unemployment rate among "the manufacturing and laboring class" in December of 1893. Breaking the data down by occupation, the surveyors found that the levels of joblessness varied widely across the city's different industries. Brewers reported virtually no one out of work—a handful of tradesmen walked an isolated picket line; the rest labored long hours meeting the increased demand for beer as a solace in hard times. Meanwhile, 90 percent of all gasmen were jobless because not only of the depression but also of changing technology. Among the city's 5,000 carpenters, about 2,000 left the city looking for employment, and one-third of those remaining still could not find steady work. Garment workers faced a 50 percent unemployment rate and a 50 percent wage reduction for those still on the job. All over the city, factories that managed to stay open worked fewer hours, and stores cut back on staff even with the holiday shopping season at hand. Employment bureaus run by charitable institutions, such as the YMCA and the Industrial Aid Society, saw hundreds more applicants in 1893 than the previous year for far fewer job placements. The authors concluded their report of the survey by posing alternatives: "The practical question now is whether we shall resort to the soup kitchens and bread carts of '73, or devise some means of furnishing the unemployed with work, and thus help them to maintain their self-respect."[41]

In the closing days of 1893, the unemployed in Boston tried to answer that question with loud demands for public works jobs. Though they obviously had little money or political power, they saw in their growing numbers the potential to voice their grievances in dramatic fashion. In late December, and again in early January 1894, organized groups of unemployed workers made several appeals to the legislature for public works projects. On February 6, more than 1,000 unemployed men gathered on Boston Common, then marched down Washington Street in the heart of the city's commercial district. They carried placards demanding that government recognize their fundamental right to a job, legislate shorter hours, and create "municipal factories where the unemployed can work for themselves." Those out of work borrowed a common trade union tactic: rally a mass of supporters and march them prominently through the political and economic heart of the community. Labor reform organizations had previously held campaign rallies, but public parades stepping off from the Common were something new for them in terms of strategy and geography.

On February 20, the protests reached a climax when 10,000 men marched from the Boston Common to the Massachusetts Statehouse. The marchers, the seemingly forgotten human flotsam of the urban economy, placed the plight of the unemployed right on the government's doorstep—both politically and literally—and demanded that the state do something about those in need of work. Here again, these aggressive tactics were something new for the labor reform campaign—this was bold public political theater, legislative lobbying with a vengeance! As protesters poured into the state capitol, even up to the chambers where the legislature stood in session, a terrified Governor Frederick Greenhalge came out of his office to address the "Committee of Ten Thousand." But the crowd chafed at the governor's noncommittal expressions of sympathy and concern. The legislature—seeing the crowd—immediately passed a motion to hear from a committee of the unemployed the following day at nine in the morning. The protesters then marched back to the Common, from which they dispersed to their homes. Though newspapers dubbed the march the "Boston Common Riot," no one reported any property damage or personal injury. The following day, and for two days afterward, forty witnesses appeared before a legislative committee testifying to the dire circumstances of the unemployed. The committee's report, and probably the fear that more mass demonstrations might follow, prompted the legislature to spend nearly half a million dollars on roads and public buildings, and to create the Massachusetts Board to Investigate the Subject of the Unemployed.[42]

The mass protests were led by two men previously unknown to the Boston labor reform community—Morrison Swift and Herbert Casson. These men did more than just wrestle intellectually with the problem of labor conflict. They waded into the masses of poor, despondent men and organized angry, hungry workers whom other labor leaders and reformers thought could not be mobilized. Morrison Swift was a thirty-seven-year-old Ohio native with an undergraduate degree from Williams College, and a PhD in political economy from Johns Hopkins. He had recently come to Boston by way of settlement houses in Philadelphia and New York, where he often advocated university extension education programs for working people. Herbert Casson was a twenty-four-year-old unordained Methodist minister from Ontario, who arrived in Boston in late summer of 1893 to work as an assistant editor on W. D. P. Bliss's *Encyclopedia of Social Reform*. Casson felt shocked by his first encounter with an urban slum and the growing poverty brought on by the depression. In addition to his efforts with Swift in mobilizing the unemployed, Casson joined a local chapter of the Socialist Labor Party and started to give lectures about his plans to form a labor church by and for working people.[43]

Swift and Casson rapidly gained public notoriety for their position at the head of the statehouse march, but both of these men also wrote extensively on a range of issues, including labor reform. Their published arguments, much like their public actions, showed them to be a new breed of bold, aggressive agitators shaking up more conventional forms of social protest in Boston. Swift, in particular, often thought big and far beyond the confines of Boston. In the summer of 1893, he proposed "A Convention of Capitalists to Solve the Labor Question." Business owners in cities across the nation would convene monthly to hear testimony from workers and "special investigators," and to elect representatives for an annual national convocation. Though Swift provided few details as to what concrete proposals might come out of such meetings, he declared that "the whole labor controversy would be placed on an absolutely new footing ... [with] confidence replacing hostility" as capitalists seized the opportunity to solve the industrial era's most pressing questions. Swift, living on Nassau Street near the city's garment district, also floated the scheme that as of May Day, 1900, all industries in the United States should be organized as industrial partnerships with joint ownership between workers and managers. Echoing the Nationalists, he urged that societies be formed across the country with that single (though immensely ambitious) goal in mind. He also hinted that workers should consider a general strike at the dawn of the new century, if capital did not accede to their demands for economic restructuring.[44]

At the height of the first cruel depression winter (1893–94), Swift turned his attention back to the immediate necessity of public employment for those out of work and destitute. He bolstered his organizing among the unemployed with forceful arguments about the responsibility of capital and the state to provide for those who had no jobs. In a pamphlet written while a resident of the Equity Union on 20 Oak Street (around the corner from his previous domicile), Swift asserted that business owners knew that

> the people were to be in want of garments this winter, [and] if they did not wish to have their own shops operated to produce these things they should have constructed other factories where the people could provide for their own needs; or since they are practically the only influential class in government they ought to have prevailed upon the government to establish these shops as permanent institutions for the unemployed and partially employed to manufacture the articles they require.... The rich should have provided the capital for these emergency shops from their unlimited store, if they were determined not to permit the existing shops to be used to produce the necessaries for the people.

Swift insisted that "when people are freezing and starving," government "must manufacture at any cost. This is where the so-called law of supply and demand obtains its only correct application; the demand is here intense, and *those who are able must supply it.*" Swift concluded that public employment was far superior to a charitable handout—workers would produce tangible goods essential for their physical well-being, and honest labor would maintain their self-esteem.[45]

Swift's colleague Herbert Casson also endorsed these proposals for government-sponsored factories in testimony before the Massachusetts Board to Investigate the Subject of the Unemployed. Casson said that the state's first task was "to assert the right of workingmen to employment," and that the unemployed "should be given employment in their own trades. A shoemaker ought not to be obliged to become a ditch digger." Furthermore, Casson urged "that those who are accustomed to work in-doors ought not to be compelled to work out-of-doors, and hitherto there has been no employment provided for those who work in-doors except out-of-doors." When the board questioned Casson about wages and hours in public enterprises, he insisted that union pay rates should prevail even if the employees worked only three days a week. When board members pressed him to explain how public businesses could sell at a competitive price in markets already glutted with surpluses and shuttered shops, Casson simply stated his belief that the demand for products could be found without putting private companies out of business. The board, unimpressed by Casson's responses or the testimony of other witnesses from across the state, refused to endorse state factories because they saw no specific plan with clear financial details for how these public enterprises would operate.[46]

In the spring of 1894, Swift organized a "Boston division" of the "Commonweal of Christ army" (often referred to in the press of the time as Coxey's Army)—a conglomeration of several cross-country unemployment marches all bound for Washington, D.C. At two o'clock in the afternoon of Sunday, April 22, Swift—as "commander" of the Boston contingent and president of the Equity Union—led a column of more than 200 workingmen once again down Washington Street. Dressed in their best clothes, the men carried banners with the words of Abraham Lincoln: "When corporations are enthroned, the wealth is in the hands of the few and the republic will fall." On the other side was a bolder inscription: "To save the republic let the people own monopoly industries." A placard stated: "Objects—Industry, Morality, Justice." When the marchers reached Boston Common (by way of Hollis and Tremont Streets), they saw 10,000 spectators gathered to see the contingent off to the nation's capital. Swift stood on a temporary platform and warned those assembled that the Commonweal army was under attack "from the enemies of labor, the monopolists." Some in the crowd clearly opposed Swift and his campaign; one group of rowdies tore banners and crushed marchers against a bandstand. Swift ordered his troops to disperse. That night, the Boston division camped out in a local park, from which police tried to evict them. The following morning, 300 men marched out of the city and headed toward Washington, D.C.[47]

When the marchers reached New York City, Swift and leaders of other New England groups issued a proclamation to the press. They called on Congress to

> provide farms or factories where the unemployed now and at all times hereafter may be able to employ their labor productively for the supply of their own wants, . . . take steps to amend the Constitution of the United States so that it shall affirm the right of everyone to have work, . . . furnish immediate employment for the unemployed by beginning the construction of good roads on a large scale throughout the country, . . . nationalize the railroads, the telegraph and mines, . . . see that all land not in actual use is thrown open to cultivation to those willing to cultivate it, . . . [and] establish a commission to investigate the desirability of nationalizing trusts.

This petition was more ambitious and comprehensive—even radical—than any demands from the larger contingents marching out of the Midwest or the Rockies. The wide-ranging document drew on familiar ideas about work relief and labor reform, as well as Nationalism and even land reform. Swift, echoing many past labor reformers, wanted to offer some scheme to nearly everyone so as to bring more supporters over to the unemployed army's cause.[48]

Once he reached Washington, Swift hoped to duplicate the methods he had used with the mass march on the Massachusetts Statehouse months earlier to bring pressure to bear on Congress. He also hoped that Congress would enact bolder economic reforms than the cautious Massachusetts legislature had produced. Arriving in late May, long after most of the "Army's" western detachments, Swift did get to testify before the U.S. House Committee on Labor. But most of his fellow "soldiers" were kept far away from the Capitol, so they exerted little influence on congressional deliberations. Frustrated and hungry, most marchers had left the city by summer's end.[49]

Swift and Coxey failed to achieve their goal of increased federal spending for public works jobs; and, not surprisingly, Congress paid no heed to their more radical demands for economic nationalization and a constitutional amendment on the right to labor for a living wage. But the unpublished transcript of Swift's congressional testimony reveals that this idiosyncratic political economist, whose brief sojourn in Boston had so unsettled the reform community, had even more to say about his innovative ideas for public expenditures and federal regulations. Testifying at two morning committee sessions—Wednesday, June 13, and Monday, June 18—Swift spoke on a wide range of subjects; he even denied being part of a plot to blow up the U.S. Capitol! Turning to the economy, Swift emphasized his idea that creating gainful employment for those out of work was a far better public policy than condescending to give the poor a meager handout. "We have adopted the principle that no man shall starve. We will not allow a man to starve when he comes and asks for alms; but we do say that we will not provide him with the means of making a living. It is an absurdity to say to a man, 'You shall be idle; and if you are idle, we will furnish you food,' while we deny him a chance to work and earn his food. In other words, the community takes out of its pocket enough to save a man from starving, and will not let labor create what saves him from starving."

Swift then went on to discuss his plans for building public workshops, which he had first proposed in his pamphlet on unemployment. He also elaborated on a scheme to store and exchange the goods produced by these factories not "for the market, but . . . for the use of the people who are idle." He again picked up on the Nationalists' call for public ownership of railroads and telegraph lines; and said that such transportation and communication networks could provide more jobs for the unemployed, especially if men went to work extending these services across more of the nation. Swift also agreed with many labor leaders that the eight-hour day would help redistribute available work, and alleviate unemployment due to both periodic depressions and technological displacement. Moreover, he advocated a very modern scheme for occupational retraining—"a system which would provide that these men thrown out of employment by inventions should not want while they are finding another trade; and if they could not get into another occupation, that the Govt. should have opportunities for enabling them to learn other trades." The congressional committee listened politely to Swift's statements and then ignored all his recommendations.[50]

Swift's peripatetic travels took him away from Washington, D.C., soon after his testimony, and eventually out to California by the later 1890s. (He returned to Boston in 1907 and led more mass protests among the unemployed in 1908 and 1914.) Herbert Casson planted his roots, at least for much of the 1890s, in Lynn, Massachusetts, a small city north of Boston, dominated by massive shoe factories. Casson went about establishing a labor church to be run entirely by and for workers. He forcefully distinguished his church from Christian Socialism, despite (or perhaps because of) his work with Bliss and the Church of the Carpenter when he first arrived in Boston. Casson believed that Bliss's congregation did not go far enough in placing the working class at the center of all its spiritual and temporal endeavors.[51]

In his published creed, *What We Believe,* Casson wondered just how strong the bridges were between reform-minded ministers in established churches and the workers they pledged to support. He believed that religious activists had to go beyond being brokers for social harmony and brotherhood, and create new independent congregations where workers' own interests would always be articulated first and foremost. Casson saw the true pro-labor minister rooted first in the house of labor, and not necessarily in a more conventional house of worship.

> Christian Socialism takes its stand in the Church as a Divinely-sanctioned institution, while the Labor Church places itself in the center of the Labor Movement, and says "God is here." Christian Socialism ... is clear-sighted enough to see the strength and final triumph of the workingmen's organizations, and it is therefore trying to scoop up the great current of the Labor Movement with its Churchly dippers into denominational tubs. It wants to put Christian labels on trades unions, and to lay hold of the unchurched masses without losing its grip on the purses of the rich. Instead of declaring itself out and out for the workingmen, it seeks to act as a go-between, and to make itself into a religious Board of Conciliation. It approaches the whole labor movement, not from the side of the worker, but from the standpoint of the benevolent aristocrat. Christian Socialism gives the poor its sympathies, but not ITSELF.... [A]nd while Christian Socialists are generally good and earnest men, they have either not the courage of their convictions, or have their vision dimmed by Churchly forms and doctrines.

Casson then offered an alternative vision of what he believed a true labor church would stand for. The church would recognize "that the great iniquity in our country is inequity." Casson saw that the

> Labor Movement in itself is religious, but it needs developing.... The essence of the Labor Movement is not selfishness, but sympathy, justice and brotherhood. When workers say "bread" they mean a thousand things.... We demand the recognition of our citizenship, our manhood, and our Divine sonship. We claim to be men and women altogether human, and not ... machines. No eight hour day, or six hour day either, will satisfy us. It is not mere wages that we want, but the right of becoming partners in our national industry.... The co-operative commonwealth is not the end of human progress, but only the beginning.

To reach this ambitious goal, Casson declared that it was "time to cease begging for paltry labor legislation, and imploring the attention of rich congregations." Since workers already had their own unions, newspapers, and political organizations; why not create their own church where their demands for social justice could be inspired by the highest moral ideals? A labor church could be a powerful educational tool, not only through Sunday School lessons about the dignity of work and the divinity of working people but also through preaching a doctrine of Christian brotherhood based in plans for a completely worker-centered cooperative national economy.

Casson also noted perceptively that a nondenominational labor church could help unite a labor movement increasingly fractured among rival ethnic groups and competing faiths. Casson believed that the "Principles of the Labor Church" would "provide a platform broad enough to hold all workingmen together, in spite of their different nationalities and organizations." At the end of his pamphlet, he listed those fundamental tenets:

1. God is the cause and strength of the Labor Movement, and whatever institution or individual opposes the Labor Movement opposes him.
2. All who are working for the abolition of wage-slavery are, consciously or unconsciously, working together with Him, and are therefore members of the real Church.
3. The improvement of personal character and of social conditions are both necessary to secure freedom from moral and social bondage.
4. All that is good in the present Christian Church, and in the history of our country, is on the side of the workingman in his struggle for Justice and Brotherhood.[52]

Casson concluded his call for a new church with an appeal rooted in the traditions of antebellum American abolitionism. He declared that "the emancipation of Labor is the greatest cause on earth; and it can be accomplished only by a great moral revolution in Society. The command of God to America is the brotherly division of wealth and labor; the real living religion of our time is to be found in the Labor Movement. The unemployed and half-paid workingmen are as unjustly oppressed as any Negro slaves, and Garrison's God is on their side." Casson believed that he had inherited that mantle of religious zeal in his labor church. He continued to work at his mission in Lynn—living in working-class neighborhoods, conducting weekly services in rented halls, and staying on the periphery of the Boston labor reform community—until his outspoken opposition to the Spanish-American War cost him the support of pro-military workers in his congregation. Casson was then left vulnerable to a new wave of criticism from those who had opposed his labor church from the start—mainstream clerics, local businessmen, and former allies in the Socialist Labor Party. He left Massachusetts in August 1898 and joined the socialist Ruskin Colony in Tennessee.[53]

Casson, like his predecessors Jesse Jones and W. D. P. Bliss, preached about an ideal society where labor reform and religious renewal were inextricably bound together. Casson's labor church represented the culmination of more than a quarter-century of Boston reformers and activists' thinking and agitating on the need for Christianity to return to Jesus' ethical teachings, and to apply those moral lessons to the workplace and the workers' own struggles for justice. The engaged, socially conscious church would save industrial society's soul and lead the way toward a new Christian economy based on brotherhood, equity, and fairness. Cross-class organizing, legislative lobbying, the eight-hour workday—all of these might be way stations on the road to Christ's kingdom on earth, but they were no substitute for deeper social and religious regeneration. Labor reform could help construct the spiritual and moral foundation for a social revolution that would touch men's and women's conscience. But in the end, it would be the radical reorientation, the profound conversion, in individual hearts and in social relations that would lead to a truly reformed world.

The links between labor reform and religious activism, forged by visionary ministers (sometimes in entirely new churches) and challenged by economic depressions and strike waves, offered an alternative model for mobilizing workers and reformers and for leading them on a spiritually uplifting journey. But not every activist or reformer in Boston embraced this renewed emphasis on spirituality; some held to more rationalist notions of radical social criticism. So, at the same time that these questions of piety and protest swirled through the Boston labor reform community, many activists and reformers continued to consider very practical worldly matters. These men and women asked simple questions—such as whether and where to build new labor reform headquarters (other than churches) so as to centralize all the organizational energy coursing through the city's tenements, workshops, streets, meeting halls, and pulpits.

6

SPACES, PLACES, AND HEADQUARTERS

Workers, Reformers, and the Search for
Common Ground, 1879–1900

DURING THE last two decades of the nineteenth century, many workers and reformers intensified their search for meeting places in Boston where they could gather on a regular basis to mobilize for social change. Ever since the Labor Reform Institute had set up Institute Hall in 1867, such sites had promoted cross-class dialogue and cooperation, organizational cohesion, and continuous political agitation beyond the more illusory enthusiasm generated by annual conferences and public rallies. Often combining the functions of a library, lyceum, and social hall, these labor reform centers strengthened the bonds of solidarity and helped attract new members to the cause. Creating central locations for labor reform activities and alliances also gave the movement more physical stability in Boston's rapidly shifting urban geography and demography. Moreover, the Boston labor reform community may have looked for such gathering places, especially in the 1880s and 1890s, because Ira Steward was no longer around to serve as a central intellectual and organizational figure in the movement. Working-class leaders now were more likely to be trade union organizers, with allegiances to their local and national bodies as well as potential interest in cross-class labor reform organizations. Thus, many reformers and activists believed that their campaign had to create meeting spaces to maintain momentum and retain a sense of shared mission. Building such gathering places would allow workers and reformers to leave behind the physical (and perhaps ideological) confines of their homes, and promote continuous efforts to break down social distances and build up stronger alliances.

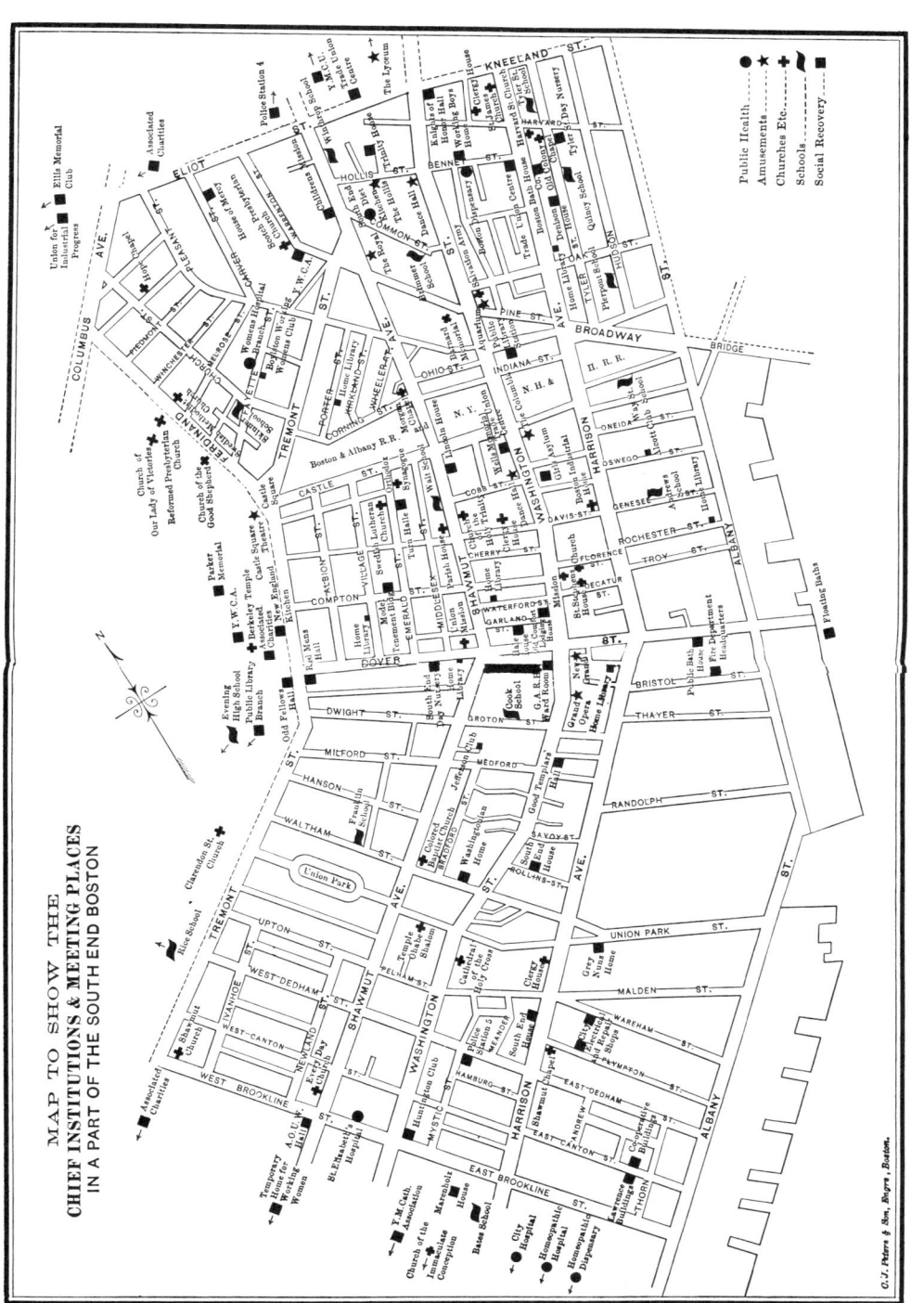

From Robert A. Woods, *The City Wilderness: A Settlement Study by Residents and Associates of the South End House* (Boston: Houghton, Mifflin, 1898).

Four institutions emerged in the 1880s and 1890s and staked some claim—either deliberately or tangentially—to the title of labor reform headquarters. The Wells Memorial Workingmen's Institute, promoted by wealthy patrons as a moral improvement society, evolved beyond that limited bourgeois vision into an open forum for cross-class debate on the labor question in late nineteenth-century America. The institute did not advocate particular reform campaigns but served as an arena for the discussion of social change in a rapidly industrializing society. The Wendell Phillips Union envisioned itself, right from its founding, as the central exchange where all reformers in Boston would share their strategies for social transformation. The Phillips Union wanted, quite consciously, to be the headquarters for all social change advocates in the city and thereby to create a more unified reform vision out of the cacophony of ideas swirling through Boston.

Two settlement houses—Andover House and Denison House—believed that they too could provide a place for workers and reformers to continue building cross-class alliances. But in these houses, gender as well as class shaped the intellectual contours and organizational dynamics of labor reform. The men at Andover House often saw their settlement as a place where dialogue across class lines could be promoted on a daily basis, and class conflicts could be mediated and defused. These men envisioned themselves as honest brokers between labor and capital, sympathetic to the rights of trade unionists while trying to settle strikes whenever possible. The women at Denison House pursued a bolder strategy by first actively organizing wage-earning women into their own union locals, then helping their immigrant working-class "sisters" navigate the often difficult relations between female labor, male trade union leaders, and middle-class social reformers. The deeper they plunged into the world of labor activism, however, the more the women of Denison House wrestled with their potentially conflicting roles as organizers, advocates, and mediators. Though they lived among the working poor, the settlement house residents could never shed their middle-class, college-educated identities and truly experience the meager, hardscrabble existence of low-paid laborers.

Finally, the location of all four institutions highlights a distinct shift in the geography of labor reform agitation in late nineteenth-century Boston. The heart of the Boston labor reform community moved from rented rooms and halls in the city's older commercial center to houses and tenements in the burgeoning immigrant neighborhoods of the South End. Workers wanted alliances that would be more active, and proactive, in the very places where they lived and worked. Labor reform organizations, in the last decades of the nineteenth century, took their campaigns directly into the shops and homes where low-wage workers toiled under the most desperate conditions and stood in dire need of justice at the workplace.

I

In the spring of 1879, friends of the recently deceased Boston minister E. M. P. Wells decided to create a living monument to their departed compatriot. They formed the Wells Memorial Association and, on June 23, opened the Wells Memorial Workingmen's Institute in rented rooms at the corner of Washington and Dover Streets in Boston's commercial district. Robert Treat Paine Jr.—one of the wealthiest men in Boston—became president of the association. Paine, writing the organization's first annual report, articulated its ideological and practical cross-class vision. His appeal for support was no radical manifesto, but it did envision an institute with both physical and intellectual space for men from all walks of life to meet and engage in vigorous and hopefully uplifting debate. Paine's model linked older concepts of labor reform, based primarily on open discussion, with the growing desire to create central locations (permanent buildings) for continual reform agitation. The institute hoped to diffuse class conflict—such as the recent railroad strikes—by encouraging cross-class contact and dialogue to discern the common moral ground that should link all men of good faith. Paine wrote: "Neither the supposed conflict of interest between capital and labor, or any separation of classes between the rich and those less well off, can be viewed by thoughtful men without feelings of profound regret. What duty or what pleasure can be more urgent than to do all we are able, not only to lessen any such conflict or separation, but to prove that a genuine sympathy unites the best men of all classes and spheres of life in strong and friendly bonds."[1]

Paine also astutely noted that "mere professions of interest by rich toward poor are seen to be empty and can do no good." Rather, "some of the men of means and culture, in a great city like Boston, [would have] to put themselves in close communication and true sympathy with the working classes, cooperating with their money in founding and maintaining an institution for the comfort and culture of all workingmen." In his concluding remarks, however, Paine revealed that he still held bourgeois notions of individual moral and economic improvement. He wanted the institute to teach workers principles such as hard work, thrift, and sobriety—values that many workers thought they had already learned quite well. Thus, the Wells Memorial— though it professed genuine concern and respect for the working classes— was still suffused with notions of noblesse oblige toward the benighted sons of toil.

> The very best use of such an institution is . . . to convince workingmen that neither it nor anything else can be of much use to men who will not help themselves, . . . that the source of most of the troubles of workingmen has been . . . their lack of appreciation of the fact that only an increase of skill can in the long run increase their earning power, and only an increase of economy can enable them to take the first step in saving, and only a persistence in saving can make them owners of their own homes and so raise them to the class of capitalists, where every intelligent American mechanic, with fair luck, at thirty years, should be.
>
> The opportunities, the methods, and the spirit of saving can be powerfully developed by this Club. The real welfare of workingmen will thus be promoted, as well as their culture and their comfort.

In his insistence that savings and self-sacrifice should be the new institute's hallmarks, Paine stood in contrast with those labor reformers and activists who advocated the reduction of working hours and an increase in working-class consumption. These divergent views of reform and social change from the top down or the bottom up would continue to compete for attention at the institute until the end of the nineteenth century.[2]

Within four years of its founding, the institute built its own Wells Memorial Building on the 900 block of Washington Street in the city's South End, thereby joining an increasing number of social reform organizations in that poor neighborhood. In the mid-nineteenth century, the South End had briefly been a fashionable home to thousands of middle-class residents. But the opening of the Back Bay to residential construction, and the depression of the 1870s, hit the South End hard. By the early 1880s, the South End's housing market steadily declined as speculators snatched up many private single-family residences and turned them into shabby boardinghouses. The district became home to a growing polyglot population of recent immigrants, who often moved in and out as their prospects waxed and waned. Irish and German families yielded over time to Canadians, and eventually east European Jews—as well as small pockets of Armenians, Greeks, Syrians, African Americans, and Chinese. These newcomers packed into dense conglomerations of cheap rental flats, looking for work in the small manufacturing firms (such as woodworking shops and steam laundries) springing up on the neighborhood's fringes, or in nearby rail yards and the city's street department depot. Reflecting Paine's vision, the institute reached out to its neighbors and evolved into a combination of workingmen's social club, moral improvement society, and night school. There was a library, recreation rooms, and bathing facilities. Also, classes in practical mechanics, a home loan and building association, and mutual health and death benefit societies all found space within the Wells Memorial Building.[3]

Yet the institute reflected more than just Paine's plans. Programs and classes often went beyond being exercises in charity and uplift for the urban poor. Workers heard ideas that transcended the standard talks about recreation and culture being good for body and soul, or the traditional refrains about hard work, sobriety, and thrift leading to middle-class status (though Paine certainly talked about those virtues). The organization's leadership promoted a policy of free debate on potentially controversial social and political issues—a far more open stance than that of many other charitable institutions which deliberately eschewed difficult questions of social justice and stuck only to pieties and personal improvement classes. Wells Memorial, at least implicitly, recognized some of the economic and ideological tensions within its own structure and vision. The institute's superintendent allowed competing ideas about social reform to be argued openly in its classrooms and lecture halls, even when some of those ideas were distasteful to the organization's wealthy trustees. Thus, workers and labor reformers claimed a share of the institute's intellectual and physical space. But the organization never assumed the role of many other labor reform groups; that is, the association was not an active advocate for any particular legislation or organizing drive. Rather, the Wells Memorial became a kind of neutral territory for the public discussion of many challenging economic and political ideas in the midst of a city wracked by class and ethnic conflicts endemic to Gilded Age urban America—a headquarters not for labor reform alone but for debating the very idea of social change in a society rapidly shifting in its economy, demography, and residential patterns.

At the institute, veteran reformers and activists (and their vocal opponents) lectured and argued with eager audiences of local workers. Edwin Chamberlin's speech "The Margin of Profit and Eight Hours" reaffirmed Ira Steward's model of decreased working hours leading to increased leisure, consumption, production, and wages. Edward Rogers closed his "Historical Base of Christian Socialism in New and Old England" by declaring, "Co-operative communities of Christian Socialists . . . would strike at the roots of the evils which disinherit the poor; competition, excessive labor and usury would disappear, and with them the main obstacle to the ownership of homes."[4]

A new generation of reformers also took advantage of the institute's open door policy to educate workers about other great questions facing industrial Boston. John Graham Brooks, a minister who would be a driving force in consumer leagues at the end of the century, gave a series of four classes on the distribution of wealth; "the question of wages. How can they be raised"; "the drift of labor organizations toward State socialism"; and "the real conflict, what can be done about it?" W. D. P. Bliss argued in his presentation "Work for the Unemployed" that "the right to work was a natural right; for existence depends upon labor. This being the case, it seemed to be the duty of society to provide work for all who might need it." Robert Woods, head of Andover House (also in the South End), gave a twelve-lecture course on the organization of labor—including trade union history, "strikes, boycotts, the eight-hour day, the living wage, women's and children's labor, the unskilled and the unemployed." Woods stated that "the object of this course was to show that the organization of labor was a natural and inevitable historical development, and to show that organized labor will move and play an important part in connection with industrial progress. . . . The great federated strike leads the way to a federated scheme of conciliation between organized employers and organized employees." Woods's course was certainly a far cry from Paine's ideal of the sober, thrifty worker striving for his own individual improvement.[5]

Many of these lecture series deliberately promoted dialogue on the labor question. A series of seven talks on the eight-hour day featured reformers, union leaders, and college professors. It was organized "as little like a debating society or a political rally as possible, in order that there might be a real sifting of the merits of different arguments, and a real exchange of views." The informal structure, and the time allotted for discussion at the end of each talk, brought out "men who are not used to making speeches and who are often the most interesting to listen to. Interruptions were allowed and encouraged within certain limits." Of course, the chairman of the program admitted that "the danger of informality is that it may degenerate into disorder, and result in everybody talking at once." Therefore, he tried, though he admitted "not always successfully, to hit the happy mean between too much government on one hand and anarchy on the other." In the end, the chair confessed that most listeners probably did not change their opinions about the eight-hour workday as a result of hearing these talks on both sides of the issue. But he was convinced that, in an era of growing public conflict between labor and capital, "to have the subject thoroughly ventilated, to find that those who disagree with you are willing to meet you and talk the matter over on common ground tends to create a . . . less bitter feeling."[6]

The institute opened its doors to dozens of working-class organizations in need of meeting space. Trade union locals, fraternal lodges, and ethnic societies all rented rooms in the Wells Memorial Building. Again, the trustees made no official endorsement of these groups, and many of the institute's wealthy backers probably disagreed with the specific platforms being promoted. But the association, until the end of the nineteenth century, believed that its open door policy promoted responsible collective action among workers, eased tension between the classes, and brought in needed income through room rentals. The trustees offered their facilities not only for labor meetings and courses on the labor question but also for mediation or arbitration sessions between employers and employees.[7]

Looking back at the end of the century on two decades of such meetings and discussions, one chronicler of the institute declared triumphantly (though perhaps somewhat sanguinely) that the Wells Memorial was the "'Clearing House' for the discussion of social questions. Here during the year the Scholar and the Trade Unionist, the Banker and Laborer, the Statesman and Ward Politician, meet and discuss, usually in a spirit of friendliness, many perplexing questions.... The relation of many of the leaders of labor in our city to the Institute and its executive officers, is one of confidence and personal friendship." Thus, the Wells Memorial Institute continued to see itself filling an important role in the Boston labor reform community—not as an organization devoted to a specific political or economic agenda but as a forum where workers could hear issues discussed in an open manner, and where disagreements did not lead to employer reprisals or physical intimidation.

By the end of the 1880s, another organization—the Wendell Phillips Union—had embarked on a different mission. The Phillips Union wanted quite deliberately to be the city's labor reform headquarters, and to try to unify those competing visions of social change that were always being debated at the Wells Memorial.[8]

II

Nearly a decade after the Wells Memorial's founding, in early 1888, twenty trade union leaders and middle-class supporters (such as Edwin Chamberlin) urged colleagues (such as Jesse Jones) to attend a meeting on Wednesday morning, February 22, in the Tremont Temple to raise money for a building to house "Labor and Reform Societies." By selecting Washington's Birthday as the date for the gathering, and proposing the name "Wendell Phillips Hall" as a living memorial to the recently deceased champion of so many causes, the organizers played on historical symbols and powerful memories in their appeal for funds to erect a central labor hall. More than fifteen years after the bitter split between Phillips and Ira Steward, and with both antagonists now deceased, most of the Boston labor reform community stood ready to forget past recriminations and pay homage to Phillips's courage and candor. Jones responded enthusiastically to the circular and noted that "to build and maintain a Wendell Phillips Hall in Boston is to do a noble work quite as honorable to those having it in charge as to him whose name it bears; and the work so done will make the name resoundingly effective for the good of man for ages to come."[9]

More than fifty people answered the call that winter morning and quickly began to argue over how the proposed building would relate to the existing Wendell Phillips Association, a group of Phillips's wealthier friends who were also casting about for a suitable memorial to the great orator. George McNeill cut through the debate and proposed that those assembled start the fundraising drive with one dollar each. More than twenty men and women opened their wallets and purses in response to McNeill's appeal. McNeill was then elected president of a new Phillips Building Association and headed a committee to confer with the existing organization and decide who would now lead the growing memorial effort.

Later that evening, influential members of the original Phillips Association, such as Lieutenant Governor (later Governor) John Brackett, addressed the assembly. The new upstart group may have been a deliberate attempt to seize the initiative for the memorial project from the more elite association, and to create a public place aimed specifically at the more progressive wing of the Boston reform community. But leaders of the earlier effort did not seem threatened by this turn of events; in fact, they publicly embraced this plebeian groundswell of support for a memorial hall. Brackett, the *Labor Leader* reported, "thought it fitting that the workingmen should initiate a movement for a hall to Phillips." Brackett then referred directly to "the continuance of Phillips' work after the emancipation of the black slaves, and said that he had the prescience to see that the work which naturally and logically supplemented the emancipation of labor in one section of the country was the elevation of labor in all sections, and that cause . . . inspired his eloquence as the anti-slavery struggle had done in his youth . . . and it ought to enlist the sympathies and support of all men in this land who honor the memory of Wendell Phillips."

Benjamin Butler also praised the memory of his friend and political supporter, and reiterated McNeill's call for common folk and small contributors to build the hall. Butler declared: "I wish that there wouldn't be more than five dollars subscribed by any one man in this hall. I want the money raised from the subscriptions of the Workingmen of this country, a five or one-cent piece from all of them would build such a hall as has never yet been raised to the Goddess of Liberty. I want the laboring men, throughout all their lodges and organizations . . . by the simplest contributions . . . [to] accomplish this object—each man having this small pittance show an appreciation which is in every man's thoughts who ever heard of . . . Wendell Phillips."[10]

The plan to raise large sums of money through myriad small contributions from humble working men and women had a certain mass appeal but also practical problems. Many local activists and reformers enthusiastically supported building a central meeting place for the city's labor reform organizations—thereby saving money on rent for union halls and creating employment in the construction trades. But donations came in slowly, and the Wendell Phillips Hall remained a dream for the project's well-to-do and more humble proponents. Three years later, in the spring of 1891, the scheme took on new life when W. D. P. Bliss proposed to "form a neighborhood or settlement in or near Boston, of those animated by a common desire in working for a truly Christian Socialism." In September, Bliss announced in *The Dawn* that he had taken the first steps in his plan by "securing a large house centrally located in Boston to be the city headquarters for the work." Christened the "Wendell Phillips Union," located at 812 Washington Street one block from the Wells Memorial Building, Bliss stated that the house would be the site for "meetings, lectures, and educational propaganda among all classes of society." Bliss and a "few fellow workers" would also reside on the premises, thereby anticipating the strategy used by settlement houses, which soon opened across the city.

The house Bliss rented had probably been built early in the postwar era, when real estate developers thought that the construction of large homes in the South End might compete with the more fashionable Back Bay neighborhood for wealthy buyers. The depression of the 1870s halted much of that residential expansion. Fortunately for Bliss, however, this house had not been subdivided by previous landlords into cheap, cramped apartments. The residence contained seventeen steam-heated rooms and two large halls—one accommodating nearly 100 people and the other even larger.[11]

Bliss deliberately took a more activist stance on social issues than the neighboring Wells Memorial; he wanted the Phillips Union to be the organizational home for all reformers. The union would be a central exchange where labor and social reform groups in Boston could gather, share ideas, and work toward common goals. Bliss envisioned that the Phillips Union, like his Church (and Brotherhood) of the Carpenter, would "recognize no class, [but] bring together the workingman, the lettered student, the woman of culture, in one true brotherhood of search and effort for social regeneration.... We call the building a Union, and mean that all classes and conditions of men shall meet here with an equal welcome." Reflecting his personal philosophy that many different roads might lead to social change, as well as Phillips's legacy of broad-based reform ideals, Bliss insisted that the house would "stand as far as possible for the union of all schools of social thought. It will not be a Nationalist house, nor a Socialist house, nor a Knight of Labor house, nor a Single Tax house; it will not even be a Christian Socialist house."

Bliss placed the house under the "general control" of the existing Wendell Phillips Association "because this organization already stands for the exact purposes of the house, the bringing of reform societies together, and ... will manage the house impartially." He gave the association exclusive use of several rooms in the house and moved *The Dawn*'s editorial offices to this new location. Bliss set up a "free reading room with library and headquarters for all kinds of reform literature." He saw this room as essential to his ideal of reformers sharing ideas and voluntarily constructing a more unified vision of social change; the library provided a physical place with intellectual space for workers to read widely and speak freely. Drawing on his own experience in various organizations, and noting their particular limitations, Bliss urged, "Let Knights of Labor come to study Nationalism, and especially let Nationalists come close to the great labor organizations." He also appealed for any of these groups to rent office space in the union.[12]

Bliss opened the Wendell Phillips Union with a week-long festival in early October 1891. Again, Bliss took great care to ensure that many institutional players in the Boston reform community had an evening to showcase their message. The first night was devoted to Phillips himself, with addresses by George McNeill and others. Subsequent evenings featured the Central Labor Union, Socialist Labor Party, Brotherhood of the Carpenter (holding its customary service, supper, and an "economic conference"), Nationalist Clubs, local assemblies of the Knights of Labor, and a "Ladies' Night" with speeches on women's rights. Every evening included food, music, and booths for selling reform literature. Bliss hoped to raise enough donations the first week to help furnish the house.[13]

Within weeks of the building's opening, representatives from various trade unions, the Brotherhood of the Carpenter, and the Phillips Association formed a management committee to oversee daily operations at the house. Several groups proposed that a cooperative bank, an employment bureau, and a lending library be established. Others asked for classes on political economy, insisting that similar institutions such as the Wells Memorial Association did not offer such courses. (The Wells Memorial did sponsor programs that brought together people from across the city to discuss contemporary social issues, and opened up its rooms for labor organizations to use. But the Wells Memorial still envisioned itself more as a workingmen's club than as a headquarters for the entire Boston reform community.) The management committee also promoted the idea of "labor suppers"; members of the Brotherhood of the Carpenter already knew about this scheme. Any labor organization or social reform group could use the facilities to hold a gathering, with food and music, to educate the public about its ideals and principles so as to increase membership. According to the prevailing logic at the union, "Rich men and business organizations have their clubs, their dinners, their suppers, and by these invite their members into solidarity of interest and of action. The Wendell Phillips Union would do the same for workingmen. If it can do this, and it can if the labor organizations choose, it will become a power in our community unequaled by any institution."[14]

By early 1892, the recently formed Wendell Phillips Woman's Club sent a petition to the state legislature asking for a "board of special commission to inquire into the condition of the laborers of the Commonwealth." The petition noted (a year before the devastating depression of 1893) the "large number of persons out of employment, so many who are regularly employed only a portion of the year, and also many who are working under conditions so unsuitable for health and moral development as to be a menace to the State." Activists at the house also took direct action to improve conditions for women garment workers. A cooperative sewing shop manufacturing children's clothing filled a large room over one of the meeting halls. About twenty-five young women worked there and shared in the shop's profits. Word of the cooperative spread quickly, and other garment manufacturers in the city felt pressure to raise wages and improve working conditions or risk losing employees to the new workshop.[15]

Despite such a promising start, the union soon faced more challenges than it could meet, and in less than two years the house was in crisis. Bliss wrote to the economist Richard Ely in the early summer of 1893, "Our work at 812 Washington St. is all broken up." Caught between demands for physical expansion and increasingly hard economic times, faced with a contagious illness that weakened him, killed his daughter, and drove many other residents away in fear, Bliss sadly concluded "that there was nothing left to do but give up the work there." The cooperative workshop moved to another location, the church searched for new quarters, and by autumn some residents were hoping to restart cooperative housing in a healthier home. But Bliss would not be part of the new scheme—he intended to limit his efforts to the Church of the Carpenter, and *The Dawn,* "which has sadly suffered not so much from lack of money as from time and strength" to edit the journal properly.[16]

The search for physical and ideological common ground in the Boston labor reform community would go on, however, with other individuals and institutions coming to the fore—especially several settlement houses that had opened their doors soon after the Phillips Union, practically in its back yard.

III

In 1892, the first settlement houses opened in several of Boston's working-class immigrant neighborhoods. By the end of the decade, organized groups of college-educated men and women—sometimes under the sponsorship of local churches—had rented or bought a dozen homes near workers' tenements throughout the city. All of these institutions brought working-class and middle-class people into close physical proximity so that the new neighbors would see each other as flesh-and-blood human beings, break down potential antagonisms, and work for social betterment. The houses were intended to function as models of justice, equity, and charity with each resident taking on his or her share of daily housekeeping duties, and striving to transform the urban poor through education and outreach. In effect, settlements aspired both to inspire their college-educated residents with a sense of duty to fellow men and women and to improve the lives of poor neighbors in the surrounding streets.

Many of the settlements in Boston (and elsewhere), however, hewed to a rather narrow definition of reform as moral uplift taught to unfortunate slum dwellers by well-intentioned urban benefactors. These houses and their resident workers—often affiliated with specific parishes or religious denominations—promoted kindergartens and daycare, boys' and girls' clubs, domestic classes in cooking and sewing for mothers, and temperance lectures for fathers. But among the earliest of Boston's settlements—especially Andover House (later renamed South End House) and Denison House—the residents pursued a more ambitious and outspoken agenda that included active participation in local labor reform campaigns. These two particular houses represented yet another deliberate effort to create space where working-class activists and middle-class reformers could come together in a genuine attempt at cross-class dialogue about shared goals for social change.[17]

Andover House opened January 1892 in a large brownstone row house at 6 Rollins Street, between Washington Street and Harrison Avenue, in the heart of Boston's South End—an ideal site for the city's first settlement. It was sponsored by an association of Andover Theological Seminary graduates interested in the ideals of "Social Christianity." (The term Social Christianity is closely linked with the Social Gospel—the concept that churches should be concerned with contemporary social problems, though not necessarily embracing the more radical doctrines of Christian Socialism.) The presiding council also included sympathetic local ministers such as Philip Moxon, but the settlement did not affiliate with any one denomination or church. Its Articles of Association specified that the settlement would "co-operate with churches, with charitable and labor organizations, and with other agencies acting for the improvement of social conditions."[18]

The settlement's "Head of the House" was Robert Archey Woods, a twenty-six-year-old native of Pittsburgh, and a recent graduate of Amherst College and the Andover Theological Seminary. Woods had been introduced to the Social Gospel by one of his professors at Amherst, Charles Edward Garman, a friend of the pioneering psychologist and pragmatist philosopher William James. He also heard President Julius Seelye of Amherst declare "that no career could be of higher service to the nation than that of the educated man who should go among the people and in the largeness of mind and heart join with them in working out the labor problem." Woods pursued his interests in sociology and social reform while at Andover under the tutelage of William Jewett Tucker, who encouraged Woods to interview labor leaders in Boston for one of his research papers. Tucker also formed the Andover House Association and urged Woods—recently returned from a postgraduate fellowship at a famous London settlement, Toynbee Hall—to take the job as head of Boston's first settlement house. Woods was described by one of his biographers as "a little over six feet tall, massive in build, with finely modeled aquiline features. Calm, affable, soft-spoken, kindly, reserved to the point of diffidence, there was that about him which made the tough-minded hesitate to stir him." This quiet yet very determined man quickly became an important player in Boston reform circles and eventually emerged (along with Jane Addams at Hull House in Chicago) as a leader of the settlement house movement across America.[19]

Woods spoke frankly about many issues, including the rights of workers and organized labor. He believed that settlements had a particular duty to reach out to what he termed the "great middle class of labor" (what sociologists today might call the urban working poor)—the 80 percent of Boston's working-class majority who were neither the destitute in need of immediate relief for their survival nor the "aristocracy of labor ... easily accessible on the basis of its ambitions." This core of the working class "scorns charity. It is indifferent to offers of advanced education." Woods saw this "working class proper [as] having the loyalties and passions of the proletariat, in one section of which is the centre of industrial unrest, in another the centre of corrupt municipal politics."

Woods argued that settlements had the "difficult and vital task" of wrestling "with the inherent organic life of the manual-labor class," seeking to understand the physical dangers and economic uncertainties these working men and women faced every day. Settlement residents would channel that class away from violence and political corruption only by confronting honestly the sources of labor's real grievances and righteous indignation. Settlements had to focus on "fellowship," not "relief" or "instruction"—building personal and institutional networks among workers and within working-class neighborhoods to find resources (material and otherwise) for improving daily life. (Today, this kind of effort could be called community organizing.) In particular, settlements had to "foster every kind of organization among workingmen that is wisely designed to strengthen their economic position."

Woods advocated "unequivocal support" for the basic principles of trade unionism—"the knowledge of industrial conditions and the healthy working-class discontent that go with it"—without necessarily giving labor leaders a blanket endorsement for everything they might say or do. Also, by virtue of their physical location as a place where educated men and women lived among the poor as neighbors, settlement houses would bring "capitalists and wage-earners, the educated class and the working class, into a just understanding of each other." These institutions would promote realistic engagement across class lines, as so many cross-class labor reform organizations tried to do, and prevent the elite from looking down on the working class as either economic objects for exploitation or sentimental objects for charity and pity.[20]

In his pioneering social survey of late nineteenth-century Boston, *The City Wilderness*, Woods expounded on his support for organized labor. Though not all workers would agree with his more sunny sweeping conclusions, many welcomed his endorsement of the trade unions' good works.

> The great improvement in all the conditions of labor that has been wrought during recent years is without any possible question the result of working-class organization. The standard wages and the regulation of hours of labor in the different trades, to the entire extent that they represent progress for the working classes, has been secured by organized action on the part of the men in those occupations.... [T]hough the trade unions have many faults to answer for, they have on the whole and in the long run distinctly served in bringing about that considerable measure of industrial peace and stability which exists in Boston.

In a lecture at another Boston settlement—Lincoln House on nearby Shawmut Avenue—Woods peered into the future of organized labor. "As trade unions become stronger," he remarked, "they will take more and more of a share in the management of industry.... They will probably begin to organize co-operative factories for themselves.... [T]he workman who at the beginning of the factory system lost his grip on the tools will regain it; though he will regain it not as an individual workman, but as a member of an industrial brotherhood in which all men work together for the good of all."[21]

Woods backed up his words with actions as Headworker at Andover House—he opened the settlement's doors to a wide variety of labor reform efforts. Within the first year, he established a regular dialogue with many of the city's trade union leaders. Residents also helped organize an employment bureau for women, lobbied for a state commission to investigate unemployment, and acted as treasurer for the Central Labor Union's Relief Committee during the depression of the mid-1890s. In late 1895, the settlement officially adopted the name South End House to acknowledge its allegiance to the neighborhood and to reaffirm its nonsectarian character. The house still had close ties with students and faculty at the Andover Theological Seminary, however, and never hid the deep religious convictions among many of its residents and supporters. Woods and others conveyed a sense of missionary zeal to bring dignity and justice to the poor and to save society, but they never engaged in any overt program of evangelizing or proselytizing in their ethnically and religiously diverse neighborhood.[22]

Whatever its name, the fourth annual report (December 1895) stated that "the settlement comes more and more into relations of friendly understanding with men engaged in the labor movement." John O'Sullivan—former seaman and streetcar driver, labor editor for the *Boston Globe,* and then president of the Central Labor Union—sat on the settlement's governing council. Residents often attended union business meetings and social gatherings, and local workers increasingly took part in "various educational meetings ... for the sake of discussing economic and social questions." Woods asserted that real cross-class intellectual interaction took place within the settlement. The college graduates in residence were "constantly exchanging with groups of workingmen the student's wider knowledge of economic questions for the worker's practical experience of industrial affairs." Indeed, the house now had a reputation as a place where workers and employers were both treated with fairness and respect, and where the residents might serve as honest brokers to mediate labor disputes. Local unions, on several occasions, asked Woods himself to serve on arbitration committees to settle strikes. At the same time, business leaders often perceived Woods as less strident in his support for labor than other local reformers—more inclined to share moderate Social Gospel ideas of compromise between classes than to publicly proclaim a potentially militant Christian Socialism—and employers therefore willingly accepted his intervention. One account said Woods used his "fairness and kindness ... [and] courtesy" to remove the "fangs of class antagonisms." Woods himself more modestly noted that "workingmen ... without any feeling of restraint meet and confer with business and professional men. Such conferences, which do much to alleviate the strain of social unrest, are occurring constantly at the House."[23]

Andover House/South End House promoted ongoing dialogue between college-educated men and workers, and arbitrated disputes between employers and various labor unions. The women at Denison House saw that many of their neighbors, especially female wage laborers, were unorganized and prone to even more exploitation on the job. Denison House residents, therefore, pursued more direct and dynamic cross-class linkages, and actively organized wage-earning women into their own trade union locals. Opening its doors less than a year after Andover House did, on December 27, 1892, Denison House was located farther east and north along Harrison Avenue—in a four-story brick duplex at 91 and 93 Tyler Street—where the South End intersected with the city's garment manufacturing district. It was established under the auspices of the College Settlements Association (CSA), an organization of women's college alumnae that raised money and recruited female residents for new settlements in cities throughout the Northeast and Midwest. The CSA believed that the rising generation of college women should put their education to good use in the service of society and its most needy members, not focus all their energy on just women's rights questions, or retreat into middle-class domesticity.[24]

Denison House's first Headworker was Emily Greene Balch, a twenty-five-year-old Bostonian and recent graduate of Bryn Mawr. Balch and many others actually wanted her college classmate Helena Dudley to take the helm of the new settlement, but Dudley could not immediately leave her post as head of the College Settlement House in Philadelphia. So Balch agreed to lead Denison House until Dudley's arrival later in 1893, though Balch continued to live at home; a decision which, she admitted, contradicted the settlement movement's basic theory and goals. Despite these limitations, she concurred with her cofounders—which included a group of Wellesley College faculty, among them the house's most prolific author on social questions, Vida Scudder—that labor reform had to be one of the institution's highest priorities. Less than a week after the settlement's opening, therefore, Balch and her coworker Kathleen Coman visited the state Bureau of the Statistics of Labor, met Charles Pidgin (the deputy chief), and requested annual reports and other publications for the house's library.[25]

Helena Dudley was older than her classmate Balch, already in her mid-thirties when she arrived in Boston in 1893, just as the city and the nation began to plunge into the nineteenth century's worst depression. Dudley recalled that "not less than 40,000 were out of work from three to eight months. Savings disappeared, furniture and clothes were pawned, charity organizations were snowed under. We listened day after day to tales of misery.... No one who has not lived through such a period among working people can fully realize how cruel and inhuman our industrial system seems." Dudley quickly abandoned the accepted settlement practice of focusing on education and uplift rather than immediate relief. Instead, she placed Denison House squarely in the struggle to find work and material necessities for the unemployed who were flooding into the South End. In particular, residents ran sewing rooms for unemployed seamstresses in donated space at the Wells Memorial Institute. But Dudley also argued that such emergency measures provided meager protection for low-wage workers facing the hardships caused by economic crises. "Relief work," she concluded, "is about as adequate as a shelter of boughs against the equinoctial storm."[26]

Dudley always insisted that real justice for workers would not come by meeting just the most pressing needs of the urban poor through charity and handouts. True reform lay in actively promoting more cross-class alliances to support workplace struggles for steady employment at a living wage and an eight-hour day, especially for the young immigrant women toiling in the squalid tenements and workshops surrounding the settlement. She wanted the influence of the house and its residents to extend far beyond setting a good example or offering enlightening classes. She wanted the settlement to be not a middle-class oasis in a desert of urban poverty but an incubator for activists and organizations that would change the city's social structure. Throwing aside almost all pretense of neutrality between social classes, Dudley made Denison House and herself as Headworker key links between the growing ranks of immigrant working women, the world of middle-class female social reformers, and the predominantly male realm of organized labor.

Dudley, true to her vision, led Denison House and its residents directly into organizing women workers before the end of 1893. More than just talking about labor activism, more than just supporting existing local unions and reform campaigns (which the men at Andover House did), the college graduates at Denison House placed themselves on the front lines in early battles to integrate women workers into the emerging national trade unions of the late nineteenth century. Denison House residents insisted that wage-earning women be organized as workers to protect their own interests on the shopfloor, rather than ministered to as objects of abject pity.

Shortly before Thanksgiving, the residents received a complaint that Knights of Labor organizers were pressuring female garment workers in nearby Kneeland Street to pay twenty-five cents and join the Knights. Vida Scudder and several others went to the local office of the United Garment Workers of America (UGWA) to get the "straight story." Organizers said that the UGWA itself was trying to make the workshop at 40 Kneeland Street a union shop where the women would have their own local and their own officers. The union's secretary stated that "they shall stand for equal pay on piece-work for men and women, and that the U.G.W. will help the women when in distress." Later that evening, nine women from the shop went to the settlement, where John O'Sullivan "explained the advantages and necessity of labor unions and advised separate organization of the women cloakmakers." The shop women then met in the dining room and reported back that "they wished to have nothing to do with the men, did not feel competent to organize by themselves or appoint a committee to see girls in other shops, but would like to do both if the ladies of the house would help them." The residents told the cloakmakers to come back the following Monday night "with as many of their friends as they could bring with a view to organizing."[27]

The next Monday evening a group of tailoresses did return to Denison House to talk about forming a union, and the local UGWA secretary (a Mr. Wilshinski) invited the women to attend a general meeting of the cloakmakers' union at America Hall (724 Washington Street, in the city's garment manufacturing and wholesaling district). Dudley and Scudder both accompanied the women to that meeting. They reported that the "women seemed suspicious and reluctant to join." Workers from one shop offered to form their own local only if one of the Denison House residents would serve as their president. One week later, Scudder went with twenty women to another meeting at the Washington Street headquarters. Under continuing pressure from the garment workers union's male leaders, who wanted female workers organized so shopowners would not use these women to undermine union wage rates, the women reluctantly formed their own local with officers drawn mainly from Denison House residents and not the shopfloor. (Scudder served as treasurer, overseeing nearly $100 inherited from a previous union.) The women workers made a calculated decision that the middle-class denizens of Denison House would be more likely to have the resources and the willingness to protect their interests—as women and as workers—than the union's male officers or even their own fellow tailoresses. These garment workers expected settlement workers to aid them not only in struggles with employers but also in potential conflicts with their union brethren. The settlement offered both leadership and the use of its facilities for local meetings, since the women seemed uncomfortable gathering at the main union hall under the watchful eyes of the citywide male hierarchy.[28]

By early 1894, Denison House residents found themselves being drawn even deeper into the organized labor movement. Dudley became a delegate from the new Garment Workers Union Local 37 to the city's Central Labor Union. In the summer, Emily Greene Balch represented the Central Labor Union at the annual meeting of the American Federation of Labor (AFL). By fall, a meeting of female garment workers had boosted union membership despite the continuing depression and falling wages. Nearly sixty women attended, and almost all of them joined Local 37. A new president was elected—Mary Kenney, thirty years old, daughter of Irish immigrants, five feet, six inches tall, broad-shouldered, with golden red hair and bright blue eyes. Kenney had extensive previous experience organizing women workers in Chicago; she also had a close association with Jane Addams and the Hull House settlement there. Both experiences made her an ideal candidate to continue building bridges between Denison House and the nascent women's labor movement. In fact, Kenney served as a transitional leader for the female garment workers as they moved from dependence on settlement residents, through having a working-class leader with connections to social reformers, to electing officers from within their own ranks. Kenney had also previously visited Boston in 1892 as the AFL's first female general organizer. She gave speeches filled with wit and enthusiasm about the advantages of trade unions—higher wages, more skilled work, real independence—to female printers, carpet weavers, and shoeworkers. She had returned in 1894 on her own to continue organizing low-wage women workers and to marry John O'Sullivan.[29]

In early October, with complaints rising against contractors who continued cutting piece rates and a strike under way, forty-five more women joined the local. The union offered collective support through especially hard times, and the hope that a settlement might be reached with at least marginally better terms for dues-paying members. One week later, on October 9, strike leaders reported that contractors throughout the city had signed new terms with male and female garment workers—a modest but nonetheless remarkable victory in the midst of the depression. By the end of the year, with another winter of little work and low wages threatening the fragile labor accord, nearly 250 union members attended a rally at the Washington Street headquarters.[30]

Thus, despite the tough times, the women of Denison House had seen the fledgling union grow rapidly in size and begin to develop its own cadre of working-class female leaders. Local 37 now claimed 700 to 800 members, out of approximately 4,000 organized garment workers in Boston. Members worked nine-hour days, instead of ten or twelve, and some workers had nearly doubled their wages in the midst of a depression! (This claim might give some indication of how low their wages had been to begin with, or how deep the first wage cuts were when the economy turned sour.) Residents still frequently attended meetings and intervened to ease tensions with the citywide male union leadership, but Local 37 was no longer just the settlement's project; it had an organizational life of its own. And Kenney, as president, drew on her own experience in labor organizing to steer this fledgling group of women workers through the sometimes stormy waters of male-dominated union politics and middle-class women's reform organizations.[31]

The women of Denison House did more than organize garment workers; they also established a Social Science Club—continuing a long tradition in the city of encouraging cross-class dialogue and debate on important socioeconomic issues. The club's biweekly meetings became a gathering place where old hands and newcomers presented papers on both the history and the current status of social reform. Robert Woods often came over from Andover House with some of his residents, once presenting a paper, "New Trade Unions." George McNeill also attended regularly. In early 1894, he spoke on women and the labor movement, the Knights of Labor, and his youthful experiences as a factory worker. McNeill—now stoop-shouldered with a shaggy beard and bald head—may have looked like a kindly professor lecturing to dutiful students, but the Denison House residents were no longer genteel college girls. McNeill certainly must have sensed their commitment to labor and social justice, and probably took keen interest in passing on his experience to a new audience.

Local labor leaders such as John O'Sullivan and Harry Lloyd also appeared frequently at club meetings. As the depression of 1893 dragged on into the following years, they urged the club to encourage even more discussion about trade unions and to actively recruit more working men to join the evening convocations. Vida Scudder noted that these working-class organizers appreciated the residents' support but did not want labor's immediate needs and struggles to be subsumed in the study of grander social theories. Scudder remembered that O'Sullivan had a "face stamped with refinement, but constantly heavy-lidded with fatigue. For he allowed himself scant sleep, and spent his nights, like many labor men, in the endless meetings, and it must be said, wranglings, that obtained in his organization." By the end of 1894, Helena Dudley took it upon herself to recruit new speakers for the club. And, returning to the idea that a settlement could be a neutral meeting ground, she suggested that businessmen and employers be invited to hear the talks as a way of promoting better labor relations in the midst of the continuing economic downturn. Despite these efforts to broaden participation in the club's deliberations, the meetings eventually attracted just several dozen regular participants from the local labor reform community, with only an occasional new face in attendance. Working women seemed to be particularly scarce at these gatherings, preferring to spend their precious free time building their own workplace organizations. The Social Science Club finally suspended its public gatherings in 1897.[32]

Denison House forged even stronger bonds between working-class activists and middle-class reformers by creating a Federal Labor Union (FLU) at the settlement. FLUs assembled workers from various small and unorganized trades into one body that reported directly to AFL headquarters, rather than going through a national trade union. The Denison House FLU (#5915), organized in early March 1894 by John O'Sullivan, translated the Social Science Club's discussions into direct action for cross-class labor reform organizing. O'Sullivan termed his strategy to organize workers—regardless of their particular craft—together with reformers into one unified local as "guerrilla warfare between the lines of industry." The FLU included George McNeill as president pro tem, Helena Dudley as vice president, and Emily Balch as financial secretary. Balch recalled that she was particularly inspired by O'Sullivan's ideal of the trade union movement as not "a struggle for material advantages for a limited class of people but . . . part of a wide-spread and many-sided effort for juster and more humane social relations everywhere." W. D. P. Bliss, Robert Woods, Harry Lloyd, Mary Kenney, and most of the house's residents also joined this FLU. In practice, the FLU initially functioned much like the Social Science Club, hearing presentations on various labor issues. But these presenters tended to be organizers (men and women) visiting from out of town who often talked about the mechanics of organizing, and working women attended these meetings in significant numbers. By the summer of 1894, the FLU began acting more like a union local—discussing fund-raising efforts to pay sick benefits for its members, and trying to help the increasing number of unemployed women.[33]

In the fall of 1894, FLU 5915 devoted a great amount of time and energy to the garment workers' strike, obviously supporting Local 37, which was linked closely with the settlement. O'Sullivan proposed that a committee from the FLU (with Woods as chair, and including Dudley and Kenney) call on contractors and urge all parties to turn the dispute over to the State Board of Arbitration; he worried that if the strike dragged on toward the end of the year, and the end of the busy season to ready the spring line of clothing, workers would lose what little leverage they had in negotiations. Before this new committee could act, employers settled the strike with favorable terms for the union, perhaps in part thanks to Denison House's efforts in organizing hundreds of female garment workers. The FLU's officers then decided to suspend further public gatherings and let the Social Science Club continue to provide the open forum for discussing reform topics. The FLU would now concentrate more of its efforts on organizing campaigns for women workers in other industries such as bookbinding (Kenney's own craft) and dry goods stores, always offering space at the settlement for meetings.[34]

Women workers continued to call on Denison House residents for support in labor struggles across the city. And sometimes the mechanisms of these labor protests—that is, the details of strikes and settlements, rather than the mechanics of organizing itself—could nearly grind to a halt and wear everyone down. Protests could become especially problematic when workers appealed to Denison House after a strike was called, rather than reaching out in advance to settlement residents in planning for a walkout. For example, in the spring of 1895, residents became involved with an ongoing strike at the Boston Gossamer Rubber Company—manufacturers of rain gear—in the Hyde Park community adjacent to the city's southern boundary. (Boston would annex Hyde Park in 1912.) Piece rates had fallen by 40 percent; the women who sewed the raincoats had to buy their own needles and thread; and the owner's son and manager, Henry Klaus, admitted that he regularly violated state law that set the factory workweek at fifty eight hours. Mary Kenney O'Sullivan (having recently married John O'Sullivan in New York, with AFL President Samuel Gompers as one of the witnesses) helped the workers organize a strike committee and chaired several protest meetings at which McNeill, Woods, Bliss, and Lloyd all addressed the strikers. Settlement residents urged Klaus to submit the dispute to the State Board of Arbitration, but he refused. The strikers stayed out over two months; the women were angry and determined, but they had little money to continue their fight into the summer.[35]

As the conflict dragged on, and settlement house residents (particularly members of the FLU) worked harder to find a resolution to the impasse, they found themselves at odds not only with a recalcitrant employer but also with many of the employees they were trying to support. The FLU pressed the State Board of Arbitration for a public meeting to hear the strikers' grievances, but the workers insisted that only employees appear before the board. Then, on May 20, the FLU sponsored a rally where workers did speak publicly about their demands, and a resolution endorsed the idea of arbitration. A second gathering approved another written resolution urging firms doing business with the Klaus factory to press the owner to mediate the dispute. After that meeting, a committee from the FLU was delegated to circulate the petition for businessmen's signatures. One member of the committee, however, John Graham Brooks, spoke directly to Klaus, "saw his books, learned that his reduction was justified, thought his business was now in good condition and the places of workers filled." Klaus "regretted that he had not arbitrated, but felt that he had meant to give his employees sufficient information about the necessity for a reduction." Following Brooks's report back to the committee, the petition was not circulated.

At another public assembly on June 6, Helena Dudley urged that the walkout be called off and cited Brooks's figures and conclusions. Though the strikers certainly knew about the FLU's long-standing support for labor organizing and for the walkout itself, the protesters would not concede the argument to their middle-class allies. The workers soundly rejected Dudley's advice. The women insisted that Klaus had never made any effort to explain why he had reduced their wages, and that they would seek employment elsewhere rather than return to his factory under present conditions. More than money was at stake for these women; they would not compromise their dignity to an employer who failed to show them any respect. The following day, at a Denison House executive committee meeting, Dudley and Vida Scudder puzzled over the "conflicting testimony" from Klaus and the workers and wondered "whether the information as to the real causes and necessity of the reduction was adequately stated to the employees when the cut was made, or at any time." They may have also asked themselves whether—in their desire to hear all sides in the dispute, assume good faith from all the parties, and uphold the ideal of peaceful negotiations—they and Brooks had been duped by Klaus into becoming unwitting agents for undermining the struggling strikers' solidarity. Mary Kenney O'Sullivan—drawing on her long experience in organizing women workers and her roots as a low-paid laborer—pressed for a mass meeting at Faneuil Hall and urged all the strikers and their supporters to turn out for one more show of unity against Klaus. Kenney O'Sullivan later recalled that the strike was eventually settled in the workers' favor. But other contemporary reports state that the walkout had fizzled by the end of June as the owners continued to stonewall the State Board of Arbitration, hired scabs, and then reopened in a new location.[36]

The Hyde Park strike, in many ways, served as a microcosm of the tensions and paradoxes that Denison House residents found in the world of labor reform. On one level, they actively organized working-class women into local unions to secure labor's basic rights on the job, and built a shared sense of women's solidarity that they believed could transcend class differences. The settlement "workers" tried to validate their new status as college-educated "working women" by encouraging working-class women toward some ideal of middle-class respectability through higher wages. On the other hand, the residents could not escape their identity as middle-class and elite college-educated women who did not completely comprehend working-class women's daily struggles and constraints. The women of Denison House put marriage, motherhood, and a middle-class home on hold to live among the poor and actively engage with social problems and social change. But they did not renounce all personal and family wealth in order to join permanently the ranks of the toiling masses.[37]

The residents committed radical acts, more radical in some ways than those of many other reformers. The women of Denison House rejected expectations about what college-educated women should do in proper society; lived among the poor and knew firsthand the problems of urban life; organized unions among working women; and dared to discuss theories such as socialism. Yet most of these college graduates, reflecting their liberal arts education and the middle-class ideals of femininity instilled in them as young girls, insisted that instruction, reasoned debate, and negotiation remained the preferred methods for changing the conditions and status of working women. The workers themselves (and organizers such as Mary Kenney O'Sullivan) had learned through hard experience that confrontation and conflict sometimes could not be avoided and had to be seen through to the end. Thus, for all the close physical proximity of settlement residents and their working-class immigrant neighbors, and relationships often built on genuine feelings of empathy and mutuality, there were still experiential gaps and divergent worldviews that would prove to be nearly insurmountable.

Looking back on nearly a decade of struggles for labor reform, and with fellow reformers and workers, Helena Dudley concluded that the "question of wages and steady employment is the crux of the whole situation.... It has been evident for several years that there is in America ... a serious problem of unemployment or irregular employment," not only in times of depression but even in "moderately good times." Drawing on her experiences with the working poor in the streets surrounding Denison House, Dudley argued that "perhaps there is no experience more embittering than that which comes to an able-bodied man, willing to work, who is faced by the alternatives of the suffering of his family and the degradation and loss of self-respect which comes from public aid." To confront this economic and moral dilemma head on, Dudley advocated not only more unions but also public works projects and "free labor bureaus to relieve unemployment and distribute labor where it may be needed." Picking up on the arguments she made when she arrived at Denison House in 1893, Dudley continued to insist that steady jobs, sturdier homes, and better schools still "bring but limited relief, for at the root of the matter is the need of more equitable distribution of wealth."

To create a truly just society, Dudley held up the ideal of a family wage based on a dominant male breadwinner—perhaps an unexpected yet frank conclusion from an independent college-educated woman who had spent the past decade supporting working women's rights to organize and earn their own livelihood. "The workman should receive wages that will raise the standard of living, wages that will enable the father to support the family without taking the child from school at fourteen, that will enable the child to get some technical training before he goes to work. These conditions obtain in the upper mechanic class which produces some of our best citizens,—better citizens than come forth from the extremes of luxury or of poverty." Dudley also drew on echoes of Christian Socialism to justify her call for a new political economy in America. "If we hold that command 'love thy brother as thyself' of real authority, we shall never be satisfied with any partial reforms. . . . We shall certainly not be satisfied that a large class of the community is put aside to do the drudgery of the world and receive few of its rewards." Rather, Dudley believed that those reformers who shared her vision always had before them "that ideal state of society which will provide for each of its members the opportunity of getting what we most prize for ourselves, a sound body, work useful and not degrading, and such intellectual food as we may be capable of taking to ourselves." But Dudley was also a pragmatist—after all, running a settlement house does require some hard-nosed decision-making and household budgeting skills in addition to a sense of social justice. She admitted "that such an ideal state is not for this generation—nor can we expect it for many a generation to come—but the ideal is placed before us in clear and imperative words."

Turning back to the role of settlements in the struggle for a better society, Dudley asserted that though "my words may seem to imply pessimism about settlement efforts, in reality I believe that such centres of democratic life are the most helpful signs of the times." The work of Denison House was certainly worthwhile, as long as residents remained what might be called practical idealists with a sense of both vision and perspective. Those who lived among the poor had to "realize that while their direct efforts are helpful, they are partial and ineffective" in driving deeper social change. Settlement houses, even those with an activist agenda such as Denison House, had to devote much of their energy to healing wounds inflicted by an unjust society rather than altering the social structure itself. Therefore, settlements were "called to use every effort to awaken the public conscience to discontent with the present conditions of poverty," for only such an inspired mass public could demand the radical political changes necessary for a truly equitable society. Dudley concluded her reflections, which were far more self-conscious and passionate than most of her brief writings, by stating, "If the work of the Settlement seems slight it may at least be considered a step toward that social state that will count all its citizens worthy of not only food and shelter for the body, but further of sufficient leisure to cultivate both mind and soul."[38]

Vida Scudder, often a more intense and politically engaged writer than her friend Helena Dudley, summed up her early years as a founder (though never a resident) at Denison House in blunt fashion. She wrote that "middle-class radicalism desperately needed to be purged of its Utopian ideology; the working-class leaders needed ... a farther vision; and the partial fusion of the two groups—the proletarian movement from below, and the activity in the middle class of many spirits aflame for justice"—was a "chief gain" of settlement work. "That fusion was far from complete," Scudder cautioned, for the true pragmatic idealist was hard to find among either workers or reformers. "But from all sides, particularly from the middle-class groups, is heard the desire for fellowship." Scudder hoped that men and women with real proletarian roots, or at least intimate knowledge of workers' lives, and genuine intellectual depth, would emerge to lead the nation toward a new political economy. And she thought that the settlement movement might be the best place to nurture such people in the midst of ongoing cross-class activism.[39]

Despite Dudley's and Scudder's hopes and ideals about social change, Denison House as an institution had turned away from labor organizing and women's workplace struggles by the end of the 1890s. Why the settlement withdrew from direct action at the point of production is not clear. The residents may have faced pressure from wealthy contributors who grew uneasy with a house at the center of union locals and strikes. The women themselves may have become more uncomfortable and distant from the increasingly poor, polyglot, and transient neighborhood surrounding the settlement. Or the denizens of Denison House may have been impatient and frustrated with internecine union conflicts and labor protests that failed to achieve their goals. After all, college graduates had the luxury of turning their energy and resources to other causes, whereas women working for wages continued to face hard times every day on the job. Despite the shift in institutional priorities, many longtime residents and leaders did not abandon their personal commitments to cross-class labor reform initiatives for women. Witness the fact that Kenney O'Sullivan, along with Dudley and Scudder and others, helped create the Woman's Trade Union League in 1903, an organization that would influence national unions and the nation's labor legislation well into the twentieth century. In the late 1890's, moreover, Dudley and other settlement leaders helped organize consumer leagues that opened up the world of nineteenth-century labor reform to new Progressive-era ideas about middle-class mobilization and economic power.[40]

The struggle to create shared space for workers and reformers in late nineteenth-century Boston took many forms—from the Wells Memorial's open forums to the Phillips Union's bold hopes for a unifying vision of social change; from the men at Andover House actively mediating labor disputes to the women at Denison House actively organizing union locals. These ongoing quests for common ground revealed a labor reform community earnestly trying to understand the complex interactions among class, gender, space, knowledge, and power in a physically expanding and increasingly heterogeneous urban society. These quests, in fact, often raised more questions than answers—questions about the city's political economy at the century's end which these workers and reformers shared with an emerging generation of Progressive social scientists and advocates.

7

NEW MODELS FOR A NEW CENTURY

Labor Reform and the Origins of the
Progressive Movement, 1891–1900

IN THE 1890s, two emerging groups in Boston—the Anti–Tenement House League and the Consumers' League of Massachusetts—stood at the crossroads of a new century, using both tactics inspired by past labor reform efforts and new techniques drawn from the emerging Progressive movement. But, faced with a burgeoning population of immigrant workers from eastern and southern Europe desperate for labor reform—thousands of men and women, speaking strange languages, who had odd customs and unusual religious practices—these organizations chose to shift away from cross-class alliances with shared leadership and toward more hierarchical associations rooted in elite economic and political power. Such leagues saw workers more as objects of reform than as partners in the cause of social justice. For some reformers, their sense of social distance and distinction was growing, and their social vision was narrowing, in a city rattled by class conflict and rife with ethnic tensions.

The anti–tenement house campaigners in Boston worked with investigators from the Bureau of the Statistics of Labor (BSL) and other state agencies, and helped draft bills to regulate (if not eradicate) "sweated" labor in garment manufacturing throughout the city's poorer neighborhoods. But, far more than most eight-hour advocates, this league also expanded its political efforts beyond the Massachusetts Statehouse and sent a paid lobbyist into the halls of the U.S. Congress with models for national labor legislation. The anti-tenement arguments combined some sympathy for recent immigrants shuttered up in "sweaters' dens" with cruder appeals to elite nativist fears of ignorant newcomers and the specter of contagion, epidemics, and revolution. Thus, opposition to tenement work often emphasized public health concerns about infected products more than justice for sick and overworked producers.

Anti–Tenement House League leaders believed that their organization, drawing especially on prominent politicians and ministers, could mobilize public support for new legislation more effectively than trade unions did. Male garment workers, for their part, also wanted to regulate unorganized sweatshops filled with low-paid young women and children. These men were far less enthusiastic about the reformers' broader plans to control all home-based manufacturing, including the labor of garment workers' own wives and children. The Anti–Tenement House League therefore evolved into an organization that championed the rights of recent immigrants to decent working conditions but made little effort to recruit those workers into a genuine cross-class alliance. Its members talked about "sweated labor" more as a problem of reform than as a pool of potential activists to bring into their campaign. As the organization's leadership ranks encompassed only a few veteran activists (such as George McNeill), this league lost out on opportunities to engage politically with new immigrants, to challenge the entire "sweating system" beyond just garment manufacturing, and to try to stop exploitation throughout the urban economy.

The Consumers' League of Massachusetts focused its labor reform efforts on the women and children working in the mercantile sector, as well as back through the supply chain to sweatshops left untouched by anti-tenement regulations. Thus, in some ways, this league addressed a familiar problem—the ongoing exploitation of a cheap labor pool that had subsidized the profits of an expanding urban economy for more than half a century. Yet in other ways, the Consumers' League developed innovative strategies and tactics. It mobilized the growing purchasing power of middle-class women in the retail marketplace to demand that employers and legislators provide better working conditions for their poorer sisters, and better-made products for the women's own homes. This league saw a distinct triadic relationship between employers, employees, and consumers in the modern commercial economy. League leaders believed that educated, enlightened shoppers should patronize only merchants who treated their help right, and buy only high-quality products labeled as having been made under safe and healthy conditions. They urged middle-class women to put their buying power on the side of the poor and vulnerable producers, even as working-class women and children usually remained outside objects of the Consumers' League's attention and not active participants in the organization's campaigns.

The Consumers' League insisted that educating middle-class shoppers about retail and factory working conditions was a crucial component of labor reform for the new century. The organized consumer movement hired paid investigators, who used the latest statistical methods from the emerging social sciences to prepare and publicize reports. The league hoped that such studies would open the eyes of merchants, shoppers, and legislators to the plight of those who worked behind the sales counters and in the back rooms. In reality, the league's research (in addition to that of the BSL) eventually did have some impact on reluctant lawmakers but little influence on recalcitrant store owners and managers.

By 1900, the Consumers' League had achieved modest success with a labor reform agenda based on lobbying for the modification of specific regulatory laws. But the league's grander vision of merchants and manufacturers flocking to produce and promote the organization's product labels and "white lists" of approved goods remained a distant dream. And once again, the objects of the league's reform efforts—working women and children—usually remained outside of the organization's membership ranks, and sometimes beyond the reach of legislative edicts or label campaigns.

I

Tenement-house "sweatshops" were a source of complaint, consternation, and controversy in cities across the late nineteenth-century United States, and Boston was no exception. Deteriorating wages (piece rates), long hours hunched over scissors and sewing machines, and cramped, ill-ventilated working conditions in clothing manufacturing led to protests among tailors and organized garment cutters in the late 1880s. Published accounts claimed that filthy workshops not only endangered the health of laboring men, women, and children but also infected the clothing sold. Governor William Russell ordered an investigation of the garment trade in early 1891 by the BSL and the District Police. The official report corroborated many of the accusations of exploitation and ill health leveled by workers and their supporters in the press and pulpit. The Massachusetts legislature then passed a bill in May 1891 to regulate tenement house manufacturing in the state and to label out-of-state goods as tenement-made. Subsequent amendments required even families working in their own quarters to get a license from the Board of Health certifying that they were making clothing under proper sanitary conditions.[1]

On March 6, 1891, at the height of the public and political agitation about sweatshops and tainted clothing, a small group of men met at 122 Boylston Street opposite the Public Gardens and organized the Anti–Tenement House

League. On September 14, at a meeting held in the Parker House hotel near the Boston Common, the new organization elected officers. The leaders included George McNeill as well as former governor John Brackett. An advisory committee of fifteen men, mostly ministers, was also elected. W. D. P. Bliss and Philip Moxon served on that committee. Despite the league's name, it was not an organization devoted to housing reform; rather, its early efforts focused on securing further legislation to regulate tenement-based manufacturing (especially the production of ready-made clothing). In its "Declaration of Principles," the league said that it stood for the idea "that the right to buy cheap is not the right to buy the lives of the working people for wages below the cost of production; that the right to sell dear is not a right to sell, at [the] price of honest goods, wearing apparel adulterated with dirt, disease, and the degradation of the people; that the right to charge rent for room to live in is not the right to charge for tenements that are packing holes for their occupants; and that the right of officials to draw salaries is not a right to be paid for failing to enforce the laws concerning fire-escapes, safe plumbing, the control of contagion and overcrowding."[2]

The league also asserted, "not as a favor but as a right," that Boston clothing manufacturers should "take immediate and efficient measures to abolish this menace to the health, wealth and morals of society, that they reverse competition and make theirs a rivalry to see who shall best serve producers and consumers, and that they bring their industry up to at least the level of the factory, which God knows is low enough." While the league believed that each individual had "a sacred right to work, . . . we have a more sacred right to save him from working harm to himself and the community." The league also declared its support for "weekly inspection, and Proof of its performance, of every room where the manufacture of wearing apparel is carried on." And, anticipating its later lobbying efforts, the league insisted "that Massachusetts may no longer serve as a dumping ground for the infected clothing made in the slums of New York—having enough of its own—we call upon the National Legislature to use against the Sweating System the national powers to regulate interstate commerce and protect the public health."[3]

Throughout 1891, the league provided information about working conditions in tenements to the state investigations, helped draft the bill regulating tenement-house labor, held rallies throughout the city, and publicly urged clergy to join the effort to regulate tenement workshops. In late November, sympathetic ministers spoke to a mass meeting at the Meionaon hall under the Tremont Temple. And twice in December, with the holiday shopping season at hand, the league invited clothing dealers from across the city to a conference "to discuss ways and means for the suppression of the tenement house sweating system." Both times, no more than a handful of merchants showed up.[4]

Right after the first of the year 1892, the league expanded the scope of its political agitation and petitioned the U.S. Congress to investigate tenement-house sweatshops in all the nation's large cities. The league's leaders realized that the sweatshop labor problem was nationwide, and deeply rooted in the industrial economy as a whole. No state law—no matter how carefully written or well enforced (and the Massachusetts legislation was said by some critics to be both full of loopholes and poorly executed)—could regulate the national market for manufacturing and selling cheap clothing. The league asked the U.S. House and Senate to do something about "these Libby prisons {Civil War prison in Richmond, Virginia} of our modern industrial system." Expanding on the prison metaphor, the petitioners wrote about the "sound of the moving machines . . . like the clanking of chains by many prisoners working at their tasks. And prisoners indeed they are, and the jailer is Hunger!" In particular, "thousands of women in our large cities have become affected by this frightful system, and are hovering between prostitution and starvation." Though certainly sympathetic to those workers exploited in sweatshops, the authors also played on elite nativist fears of ignorant immigrants and "bloody revolutions" in their appeal to the Congress. "These are the class that will ultimately bring sorrow and destruction to our civilization," the petitioners warned, "for their grinding slavery is such that they have only their miserable lives to lose and everything to gain by rising and instituting a reign of pillage and murder."[5]

To buttress its claims of degradation, the league cited a British Parliamentary report on the sweating system, and another petition for an investigation from the American Federation of Labor (AFL). The authors also pointed out that "mechanics all over the land, who already feel the approaching decay of their trade from the same causes that have brought the clothing trade to its deplorable condition," would support congressional investigation and action. The league closed its lengthy petition with a gloomy prediction for the politicians if they chose not to legislate—something even more frightening than losing an election. Hitting hard on themes of modern science, public health, and near-biblical pestilence (which seemed to strike a deeper chord with Congress than appeals for laboring people to have decent working conditions), the authors wrote: "We lay no claim to prophetic insight, but reason tells us that unless prompt action is speedily taken, Nature will rectify the evils of the tenement house system, where diseases fester, by a great plague which will sweep over the country sparing neither high nor low. This is no exaggeration, for the conditions are ripe and the germs of disease are rapidly being disseminated throughout the country.... This natural process of a plague seems to be the only cure for the sweating system unless Congress shall act."[6]

In addition to its dramatic pleas and petition, the league dispatched its secretary, John Crowley, to Washington to personally lobby senators and representatives for national action on tenement-house labor. Crowley had campaigned publicly against sweatshops since 1889 when, as a twenty-seven-year-old immigrant from England with nearly a decade's experience in the garment industry, he was elected secretary of the Clothing Pressmen's Union in Boston. Crowley then organized a coalition of mostly immigrant pressmen, tailors, cutters, trimmers, and sewing machine operators—the Boston Clothing Trade Advisory Board—to speak out in opposition to tenement-house work. Unionized garment workers (mostly men) particularly favored laws that would shut down unorganized sweatshops employing large numbers of low-paid young women and children. These men showed far less enthusiasm for reformers' efforts to regulate household garment work where the tailors' wives and children did the finishing. Workers and reformers may well have agreed that the ultimate goal was for men to earn enough so that the rest of their families would not have to toil under tenement sweatshop conditions. But workers also knew the current reality—family labor was often a necessity for family survival in an urban economy of increasingly intense piecework and falling piece rates. Thus, legislating such homework out of existence could lead to more rather than less hardship for such hard-pressed families.

Crowley headed an investigation of sweatshops in New York City that led to a public exposé on Labor Day and the first clothing trade label. (Union labels were a forerunner of the legislatively mandated inspectors' tags.) He also worked with the Massachusetts state investigation in 1891 and became secretary of the Anti–Tenement House League at its inception. As secretary, Crowley helped write most of the league's public statements, including its appeals to clergy and a letter to the local postmaster warning him that letter carriers wore uniforms made in "reeking tenement houses." Crowley drew on his own experience of working and organizing in the garment industry to serve as the league's key spokesman. But he also became convinced that the league itself, a labor reform organization filled with sympathetic ministers and politicians, would mobilize public opinion and legislation even more effectively than trade unions. And he now endorsed the broader efforts to regulate all tenement and home-based garment manufacturing, which did not endear him to his union brethren.[7]

Senator George F. Hoar (Republican, Massachusetts), an honorary vice president of the league, encouraged Crowley to draft a national bill regulating tenement-made clothing. Crowley's proposed legislation echoed Massachusetts law with its provisions for clothing labels, inspectors appointed by the secretary of the treasury, and a ban on the interstate sale of any clothing manufactured under unhealthy or unsafe conditions. Hoar then presented the bill to the Senate, where it was referred to the Committee on Education and Labor.[8]

Meanwhile, in March and April of 1892, the House Committee on Manufacturers sent a subcommittee including Congressman Sherman Hoar (Republican, Massachusetts) to Boston and New York to hear testimony about sweatshop conditions from workers and merchants in the clothing industry. On April 12, at the post office building on State Street in the heart of the city's financial district, Crowley testified before the three-man panel. In an effort to press the case for a nationwide law, Crowley bluntly criticized the shortcomings of the Massachusetts statute that he had promoted less than a year earlier. He stated that at least 150 sweatshops in Boston did contract work for the "best firms" in the city, and that despite the legislation recently enacted, conditions continued to deteriorate. The presence of inspectors, Crowley argued, merely gave manufacturers an excuse to claim that their garments were now clean and safe, even when everyone in the industry knew that many establishments had yet to be examined. Moreover, even if particularly nefarious tenement workshops were shut down, subcontractors moved their operations to cramped rental space in old warehouses, and the sweating system went on unabated. Crowley insisted on national legislation to standardize labels so consumers could know where clothing was made. "The advantage we would get," he stated, "would be that plate glass and marble" in a department store "couldn't be a substitute for cleanliness." Under the present system, "purchasers are deceived. They pay their money under false pretenses.... If they knew where the clothing was made they wouldn't touch it with a 40 foot pole." Crowley also argued for legislation to license all garment manufactories, for license numbers to appear on all the clothing labels, and for a "law to hold the owner of property responsible for filthy and overcrowded conditions."[9]

The House subcommittee published its report in early 1893, including graphic testimony from Crowley and dozens of others intimately connected with sweatshops. But the committee merely recommended that Congress enact some form of legislation "to prevent interstate commerce in articles of clothing or personal wear made under unhealthy conditions of manufacture ... with least interference with the business of the citizen, and least exercise of Federal jurisdiction." By 1894, Hoar's bill still languished in a Senate committee, and the House had yet to act on its own vague committee recommendations. (The nation's plummeting economy may have added to the legislative inertia on regulation of the garment industry.) The league, with offices now at 53 Chandler Street on the northern fringe of the city's South End, responded to this stagnant climate by conducting its own investigations of children under fourteen being employed in local manufacturing sites, workplaces without fire escapes, and sweatshops with unhealthy working conditions. The league also dispatched Crowley again to Washington. He conferred with Senator Hoar and Senator James H. Kyle (Populist, South Dakota), chair of the Committee on Education and Labor, and drafted another bill for the committee in April. Crowley also met with Congressman John DeWitt Warner (Democrat, New York), who had chaired the House subcommittee. Warner agreed with Crowley that the earlier hearings supported all the arguments against sweatshop labor. But Warner's committee had held back on legislation to see if newly enacted state regulations would have any effect on the problem of tenement-house manufacturing. Now, however, realizing that state laws could not cope with a national problem like sweatshops and the interstate sale of substandard garments, Warner endorsed Crowley's efforts to draft national legislation.[10]

As Crowley worked the halls of Congress trying to move an anti-sweatshop bill out of committee, he also tried to restore his reputation following a torrent of recent criticism from old labor union colleagues back in Boston. Shortly after the first of the year, 1894, the president and secretary of District Council No. 2, United Garment Workers of America, sent a letter to the league's president (Rev. A. A. Miner). The union leaders cautioned the league that it "was a farce as it now exists" and "its actions [were] regarded with suspicion and distrust" because its secretary, Crowley, had been expelled from the union for "misappropriation of funds and many other offenses." This expulsion had occurred back in March 1891, the same month in which the league was formed. The UGWA had charged Crowley with selling union labels for his own personal profit without regard to working standards or wage rates. (The union may also have been angry with Crowley for joining the reformers' campaign to control all home-based garment manufacturing, including the finishing of clothing done by families in their own apartments.) At present, the union leaders wrote, "we can expect nothing" from Crowley, for he had been "tried and found wanting when in the ranks of the working class."

In the same letter, the union also claimed that it had previously warned the league about Crowley's misdeeds. In fact, this correspondence may have been part of an ongoing dispute between Crowley and certain local labor leaders whom he accused of being bought off by clothing manufacturers. The UGWA officers concluded that the league had chosen to stand by its secretary and thereby risk its credibility among Boston workers. They asserted that the money raised by the league was now "wasted in supporting in scheming idleness a man who neutralizes all your efforts." The union asked for "an impartial committee to investigate" its charges "in the name of the seamstress toiling far into the night and periling her honor for bread in the sweaters dens . . . in the name of the little children whose babyhood is but an apprenticeship to the degrading labor of later years."[11]

Neither Crowley nor the league took these charges lying down. The league appointed a committee to investigate the matter, and Crowley vigorously defended himself. On February 5, one month after the union sent its letter to the league, Crowley wrote to George McNeill trying to get a written copy of the accusations leveled against him. Crowley knew that McNeill was a member of the investigating committee, as well as a man with impeccable credentials in both union halls and the entire Boston labor reform community. Crowley felt stonewalled by the league leadership, and wanted his day in the court of public opinion as soon as possible. He confidently told McNeill: "I do not want a particle of sympathy, or the slightest consideration that may not be given to the other side. All I ask for is prompt action and a fair trial. The fact is that the good name of the League is being jeopardized and dragged in the mud . . . and delay in this trial means more time to inject poison and more time for it to take effect. Whether this thing goes my way or another I want it settled right off. This delay is intolerable."[12]

With Crowley under investigation, the league's executive committee carefully reviewed all the secretary's official actions; Crowley chafed under the committee's close watch. The same day he wrote to McNeill, he also penned a letter to another member of the investigating committee, A. A. Carlton. Crowley pleaded that he was "anxious and ready to go on with the work of the League." But under the new arrangements giving the executive committee direct control over everything he did, Crowley warned that "it will not be my fault if being ready to work I am not authorized to do anything." Crowley was especially indignant that his fund-raising efforts for the league, from which he appears to have drawn a commission to support himself and his wife, now hung under a cloud of suspicion because of the garment workers' accusations. "I have told you in minute detail," he insisted to Carlton, "why and wherefore the collecting of money thro' circulars cannot be done on a decent scale without an outlay of at least $25 weekly. My position on this question is familiar to the Rev. Mr. Bliss and I believe to McNeill." Crowley seemed particularly exasperated because the more money he raised in difficult personal and economic circumstances, and the more commission he earned, the more he was criticized for his efforts! The strain was showing in his letter and, he implied, affecting his wife: "Why don't your committee let me know just exactly what they want me to do? I have collected nearly or quite $1500 in less than three months and received nothing but criticism for my pains. The cry was: 'It's a fine thing for you and Mrs. Crowley.' Yes, it was, only I am afraid that the 'fine thing' is going to cost Mrs. Crowley her life. You may rest assured that if I again take charge of collecting money, it will be in my own way; and without the slurs I have received in the past."[13]

Crowley survived the attacks on his reputation and retained his position as secretary; but he and the league never persuaded Congress to make the Massachusetts legislation regulating tenement-house labor a model for national law. Draft bills continued to linger on in committees. Crowley and the league's political struggles also revealed deeper tensions and limitations within their efforts to build alliances to eliminate labor exploitation.

On the one hand, the league championed some of the poorest, most exploited workers in Boston, and their demands for decent working conditions. Many garment workers were recent Catholic immigrants from Italy, or Jews from Poland and Russia. The 1891 BLS report on contract labor in the clothing industry found that nearly 80 percent of contractors surveyed were "Hebrew," and 60 percent of employees were either Jews or Italians. BLS officials admitted that the figures did "not represent the total number of employees engaged on contract work in the city, [but] they may be considered to represent the relative preponderance of the different nationalities employed." These workers were usually physically and culturally isolated from the rest of the city, as they clustered in the cheap rental flats of the South End and North End. Sympathetic reformers often still seemed ill at ease with these foreigners' strange languages, customs, and religions. And the emerging garment workers' unions debated whether it was even possible to organize the newcomers. Whole families—fathers, mothers, and small children—scratched out a living in their own cramped tenements, or trudged off to work long hours in a nearby sweater's den. The law attempted to eliminate the worst specimens of crowded, filthy, and ill-ventilated tenement workshops, despite problems with enforcement because of a small and chronically overwhelmed staff of state inspectors. And, in fact, basic sanitary and working conditions often did improve when the law *was* enforced, but the wages of these unskilled immigrant workers usually remained abysmally low.[14]

On the other hand, the league did not often try to recruit these newcomers into the organization itself. Even though it is true that the anti-tenement campaigners did not join the nativist, immigration-restriction efforts of the late nineteenth century, neither was their sympathy for recent arrivals all-encompassing. Helping exploited workers was one thing; building a coalition with them was another matter. Cross-class alliances seemed to founder not on questions of skill, occupation, or even immigrant status itself, but on specific ethnicities and religions. Protestant reformers and workers were less than comfortable building organizational links with Catholic and Jewish immigrants. Therefore, league leaders—even veteran activists such as McNeill and Crowley—lacked the perspective of these most recent arrivals, and did not always consider the economic and social consequences of their reform campaign. For example, if tenement-house labor were eliminated completely, would the unemployed families receive assistance in finding new jobs and maintaining cohesive households? Would immigrant fathers ever earn enough money so that their wives and children would not have to take in piecework? Moreover, despite the occasional rhetorical blurring between tenement-house labor, sweatshops, and the "sweating system," the league's campaigns focused almost solely on labor in tenement apartments and districts (especially garment manufacturing). Thus, state legislation eventually licensed and closely regulated much of this tenement-house labor, including work done by families in their own living quarters. But the law included many loopholes in defining exactly what sites were to be controlled; production done in nearby workshops or warehouses, often just as squalid and poorly remunerated, went on virtually unchecked.[15]

Several perceptive state officials noted these limitations in legislation, and in the league's arguments, when they confronted every day a complex network of sweated industries beyond the tenements. Factory inspector John Plunkett observed that the anti–tenement labor campaign merely scratched the surface of exploitation in the burgeoning urban economy. He pointed out that the sweating system "has been imposed in other industries for years upon the unfortunate immigrant coming to this country, particularly at periods when an immense number of one class or nationality is forced to come here on account of persecutions or for other causes from European countries. It was and is successfully imposed today upon what is called the unskilled laborer, in the building of railroads, streets, sewers, and [the] like. So we find that legislation was not enacted against the sweating system, but against the tenement-house system of manufacture, which was but the effect of the sweating system in the clothing industry." Horace Greeley Wadlin, chief of the Massachusetts Bureau of the Statistics of Labor in the 1890s, argued that the key underlying motive for laws "against the manufacture of clothing in filthy and presumably disease-infected tenements . . . was the protection of the public against an infected product, rather than the protection of the workers against the exaction of the sweater. It was, in fact, sanitary legislation rather than industrial legislation that was sought." Thus, Wadlin and Plunkett both concluded that although the anti-tenement legislation had an impact within its modest sphere of industrial influence, these laws did not lift many other workers out of the sweaters' dens because they did not tackle exploitation in the urban economy as a whole.[16]

II

The Anti–Tenement House League, whatever its limitations, also anticipated arguments that would help to shape yet another new labor reform organization in late nineteenth-century Boston: the Consumers' League of Massachusetts. One article in the Anti–Tenement House League's newspaper, *American Home Life,* from December 1893, pointed out that "people who enjoy fair incomes and have comfortable homes do not realize or stop to consider that, when they look over the advertisements for 'bargains' in clothing or manufactured articles generally, they are offering a premium on the encouragement of long hours and poor pay to their less fortunate brothers and sisters. The firms that undersell their rivals are usually firms who are merciless in their demands upon their employees." The league urged its readers to use their purchasing power and selective shopping practices to encourage better labor conditions. "Pay a fair price for the articles you buy, and buy them where fair wages are paid for the labor of the employees, and you are encouraging fair treatment to all and an increased prosperity to their country at large which means also, you in particular." Seeing that women often made daily shopping decisions for the family, the article concluded that these wives and mothers should "interest themselves in the work of benefiting their less fortunate sisters by dealing only with such firms as pay employees wages as will permit them to exist without selling their womanhood." Four years later, the Consumers' League of Massachusetts would extend these ideas about patronizing ethical, fair-minded merchants and mobilize large numbers of middle-class women into a powerful constituency for labor reform.[17]

The Consumers' League movement also had roots in the growing labor reform efforts of working girls' (women's) clubs across Boston. These clubs began in the mid-1880s as a means for wealthy women to sponsor groups of clerical workers, retail employees, seamstresses, or other urban working women. Early clubs often focused on self-improvement classes emphasizing personal appearances and social graces. In theory, the clubs were also supposed to teach self-reliance and self-government, but well-to-do benefactors sometimes tried to use their power of the purse to exert more control over these groups than working women wanted. Thus, hopes for working-class independence, or even cross-class cooperation, often collided with paternalism and power grabs. By the mid-1890s, faced with the same harsh economic conditions confronting all cross-class organizations, some working girls' clubs began to shift their emphasis from personal uplift to discussions of reforming the industrial economy and meeting their members' immediate needs for jobs. Moreover, some club leaders insisted that, no matter what wealthy sponsors might want to say, it was now incumbent upon wage-earning women to set this new agenda.[18]

Reflecting this shift in emphasis, the Massachusetts Association of Working Women's Clubs threw its support, in late 1895, behind the campaign for an eight-hour workday in dry goods stores throughout Boston. Individual clubs circulated petitions in the first months of 1896, calling for earlier closing hours, and "thousands of thoughtless women thus learned the inhumanity of late shopping." Moreover, so as "not to antagonize the heads of the large mercantile establishments," club officers also interviewed store owners to solicit the business leaders' opinions and encourage their cooperation. By the end of the year—retailers being especially sensitive to public demands—many shops now opened at 8:30 a.m., closed at 5:30 p.m., and gave their help an hour's lunch break at noon. One club leader echoed earlier eight-hour advocates: she concluded that shorter hours led to "*increased personal efficiency*" among the retail staff, and "that there had been no falling off of sales in consequence."[19]

The association also investigated the system of fines for tardiness and carelessness in stores and factories in May 1896. They concluded that such penalties were not excessive but did recommend that employers put all proceeds into a "General Benefit Fund" to reduce any ill feeling about the system. In that same spring, the association helped to organize the Women Clerks' Benefit Association and by the following year, this clerks' union was pursuing its own citywide campaign to eliminate fines.[20]

The association also reported, in 1897, that many clubs were now discussing "the necessity of a higher conception of the relations between employer and employee, buyer and seller." This interest in reforming economic relationships "was especially manifested in the deep impression made on" wage-earning women "by the idea of the 'Consumers' League.'" O. M. E. Rowe, from the Shawmut Club (founded in 1886 on Shawmut Avenue in the city's South End), argued that "associations of clubs may do a larger work to advance shorter hours. Perhaps the next step may be a cordon of consumers' leagues from Maine to California. There are large areas of sweat-shops, petty retailers, bakeries and small industries, which evade the law and grind relentless hours of toil. They are still untouched by the great movement for a short work-day." Rowe's fellow "club worker" and statewide director, Edith Howes, added: "Are not those of us who work in our clubs, side by side with women who are oftentimes the victims of the desire for bargains, allied to this movement, as other women cannot be? Do not all these questions come to us with a force, and with an appeal, that cannot come to those whose friends are not the workers who are suffering?"[21]

In early spring 1897, near the time when Rowe and Howes gave their speeches, John Graham Brooks called a meeting in Association Hall with fellow ministers, labor leaders (such as John O'Sullivan), settlement house workers (such as Robert Woods), and others to discuss forming a Consumers' League in Boston. Brooks would quickly emerge as one of the key figures in this Consumers' League; even though the organization was designed to mobilize middle-class women to use their growing consumer power to leverage better working conditions for women and children, especially those laboring in retail stores and sweatshops. Brooks was fifty years old, a graduate of Oberlin College and the Harvard Divinity School, and an ordained Unitarian minister. By the mid-1890s, he had left the pulpit to serve as a traveling strike investigator for the U.S. Department of Labor. He also lectured and wrote on a wide range of reform issues, including old age pensions, workmen's compensation, cooperatives, and settlement houses.[22]

In May 1897, a committee recommended that a new league be formed around the following objectives: "*first,* to promote and to foster intelligent and conscientious buying; *second,* to improve conditions of retail shops by recommending those which offer good conditions to their employees; and *third,* indirectly to improve the conditions under which goods are produced by increasing and formulating the demand for those produced under proper conditions." The committee also stated that in order to reach its goals, the league should collect and publish information about existing shop conditions, and the "willingness of retail dealers to supply and certify to goods produced under proper conditions." The committee urged that Edith Howes take on the task of collecting information about labor conditions in Boston's retail sector, and that she work with her own Massachusetts Association of Working Women's Clubs which already had investigating experience in this arena.[23]

In September 1897, the league—meeting now at 264 Boylston Street, headquarters of the Women's Educational and Industrial Union (WEIU)—organized a standing Investigating Committee (with Edith Howes as temporary chair) to "inform themselves, by consultation with Chief [Rufus] Wade and inspectors, of the conditions, in Boston, of the manufacture of white goods and cloaks." The new committee would also talk with local department store managers to ascertain "their opinion of a proper estimate of a fair house" and "what goods they will guarantee as made under good conditions." If granted permission, the committee planned to visit workrooms to see whether they were in compliance with Massachusetts factory laws, "whether their prevailing wages are reasonable," and whether employees had a regular lunch hour, vacation with pay, or overtime pay. One month later, the league decided that even if merchants guaranteed the products as made under good conditions, it would "approve no goods without investigating the conditions of their manufacture. Miss Howes was asked to obtain . . . lists of goods which retail stores suppose to be 'made under fair conditions,' with the names of the places of manufacture." The league also started inquiring into the possibility of hiring inspectors to take on what could be a long list of such goods and manufacturers.[24]

While the Boston league was taking shape, Brooks published a pamphlet on consumers' leagues in 1897. He noted where such organizations were already making a difference in the retail trade, similar to the working girls clubs' efforts in Massachusetts. "At the point where the retail sale of goods is carried on, it is already proved that consumers may exercise an influence in their buying. They may induce employers to correct certain obvious evils— imperfect sanitary arrangements, lack of seats, and appropriating fines by the firm instead of turning them into benefit funds. Especially may these things be done where no laws for mercantile establishments exist, or, if existing, are poorly administered." In fact, Brooks admitted that some readers might find the need for a league in Boston less than compelling, since the city's leading retail stores and the state's factory legislation (which often also covered retail industries) stood far in advance of those in many other locales. But, Brooks asked, "shall our own League aim to lift the standard still higher?—to ask for fewer hours, longer vacations, better sanitation?" Though all these were laudable goals, Brooks was cautious: "As the conditions of labor in our stores now are, and as the laws are at present enforced, no body of citizens would be likely to unite in such an effort" to merely raise the bar a little higher. Meanwhile, demands for a minimum wage law, or "equal pay for equal work" for men and women, remained so ill-defined and controversial that Brooks was even more skeptical about assembling a coalition to press for their enactment. "What then remains to justify the formation of a League?" he asked. In answering this question, Brooks proved to be more ambitious than some of his fellow committee members. He wanted to mobilize even more consumer power to reach beyond the sales counter, beyond improving the lives of retail workers, back through the supply chain to the point of production. "The deeper and graver evils are not at the selling points, but where the goods are made," Brooks argued. "It was abundantly worth while to lessen the abuses of the store. Is it worth while to attempt the far harder task of attacking the evils at their source? This question our League has to face."

Brooks saw that his key challenge was to build a new organization that would coordinate the purchasing power of individual consumers into a unified reform movement to demand both better products and better working conditions for producers. "Can we get through the store to the sweater's den?" he asked. "Can we organize our buying so as to make the pinched and meager life of the sweated worker (often of the sweater as well) more tolerable and more hopeful? If it is true that we make what we buy and determine in large measure the conditions of labor from which the product comes, can we make practical use of the fact? Can we apply the principle in our shopping and our spending so as to stimulate the production of better and more honest products, together with the improved conditions of labor that usually accompany better workmanship and better goods?"

Brooks believed that the answer to all those questions lay in the Consumers' League, which would educate buyers—through meetings, lectures, leaflets, and investigative reports—about where and how their purchases were produced, the risks to both workers and buyers from shoddy goods made in poor conditions, and the need for retailers to certify their goods as well made and produced under decent working conditions. "The end and aim of the Consumers' League" was to create a "white list" (as opposed to the blacklist used against working-class activists) not only of stores that treated their help well but also "of properly made and fairly paid goods." The league would make that list "known to the greatest number of buyers,—to persuade them to practice the new economic virtue of creating excellence by buying excellence." The league would try to avoid coercion or boycotts, and instead encourage the patronage of fair merchants and manufacturers. Store owners, faced with such a well-educated and responsible buying public, would not only ensure that the goods they sold met the league's standards but also proclaim the white list in all their advertising. The growing demand for such goods—"well made and well paid"—would prompt all wholesalers, distributors, and manufacturers to abide by the higher working standards: benchmarks of quality and fairness that consumers would come to insist on, and labor would obviously welcome. Over time, everyone in the supply chain would actively seek out the league's inspection and endorsement, through the white list and labels on individual articles.

Brooks also looked at the consumer movement's potential costs, and stated emphatically that "we are not necessarily asking the purchaser to pay a higher price for his goods. *The League is not a movement against cheapness AS cheapness,* but only against the cheapness which is bound up with dangerously low surroundings." Brooks confidently surmised that the "application of science and machinery," especially in regulated factories as opposed to tenement sweatshops, and even with "higher wages and fewer hours," would make "extreme cheapness possible without necessarily taking it out of the laborer." Moreover, Brooks argued, "it is now an accepted economic fact that low wages and bad conditions do not as a rule give us the cheap products. An overwhelming proportion of the cheapest products are made by those who work under best conditions and with far higher wages and fewer hours than would be found in the squalid quarters of the sweater. . . . This is the cheapness of which we cannot have too much; especially the poor cannot have too much of it." But low wages, driven only by selfish consumer demand for the lowest price possible regardless of quality or consequence, often forced the working poor to go to the state or private charity for handouts to supplement their unjustly meager earnings—this kind of cheapness hurt workers and the nation. Those cheap goods were a bargain bought at the expense of a weaker person's time, money, and health. And such cheap labor imposed higher social and economic costs on public health and safety, as well as on the public purse.

Looking to the consumer campaign ahead, Brooks cautioned his readers: "The real difficulties are not outside of us, in the store, or workshop; the difficulties most to be feared are in themselves as careless and indifferent buyers. The league is an occasion for our own instruction in this new and much needed morality." Brooks added that the movement should be "an education of our economic desires as these pass into purchases. It is to teach us how to 'want' right things, rightly made. It is to teach us the ways through which an 'organized buying of the best' reacts upon the worker's life. It is to teach us how to buy, so that the strain, the burden, the squalor of much of the industrial life about us may be diminished." With such an ambitious educational agenda, Brooks also asked himself, "Can a sufficient number of buyers be taught to care?—a number considerable enough to show the store-keeper that the movement is serious?" Though he had no ready answer, and he counseled patience with what he saw as a slow change in public morality, Brooks hoped that the movement would eventually grow large enough to be a force in politics and in shaping public policy on labor and consumer issues.[25]

In early 1898, the Consumers' League of Massachusetts claimed over 1,000 members and invited Boston merchants to a public meeting on February 2 (again at Association Hall). The league wanted to gather "not in a spirit of interference or coercion, but for the purpose of educating a great body of shoppers to a better and keener sense of personal responsibility, and to a more intelligent use of their influence" in the marketplace. At the meeting, the league presented its constitution. Its principles echoed what Brooks had written the previous year—"since the demand of consumers determines the nature of production, an intelligent recognition of their responsibility and influence is the duty of the purchasing public. [And] an amelioration of the deplorable condition surrounding many producers and distributors of manufactured goods can be affected by the association of persons who endeavor to buy articles of good quality made and sold under just and wholesome conditions." The league's officers included Brooks, Helena Dudley, and Robert Woods; Edith Howes became the first president. An active executive committee managed the league's funds, directed investigations into working conditions at factories and stores, maintained a label for goods made and sold under league standards, oversaw the publication of reports, and provided lectures to local chapters.[26]

The executive committee also soon had to address a potentially difficult matter—the relationship between a Consumers' League label and a trade union label on the same product. The committee ruled that the league "should further the interests of the trades-union label by publishing details of its use, by investigating trades-union shops and by adopting trades-union standards of wages, without however requiring the trades-union label as requisite to the Consumers' League label." In later discussions, the committee continued to insist that it was "willing to consider the Trades' Union standard of hours and wages in determining the conditions which should prevail in any shop endorsed by" the league, but it objected to the "adoption of the Trades' Union standard as the sole test." Meanwhile, many activists expressed concern that the league was taking a union (label) strategy aimed at working-class consumers, signifying that shop conditions were acceptable to labor, and substituting a campaign for middle-class consumers and their approval of products and production.[27]

In late November 1898, the league discussed the efforts of Helena Dudley and the Federal Labor Union (FLU) at Denison House to secure a sixty-hour work week in mercantile establishments. (The plan would adapt the state's existing fifty-eight-hour law regulating the textile industry to women and children working in stores.) Working girls' clubs had already pressed for voluntary adoption of the eight-hour day in many Boston stores, but there was no legal provision securing such standards throughout the city or state. Some large retailers, already working on shorter weekly hours, liked the idea that all their competitors across the state would fall under the same legal restrictions. But this new legislative effort would not pressure stores into set hours or early closings; rather, the law would stipulate a maximum work week, and still leave each merchant free to determine specific hours of operation and each worker's schedule.[28]

The FLU already had statistical ammunition for its lobbying efforts from the league's recently published reports on working conditions in Boston stores. The league hired a Harvard postgraduate student in economics, MacKenzie King (who decades later would become prime minister of Canada), to interview young women who had worked in dry goods stores, bakeries, and other small shops around Boston during the past summer of 1898. King wrote in his diary, "The confidence these working girls put in me is touching, pretty girls most of them young & even innocent, they tell me their hours & wages as if I were their friend." The following day King reflected on the moral dimensions of overwork in these small shops. "Surely these are the people who will ask 'When Lord' when they are told I was hungered and ye gave me to eat. Are not the working classes by reason of their work nearer to fulfilling the fundamental laws of . . . [Christ]ian life than any other." King repaid the workers' trust and perseverance when he concluded in his public report that consumers could make a difference in these young women's lives—could demand shorter hours and better working conditions—through selective shopping and political lobbying:

> The position of the conscientious consumer seems plain. Granted that such a limitation of hours appears to him to be necessary and fair, he should, as a private citizen, seek so to direct his own acts of purchase that the desired result might be obtained by voluntary effort alone. As a public citizen, he should see to it that attempts at right dealings by some are not frustrated by the acts of those unwilling that such should be observed; or that the health and happiness of employees be sacrificed to mere pecuniary gain: in achieving this end he may bring to his aid, should he require it, the necessary legislation.[29]

The Denison House residents wanted to make sure that the league did not plan to lead this legislative campaign for shorter working hours. Though it is possible that some at Denison House wanted the league to shoulder more of this effort, the league's executive committee responded that it was "unanimously desirous of having the Federal Labor Union direct the work toward gaining the sixty-hour law." A motion to formally endorse the effort was tabled, however, when Robert Woods "expressed the opinion that the committee had no right in any way to pledge its constituency to this movement, and the fear that the effort for a sixty-hour law might alienate some of our members." Woods may have been thinking particularly of several local merchants who had been cooperating closely with the league in its investigations, and promoting the idea of a league label on certain products, but who also remained leery of having legislative mandates imposed on their establishments. The executive committee took up the sixty-hour law again in December. Despite Woods's urging that the league treat this legislative effort with the same qualified attitude it held toward union labels, the committee voted to officially endorse the law and offer any relevant information its investigators collected to Dudley and the FLU in support of their lobbying.[30]

By the fall of 1899, the FLU at Denison House seemed to be flagging in its efforts to push the sixty-hour bill. The league considered taking a more forceful stand to pick up the legislative slack, and to distract attention from its own failing campaign to promote the white list and label program. The executive committee—now meeting at 129 Mt. Vernon Street on fashionable Beacon Hill near the statehouse—asked Woods to "find out the present attitude of the Labor Union" on the legislation, and requested other members to draw up a new version of the bill for the league to sponsor. Edith Howes spoke with Governor-elect W. Murray Crane in mid-December, but he told her that he would not press for a sixty-hour bill in his inaugural address. The league and other proponents then decided to bypass the governor's office and go directly to the legislature at its next session. With that strategy in mind, Emily Greene Balch joined the executive committee and became chair of a committee to manage the lobbying effort for the sixty-hour bill. Fellow committee members, such as Edith Howes and Helena Dudley, helped press the legislative initiative. Though the league continued to proclaim its white list and label campaigns, it actually had more success persuading legislators than store owners to support its agenda on shorter hours in mercantile establishments. Balch and her committee saw their bill signed into law in 1900.[31]

The Consumers' League would build on these targeted legislative successes and prove to be an influential model for Progressive-era labor reformers, sometimes more influential than its colleagues in the settlement houses. The league committed itself to investigating working conditions in manufacturing and mercantile businesses, educating its members about those conditions and the power of consumers to change them, and agitating in the marketplace and in the political arena to secure better-made products and better-paid producers. The league reached out to struggling women and children toiling in workshops and stores, though usually more as objects of reform than as partners in a cross-class movement. Meanwhile, the league also carefully cultivated alliances in high places with wealthy backers and influential politicians. The group used the new tools of social science investigations to uncover age old abuses in labor standards. And the organization embraced the growing world of middle-class consumption as a powerful economic weapon in the moral struggle for workers' rights to a living wage and a safe place to labor.

The league also provided a prologue to new organizational structures for a new century—a labor reform group with fewer workers in its leadership ranks, and more emphasis on middle-class expertise and economic power mobilized to serve the needs of struggling toilers. Although the league was not an entirely elite institution, its officers made fewer efforts to share power horizontally across class lines, and focused more on a vertical top-down approach to addressing labor problems. Legislative lobbying was more often done on workers' behalf, than in a coalition with labor. And the executive committee, often meeting in the homes of wealthy league officers, wielded great decision-making power. Thus this organization, though it had some close ties with the settlement houses, chose to distance itself physically from the workers whose cause it purported to champion. This league urged consumers to use their pocketbook power to demand better products and better treatment for producers laboring unseen in back rooms. But there was far less discussion of reaching across class lines to build alliances with the "dangerous" classes living in dangerous neighborhoods. Informed shoppers acting as moral agents in the marketplace, rather than workers protesting in the city's streets, seemed to offer a more peaceful path to social reform.

Middle-class reformers, many of them increasingly uneasy about creating coalitions with the growing number of immigrant workers, independent-minded trade unionists, and radical socialists, tried to keep control of the new organizations in the hands of those with more economic resources and political power. These reformers were now more likely to talk with one another, and talk down to workers, telling them what was best for their future. Meanwhile, working-class activists, many of them increasingly skeptical about alliances that continued to press for labor reform mainly through legislation, listened intently to trade union warnings about the power of the government to issue labor injunctions and send in the army as strikebreakers. Both reformers and workers, thus, discussed the labor problem and labor reform more within their own circles than in coalitions that cut across class lines. The emerging labor reform organizations in the new century often had more hierarchical leadership structures and more constricted ideals about changing society; they became more willing to settle for small legislative victories and less likely to speak their version of truth to power. The world of nineteenth-century labor reform—often openhearted, optimistic, even naive in the face of continuing struggles to hold together cross-class alliances, to share organizational power, to build a campaign that could both immediately improve workers' lives and offer a vision of broad social change—was coming to an end.

EPILOGUE

BOSTON AT the dawn of the twentieth century was certainly a different city in many respects from its antebellum ancestor. The previously modest-sized port had expanded nearly tenfold in population, and nearly thirty times in physical size. By 1900, immigrants and their children—many of them now Catholics and Jews from southern and eastern Europe—constituted nearly three-quarters of the city's inhabitants. These newcomers often flooded into the cramped flats and boardinghouses of the South End and North End, and toiled long hours in nearby sweatshops, despite the efforts of tenement house opponents to stamp out such egregious working conditions. Boston—like most American cities at that time—was a land of sharp contrasts in living conditions, and growing physical distances between the social classes.

Not surprisingly, given this changing landscape of stark class relations, labor reform organizations in Boston also often looked quite different from their antebellum predecessors. The men and women who formed associations such as the NEA and the NEWA in the 1830s and 1840s came from a range of social, educational, and economic backgrounds—mechanics, "millgirls," and ministers all had a role in leading these alliances. The groups sponsored a constant stream of conventions where those assembled debated labor reform in the broadest terms possible. In the midst of building these coalitions and of linking labor reform to a wider universe of social action, however, these pioneers sometimes lost opportunities to press the case for practical gains at the workplace. Though the demand for a shorter workday could be heard at nearly every meeting, these associations never brought all their organizational energy to bear on that essential need.

By 1900, the women and men who led organizations such as the Anti-Tenement House League and the Massachusetts Consumers' League often came from wealthier families. These groups frequently employed educated experts to investigate the conditions of labor and propose legislative remedies for specific problems. The cry for shorter working hours could still be heard in the city's tenements and sweatshops, but the eight-hour campaign had to share the stage with other labor reform strategies. What these leagues achieved in legal victories, however, came at a price: a narrowed vision of social change and a constricted leadership of the coalitions.

To be sure, these changes across nineteenth-century Boston were uneven and sometimes halting. Well into the 1890s, for example, the college-educated women at the Denison House settlement actively organized female wage workers and even served as leaders of union locals. And W. D. P. Bliss's Church of the Carpenter gathered workers and reformers together for spiritual, social, and political communion. Thus, even as expert-driven, hierarchical labor reform organizations assumed a more prominent role in Boston, remnants of earlier cross-class models still could be found in the city's neighborhoods and churches.

In Boston's labor reform scene at century's end, with its pastiche of labor reform groups looking to both the past and the future for their inspiration, unexpected ironies and paradoxes abounded. When reformers assumed command of some labor reform efforts, they proved to be anything but dreamy idealists. Groups such as consumers' leagues often narrowed their focus to legislative agendas carefully crafted by lawyers and industrial experts drawing on field research and the emerging social sciences. Meanwhile, purportedly pragmatic workers got what they wished for in limited doses, as the state increased its regulation of working hours and shopfloor conditions (in some industries). Yet many of these same workers were not content with just modest legislative victories. They still believed in a broader vision of social justice and did not intend to hand over the ongoing campaign for labor reform to organizations dominated by middle-class reformers and experts.

The struggles of labor reformers and activists in nineteenth-century Boston to construct stable alliances and strive for social change can offer lessons to coalition builders today. Creating cross-class organizations was, and is, just plain hard work. To bring men and women together from varying economic, educational, and social backgrounds, and get them to agree (if ever) on a common agenda and a shared strategy for achieving organizational goals, takes a great amount of time and patience. Organizing is never done in a vacuum; every member of a coalition brings to every meeting his or her own assumptions about what needs to be done and how best to do it. And those assumptions are shaped by each individual's economic needs, social values, and political calculations.

The labor reform organizations in nineteenth-century Boston faced many of the same questions that alliances for social change confront today: First of all, who should lead these groups? Should the struggle be focused on immediate problems or on a long-term vision for structural reform? Should the coalition craft a broad agenda that tries to appeal to many diverse constituencies, or zero in on one issue that all can agree on, with the hope that success in that one endeavor may begin to build momentum toward more ambitious goals? To make matters even more challenging, any organization that tackles a complex issue like labor reform—seeking to give workers more time and money, and more control over the terms and conditions of their labor—will certainly face opposition from entrenched economic and political forces with an abiding interest in preserving the status quo of unequal wealth and power.

All these challenges and obstacles are certainly not unique to cross-class labor reform organizations, or to nineteenth-century Boston. Yet what women and men did in that city through nearly seventy years of organization building and rebuilding reflected their abiding faith that the ideals of equality and justice would eventually prevail in the face of human frailty, selfishness, and indifference. Labor reform alliances in Boston never did find that right balance between talking and doing, between addressing immediate needs and working toward long-term change. But many workers and reformers never stopped believing that they would someday create the organization that would bring everyone together on a common agenda and a shared struggle, and keep them all together for the long haul.

The sparks of such ideals and hopes have never been extinguished completely; they remain to be found and reignited in communities throughout the nation. Organizing across class lines for social change may appear to be even more difficult now than it was for those nineteenth-century Bostonians who strove over and over again to create such coalitions. The gap between classes has grown wider in recent years, even as so many in our society continue to deny the existence of class itself. In today's often hostile political climate, who will take the time necessary to build alliances based on patience, trust, and shared leadership? Those who try to answer that question would do well to recall how men and women in nineteenth-century Boston fought against the forces of antagonism and pessimism, often with only meager economic and technological resources at their command. Contemporary activists and reformers could learn much from their predecessors in Boston—both cautionary tales of lost opportunities, and inspiring examples of endurance in the pursuit of social justice.

ABBREVIATIONS

ABIR	American Bureau of Industrial Research
AFL	American Federation of Labor
BLRA	Boston Labor Reform Association
BSL	Massachusetts Bureau of the Statistics of Labor
BTU	Boston Trades Union
CLU	Christian Labor Union
CSA	College Settlements Association
DEV	*Daily Evening Voice*
FLU	Federal Labor Union
LFLRA	Lowell Female Labor Reform Association
LRLNE	Labor Reform League of New England
NEA	New England Association of Farmers, Mechanics, and other Working Men
NELRL	New England Labor Reform League
NEWA	New England Workingmen's Association
UGWA	United Garment Workers of America
VOI	*Voice of Industry*
WEIU	Women's Educational and Industrial Union

NOTES

Introduction

1. Labor *reform* organizations should be considered as distinct from the labor movement composed of trade unions. Certainly, some workers were also involved in various trade unions, and some reformers also supported unions, but this study is concerned with these individuals' participation in cross-class labor reform efforts.

2. Martin J. Burke, *The Conundrum of Class: Public Discourse on the Social Order in America* (Chicago: University of Chicago Press, 1995), xii, 165.

3. It should be noted that, with a brief exception in the mid-1830s, cross-class labor reform organizations in Boston did not recruit middle-class members from the ranks of business owners, manufacturers, managers, foremen, etc. Organizing across class lines did not usually entail organizing across the social relations of production in industry, though occasionally labor reform groups in the late nineteenth century functioned as arbitrators to bring employees and employers together, and defuse strikes and protests.

4. Richard T. Ely, *The Labor Movement in America* (New York: Thomas Crowell, 1886), 50–52, 171–77. Also see Richard T. Ely, *Ground under Our Feet: An Autobiography* (1938; rpt. New York: Arno Press, 1977); and Benjamin Rader, *The Academic Mind and Reform: The Influence of Richard T. Ely in American Life* (Lexington: University Press of Kentucky, 1966). It should also be noted that Ely, soon after he published *The Labor Movement,* began a steady drift away from his outspoken support for organized labor and his social reform activism, and toward a more moderate position as a detached scholar of political economy.

5. George E. McNeill, *The Labor Movement: The Problem of Today* (1887; rpt. New York: Augustus M. Kelley, 1971), 77–79, 99–110, 137–54. Also see Robert Montgomery, "'To Fight This Thing till I Die': The Career of George Edwin McNeill," in *Culture, Gender, Race, and U.S. Labor History,* ed. Ronald Kent et al. (Westport, CT: Greenwood Press, 1993), 3–23.

6. Philip S. Foner and Brewster Chamberlain, eds., *Friedrich A. Sorge's Labor Movement in America: A History of the American Working Class from Colonial Times*

to 1890 (Westport, CT: Greenwood Press, 1977), 55–56, 72–73, 88–98, 100–102, 109–14, 125–43, 152–63, 166–67.

7. Charles E. Persons, "The Early History of Factory Legislation in Massachusetts from 1825 to the Passage of the Ten Hour Law in 1874," in *Labor Laws and Their Enforcement with Special Reference to Massachusetts*, ed. Susan M. Kingsbury (New York: Longman, Green, 1911), 3–129.

8. Frank T. Carlton, "Ephemeral Labor Movements, 1866–1889," *Popular Science Monthly* 85 (1914): 487–503.

9. John R. Commons et al., *The History of Labour in the United States*, vols. 1 and 2 (New York: Macmillan, 1918). Also see John R. Commons, *Myself: The Autobiography of John R. Commons* (1934; rpt. Madison: University of Wisconsin Press, 1963); Lafayette Harter, *John R. Commons: His Assault on Laissez-Faire* (Corvallis: Oregon State University Press, 1962); Maurice Isserman, "'God Bless Our American Institutions': The Labor History of John R. Commons," *Labor History* 17 (Summer 1976): 309–28; Leon Fink, "'Intellectuals' versus 'Workers': Academic Requirements and the Creation of Labor History," *American Historical Review* 96 (1991): 395–421; Ellen Fitzpatrick, "Rethinking the Intellectual Origins of American Labor History," *American Historical Review* 96 (1991): 422–28.

10. Norman Ware, *The Industrial Worker, 1840–1860: The Reaction of American Industrial Society to the Advance of the Industrial Revolution* (Boston: Houghton, Mifflin, 1924), quotations on xvii.

11. David Montgomery, *Beyond Equality: Labor and the Radical Republicans, 1862–1872* (1967; rpt. Urbana: University of Illinois Press, 1981), quotation on x.

12. Montgomery, *Beyond Equality*, 219.

13. Carl Guarneri, *The Utopian Alternative: Fourierism in Nineteenth-Century America* (Ithaca, NY: Cornell University Press, 1991), especially chapter 11, quotation on 293–94.

14. Teresa Murphy, *Ten Hours' Labor: Religion, Reform, and Gender in Early New England* (Ithaca, NY: Cornell University Press, 1992).

15. Bruce Laurie, *Beyond Garrison: Antislavery and Social Reform* (New York: Cambridge University Press, 2005), chapter 4; Sarah Deutsch, *Women and the City: Gender, Space, and Power in Boston, 1870–1940* (New York: Oxford University Press, 2000). See also John T. Cumbler, *From Abolition to Rights for All: The Making of a Reform Community in the Nineteenth Century* (Philadelphia: University of Pennsylvania Press, 2008), for a portrait of the more elite reform community in mid-nineteenth-century Boston, many of them former Garrisonian abolitionists.

16. This book examines organizational records and minutes, pamphlets and proclamations, convention proceedings and resolutions, and reports in the contemporary labor press to paint a complex portrait of dynamic organizations that continually formed, flourished, faded, and often reconstituted themselves as new entities. Thus, the key to understanding these organizations is to capture their debates and arguments not only through middle-class eyes and ears but also from working-class sources

whenever possible, so as to see whether these coalitions maintained authentic cross-class alliances.

The sources used here strove to convey, wherever possible, both the public and the private "voice" of cross-class labor reform organizations, their leaders, and their rank and file. Books and pamphlets captured arguments from the alliances' most articulate orators; newspapers recruited, informed, and mobilized the membership by reporting debates on resolutions and elections of officers; minute books (where they survive) often revealed daily activities; and personal correspondence conveyed the private musings of some prominent activists and reformers.

This study also emphasizes prescriptive literature that articulates individual and organizational ideas for labor reform. A large body of writing often includes detailed descriptive reports critiquing labor under industrial capitalism. But this book focuses on what labor reformers and activists had to say about specific schemes for improving working conditions and advancing the status of working people, and how they organized and struggled to achieve their goals.

1. Awakenings

1. *Columbian Centinel* (Boston), February 15, 1832, in *A Documentary History of American Industrial Society,* ed. John R. Commons et al., 11 vols. (Cleveland: Arthur H. Clark, 1910–11), 5:192. The Boston meeting of the association had been arranged, and a constitution drafted, at a previous meeting in Providence, Rhode Island, on December 5, 1831, but there are no records extant from that gathering. The constitution was ratified, and the association formally established, at the February 1832 meeting in Boston. See Teresa Murphy, *Ten Hours' Labor: Religion, Reform, and Gender in Early New England* (Ithaca, NY: Cornell University Press, 1992), 32–37, for a detailed discussion of the NEA's origins.

2. Thomas O'Connor, *The Athens of America: Boston, 1825–1845* (Amherst: University of Massachusetts Press, 2006), 26–28; Carroll Wright and Horace Wadlin, "The Industries of the Last Hundred Years," in *The Memorial History of Boston,* vol. 4, ed. Justin Winsor (Boston: Ticknor, 1881), 86–87.

3. O'Connor, *Athens of America,* 37; Oscar Handlin, *Boston's Immigrants, 1790–1880: A Study in Acculturation* (1941; rpt. New York: Atheneum, 1974), 26; Sam Bass Warner Jr., *Streetcar Suburbs: The Process of Growth in Boston (1870–1900)* (Cambridge, MA: Harvard University Press, 1962), 5.

4. See S. A. Eliot, "Public and Private Charities of Boston," *North American Review* 56 (July 1845): 141–42, for a partial list of charitable and reform organizations in Boston around 1830. See also Thomas O'Connor, *The Hub: Boston Past and Present* (Boston: Northeastern University Press, 2001), 94–99; and Johann Neem, *Creating a Nation of Joiners: Democracy and Civil Society in Early National Massachusetts* (Cambridge, MA: Harvard University Press, 2008), chapters 4 and 6.

5. Proceedings of the New England Association of Farmers, Mechanics, and Other Working Men (1832), in *Official Hand Book of the Rhode Island District Assembly 99*

Knights of Labor (Providence, RI: District Executive Board, 1894), 40–41. These proceedings were first reported in the *New England Artisan,* February 23, 1832.

6. Proceedings of the New England Association, 41–42.

7. Proceedings of the New England Association, 41; *New England Artisan,* March 1, 1832.

8. Proceedings of the New England Association, 43. Also see John R. Commons et al., *The History of Labour in the United States* (New York: Macmillan, 1918), 1:310–12, for more on the ten-hour strikes that did take place in 1832.

9. Proceedings of the New England Association, 44–45. The term "committee of vigilance" was a clear allusion to similar Revolutionary-era organizations that enforced community agreements and pro-Patriot policies.

10. For an extensive discussion of the links between working hours, education, self-improvement, and citizenship, see William F. Hartford, *Money, Morals, and Politics: Massachusetts in the Age of the Boston Associates* (Boston: Northeastern University Press, 2001), 67–77.

11. *Workingmen's Advocate,* September 15, 1832; *Free Enquirer,* September 22, 1832; *New England Artisan,* October 11, 1832; *First Annual Report of the Massachusetts Bureau of Statistics of Labor* (Boston: Wright and Potter, 1870), 93–94; Edward Pessen, *Most Uncommon Jacksonians: The Radical Leaders of the Early Labor Movement* (Albany: State University of New York Press, 1967), 17.

For more on Luther, see Carl Gersuny, "Seth Luther—The Road from Chepachet," *Rhode Island History* 33 (1974): 47–55; and Louis Hartz, "Seth Luther: Working Class Rebel," *New England Quarterly* 13:3 (1940): 401–18.

12. *Proceedings of the Working-Men's Convention* (1833), 1, 6, 7, 25, 28, 31; Commons et al., *History of Labour,* 1:316.

13. *New England Artisan,* November 9, 1833; March 22, 1834. Eight hundred women went on strike in February 1834 to protest reduced piece wages in Lowell mills. See Thomas Dublin, *Women at Work: The Transformation of Work and Community in Lowell, Massachusetts, 1826–1860* (New York: Columbia University Press, 1979), 89–98; and David Zonderman, *Aspirations and Anxieties: New England Workers and the Mechanized Factory System, 1815–1850* (New York: Oxford University Press, 1992), 200–204.

14. Henry Carey, *Select Excerpta,* IV, 435, quoted in Commons et al., *History of Labour,* 1:306.

15. *National Trades' Union,* November 1, 1834; Murphy, *Ten Hours' Labor,* 51; Arthur B. Darling, "The Workingmen's Party in Massachusetts, 1833–1834," *American Historical Review* 24 (1923): 81–86; and Ronald Formisano, *The Transformation of Political Culture: Massachusetts Parties, 1790s–1840s* (New York: Oxford University Press, 1983), 227–36.

16. *The Man,* March 12, 1834, in *Documentary History of American Industrial Society,* 6:95; *The Man,* May 30, 1834, quoted in Commons et al., *History of Labour,* 1:379–80. The Boston Trades Union was not as open minded on the question of admitting women workers as it was on masters. Women could join only if their labor organizations were represented by men! See Murphy, *Ten Hours' Labor,* 50–51.

For more on the debate among antebellum reformers over the meaning of labor and the definition of workers, see Jonathan Glickstein, *American Exceptionalism, American Anxiety: Wages, Competition, and Degraded Labor in the Antebellum United States* (Charlottesville: University of Virginia Press, 2002), 117–30.

17. *National Trades' Union,* May 16, 1835.

18. Theophilus Fisk, *Capital against Labor* (Boston: Daily Reformer Office, 1835), 9, 11–14; Pessen, *Most Uncommon Jacksonians,* 42, 92; Commons et al., *History of Labour,* 1:388–89.

19. Seth Luther, *An Address Delivered before the Mechanics and Working-men of the City of Brooklyn . . .* (Brooklyn, NY: Spooner, 1836), 21.

20. *Mechanic* (Fall River), May 25, and July 13, 1844.

21. Philip Foner, "Journal of an Early Labor Organizer," *Labor History* 10 (Spring 1969): 205–27; Bruce Laurie, *Beyond Garrison: Antislavery and Social Reform* (New York: Cambridge University Press, 2005), 128; also see Murphy, *Ten Hours' Labor,* 137–42, 147–52, 165, 191.

22. *Boston Laborer* and *Manchester Operative,* in *Mechanic,* August 3, 1844; *New England Operative,* in *Mechanic,* August 31, 1844; *Mechanic,* September 14 and 21, 1844.

23. Letter of Ralph Waldo Emerson to Thomas Carlyle, October 30, 1840, in *The Correspondence of Thomas Carlyle and Ralph Waldo Emerson,* ed. Charles E. Norton (Boston: James R. Osgood, 1883), 1: 308–9; O'Connor, *Athens of America,* 152; Handlin, *Boston's Immigrants,* 239.

24. *Mechanic,* October 26, 1844; *Working Man's Advocate* (New York), October 19, 1844, in *Documentary History of American Industrial Society,* 8:91–95. For a further discussion of the links between land reform and workers' organizations, see Helene Zahler, *Eastern Workingmen and National Policy, 1829–1862* (New York, 1941). For an extensive analysis of the Associationist movement and labor reform, see Carl Guarneri, *The Utopian Alternative: Fourierism in Nineteenth-Century America* (Ithaca, NY: Cornell University Press, 1991), especially chapter 11. Also see Anne C. Rose, *Transcendentalism as a Social Movement, 1830–1850* (New Haven, CT: Yale University Press, 1981), 155–60; Charles Crowe, *George Ripley: Transcendentalist and Utopian Socialist* (Athens: University of Georgia Press, 1967), 209–15; and Sterling Delano, *Brook Farm: The Dark Side of Utopia* (Cambridge, MA: Harvard University Press, 2004), 186–89, 230–32, 280–81.

This study explores the links between Associationists and cross-class labor reform organizations such as the NEWA. Guarneri also discusses the cross-class membership rolls at Fourierist communities (phalanxes) and the Associationists' experiments with communal labor. But those experiments usually did not influence broader labor reform efforts (such as the ten-hour movement) outside the utopian communities, despite the Associationists' fervent hopes. Thus, when Associationists wanted to shape that broader campaign, they took time away from their communal duties and joined groups such as the NEWA.

Although the NEWA opened its convention to a wide variety of reformers, it drew the line at Horace Seaver, editor of the freethought newspaper *Investigator*. Seaver and his newspaper supported labor reform, but the delegates worried that seating a known "infidel" in their midst might stir up both internal arguments and external condemnation against their organization. See Jama Lazerow, *Religion and the Working Class in Antebellum America* (Washington, DC: Smithsonian Institution Press, 1995), 41.

25. *The Awl* (Lynn), October 23, 1844, in *Documentary History of American Industrial Society*, 8:96–99.

26. *Weekly Bee*, October 19, 1844, in Teresa Murphy, "The Petitioning of Artisans and Operatives: Means and Ends in the Struggle for a Ten-Hour Day," in *American Artisans: Crafting Social Identity*, ed. Howard Rock et al. (Baltimore, MD: Johns Hopkins University Press, 1995), 90.

27. *The Awl*, October 23, 1844. The resolution on producer cooperatives, although it did not garner great attention at the meeting, reflected a broader impulse in the region. By the end of the year, a committee of the Boston Mechanics' and Laborers' Association recommended the formation of an "Industrial Association" whereby workers would "own their own shops and factories; work their own stock, sell their own merchandise, and enjoy the fruits of their own toil. Our Lowells must be owned by the artisans who build them, and the operatives who run all the machinery and do all the work. And the dividends, instead of being given to the idle parasites of a distant city, should be shared among those who perform the labor." The committee proposed an ambitious plan to petition the legislature to incorporate this association with a capital stock up to one million dollars! A "Unitary Edifice" (perhaps akin to a Fourierist phalanstery) would be constructed for workshops, meeting halls, and community stores.

Producer cooperatives may have been particularly attractive to artisans who were just beginning to feel the pinch of industrial production; and who therefore wanted to retain their craft skills while still competing in an increasingly stratified economy. But these grand schemes never came to fruition, and the cooperative movement— along with its supporters in the NEWA—soon shifted the focus to protective union consumer stores. See *Working Man's Advocate*, January 11, 1845, in *Documentary History of American Industrial Society*, 8:263–65; and Edwin C. Rozwenc, *Cooperatives Come to America: The History of the Protective Union Store Movement, 1845–1867* (1941; rpt. Philadelphia: Porcupine Press, 1977), 24–26.

28. *The Awl*, April 5, 1845, in *Documentary History of American Industrial Society*, 8:99–106; *The Mechanic*, April 1, 1845; Letter of Horace Greeley, New York, to C. A. Dana, October 10, 1842, Horace Greeley Papers, Manuscript Division, Library of Congress, Washington, DC; Frances Early, "A Reappraisal of the New England Labour-Reform Movement of the 1840s: The Lowell Female Labor Reform Association and the New England Workingmens Association," *Social History* (Canada) 13 (1980): 40.

29. *Voice of Industry* (*VOI*), June 5, 1845; *Harbinger* (Brook Farm), June 14, 1845. See Murphy, *Ten Hours' Labor*, 203–6, for another analysis of Bagley's speech emphasizing how Bagley used concepts of history and the notion of separate spheres.

Also see Helena Wright, "Sarah G. Bagley: A Biographical Note," *Labor History* 20 (Summer 1979): 398–413; Teresa Murphy, "Sarah Bagley: Laboring for Life," in *The Human Tradition in American Labor History*, ed. Eric Arnesen (Wilmington, DE: Scholarly Resources, 2004), 31–45; and Teresa Murphy, "Sarah Bagley," in *American National Biography*, ed. John Garraty and Mark Carnes (New York: Oxford University Press, 1999), 1:869–70.

30. For an extensive discussion of reform and concepts of women's benevolence, see Lori D. Ginzberg, *Women and the Work of Benevolence: Morality, Politics, and Class in the Nineteenth-Century United States* (New Haven, CT: Yale University Press, 1990).

31. Zonderman, *Aspirations and Anxieties*, 223–24.

32. *VOI*, June 12, 1845; *Harbinger*, June 21, 1845.

33. *VOI*, June 12, 1845.

34. *VOI*, September 18, 1845. For more on William Young and his work with the NEWA and *VOI*, see Jama Lazerow, "Religion and Labor Reform in Antebellum America: The World of William Field Young," *American Quarterly* 38 (Summer 1986): 265–86. Lazerow argues that Young's personal history is typical of many antebellum labor activists: born 1821 in the rapidly changing New England countryside, as a young man he gravitated to the emerging mill towns, where he came of age during the depression of the late 1830s and early 1840s. Struggling to secure a competence, he drifted from farming to dentistry and eventually to harnessmaking.

35. *VOI*, September 18, 1845.

36. *VOI*, September 18, 1845.

37. *VOI*, September 18, 1845; *Harbinger*, September 24, 1845.

38. *VOI*, November 7 and 21, 1845. It should be noted that the NEWA was not the only group advocating a ten-hour law. Numerous local labor reform groups and workers' associations sent petitions to the Massachusetts legislature asking that the state use its power to regulate corporations and enforce a legal ten-hour day. Female factory operatives from Lowell even testified before a legislative panel in 1845. But the committee's final report declined to endorse any law infringing on the sacrosanct ideal of free contracts or putting the state's industries at what lawmakers perceived was an unfair competitive disadvantage. See Commons et al., *History of Labour*, 1:536–43; Norman Ware, *The Industrial Worker, 1840–1860* (1924; rpt. Chicago: Quadrangle, 1964), chapter 8; and Charles E. Persons, "The Early History of Factory Legislation in Massachusetts from 1825 to the Passage of the Ten Hour Law in 1874," in *Labor Laws and Their Enforcement with Special Reference to Massachusetts,* ed. Susan M. Kingsbury (New York: Longman, Green, 1911), 23–54, for a survey of the ten-hour movement during the 1840s.

39. *VOI*, January 23, 1846. For more on John Cluer's labor activism, see Murphy, *Ten Hours' Labor*, 184–87; Persons, "Early History of Factory Legislation," 39–41; Zonderman, *Aspirations and Anxieties*, 247; David R. Roediger and Philip S. Foner, *Our Own Time: A History of American Labor and the Working Day* (New York: Greenwood Press, 1989), 60–61; and Mary Blewett, *Constant Turmoil: The Politics of*

Industrial Life in Nineteenth-Century New England (Amherst: University of Massachusetts Press, 2000), 84.

40. *VOI*, April 3 and 10, 1846. By June 1846, Luther was committed to an insane asylum; he remained in various institutions until his death in 1863. See Gursuny, "Seth Luther—The Road from Chepachet," 54; and Hartz, "Seth Luther: Working Class Rebel,"409. For more on the stretch-out and speed-up in antebellum textile mills, see Dublin, *Women at Work*, 109–11, 137–38, 156–57; and Zonderman, *Aspirations and Anxieties*, 32–34.

41. *VOI*, September 25, October 2 and 9, 1846.

42. *VOI*, January 22 and February 12, 1847; *The Condition of Labor. An Address to the Members of the Labor Reform League of New England . . . by One of the Members*, (Boston: Author, 1847); Early, "A Reappraisal of the New England Labour-Reform Movement of the 1840s," 50.

43. Senate Unpassed Papers, Box 302, #12,232, Massachusetts State Archives, Boston; Early, "Reappraisal," 50. Also see Persons, "Early History of Factory Legislation," 24–28, 42–46, 52, for more on the ten-hour petitions in general and this one in particular; and see Murphy, *Ten Hours' Labor*, 154–63 for an extended analysis of the act of petitioning within the context of the ten-hour movement as a whole during the 1840s.

This study focuses more on the connections, or lack thereof, between the NEWA and the ten-hour movement than on the frequently hostile political climate in the Massachusetts legislature toward this lobbying campaign.

44. *VOI*, July 30, 1847.

45. *VOI*, January 14, 1848; Guarneri, *The Utopian Alternative*, 303; Mark Lause, *Young America: Land, Labor and the Republican Community* (Urbana: University of Illinois Press, 2005), 15.

46. *VOI*, January 28, 1848. For more on the Washingtonians, see Murphy, *Ten Hours' Labor*, chapter 5. Although the league insisted that it was still following a regular schedule of quarterly meetings, there are no records of a convention in fall 1847.

47. *VOI*, March 31, 1848; Early, "Reappraisal," 53.

48. The *VOI*, the NELRL's primary organ, ceased publication in late March or early April, 1848. The newspaper's demise was linked to the league's collapse. See Roediger and Foner, *Our Own Time*, 62–64, on the league's decline and the entire ten-hour movement's dissipation in the late 1840s.

49. Commons et al., *History of Labour*, 1: chapter 4; Persons, "Early History of Factory Legislation," 23–54; and Ware, *The Industrial Worker*, chapters 8 and 14, remain the classic formulations of this argument about the antagonism and conflicts between unrealistic middle-class reformers and hardheaded pragmatic workers within organizations like the NEWA. Clearly, tensions and debates emerged, but the battle lines between workers and reformers were rarely drawn as quickly and starkly as these scholars contend.

2. Keeping the Flame Alive

1. *Harbinger,* May 27, 1848; George McNeill, ed., *The Labor Movement: The Problem of Today* (1887; rpt. New York: Augustus Kelley, 1971), 115.

2. Carroll Wright and Horace Wadlin, "The Industries of the Last Hundred Years," in *The Memorial History of Boston,* vol. 4, ed. Justin Winsor (Boston: Ticknor, 1881), 89–91; Jane H. Pease and William H. Pease, *Ladies, Women, and Wenches: Choice and Constraint in Antebellum Charleston and Boston* (Chapel Hill: University of North Carolina Press, 1990), 45–46.

3. Historians have often asserted that the reform movements of the 1840s dissipated in the political crises of the 1850s. For example, Ronald Walters, in *American Reformers, 1815–1860* (New York: Hill and Wang, 1978), argues that reform efforts throughout the United States declined in the 1850s because of increasing sectional tensions and the emphasis on abolitionism above any other issue. He specifically states that the labor movement of the 1850s centered on emerging trade unions, and not on the ten-hour campaign or any broader efforts for labor reform. Clearly, however, the evidence from Boston shows that labor reform was very much alive well into the 1850s.

4. *Spirit of the Age,* September 29, 1849, in *A Documentary History of American Industrial Society,* ed. John R. Commons et al., 11 vols. (Cleveland: Arthur H. Clark, 1910–11), 8:279–81. See also Carl Guarneri, *The Utopian Alternative: Fourierism in Nineteenth-Century America* (Ithaca, NY: Cornell University Press, 1991), 316.

5. *Spirit of the Age,* January 19, 1850, in *Documentary History of American Industrial Society,* 8:281–84.

6. *Protective Union,* January 5, 1850.

7. Edwin Rozwenc, *Cooperatives Come to America: The History of the Protective Union Store Movement, 1845–1867* (1941; rpt. Philadelphia: Porcupine Press, 1977), 64; *Protective Union,* April 13 and May 4, 1850.

8. *Protective Union,* May 18, June 1, and June 29, 1850.

9. *Protective Union,* September 14 and 21, 1850.

10. *Protective Union,* October 19, 1850. Also see Guarneri, *The Utopian Alternative,* 318–19; and Henry Schreiber, "The Working People of Boston in the Middle of the Nineteenth Century" (PhD diss., Boston University, 1950), 188–92.

11. For more on the political transformation of the ten-hour movement in the 1840s and 1850s, especially the links between labor reform and antislavery politics, see Bruce Laurie, "The 'Fair Field' of the 'Middle Ground': Abolitionism, Labor Reform, and the Making of an Antislavery Bloc in Antebellum Massachusetts," in *Labor Histories: Class, Politics, and the Working-Class Experience,* ed. Eric Arnesen et al. (Urbana: University of Illinois Press, 1998), 45–70; and Bruce Laurie, *Beyond Garrison: Antislavery and Social Reform* (New York: Cambridge University Press, 2005), chapter 4.

For more on the dynamics between men and women in the ten-hour movement during both the 1840s and 1850s, see Thomas Dublin, *Women at Work: The Transformation of Work and Community in Lowell, Massachusetts, 1826–1860* (New York:

Columbia University Press, 1979), chapters 7 and 12; Teresa Murphy, *Ten Hours' Labor: Gender, Religion, and Reform in Early New England* (Ithaca, NY: Cornell University Press, 1992), chapters 6 and 8; and David Zonderman, *Aspirations and Anxieties: New England Workers and the Mechanized Factory System, 1815-1850* (New York: Oxford University Press, 1992), chapter 8.

Norman Ware argued that as the ten-hour movement became more "political" in the 1850s, it became dominated by middle-class philanthropists to the near exclusion of workers. Ware ignored both the movement's political dimensions in the preceding decade and the strong presence of working-class activists throughout the antebellum period, even as some politicians took a growing interest in the issue of shorter working hours. See Norman Ware, *The Industrial Worker, 1840-1860* (1924; rpt. Chicago: Quadrangle Books, 1964), 125-26.

12. Massachusetts Legislative Document, House No. 153, 1850. For more on this coalition in the Massachusetts legislature, see Kevin Sweeney, "Rum, Romanism, Representation, and Reform: Coalition Politics in Massachusetts, 1847-1853," *Civil War History* 22 (July 1976): 116-37; and Laurie, *Beyond Garrison*, 190-91.

13. Massachusetts Legislative Document, House No. 185, 1852; entry on William S. Robinson, in *Dictionary of American Biography*, vol. 16, ed. Dumas Malone (New York: Scribner, 1935), 58-59; Laurie, *Beyond Garrison*, 164-68. See also William F. Hartford, *Money, Morals, and Politics: Massachusetts in the Age of the Boston Associates* (Boston: Northeastern University Press, 2001), 173-77. For more on the political context of this bill, see John Mulkern, *The Know-Nothing Party in Massachusetts: The Rise and Fall of a People's Movement* (Boston: Northeastern University Press, 1990), 38-39.

14. *The Hours of Labor. Address of the Ten Hours State Convention* (Boston: Ten Hours State Committee, 1852), 16; Mark Voss-Hubbard, *Beyond Party: Cultures of Anti-Partisanship in Northern Politics before the Civil War* (Baltimore, MD: Johns Hopkins University Press, 2002), 81-82.

Also see John R. Commons et al., *The History of Labour in the United States* (New York: Macmillan, 1918), 1:545-46. Commons refers to an Industrial League's meeting in October 1851, and another Ten Hour State Convention in January 1852 which prompted the legislative reports in April. There are no records of either of these meetings being held, although the document *Hours of Labor* does make passing reference to a convention on January 28, 1852.

15. *The Hours of Labor*, 1. Political abolitionists also often followed this strategy, publicly querying candidates as to their stand on abolishing chattel slavery.

16. *The Hours of Labor*, 1-2.

17. *The Hours of Labor*, 4-5; Laurie, *Beyond Garrison*, 207.

18. Paul Goodman, "The Politics of Industrialism: Massachusetts, 1830-1870," in *Uprooted Americans: Essays to Honor Oscar Handlin*, ed. Richard Bushman et al. (Boston: Little, Brown, 1979), 193.

19. Oscar Handlin, *Boston's Immigrants, 1790-1880: A Study in Acculturation* (1941; rpt. New York: Atheneum, 1974), 51-52, 56, 59-61, 93-94.

20. Albert Wright is one possible example of a legislator who switched allegiances. Wright was a printer from South Boston and an activist in the labor reform movement of the 1840s, as well as a longtime supporter of ten-hour bills in the Massachusetts State Senate. Yet he suddenly spoke against legal limits on the workday in 1855, when the Senate debated a ten-hour bill that had already passed the House by a large margin. Wright's new-found opposition may have been linked to his growing alliances with small manufacturers in his district, men who saw the law as an unnecessary intrusion into what they believed were peaceful labor relations. Or Wright may have been caught up in the nativist sentiments of the period, given his longstanding skepticism toward the Catholic Church in Boston, and decided he had little interest in applying legislative remedies to Irish immigrants' working conditions (even though the Know-Nothings strongly supported the ten-hour law, regardless of whom it benefited). Or perhaps the skeptics were right: they noted that when Wright merged his printing firm in 1857 to form Wright and Potter, he just happened to get the lucrative state printing contract. Ironically, the firm held the contract for more than two decades, and published later reports on successful ten-hour legislation as well as the pioneering studies of the Bureau of the Statistics of Labor. When questioned about his change in course, Wright defended himself in the pages of his own newspaper by claiming that American workers had the right to negotiate their own contracts free from government interference. See Mulkern, *Know-Nothing Party in Massachusetts*, 214, n. 87; Voss-Hubbard, *Beyond Party*, 158–59; and Paul Foos, "Reform Politics in 1850s Massachusetts, and the Hours of Labor Controversy" (graduate seminar paper, Yale University, 1992; in author's possession).

21. See Mulkern, *Know-Nothing Party in Massachusetts*; and *Speech of Honorable E. C. Baker, of Middlesex, on the Bill to Regulate the Hours of Labor in Incorporated Establishments. Delivered to the Senate of Massachusetts, April 13, 1855* (Boston: Wm. White, 1855). For brief discussions about the political context of these debates in the mid-1850s, see Ronald Formisano, *The Transformation of Political Culture: Massachusetts Parties, 1790s–1840s* (New York: Oxford University Press, 1983), 336–40; and Carl Siracusa, *A Mechanical People: Perceptions of the Industrial Order in Massachusetts, 1815–1880* (Middletown, CT: Wesleyan University Press, 1979), 200. Also see David Roediger and Philip Foner, *Our Own Time: A History of American Labor and the Working Day* (New York: Greenwood Press, 1989), chapter 4. Finally, the best overview of all ten-hour politics in the 1850s remains Charles E. Persons, "The Early History of Factory Legislation in Massachusetts from 1825 to the Passage of the Ten Hour Law in 1874," in *Labor Laws and Their Enforcement, with Special Reference to Massachusetts*, ed. Susan M. Kingsbury (New York: Longman, Green, 1911), 55–89. It should be noted that all these references focus on how political parties approached the ten-hour workday, rather than (my emphasis) on labor reform arguments outside the legislature.

22. Handlin, *Boston's Immigrants*, 239; Thomas H. O'Connor, *Civil War Boston: Homefront and Battlefield* (Boston: Northeastern University Press, 1997), 162.

23. "Systematic Labor-Reform Movement," typescript of leaflet, Ira Steward Papers, State Historical Society of Wisconsin, Madison; Commons et al., *History of*

Labour, 2:88; entry on Ira Steward, in *Dictionary of American Biography*, 18:1–2; Lawrence Glickman, "Ira Steward," in *American National Biography*, vol. 20, ed. John Garraty and Mark Carnes (New York: Oxford University Press, 1999), 734–36. See Foner and Roediger, *Our Own Time*, 82, for a discussion of machinists and molders often taking the lead in eight-hour agitation, given technological changes in their workplaces.

For more on Steward's economic and political arguments in support of the eight-hour workday, which he developed from 1865 until his death in 1883, see chapters 3 and 4.

24. *Daily Evening Voice* (*DEV*), December 23, 1864, and May 4, 1865; *Eighth Annual Report of the Bureau of Statistics of Labor, March 1877* (Boston: A. J. Wright, State Printer, 1877), 88–89. In the spring of 1865, the BLRA was incorporated, an unusual step for a labor reform organization. The incorporation may have been related to the association's early interest in cooperative consumer purchasing. In particular, responding to the high cost of coal during wartime winters, the association formed a fuel purchasing network for its members.

25. Extract from report of BLRA in *DEV*, December 7, 1864.

26. Letters of Ira Steward, n.d., n.p., to Wendell Phillips, Wendell Phillips Papers (Ms Am 1953), Houghton Library, Harvard University.

27. Philip Foner, "A Labor Voice for Black Equality: The *Boston Daily Evening Voice*, 1864–1867," *Science and Society* 38 (1974): 304–25. Foner's article focuses on the newspaper's efforts to promote trade union activism and organizing across racial lines, a campaign well ahead of its time.

28. *DEV*, January 4, 1865.

29. *DEV*, January 26 and March 27, 1865.

30. *DEV*, October 4 and December 16, 1865.

31. *DEV*, April 4 and December 4, 1865.

32. *DEV*, April 6 and July 26, 1865.

33. *DEV*, February 24, March 18, April 8, and June 28, 1865; James Harvey Young, "Anna Dickinson," in *Notable American Women, 1607–1950: A Biographical Dictionary*, vol. 1, ed. Edward T. James et al. (Cambridge, MA: Belknap Press of Harvard University Press, 1974), 475–76; Kathleen Berkeley, "Anna Dickinson," in *American National Biography*, 6:557–59.

See also J. Matthew Gallman, *America's Joan of Arc: The Life of Anna Elizabeth Dickinson* (New York: Oxford University Press, 2006), 69–71, 100. It should be noted that in the early 1870s, Dickinson castigated labor union leaders for turning their backs on unskilled workers, including many women and recent immigrants. Her solution to the "labor problem" was government training schools for poor boys and girls, not legal protection for trade unions.

3. Acts of Commission

1. George McNeill, ed., *The Labor Movement: The Problem of Today* (1887; rpt. New York: Augustus Kelley, 1971), 127.

2. *Daily Evening Voice* (*DEV*), January 10, 1865.

3. *DEV*, March 9, 1865.

4. *DEV*, March 13, 1865. For a careful analysis of government investigative reports, see Oz Frankel, *States of Inquiry: Social Investigation and Print Culture in Nineteenth-Century Britain and the United States* (Baltimore, MD: Johns Hopkins University Press, 2006). Whereas Frankel focuses on the commissions' investigations and publications, this study concerns itself more with labor reform organizations and their interactions with these legislative inquiries.

5. David Montgomery, *Beyond Equality: Labor and the Radical Republicans, 1862–1872* (1967; rpt. Urbana: University of Illinois Press, 1981), 122, 124.

6. Edward H. Rogers, Autobiography, State Historical Society of Wisconsin, Madison; *DEV*, April 5, 12, 15, 29, 1865. The various commissions and committees investigating the hours of labor in Massachusetts often took testimony, and sent out circulars seeking responses from workers and employers. But commissioners usually did not conduct on-site visits to examine working conditions.

7. *DEV*, April 7, 1865.

8. *Fincher's Trade Review*, April 22, 1865, typescript in American Bureau of Industrial Research (ABIR) Papers, State Historical Society of Wisconsin, Madison.

9. Massachusetts Legislative Document, House No. 259, 1865. The committee, reflecting its name and original charge, also devoted considerable attention to drafting legislation for the regulation of apprenticeships. Edward Rogers, with his ties to trade unions and the Workingmen's Assembly, wrote the report and bill on that issue (Massachusetts Legislative Document, House No. 256, 1865). Labor reform organizations in Boston did not give much attention to apprenticeship laws, and many activists continued to argue that an eight-hour workday would do more to improve all workers' status, not just skilled trades and their apprentices. For a thorough examination of the apprenticeship question and legislation, and how later reformers and historians have often ignored that part of the committee's deliberations, see John Potter, "The Attempt to Restore the Legal Enforcement of Apprenticeship in Massachusetts in 1865" (paper presented at the annual meeting of the Social Science History Association, Washington, DC, 1997).

10. *The Liberator*, June 9, 1865, typescript in ABIR Papers. Steward made nearly identical arguments in a series of resolutions presented to a meeting at the Hopedale utopian community; see *DEV*, August 4, 1865.

11. *DEV*, June 22, 1865.

12. Ira Steward, *The Eight Hour Movement: A Reduction of Hours is an Increase of Wages* (Boston: Boston Labor Reform Association, 1865), quotation on 4. See *DEV*, September 26, 1865, for an enthusiastic review of Steward's lecture at Kent Hall on Hanover Street, sponsored by the Grand Eight Hour League.

13. For extensive discussions of Steward's theories and their intellectual context, see *A Documentary History of American Industrial Society,* ed. John R. Commons et al., 11 vols. (Cleveland: Arthur H. Clark, 1910–11), 9:24–33; Montgomery, *Beyond Equality,* 249–60; Dorothy W. Douglas, "Ira Steward on Consumption and Unemployment," *Journal of Political Economy* 40 (August 1932): 532–43; Hyman Kuritz, "Ira Steward and the Eight Hour Day," *Science and Society* 22 (1956): 118–34; David Roediger, "Ira Steward and the Anti-Slavery Origins of American Eight-Hour Theory," *Labor History* 27 (Summer 1986): 410–26; Lawrence Glickman, *A Living Wage: American Workers and the Making of Consumer Society* (Ithaca, NY: Cornell University Press, 1997), chapter 5; and Lawrence Glickman, "Workers of the World, Consume: Ira Steward and the Origins of Labor Consumerism," *International Labor and Working-Class History* 52 (Fall 1997): 72–86.

My study does not repeat these analyses of Steward's political economy but links his ideas with his organizational activism and leadership of the Boston labor reform community.

14. Steward, *The Eight Hour Movement,* 7, 13, 18, 24.

15. *DEV,* July 14, 1865; entry on Henry Ingersoll Bowditch, in *Dictionary of American Biography,* vol. 2, ed. Allen Johnson (New York: Scribner, 1928), 492–94; John Harley Warner, "Henry Ingersoll Bowditch," in *American National Biography,* vol. 3, ed. John Garraty and Mark Carnes (New York: Oxford University Press, 1999), 267–69; entry on Franklin Sanborn, in *Dictionary of American Biography,* 16:326–27; Robert Burkholder, "Franklin Sanborn," in *American National Biography,* 19:237–38; Robert Cutler, "An Unpublished Letter of M. A. Bukunin to R. Solger," *International Review of Social History* 33 (1988): 217; Lawrence Goodheart, *Abolitionist, Actuary, Atheist: Elizur Wright and the Reform Impulse* (Kent, Ohio: Kent State University Press, 1990). Also see John T. Cumbler, *From Abolition to Rights for All: The Making of a Reform Community in the Nineteenth Century* (Philadelphia: University of Pennsylvania Press, 2008), for an extensive discussion of Henry Ingersoll Bowditch and his place in the broader Brahmin reform community of mid-nineteenth-century Boston.

16. *DEV,* October 21, 26, and November 2, 9, 18, 23, 1865.

17. Remarks of Ira Steward, Transcript of Hearings, November 30, 1865, 48, 53, 54, Massachusetts Commission on Hours of Labor, 1865, Massachusetts State Archives, Boston.

18. *DEV,* November 3, 1865.

19. *DEV,* November 3, 1865; Donald K. Springen, "Labor's Political Allies," in *The Rhetoric of Protest and Reform, 1878–1898,* ed. Paul H. Boase (Athens: Ohio University Press, 1980), 74.

20. *Remarks of Wendell Phillips at the Mass Meeting of Workingmen in Faneuil Hall, Nov. 2, 1865* (Boston: Voice Printing and Publishing, 1865), 5, 8, 10–21; quotations on 16, 19–20.

21. Oscar Sherwin, *Prophet of Liberty: The Life and Times of Wendell Phillips* (New York: Bookman Associates, 1958), 576–78; Roediger, "Ira Steward," 422. For more

on abolitionists supporting the postwar labor reform campaign, see Timothy Messer-Kruse, *The Yankee International: Marxism and the American Reform Tradition, 1848–1876* (Chapel Hill: University of North Carolina Press, 1998), 31–36.

Phillips's address at Faneuil Hall was not his first public statement in support of the postwar labor reform effort. In early March 1865, speaking in Portland, Maine, on "Capital and Labor," he had made an extensive argument about the harmony of labor and capital and sketched out some of the ideas he would develop in his later speech: "The first and cardinal idea with which we should enter this work is that Capital and Labor are not enemies, but friends; more than this, twins; more than this, Siamese twins, they cannot live a separate life. They are almost identical, being only parts of the same whole. Capital is only the labor of yesterday which has not been consumed, and Labor is only the capital of today that has not been refunded. Capital is but frozen, crystallized labor, and labor is but capital dissolved and become active. There cannot be a war against the same thing in its different stages.... What is Labor? Labor is a man's time, a man's capital, a man's means of working.... There is no antagonism—the one can hardly exist without the other.... [W]e are endeavoring, not to fight Capital, but to study the relations between Capital and Labor. Let this idea be the entering wedge of this discussion, which is to agitate the next thirty years" (*DEV*, March 7, 1865).

22. Report of the Special Commission on the Hours of Labor, and the Condition and Prospects of the Industrial Classes, Massachusetts Legislative Document, House No. 98, 1866, 4, 9–11, 16, 24, 25–28, 49.

23. Report of the Special Commission, 1866, 49–50; Nancy Cohen, *The Reconstruction of American Liberalism, 1865–1914* (Chapel Hill: University of North Carolina Press, 2002), 34–37; Montgomery, *Beyond Equality*, 266–68.

24. *DEV*, March 2, 3, 5, 6, 1866; Letter of Edward H. Rogers to Rev. W. P. Tilden, n.d., in Correspondence, Massachusetts Commission on Hours of Labor, 1865, Massachusetts State Archives.

25. *DEV*, March 23 and April 7, 1866. The *DEV* appeared to be backpedaling from some of its earlier fiery rhetoric in support of the eight-hour day. The newspaper may have taken this more conciliatory stance because it had become the official organ of the moderate, trade-union-dominated Workingmen's Assembly. The assembly still considered itself a rival to Steward's Labor Reform Association, which insisted on a compulsory eight-hour law binding on employers.

26. The fund-raising letter was published in *DEV*, April 28, 1866. Also see *DEV*, July 20, August 10, September 8, October 12, 13, 18, 26, and November 1, 1865, and February 8 and April 6, 1866, for meetings of the Grand League and its local affiliates.

27. *DEV*, April 28, 1866.

28. Massachusetts Legislative Document, House No. 44, 1867, 4.

29. Rogers, Autobiography; *Boston Sunday Globe,* February 5, 1905, clipping in Rogers Papers, State Historical Society of Wisconsin; entry on Amasa Walker, in *Dictionary of American Biography,* 19:338–39; Lawrence Moss, "Amasa Walker," in *American National Biography,* 22:485–87; Philip Giles, "Workingman and Theologian:

Edward Henry Rogers (1824–1909) and the Impact of Evangelicalism on the Making of the American Working Class" (PhD diss., University of Rochester, 1990).

Rogers wrote that Ira Steward coveted his position on this new commission and sent him innumerable letters attacking his integrity, which he threw out without even showing them to his colleagues. (One letter from Steward to this commission has survived, but it contains rather general arguments about reform.) As relations between the two reformers deteriorated, associates in the eight-hour leagues arranged for Steward to visit Rogers in his statehouse office, where Steward grudgingly apologized for the tone of his correspondence. Later, Steward did praise Rogers's minority commission report. See Rogers, Autobiography; and Correspondence, Massachusetts Committee on Hours of Labor, 1866, Massachusetts State Archives.

30. *DEV,* October 2 and 12, 1866; *Boston Weekly Voice,* October 18, 1866, typescript in ABIR Papers. Phillips's refusal to run for Congress in 1866 was probably due in part to his antipathy toward party politics, and his reluctance to undermine the Republican Party when it was struggling with Reconstruction in the southern states. Also, Phillips may have seen this workingmen's party as basically a local affair, not a fully developed political movement for statewide labor reform.

For more on Guiney's campaign, and the unsuccessful efforts to create a stable political coalition between Irish immigrants, labor reformers, and Radical Republicans, see James Green, *Boston Workers: A Labor History* (Boston: Boston Public Library, 1979), 50–51. Also see Montgomery, *Beyond Equality,* 269–73.

31. Massachusetts Legislative Document, House No. 44, 1867, 1–40; Moss, "Amasa Walker," in *American National Biography,* 22:485–87.

32. Massachusetts Legislative Document, House No. 44, 1867, 100–101, 116, 122, 141; Montgomery, *Beyond Equality,* 292.

Rogers wrote in his autobiography that William Hyde was particularly upset with his minority report. He explained away Hyde's opposition as the grumbling of an old man enamored of currency reform, and still holding grudges against working-class mobs from his days as a Garrisonian abolitionist in the 1830s. Rogers also claimed that Governor Bullock was disappointed in the majority report and sympathetic to the eight-hour day, but the governor made no public statements to that effect. See Rogers, Autobiography.

Rogers also wrote a brief pamphlet sketching out some of the ideas he developed in his minority report: *Reasons for Believing That the People Will Use Leisure Wisely. with a Statement of the Character of the Eight Hour Movement. By a Workingman* (Boston: Voice Printing and Publishing, 1866).

One correspondent to the *DEV* endorsed Rogers's moderate stand and gave a backhanded slap to other labor reformers: "The few reformers who have asked for more" than Rogers's proposed law "stand relatively to the mass of petitioners, about as Mr. Wendell Phillips does to the Republican party" (*DEV,* March 12, 1867).

33. Minutes of December 11 and 26, 1866, and January 26, February 19, and March 19, 1867, Minute Book, Workingmen's Institute of Boston, Massachusetts Historical Society, Boston.

34. "Middleton" (George Gunton), biographical sketch of George McNeill, *Labor Standard*, July 28 and August 4, 1877; W. D. P. Bliss, "George E. McNeill," *American Fabian* 1 (November 1895): 5–7; Frank K. Foster, "George Edwin McNeill. A Memorial," *Massachusetts Labor Bulletin* 12 (September 1907): 83–98; Letter of Ira Steward, West Somerville, Massachusetts, to Friedrich Sorge, March 13, [1876/77], Steward Papers, State Historical Society of Wisconsin. See also Robert R. Montgomery, "'To Fight This Thing till I Die': The Career of George Edwin McNeill," in *Culture, Gender, Race, and U.S. Labor History*, ed. Ronald C. Kent et al. (Westport, CT: Greenwood Press, 1993), 4–8.

35. Minutes of April 2, 30, and July 2, 1867, Minute Book, Workingmen's Institute of Boston.

36. Minutes of November 19, December 24, 31, 1867, and February 4, June 2, 9, 16, 30, and July 7, 1868, Minute Book, Workingmen's Institute of Boston.

37. Minutes of March 17, July 7, and August 25, 1868, Minute Book, Workingmen's Institute of Boston.

38. Minutes of September 1, December 15, 29, 1868, Minute Book, Workingmen's Institute of Boston.

39. Minutes of January 19, February 9, 23, and March 2, 1869, Minute Book, Workingmen's Institute of Boston. Also see *American Workman*, May 1, June 5, 19, 1869, for detailed reports on several meetings that considered a number of issues, including the hours of labor and woman suffrage.

40. Minutes of August 17, 31, and September 7, 1869, Minute Book, Workingmen's Institute of Boston. Also see *American Workman*, September 18, 1869, for a report on one of the eight-hour hearings for Boston city workers.

41. Minutes of October 5, November 16, 30, and December 21, 1869, Minute Book, Workingmen's Institute of Boston.

Steward and McNeill may have pulled away from the institute not only because of internal problems with finances and leadership but also because they had recently formed the Boston Eight Hour League to press their key demand for reduced working hours. For more on this league, see chapter 4.

42. Minutes of December 28, 1869, January 4, 11, February 1, 15, and March 8, 1870, Minute Book, Workingmen's Institute of Boston.

43. Minutes of May 31, 1870, Minute Book, Workingmen's Institute of Boston. The political discussion at this meeting may also have been motivated by the work of the Massachusetts Labor Reform Party, founded the previous fall. For more on this party, see chapter 4.

44. Minutes of June 21, 1870, Minute Book, Workingmen's Institute of Boston. An account book from the Workman Hall Company (1870–74) shows that other labor organizations continued to rent rooms at the headquarters into late 1870 and through 1871—including the Massachusetts State Labor Union, Labor Reform Ward and City Committees, Section 20 of the International Workingmen's Association, and the Knights of St. Crispin. See Account Book, Workman Hall Company, 1870–74, Massachusetts Historical Society, Boston.

45. *DEV*, January 17, 1867; Mary Blewett, *Constant Turmoil: The Politics of Industrial Life in Nineteenth-Century New England* (Amherst: University of Massachusetts Press, 2000), 105–6.

46. Ira Steward, *The Meaning of the Eight Hour Movement* (Boston, 1868), 7, 8, 11, 12, 14.

4. The Generation of 1869

1. *Workingmen's Advocate,* January 16, 1869.

2. "The Life of Benjamin R. Tucker, Disclosed by Himself in the Principality of Monaco at the Age of 74," 85, Benjamin Tucker Papers, Manuscripts and Archives Section, New York Public Library; *The Word,* February 1884; Martin Henry Blatt, *Free Love and Anarchism: The Biography of Ezra Heywood* (Urbana: University of Illinois Press, 1989), especially chapters 1–3; William O. Reichert, *Partisans and Freedom: A Study in American Anarchism* (Bowling Green, OH: Bowling Green University Popular Press, 1976), 289–93; James J. Martin, *Men against the State: The Expositors of Individualist Anarchism in America, 1827–1908* (DeKalb, IL: Adrian Allen Associates, 1953), 110–25.

3. E. H. Heywood, *The Labor Party: A Speech Delivered before the Labor Reform League of Worcester, Mass.* (New York: Journeymen Printers' Co-operative Association, 1868), 3, 9, 12, 13, 17.

In another speech, "The Emancipation of Labor," delivered in Biddeford, Maine, on August 31, 1868, Heywood went so far as to suggest that workers might vote the Democratic ticket in the upcoming presidential campaign if the party would support specific issues like the eight-hour day. Heywood's suggestion was unusual advice for an ardent abolitionist and avowed skeptic of the established parties, but his remarks demonstrate his willingness to shake up the established political order so as to secure workers more leverage in the electoral arena.

4. Heywood, *The Labor Party,* 13–14, 15, 20.

5. *New York World,* January 30, 1869; *The Revolution,* February 11, 1869. This section traces the league's development by focusing on some of its most significant meetings and statements but is not intended to be a complete chronological catalogue of convention proceedings.

6. *The Revolution,* February 11, 1869; *Workingman's Advocate,* February 13, 1869.

7. *New York World,* May 27, 1869. See also *American Workman,* June 5 and July 3, 1869.

8. *New York World,* May 27, 1869. The practice of appointing committees at conventions to prepare resolutions was quite common with the Labor Reform League of the 1840s. But this later league always had resolutions prepared in advance, and usually Heywood wrote them with the executive committee's approval.

9. *New York World,* May 27, 1869. See Sidney H. Morse's essay on "The Labor Question" (*The Word,* April 1875) for a perceptive discussion of the distinctions between the "eight hour school" of labor reform and the "equity" school, which focused on the concept of just prices and fair exchange.

10. *New York World,* May 27, 1869.

11. *New York World,* May 27, 1869.

12. *American Workman,* June 26, 1869.

13. *American Workman,* August 21, 1869. Heywood's statement may have been motivated, in part, by reports that a Labor Reform Party would be formed in advance of the fall elections. For more on this party, which assembled in late September, see section IV of this chapter.

14. *American Workman,* August 21, 1869.

15. *Workingman's Advocate,* October 23, 1869. For more on the Boston Eight Hour League, see below.

16. "Life of Benjamin R. Tucker," 87; Reichert, *Partisans and Freedom,* 142; Martin, *Men against the State,* 202. Tucker's remarks about printed resolutions never being officially endorsed, and speeches often lost in summary press accounts, are borne out by newspaper reports of the league's meetings. The most detailed information available about the league's activities remains the numerous published resolutions. Although these statements usually were not subject to a formal vote at the meetings, they did reflect what the league's leadership was thinking at the time.

17. *New York World,* January 26, 1870.

18. *New York World,* January 26, 1870. For more on Jennie Collins, see Laura Vapnek, *Breadwinners: Working Women and Economic Independence 1865–1920* (Urbana: University of Illinois Press, 2009), chapter 1.

19. *Workingman's Advocate,* May 28, 1870.

20. *Workingman's Advocate,* February 4, 1871.

21. *The Word,* May 1872.

22. *The Word,* July 1873.

23. *The Word,* April and July 1874. Heywood's criticism of the Massachusetts Bureau of the Statistics of Labor may have been prompted by leadership changes that made the agency less sympathetic to labor reform. For more on the bureau, see section III of this chapter.

24. *The Word,* December 1875.

25. *The Word,* June 1877, March 1880. It is possible that the NELRL continued to meet after 1886, but no records exist of any further convention proceedings.

26. *American Workman,* August 21 and September 25, 1869; Margaret Bendroth, *Fundamentalists in the City: Conflict and Division in Boston's Churches, 1885–1950* (New York: Oxford University Press, 2005), 21. Also, see *Boston Eight Hour League, Its Objects and Work* (Boston: Boston Eight Hour League, 1872) for background on the league's founding.

27. Leaflet, "Mass Convention under the Auspices of the Boston Eight-Hour League" (1870), Boston Public Library. As for the convention itself, it met on May 18, but only one brief report of its proceedings provides summaries of several speeches given by McNeill, Steward, and others. See *American Workman,* May 28, 1870.

28. *Workingman's Advocate,* March 11, 1871; *National Standard,* June 10, 1871.

29. Fundraising Circular, Boston Eight Hour League, November 20, 1871, Boston Public Library.

30. Leaflet, "Free Hall for Working-men and Working-women. Plan and Estimates," n.d., Boston Public Library; leaflet, "Head Quarters Labor Movement in Massachusetts," Boston, May 30, 1873, Boston Public Library; *Boston Eight Hour League, Its Objects and Work,* 8–9. The 1872 pamphlet also reprints the texts of the fund-raising circular and plan for the hall, as well as a list of contributors to the fund—including former governor William Claflin, Mayor William Gaston, and Senator Charles Sumner, each of whom gave $50. Wendell Phillips and Benjamin Butler helped to underwrite the league's conventions.

31. "Protest of the Boston Eight Hour League against the repeal or amendment of the National Eight Hour Law," [April 4, 1872], U.S. Senate Committee on Education and Labor, Senate Papers, 42A-H7, Record Group 46.16, National Archives, Washington, DC.

32. *American Workman,* June 19, 1869.

33. *The Commonwealth,* June 1, 22, 1872, typescripts in ABIR Papers, State Historical Society of Wisconsin, Madison; *Boston Globe,* May 30, 1872, and *New York World,* May 30, 1872, both cited in Timothy Messer-Kruse, "Eight Hours, Greenbacks, and 'Chinamen': Wendell Phillips, Ira Steward, and the Fate of Labor Reform in Massachusetts," *Labor History* 42 (May 2001): 133–34. Oliver, McNeill and the Bureau of the Statistics of Labor are discussed further below.

34. *The Commonwealth,* June 29, 1872, typescript in ABIR papers. Ezra Heywood recalled that Phillips gave him similar instructions, probably at the same rally in 1866: "Don't discuss debt, don't meddle with money or land questions but stick to eight hours." By 1872, Heywood reported, Phillips had changed his mind "and talked little but finance afterwards!" But Phillips refused Heywood's invitation to become a regular participant again in the New England Labor Reform League, where financial reform was central to the debates. Phillips replied: "After one has worked 40 years, served in 20 movements & been kicked out of all of them he rather likes to paddle his own canoe!" *The Word,* February 1884.

35. *The Commonwealth,* June 29, 1872. Timothy Messer-Kruse, "Eight Hours, Greenbacks, and 'Chinamen,'" has also extensively studied the Phillips-Steward schism and come to some similar conclusions. He too finds that the split was not a simple matter of the rich patrician versus the humble mechanic, though he does not consider personality conflicts and the struggle over who would be the public spokesman for the labor reform movement. Messer-Kruse also does a superb job dismantling previous explanations in the literature about Phillips becoming an avid Greenbacker and Steward disowning him for that apostasy. But there are some indications that Phillips was expressing more interest in financial reform as a whole (not just greenbacks), schemes that Steward rejected when he left the New England Labor Reform League.

Messer-Kruse sees the root of this split in an intense debate over the rights of Chinese laborers in the United States. Steward argued for harsh restrictions, whereas Phillips insisted on civil rights for all. This ideological analysis is quite convincing on an intellectual level, but it does not address the ramifications of the split for other cross-class organizations or for other labor reform issues.

Finally, Messer-Kruse argues that Phillips and Steward divided over their fundamental philosophies of reform—Phillips holding a more universal reform vision and Steward advocating a more reductionist stance. Again, this is a perceptive observation, but it ends up being rather hard on Steward and rather easy on Phillips—as opposed to previous generations of scholars who blamed Phillips for turning his back on the labor reform movement. Phillips's broad conception of reform was indeed often bold and courageous, but it ran the risk of becoming disorganized and unfocused, as Steward had observed in the New England Labor Reform League. Meanwhile, Steward's continued insistence on the primacy of the eight-hour day could appear monomaniacal at times. But Steward never intended to make a narrow argument just about working hours; his efforts were always based on the idea that a shorter workday was the necessary first step down the road toward social transformation.

36. George E. McNeill, ed., *The Labor Movement: The Problem of Today* (1887; rpt. New York: Augustus Kelley, 1971), 144–45.

37. Ira Steward, *Poverty* (Boston: Boston Eight Hour League, 1873), 26–31.

38. "Eight Hour League Convention," *Equity* 1 (June 1874): 20, 21. Given these criticisms, it is surprising that Ezra Heywood spoke at this annual meeting of the Eight Hour League—something that he rarely did. He "said that while he differed as to the measures, he was in harmony with the LEAGUE, so far as it aimed to benefit working people, and lift them from their condition of poverty."

39. *The Socialist*, June 17, 1876.

40. Letter of Ira Steward to Friedrich Sorge [Spring 1877], Steward Papers, State Historical Society of Wisconsin.

41. *Labor Standard*, June 9, 1878; E. E. Spencer, "Ira Steward," *Prospect Union Review* 3 (November 20, 1895): 11–14.

42. Letter of Ira Steward to Friedrich Sorge, March 14 [1877], Steward Papers; Lawrence Glickman, "Ira Steward," in *American National Biography*, vol. 20, ed. John Garraty and Mark Carnes (New York: Oxford University Press, 1999), 734–36; entry on Ira Steward, in *Dictionary of American Biography Dictionary*, vol. 18, ed. Dumas Malone (New York: Scribner, 1936), 1–2.

For an extensive discussion of the eight-hour movement's broader arguments across the nation, including those of Steward and the league, see Alexander Yard, "A Fair Day's Work: The Shorter Hours Movement, Labor Reformers, and American Political Culture, 1865–1916" (PhD diss., Washington University, 1994), especially chapters 1–3. Also see Rosanne Currarino, "'To Taste of Life's Sweets': The Eight-Hour Movement and the Origins of Modern Liberalism," *Labor's Heritage* 12 (Spring/Summer 2004): 22–23.

43. *Fourth Annual Report of the Massachusetts Bureau of Statistics of Labor* (Boston: Wright and Potter, 1873), 5, 7–9; Edward H. Rogers, Autobiography, Rogers Papers, State Historical Society of Wisconsin.

44. *Seventh Annual Report of the Massachusetts Bureau of Statistics of Labor* (Boston: Wright and Potter, 1876), 280; William R. Brock, *Investigation and Responsibility: Public Responsibility in the United States, 1865–1900* (Cambridge, UK: Cambridge

University Press, 1984), 148–51; Wendell D. MacDonald, "The Early History of Labor Statistics in the United States," *Labor History* 13 (Spring 1972): 267–73; Henry F. Bedford, ed., *Their Lives and Numbers: The Condition of Working People in Massachusetts, 1870–1900* (Ithaca, NY: Cornell University Press, 1995), 3–7; Jesse Jones, *Henry K. Oliver* (Boston, 1886); entry on Henry K. Oliver, in *Dictionary of American Biography*, 14:18–19.

Boston labor reform organizations were not extensively involved in the legislation regulating working hours and schooling for children in factories. Most labor reformers did not oppose the new laws but did not give them a high priority in their lobbying efforts, probably because they saw such enactments as merely partial measures compared with a comprehensive eight-hour law.

45. *Fourth Annual Report of the Massachusetts Bureau of Statistics of Labor*, 1873, 9–10; Massachusetts Legislative Document, Senate No. 279, 1870; *Labor Standard*, August 4, 1877. Also see James Leiby, *Carroll Wright and Labor Reform: The Origins of Labor Statistics* (Cambridge, MA: Harvard University Press, 1960), 55–59. For an extensive analysis of the bureau's investigations of working women throughout the nineteenth century, see Henry F. Bedford, "Good Men and 'Working Girls': The Bureau of Statistics of Labor, 1870–1900," in *Women of the Commonwealth: Work, Family, and Social Change in Nineteenth-Century Massachusetts*, ed. Susan L. Porter (Amherst: University of Massachusetts Press, 1996), 85–98.

46. *First Annual Report of the Massachusetts Bureau of Statistics of Labor* (Boston: Wright and Potter, 1870), 196–98; *Second Annual Report of the Massachusetts Bureau of Statistics of Labor* (Boston: Wright and Potter, 1871), 550–68; *Fourth Annual Report of the Massachusetts Bureau of Statistics of Labor*, 1873, 260–63, 350–53, 461–67, 488, 501–3. This Fourth Annual Report also contained Steward's essay, "Poverty," which the Boston Eight Hour League subsequently reprinted.

47. *Fourth Annual Report of the Massachusetts Bureau of Statistics of Labor*, 1873, 13–18.

48. *The Worker*, January 26, 1873; *Workingman's Advocate*, February 1, 1873.

49. Leaflet, "To the Friends of Labor Investigation in Massachusetts," Boston, February 25, 1873, New England Depository Library.

50. *Workingman's Advocate*, March 15, 1873; Massachusetts Legislative Document, House No. 383, 1873; Leiby, *Carroll Wright and Labor Reform*, 62–69; Brock, *Investigation and Responsibility*, 154–55; Bedford, *Their Lives and Numbers*, 7–11, 49, 226; Edwin Gabler, "Gilded Age Labor in Massachusetts and Illinois: Statistical Surveys of Workingmen's Families," *Labor's Heritage* 4 (Fall 1992): 4–21. Also see Horace G. Wadlin, *Carroll Davidson Wright: A Memorial* (Boston: Wright and Potter, 1911).

In 1874, after his dismissal from the BSL, McNeill was appointed deputy state constable to oversee laws governing the education of children employed in factories—Oliver's old job! His 1875 report (Massachusetts Legislative Document, Senate No. 50) contained recommendations for stronger laws and stricter enforcement, but McNeill did not press his ideas in the Boston labor reform community.

51. Francis A. Walker's letter is quoted in "a Letter from the Commissioner of Labor to the Honorable Secretary of the Interior, Declaring the Policy of the Bureau," February 4, 1885 (printed copy), Department and Bureau Forms, Records of U.S. Bureau of Labor Statistics, Record Group 257, National Archives, Washington, DC.

52. One exception to Wright's reluctance to propose reforms was the Bureau's *Sixth Annual Report* (1875), the second written under his direction and thus early in his career as a labor statistician. Although Wright did not support any further reduction in the hours of labor beyond the recently enacted ten-hour law (1874), he did urge that child labor be banned from factories. He also endorsed previous recommendations regarding machine safety, ventilation, and factory inspection, though he never supported Oliver and McNeill's arguments for cooperatives. He summed up his ideas in a model Factory Act that he recommended to the legislature. See *Sixth Annual Report*, 177–87. Also see John F. McClymer, "How to Read Wright: The Equity of the Wage System and the Morality of Spending," *Hayes Historical Journal* 8 (Winter 1989): 37–43, for a discussion of Wright's brief but bold foray into the concept of a minimum-wage law.

53. John R. Commons et al., *History of Labour in the United States* (New York: Macmillan, 1918), 2:140; *Labor Standard*, August 4, 1877.

Since the *national* labor reform party was not organized until 1871, the Massachusetts party clearly was not established as a state auxiliary of that body.

54. *American Workman*, October 2, 1869; *Workingman's Advocate*, October 30, 1869.

The shorter-hours plank, reflecting the presence of so many factory workers, called for a law compelling all manufacturing corporations to run on a ten-hour day or surrender their charters. See *American Workman*, January 15, 1870.

55. Edward Rogers, *Is It Expedient to Form a Political Party in the Interest of Labor?* (Chelsea, MA, 1869); Rogers, Autobiography.

56. *Workingman's Advocate*, November 20, 27, 1869; Nathan Fine, *Labor and Farmer Parties in the United States, 1828–1928* (New York: Rand School of Social Science, 1928), 29.

Since reports vary as to exactly which legislators belonged to the Labor Reform Party, or endorsed its platform, and since the Journals of the Massachusetts House and Senate did not record the party affiliation on votes, it is difficult to determine the precise impact of this party on key legislation. The discussion in this section focuses on the party's nominations, platforms, and electoral campaigns.

57. *American Workman*, September 17, 1870. Two recent controversies also prompted debates on the convention floor. Reports that a shoe manufacturer in the far western Massachusetts town of North Adams had hired Chinese laborers sparked the Crispin delegates to demand a strong resolution against the importation of "coolie labor." Cummings's committee drafted a carefully worded proclamation which stated "that while we welcome voluntary emigrants from every clime, and pledge them the protection of our laws and equal opportunity in every field of industry, still we are inflexibly opposed to the importation, by capitalists, of laborers from China and elsewhere,

for the purpose of degrading and cheapening American labor, and will resist it by all the legal and constitutional means in our power." The use of state militiamen to suppress labor protest in Fall River also prompted the convention to pass a supplementary resolution condemning the use of "State constabulary and militia to overawe and persecute the laborers of Massachusetts, under the specious pleas of riot and disorder." For more on the controversy over Chinese workers, see Anthony W. Lee, *A Shoemaker's Story* (Princeton, NJ: Princeton University Press, 2008).

58. Letter of Wendell Phillips, Boston, to Charles Cowley, September 12, 1870, quoted in George Austin, *Life and Times of Wendell Phillips* (Boston: Wilson Brothers, 1884), 258–60.

59. *American Workman*, October 29, 1870, typescript in ABIR Papers; Carlos Martyn, *Wendell Phillips: The Agitator* (New York, 1890), 380; Irving H. Bartlett, *Wendell Phillips: Brahmin Radical* (Boston: Beacon Press, 1961), 353.

Not everyone believed Phillips's protestations that he was in the campaign primarily to educate and organize the laboring masses. Emily Grew, a close personal friend, chided Phillips before he had even been nominated for governor: "It seems like a deplorable descent from the high moral vantage ground, for you to step into such a post"; people were starting to assume "that personal political advancement is one of your aims." Letter of Emily Grew to Wendell Phillips, August 12, 1870, quoted in James Brewer Stewart, *Wendell Phillips: Liberty's Hero* (Baton Rouge: Louisiana State University Press, 1986), 299.

60. Richard Abbott, "Massachusetts: Maintaining Hegemony," in *Radical Republicans in the North: State Politics during Reconstruction*, ed. James Mohr (Baltimore, MD: Johns Hopkins University Press, 1976), 15; Stewart, *Wendell Phillips: Liberty's Hero*, 299–300. For an extensive statistical analysis of the labor reform vote in 1869 and 1870, see Dale Baum, *The Civil War Party System: The Case of Massachusetts, 1848–1876* (Chapel Hill: University of North Carolina Press, 1984), 146–47, 150–55.

61. *American Workman*, February 4, 1871, typescript in ABIR Papers.

62. *American Workman*, October 7, 1871, typescript in ABIR Papers.

63. Austin, *Life and Times of Wendell Phillips*, 263–67; Phillips's speech is quoted on 267.

64. *American Workman*, October 7, 1871; Abbott, "Massachusetts: Maintaining Hegemony," 20; Austin, *Life and Times of Wendell Phillips*, 268.

65. *Workingman's Advocate*, November 18, 1871. A modern biographer of Phillips, James Brewer Stewart, has argued that the Labor Reform Party campaign of 1870 was really part of Phillips's scheme to build momentum for Butler's election in 1871. See Stewart, *Wendell Phillips: Liberty's Hero*, 298.

66. *Workingman's Advocate*, April 13, May 4, and October 26, 1872.

67. *Workingman's Advocate*, June 7 and August 16, 1873.

68. Charles E. Persons, "The Early History of Factory Legislation in Massachusetts from 1825 to the Passage of the Ten Hour Law in 1874," in *Labor Laws and Their Enforcement with Special Reference to Massachusetts*, ed. Susan M. Kingsbury (New York: Longman, Green, 1911), 123–25.

69. *Workingman's Advocate*, July 11, 18, and October 24, 1874; "The New Labor Party," *Equity* 1 (November 1874): 61-62.

70. Letter of Wendell Phillips, Boston, to G. J. Holyoake, July 22, 1874, quoted in Austin, *Life and Times of Wendell Phillips*, 304-6.

71. Oscar Sherwin, *Prophet of Liberty: The Life and Times of Wendell Phillips* (New York: Bookman Associates, 1958), 633-35; Lorenzo Sears, *Wendell Phillips: Orator and Agitator* (New York, 1909), 314.

Phillips also ran for governor on the Greenback Party ticket in 1877. He received support from some workers active in local socialist politics, but Steward and the eight-hour activists continued to staunchly oppose both Phillips and currency reform. See Kenneth Fones-Wolf, "Boston Eight Hour Men, New York Marxists, and Emergence of the International Labor Union: Prelude to the AFL," *Historical Journal of Massachusetts* 9 (1981): 53.

72. Letters of Ira Steward, West Somerville, Massachusetts, to Friedrich Sorge, December 4, 1876, and March 1, 1877, Steward Papers. For more on Henry Delano and Jesse Jones, see chapter 5.

73. *Labor Leader*, April 10, 1897. For more on the Christian Labor Union, see chapter 5.

Part II

1. Oscar Handlin, *Boston's Immigrants, 1790-1880: A Study in Acculturation* (1941; rpt. New York: Atheneum, 1974), 212-13; Sam Bass Warner Jr., *Streetcar Suburbs: The Process of Growth in Boston (1870-1900)* (Cambridge, MA: Harvard University Press, 1962), 6; David Ward, *Cities and Immigrants: A Geography of Change in Nineteenth Century America* (New York: Oxford University Press, 1971), 76; Stephen Thernstrom, *The Other Bostonians: Poverty and Progress in the American Metropolis, 1880-1970* (Cambridge, MA: Harvard University Press, 1973), 11, 113.

2. Warner, *Streetcar Suburbs*, 17, 19, 163; Thomas O'Connor, *Bibles, Brahmins, and Bosses: A Short History of Boston* (Boston: Boston Public Library, 1984), 120-21; Thomas O'Connor, *The Hub: Boston Past and Present* (Boston: Northeastern University Press, 2001), 144.

5. Piety and Protest

1. [Justice to Labor], printed invitation, Boston, June 17, 1872, Boston Public Library.

2. *Live to Help Live. An Address from Friends of the Workingman, to the Pulpit, the Platform, and the Press, in the United States of America* (Boston: Conference of Labor Reformers, 1872), 4, 7, 10, 11.

There is one report that, shortly after New Year's Day, 1873, Linton and others met again at 14 Bromfield Street to form a Societal Reconstruction Association. This meeting may have been an attempt to create yet another organization out of the previous year's conference, but there are no further accounts of this association. See *Workingman's Advocate*, January 18, 1873.

3. *Live to Help Live*, 3, 13.

4. Halah H. Loud, "Biographical Sketch of the Reverend Jesse Henry Jones," in Jesse Jones, *Joshua Davidson Christian* (New York: Grafton Press, 1907), vii–xiv.

Henry May, *Protestant Churches and Industrial America* (1949; rpt. New York: Octagon Books, 1963), 75–79, and Arthur Mann, *Yankee Reformers in the Urban Age* (Cambridge, MA: Harvard University Press, 1954), 87–89, both paint Jones as an orthodox Christian zealot and utopian communist. But Jones's own writings portray a man wrestling with both utopian visions and practical ideas for labor reform. In fact, Jones proved to be more pragmatic than some of the other religious activists in his organizations.

5. Jones, *Joshua Davidson*, 129, 130, 139, 140. Jones's pronouncements on labor reform were published posthumously in this book, which claims to be "a parable" about a minister, Joshua Davidson, "as told by his body servant." Though Jones chose to discuss his ideas in this thinly veiled and semifictitious autobiographical account, he included verbatim material from pamphlets written decades earlier. Therefore, the supposed speeches and sermons of Joshua Davidson are certainly a fair reflection of Jones's thoughts on religion and labor reform in the latter third of the nineteenth century.

6. Jones, *Joshua Davidson*, 220–22. Jones promoted many of these same ideas about industrial democracy and workers' cooperatives in his essay "The Labor Problem," *International Review* 9 (July 1880): 51–68. For more on Jones's ideas about economics and class relations, see Martin J. Burke, *The Conundrum of Class: Public Discourse on the Social Order in America* (Chicago: University of Chicago Press, 1995), 148–49.

7. Jones, *Joshua Davidson*, 223–25.

8. Philip L. Giles, "Workingman and Theologian: Edward Henry Rogers (1824–1909) and the Impact of Evangelicalism on the Making of the American Working Class" (PhD diss., University of Rochester, 1990), 148–52.

9. For previous surveys of the CLU, see James Dombrowski, *The Early Days of Christian Socialism in America* (New York: Columbia University Press, 1936), chapter 7 (77–83), which emphasizes the group's articulation of Christian Socialism. Charles Hopkins, *The Rise of the Social Gospel in American Protestantism, 1865–1915* (New Haven, CT: Yale University Press, 1940), 42–49, disagrees with Dombrowski's interpretation and sees the CLU as motivated primarily by a less focused sense of Christian humanitarianism. Hopkins also argues that the CLU's real importance lay in its links with Social Gospel ministers of the 1880s and 1890s. Also see Aaron Abell, *The Urban Impact on American Protestantism, 1865–1900* (1943; rpt. Hamden, CT: Archon, 1962), 21–26; and Robert H. Craig, *Religion and Radical Politics: An Alternative Christian Tradition in the United States* (Philadelphia: Temple University Press, 1992), 18–28. Much of this previous scholarship focuses on the CLU's economic theories and religious ideas, not on its role in the Boston labor reform community's organizational development.

Also see Robert C. Reinders, "T. Wharton Collens and the Christian Labor Union," *Labor History* 8 (Winter 1967): 53–70, for a biographical account of the Louisiana lawyer who provided substantial financial backing for the CLU and its publications. Collens added his distinctive brand of southern Catholic theology to articles that he wrote for CLU journals.

10. Reinders, "T. Wharton Collens and the Christian Labor Union," 59. There are no extensive accounts of the proceedings from either of these "Bible Labor Reform Conventions."

11. *Workingman's Advocate,* January 2, 1875; handbill, "The Christian Labor Union of Boston" (handwritten date, probably by Edward Rogers, February 1875), Edward Rogers Papers, State Historical Society of Wisconsin, Madison.

Jones also sketched out a model agreement for an "Industrial Copartnership"— part of a brief paper published in the *Fourth Annual Report of the Massachusetts Bureau of Statistics of Labor,* 1873, 356–63—where employers and employees could both invest in a company and share in the profits.

12. *Address of Edward H. Rogers Before the Christian Labor Union, in the Vestry of Park St. Church, Boston, May 27th, 1873* (Boston: W. C. Allan), 2, 4.

13. "Our Ideal," and "The Two Methods," *Equity* 1 (April 1874): 1–3.

14. "The Remedy," *Equity* 1 (August 1874): 33–34; "What Shall We Do Now?" *Equity* 1 (December 1874): 65–66.

15. "The End," *Equity* 2 (December 1875): 28; Reinders, "T. Wharton Collens and the Christian Labor Union," 64–68.

In the fall of 1879, as his second publishing venture collapsed, Jones continued to declare his allegiance to Republican Party politics. He wrote a letter to the *Labor Standard* (October 11, 1879) urging workers to vote the Republican ticket because that party had enacted laws establishing the BSL, the ten-hour day, and the factory inspection system. The newspaper's editor, George Gunton, accused Jones of distorting the historical record by giving Republicans credit for bills that legislators approved very reluctantly only after years of agitation and struggle.

16. Edwin M. Chamberlin, *Sovereigns of Industry* (Boston: Lee and Shepard, 1875), 164–65. The Sovereigns of Industry had a strong presence in the western Massachusetts cities of Worcester and Springfield during the 1870s. They fashioned themselves to be the industrial equivalent of the Grange movement (the Patrons of Husbandry) and set up numerous cooperative stores modeled on the Protective Union's previous efforts in the 1840s and 1850s. John Orvis was a traveling lecturer for the Sovereigns, and George McNeill served as a state officer, but the organization did not have much influence in the Boston labor reform community. See Steve Leiken, *The Practical Utopians: American Workers and the Cooperative Movement in the Gilded Age* (Detroit, MI: Wayne State University Press, 2005), 19–23.

17. Chamberlin, *Sovereigns of Industry,* 5, 6, 68–69, 164–65. For more on Chamberlin's ideas about class, see Burke, *Conundrum of Class,* 144–46.

18. Robert V. Bruce, *1877: Year of Violence* (1959; rpt. Chicago: Quadrangle Books, 1970), 34–36, 41, 232, 261; see also Philip S. Foner, *The Great Labor Uprising of 1877* (New York: Monad Press, 1977), 25–26. The following discussion focuses not on details of the strike itself but rather on how labor reformers in Boston tried to understand this large-scale protest in the context of their ideas about social change.

19. Ezra Heywood, *The Great Strike: Its Relation to Labor, Property, and Government*. (Princeton, MA: Co-operative Publishing, 1878), 1, 3–5, 11, 19, 22–23. Also see Burke, *Conundrum of Class*, 146–47; William O. Reichert, *Partisans of Freedom: A Study in American Anarchism* (Bowling Green, OH: Bowling Green University Popular Press, 1976), 291–92; James J. Martin, *Men against the State: The Expositors of Individual Anarchism in America, 1827–1908* (DeKalb, IL: Adrian Allen Associates, 1953), 121–22.

20. Jones, *Joshua Davidson*, 292, 293–94. Jones proposed a far more modest solution than Heywood's grand vision for eliminating private property. Jones argued for government ownership of railroad track lines, though not necessarily the rolling stock. And he urged that all railroad workers be organized into a "public-service civil army" with job security, higher wages, and the eight-hour workday (296).

21. *Labor Standard*, May 5, 1880.

22. *Chicago Tribune*, June 30, 1878, typescript—"The Labor Movement of 1878 in Chicago"—includes excerpts from both McNeill's interview and his rally speech.

23. Jama Lazerow, "'The Workingman's Hour': The 1886 Labor Uprising in Boston," *Labor History* 21 (Spring 1980): 202–4, 217. Here again, the focus of my discussion is not on the strike itself—which Lazerow has carefully described and analyzed—but on how Boston labor reformers made sense of this renewed conflict.

The Central Labor Union of Boston consistently promoted a broad labor reform agenda. But the organization was a coalition of local trade unions and did not actively recruit a cross-class membership. District Assembly 30 (Knights of Labor) can be considered, in some ways, a labor reform organization with a cross-class membership, even as it also resembled a trade union federation deeply involved with strikes and boycotts; several prominent activists and reformers, such as George McNeill and Jesse Jones, held leadership roles. But surviving reports from local Knights assemblies in Boston are concerned mostly with internal organizational disputes and national proposals having little direct connection to the Boston labor reform community. For more on District Assembly 30, see Mann, *Yankee Reformers in the Urban Age*, 178–83.

24. Entry on Phillip Moxon, in *Dictionary of American Biography*, vol. 13, ed. Dumas Malone (New York: Scribner, 1934), 301–2; George H. Shriver, "Phillip Moxon," in *American National Biography*, vol. 16, ed. John Garraty and Mark Carnes (New York: Oxford University Press, 1999), 47; *American Home Life* 3 (December 1893): 4.

25. Philip S. Moxon, "The Industrial Revolution: A Sermon," *The Watchman*, May 20, 1886 (subsequently published as a pamphlet—pages 7–11, 15). For an extensive discussion of how clergymen across the nation approached the strikes of 1886 with great circumspection, see Carl Warren Griffiths, "Some Protestant Attitudes on the Labor Question in 1886," *Church History* 11 (June 1942): 138–48.

26. *Labor Leader*, January 19, 26, and April 6, 1889. See also *Report for 1889 of the Legislative Committee of the State Conference of Central Labor Unions*, n.p., n.d., 5.

27. *Labor Leader*, January 18, 1890.

28. *Labor Leader*, January 25, 1890.

29. George McNeill, "Eight Hours," *The Dawn* 2 (May 1890): 20–25; quotations on 20, 24, 25.

30. *Labor Leader,* March 15, 1890.

31. There is a substantial body of literature on Bliss's life and work as a Christian Socialist, but much of this previous scholarship has reviewed and critiqued his broad theological and political arguments; it has not focused extensively on Bliss's personal, intellectual, and institutional connections to the Boston labor reform community. See Dombrowski, *The Early Days of Christian Socialism in America,* 96–106; Hopkins, *The Rise of the Social Gospel in American Protestantism, 1865–1915,* 173, 176–83; May, *Protestant Churches and Industrial America,* 241–47; Howard Quint, *The Forging of American Socialism: Origins of the Modern Movement* (Columbia: University of South Carolina Press, 1953), 109–19; Mann, *Yankee Reformers in the Urban Age,* 90–95; Christopher L. Webber, "William Dwight Porter Bliss (1856–1926): Priest and Socialist," *Historical Magazine of the Protestant Episcopal Church* 28 (March 1959): 9–39; Albert Fried, *Socialism in America: From the Shakers to the Third International, a Documentary History* (New York: Doubleday, 1970), 336–41; Richard Dressner, "Christian Socialism: A Response to Industrial America in the Progressive Era" (PhD diss., Cornell University, 1972), 37–105; Peter J. Frederick, *Knights of the Golden Rule: The Intellectual as Christian Social Reformer in the 1890s* (Lexington: University Press of Kentucky, 1976), 81–98; Richard Dressner, "William Dwight Porter Bliss's Christian Socialism," *Church History* 47 (1978): 66–82.

32. *Labor Leader,* July 9, 1887. Bliss's essay was originally published in *Work and Wages* for June 1887. See also *Labor Leader,* August 27, 1887.

33. Rev. W. D. P. Bliss, "Be Practical," *The Dawn* 1 (August 15, 1889): 1–2.

Bliss edited *The Dawn* from its founding in May 1889 to its close in March 1896. In December 1890, Bliss assumed ownership of the magazine so he could emphasize his interests in Christian Socialism, politics, and the labor movement, rather than more general discussions of liberal Christianity and church reform. He may also have taken control of the paper because the local Society of Christian Socialists was apparently folding after just one year in existence. See Dombrowski, *The Early Days of Christian Socialism in America,* 108; Quint, *Forging of American Socialism,* 117.

It should also be noted that Bliss's cofounder in the Society of Christian Socialists was Francis Bellamy, a Baptist minister and cousin of the famous utopian novelist Edward Bellamy. See Sylvia Bowman, *Edward Bellamy* (Boston: Twayne, 1986), 116.

34. Rev. W. D. P. Bliss, "What Is Christian Socialism?" *The Dawn* 1 (January 15, 1890): 1–3, and *The Dawn* 1 (February 1890): 1–3.

35. *Labor Leader,* July 13, 1889. Frank Foster—editor of the *Labor Leader*—attended the same Nationalist Club meeting. He too sharply criticized the group's failure to grasp the immediate problems facing workers and their organizations. Foster also referred to correspondence from George Gunton, who urged eight-hour advocates to steer clear of the "Boston craze." *Labor Leader,* July 19, 1889.

See also Quint, *Forging of American Socialism,* 98–102, 114–15; and Everett MacNair, *Edward Bellamy and the Nationalist Movement, 1889–1894* (Milwaukee, WI:

Fitzgerald, 1957), 61–62 for details of the Nationalists' often convoluted debates over supporting labor unions and the eight-hour workday. MacNair theorized that McNeill may have influenced Bliss to press the Boston Nationalists to finally issue a public endorsement of the shorter working day.

Franklin Rosemont argued that Edward Bellamy himself was more sympathetic to organized labor and its demands. When Bellamy assumed a more direct role in the Nationalist movement and its publications, in the early 1890s, he advocated stronger links with workers. Despite Rosemont's claims, there is no evidence that the Boston Nationalist Clubs played a significant role in the labor reform campaign. Franklin Rosemont, "Bellamy's Radicalism Reclaimed," in *Looking Backward, 1988–1888: Essays on Edward Bellamy,* ed. Daphne Patai (Amherst: University of Massachusetts Press, 1989), 158–59.

36. "Christian Socialism: II. What Christian Socialists Believe Should Be Done Now," *The Dawn* 4 (October 1892): 5–9, quotations on 5. Although this essay has no byline, significant portions are copied from previous articles written by Bliss.

37. "Christian Socialism: II. What Christian Socialists Believe Should Be Done Now," 6, 7. Peter Frederick, in particular, argued that Bliss was too much of an intellectual, and too interested in vague schemes for building unity among all reformers, to really confront working-class problems. While there is some truth to this criticism, especially for the period after 1895, the record of Bliss's writings and activities for the late 1880s and early 1890s demonstrates that he had a strong interest in building organizational links to specific labor activists (such as his friend George McNeill) and specific labor reform issues (such as the eight-hour workday) in Boston.

38. Quint, *Forging of American Socialism,* 117; *Labor Leader,* April 12, 1890.

39. *Journals of the Annual Convention of the Episcopal Diocese of Massachusetts, 1894–96;* W. D. P. Bliss, "The Church of the Carpenter and Thirty Years After," *Social Preparation for the Kingdom of God* 9 (January 1922): 12–15; Letter of W. D. P. Bliss, Boston, to Richard Ely, September 18, 1892, Richard Ely Papers, State Historical Society of Wisconsin. See chapter 6 for more on the Wendell Phillips Union, Andover House, and Robert Woods.

40. W. D. P. Bliss, "The Church of the Carpenter," *My Neighbor: A Monthly Journal of the Episcopal City Mission* 2 (January 1893): 2–5, quotation on 4; Vida Scudder, *On Journey* (New York: Dutton, 1937), 165; copy of Letter of W. D. P. Bliss, Roslindale, Massachusetts, to Edward Rogers, April 30, 1896, Edward Rogers Papers; Dressner, "Christian Socialism," 62–63. The dinners were sponsored by a separate parish guild—the Brotherhood of the Carpenter—which also promoted interdenominational dialogues. Meanwhile, the church itself became an official mission of the Massachusetts Episcopal diocese.

41. "The Unemployed in Boston," *Andover House Bulletin,* No. 2, December 6, 1893.

42. Herbert Casson, *The Story of My Life* (London: *Efficiency Magazine,* n.d.), 46–49; Alexander Keyssar, *Out of Work: The First Century of Unemployment in Massachusetts* (Cambridge, UK: Cambridge University Press, 1986), 225–28, 249.

43. William O. Reichert, "The Melancholy Political Thought of Morrison I. Swift," *New England Quarterly* 49:4 (1976): 542–43; Leslie Wharton, "Herbert N. Casson and the American Labor Church, 1893–1898," *Essex Institute Historical Collections* 117:2 (1981): 120–21, 125; W. Fitzhugh Brundage, *A Socialist Utopia in the New South: The Ruskin Colonies in Tennessee and Georgia, 1894–1901* (Urbana: University of Illinois Press, 1996), 55–58.

44. *Open Court* 7 (June 15, 1893): 3701–2; *Labor Leader*, May 6, 1893. Not surprisingly, the elitist Nationalists became quite uncomfortable with Swift's more plebeian and radical pronouncements and public activities. Sylvester Baxter wrote to Edward Bellamy in February 1894 during the unemployment marches: "It is a pity that fellows like Swift get hold of our ideas in a half-baked sort of way! The Governor acted as much like a fool as Swift did, however." Edward Bellamy Papers, Houghton Library, Harvard University.

45. Morrison I. Swift, *Capitalists Are the Cause of the Unemployed* (Boston, 1894), 11.

The Equity Union opened its doors in November 1893 as a combination reformist commune and settlement house—yet another attempt to establish a headquarters for Boston reformers. The Union set aside Tuesday evenings for meetings on municipal work projects for the unemployed, and Swift gave lectures on political economy to working men on Wednesday evenings. The organization also sponsored one of Swift's public meetings for unemployed workers, this one shortly before Christmas 1893 at Faneuil Hall. See Daybook, 1893–94, vol. 1, 56, 83, November 15, December 17, 1893, Denison House Records, Schlesinger Library, Harvard University. (There are no surviving records from the Equity Union.)

For more on settlement houses, and other efforts to create central meeting places for Boston labor reformers and activists, see chapter 6.

46. Report of the Massachusetts Board to Investigate the Subject of the Unemployed, Massachusetts Legislative Document, House No. 50, February 1895, 104–6. Edward Bellamy sent the Board an extended communication (109–11) detailing his plans for creating self-sustaining colonies of unemployed workers producing enough goods in factories and farms to support themselves through exchange at public stores. Bellamy saw his scheme as both a solution to chronic unemployment in an industrial economy and a model for how a larger nationalized society might operate. Casson, and especially Swift, echoed some of Bellamy's ideas about workers supporting themselves in a kind of self-contained economic system. But Bellamy did not work directly with the unemployed or with labor reformers in Boston during the depression.

47. Henry Vincent, *The Story of the Commonweal* (1894; rpt. New York: Arno Press, 1969), 204–6; Keyssar, *Out of Work*, 229–30.

48. *Public Opinion* 17 (1894): 137, quoted in Donald McMurray, *Coxey's Army: A Study of the Industrial Army Movement of 1894* (Boston: Little, Brown, 1929), 228.

49. Keyssar, *Out of Work*, 231. For broader accounts of the march on Washington in 1894, see Carlos Schwantes, *Coxey's Army: An American Odyssey* (Lincoln: University

of Nebraska Press, 1985); and Lucy G. Barber, *Marching on Washington: The Forging of an American Political Tradition* (Berkeley: University of California Press, 2002), chapter 1.

50. Docket Book, U. S. House Committee on Labor, 53rd Congress, 2nd session, page 8, June 6, 13, 18, 1894, Record Group 233.11, National Archives, Washington, DC; Statement of Mr. Morrison I. Swift, of Boston, Mass., June 13, 1894, pages 7, 8, 9, 17; June 18, 1894, pages 9, 18, U.S. House Committee on Labor, House Papers, 53A-F23.2, Record Group 233.11, National Archives, Washington, DC [corrected stenographer's report].

51. Keyssar, *Out of Work,* 231; Wharton, "Herbert N. Casson and the American Labor Church, 1893–1898," 121–23.

52. Herbert N. Casson, *What We Believe* (Lynn, MA: Webster-Eaton Press, n.d.), 3, 5–6, 7, 12. In his 1898 publication, *Red Light,* Casson enunciated four other, more ethereal "Labor Church Principles": "1. To remove religious superstition and to develop the moral nature of the Labor Movement. 2. To promote social intercourse, and practical co-operation. 3. To prepare for the social crisis by educating ourselves and others. 4. To proclaim the Co-operative Commonwealth as the ideal of society."

Casson also published "The Ten Commandments of the Labor Movement" as part of his plan to create a bold new perspective on religion for working people. Among these commandments were "1. Thou shalt earn thine own living, and not live on rent, profits, or interest. . . . 6. Thou shalt treat private luxury as immoral, as long as poverty exists. . . . 7. Thou shalt resist and overthrow all injustice, tyranny and social evil."

53. Casson, *What We Believe,* 10–11; Wharton, "Herbert N. Casson and the American Labor Church, 1893–1898," 135–36. Casson claimed in his autobiography, *Story of My Life* (50–51, 64), that he hoped to construct a new kind of socialism, and teach workers about efficiency and political responsibility, but his published writings in the 1890s focus on the labor church.

6. Spaces, Places, and Headquarters

1. *First Annual Report of the Wells Memorial Association* (Cambridge, MA: Riverside Press, 1880), 14; *Tenth Annual Report of the Wells Memorial Association* (n.p., 1889), 1.

2. *First Annual Report of the Wells Memorial Association,* 14–15.

3. *Tenth Annual Report of the Wells Memorial Association,* 4; *Fifteenth Annual Report of the Wells Memorial Association* (Boston, 1894), 13; James Green, *Boston Workers: A Labor History* (Boston: Boston Public Library, 1979), 56; Sam Bass Warner Jr., *Streetcar Suburbs: The Process of Growth in Boston (1870–1900)* (Cambridge, MA: Harvard University Press, 1962), 97. For more on social reform organizations in the South End, see Robert A. Woods, *The City Wilderness: A Settlement Study by Residents and Associates of the South End House* (Boston: Houghton Mifflin, 1898), chapter 11.

In 1893, the institute began to admit women as members, but the organization's basic programs and leadership did not change significantly through the 1890s.

4. *Ninth Annual Report of the Wells Memorial Association* (Boston: Crosby, 1888), 4; *Twelfth Annual Report of the Wells Memorial Association* (Boston: Stillings, 1891), 27.

5. *Eighth Annual Report of the Wells Memorial Association* (n.p., 1887–88), 9; *Twelfth Annual Report of the Wells Memorial Association,* 26; *Sixteenth Annual Report of the Wells Memorial Association* (Boston, 1895), 21. For more on Brooks and the Consumers' Leagues, see chapter 7. Woods and Andover House are discussed later in this chapter.

6. *Eleventh Annual Report of the Wells Memorial Association* (Boston: Crosby, 1890), 20–21.

7. *Tenth Annual Report of the Wells Memorial Association,* 16; *Fifteenth Annual Report of the Wells Memorial Association,* 14–15; *Wells Memorial Institute, Its Twenty Years of Service in the City of Boston, 1880–1900* (n.p., n.d.), 13.

8. *Wells Memorial Institute, Its Twenty Years of Service in the City of Boston, 1880–1900,* 21.

9. Circular, "Wendell Phillips Hall"; Letter of Jesse Jones, North Abington, Massachusetts, February 4, 1888, Massachusetts Labor Party Correspondence, Boston Public Library.

10. *Labor Leader,* February 25, 1888.

11. "Wendell Phillips Union," *The Dawn* 3 (September 1891): 3. Most of the reports in *The Dawn* carry no byline but were probably written by Bliss.

12. "Wendell Phillips Union," 3.

13. "Grand Opening Festival of the Wendell Phillips Union," *The Dawn* 3 (October 1891): 3.

14. "The Wendell Phillips Union, Opened at 812 Washington St., A Success," *The Dawn* 3 (November 1891): 6–7.

15. "The Wendell Phillips Movement," *The Dawn* 3 (February 1892): 12; Katherine Pearson Woods, "Progressive Methods of Church Work, XI—The Church of the Carpenter," *Christian Union,* August 27, 1892, 383–84.

16. Letter of W. D. P. Bliss, Roslindale, [Massachusetts], to Richard Ely, June 6, 1893, Ely Papers, State Historical Society of Wisconsin, Madison.

17. John Gavit, comp., *Bibliography of College, Social, and University Settlements,* 3rd edition (Cambridge, MA: Co-operative Press, 1897), 25–50; Caroline Montgomery, comp., *Bibliography of College, Social, University and Church Settlements,* 4th edition (New York, 1900), 22–26.

The following discussion focuses on the role played by Andover House and Denison House in the Boston labor reform community of the 1890s. For broader overviews of the settlement movement's impact on urban politics, culture, and the built environment, see Allen F. Davis, *Spearheads for Reform: The Social Settlements and the Progressive Movement, 1890–1914* (1967; rpt. New Brunswick, NJ: Rutgers University Press, 1984); and Mina Carson, *Settlement Folk: The Evolution of Social Welfare Ideology in the American Settlement Movement, 1885–1930* (Chicago: University of Chicago Press, 1990).

18. "Social Christianity—The Andover House Association," *Andover Review*, January 1892, 82–85; Articles of Association, Andover House Association, Circular No. 3, n.d.

19. Entry on Robert A. Woods, in *Dictionary of American Biography*, vol. 20, ed. Dumas Malone (New York: Scribner, 1936), 503–4; Clyde McDaniel Jr., "Robert A. Woods," in *American National Biography*, vol. 23, ed. John Garraty and Mark Carnes (New York: Oxford University Press, 1999), 815–16; Arthur Mann, *Yankee Reformers in the Urban Age* (Cambridge, MA: Harvard University Press, 1954), 115–16.

See William Jewett Tucker, "The Work of the Andover House in Boston," *Scribner's Magazine* 13 (March 1893): 357–72, for Tucker's appraisal of the settlement.

20. Robert A. Woods, "University Settlements: Their Point and Drift," *Quarterly Journal of Economics* 14 (October 1899): 72–73, 77; *South End House: A University Settlement, 1892–1899* (n.p., n.d.), 3; Woods, *The City Wilderness*, 284.

21. Woods, *The City Wilderness*, 282; Robert A. Woods, "The Story of Labor. Paper II," *Lincoln Review* 1 (May 1896): 74. *City Wilderness* was, in some ways, Woods's challenge to theories of objective social science which insisted that empirical research and reform advocacy could not go together.

22. Andover House Association, Third Yearly Report, Circular No. 11, December 1894, 6–8; "The Andover House Association Hereafter to be Called The South End Association. Change of Name," Circular No. 12, November 1, 1895; South End House Chronology 1891–1901, South End House Association, *Tenth Annual Report* (Boston, 1902), 34–36. See chapter 5 for more on the depression of 1893 and the labor reform movement in Boston.

23. South End House Association, *Fourth Yearly Report of the Settlement* (n.p., 1895), 6–7; *South End House: A University Settlement, 1892–1899*, 7; South End House Association, *Sixth Yearly Report of the Settlement* (n.p., 1898), 1–4; Eleanor Woods, *Robert Woods: Champion of Democracy* (Boston: Houghton Mifflin, 1929), 101, 104.

See Edward S. Shapiro, "Robert A. Woods and the Settlement House Impulse," *Social Service Review* 52 (June 1978): 215–26. Shapiro argues that Woods's settlement work was essentially conservative in trying to restore traditional New England notions of community, face-to-face dialogue, and social reconciliation in the emerging heterogeneous modern city.

24. Gavit, *Bibliography of College, Social, and University Settlements*, 22.

25. Sandra Opdycke, "Emily Greene Balch," in *American National Biography*, 2:39–40; Mercedes M. Randall, *Improper Bostonian: Emily Greene Balch* (New York: Twayne, 1964), 82; Denison House Records, January 1893, Box 1, Folder 4, Schlesinger Library, Harvard University.

26. Jane Rosenberg, "Helena Stuart Dudley," in *Biographical Dictionary of Social Welfare in America*, ed. Walter Trattner (Westport, CT: Greenwood Press, 1986), 252–54; Kathleen Nutter, "Helena Stuart Dudley," in *American National Biography*, 7:8–9; Helena S. Dudley, Twenty-fifth Reunion Statement, c. 1914, 1, Bryn Mawr College Archives, quoted in Kathleen Banks Nutter, *The Necessity of Organization: Mary Kenney O'Sullivan and Trade Unionism for Women, 1892–1912* (New York: Garland,

2000), 27, 29; Helena S. Dudley, "Relief Work Carried on in the Wells Memorial Institute," *Annals of the American Academy of Political and Social Science* 5 (1895): 396.

27. Daybook, 1893–94, vol. 1, 59–60, November 21, 1893, Denison House Records. These women garment workers were employed usually in workshops and small factories. Much of the large-scale tenement manufacturing of clothing had been suppressed by the efforts of the Anti-Tenement House League and state inspection laws starting in 1891. But mothers and small children continued to do piecework at home for clothing contractors. For more on the Anti-Tenement House League, see chapter 7.

28. Daybook, 1893–94, vol. 1, 65, 71–72, November 27, December 4, 1893, Denison House Records (the term "garment worker," "cloakmaker," and "tailoress" were used interchangeably in the daybrook when describing these women workers); Sarah Deutsch, *Women and the City: Gender, Space, and Power in Boston, 1870–1940* (New York: Oxford University Press, 2000), 166–67. Deutsch also points out that there was ethnic tension between the largely Irish tailoresses and the Russian/Polish Jewish male union leaders.

29. Daybooks, 1893–94, vol. 1, 117, February 4, 1894, and 1894–97, vol. 2, 20, 137, July 1 and September 28, 1894, Denison House Records; Kathleen Banks Nutter, "Organizing Women during the Progressive Era: Mary Kenney O'Sullivan and the Labor Movement," *Labor's Heritage* 8 (Winter 1997): 18–37; Kathleen Nutter, "Mary Kenney O'Sullivan," in *American National Biography*, 16:816–17; Eleanor Flexner and Janet Wilson James, "Mary Kenney O'Sullivan," in *Notable American Women 1607–1950: A Biographical Dictionary*, vol. 2, ed. Edward T. James et al. (Cambridge, MA: Belknap Press of Harvard University Press, 1971), 655–56.

30. Daybook, 1894–97, vol. 2, 139, 142, 179, October 3 and 9, December 19, 1894, Denison House Records; Deutsch, *Women and the City*, 174–77.

31. Daybook, 1894–97, vol. 2, 190, January 11, 1895, Denison House Records; Deutsch, *Women and the City*, 177. The Wells Memorial Institute and the Women's Educational and Industrial Union (WEIU) also supported efforts to organize women garment workers and sponsored several meetings at their headquarters. The WEIU had a legal service to help working women collect wages owed to them and was especially concerned that contractors in the clothing industry were trying to stay in business by delaying payments to their employees. Overall, however, the WEIU remained interested more in vocational training and job placement than in labor reform activism.

32. Daybooks, 1893–94, vol. 1, 115, 130, 136, February 1, March 1, 15, 1894, and 1894–97, vol. 2, 5, May 4, 1894; Minutes of the Executive Committee, 1892–95, 87–90, December 11, 1894, and January 8, 1895, Denison House Records; Vida Scudder, *On Journey* (New York: Dutton, 1937), 154–55.

33. Daybooks, 1893–94, vol. 1, 131, March 3, 1894, and 1894–97, vol. 2, 115–16, August 28, 1894, Denison House Records; John Kennealy's account of O'Sullivan's lecture on the AFL before the Social Science Club, *Prospect Union Review* 1 (April 4, 1894): 5, 7; Balch quoted in Randall, *Improper Bostonian: Emily Greene Balch*, 83.

34. Daybook, 1894–97, vol. 2, 133–35, 157, September 25, November 8, 1894, Denison House Records.

35. Daybook, 1894–97, vol. 2, 219–20, April 13, 1895, Denison House Records.

36. Minutes of the Executive Committee, 1892–95, 111–13, June 7, 1895, Denison House Records; Mary Kenney O'Sullivan, Autobiography, 137–38, Collection VIII, Papers of the Women's Trade Union League and Its Principal Leaders (Woodbridge, CT: Research Publications, 1981), microfilm; Nutter, *Necessity of Organization,* 44–46.

37. For more on how women used settlement houses to challenge concepts of private and public space, see Sarah Deutsch, "Reconceiving the City: Women, Space, and Power in Boston, 1870–1910," *Gender and History* 6 (August 1994): 202–23.

38. Helena S. Dudley, "The Scope of the Settlement," *Eleventh Annual Report of the College Settlement Association* (Boston: Bliss, 1900), 23–25.

39. Scudder, *On Journey,* 171.

40. Nutter, *Necessity of Organization,* chapter 3.

7. New Models for a New Century

1. John E. Griffin, "Operations of the Law in Massachusetts Relating to the 'Sweating System,'" in *Papers Read at the Sixth Annual Convention of the International Association of Factory Inspectors of North America* (1892), republished in Seventh Annual Report of the Factory Inspector of New York, Assembly Document 63, vol. 9, 1893, 669–76; John Plunkett, "Sweat Shops in Massachusetts," in *Speeches and Papers Read at the Twelfth Annual Convention of the International Association of Factory Inspectors of North America* (1898), republished in Thirteenth Annual Report of the Factory Inspector of New York, Assembly Document 51, vol. 7, 1899, 781–84; Eileen Boris, *Home to Work: Motherhood and the Politics of Industrial Homework in the United States* (Cambridge, UK: Cambridge University Press, 1994), 49–60; Geoffrey Blodgett, *The Gentle Reformers: Massachusetts Democrats in the Cleveland Era* (Cambridge, MA: Harvard University Press, 1966), 133–38.

This study does not focus on working conditions within tenement house sweatshops, or on the details of regulatory legislation and its enforcement. The emphasis is on the Anti–Tenement House League's efforts in mobilizing reformers and legislators to regulate this particular labor system.

2. *History and Report of the Work of the Anti–Tenement House League, from its Organization to October 1, 1894* (Boston: A. T. Bliss, 1894), 9, 79; Boris, *Home to Work,* 60–65.

3. *History and Report of the Work of the Anti–Tenement House League,* 80–81.

4. *History and Report of the Work of the Anti–Tenement House League,* 16–19.

5. Petition of Anti–Tenement House League, January 4, 1892, 2–6, 9, U.S. Senate Committee on Education and Labor, Senate Papers, 52A-J8.5, Record Group 46.16, National Archives, Washington, DC.

6. Petition of Anti–Tenement House League, 7–11. John Crowley, secretary of the league, wrote an article for the *Labor Leader* (May 9, 1891) which also used the image of a nationwide plague as the motivating force for some future legislation placing the entire clothing industry under government control. Crowley, borrowing a page from

Edward Bellamy's *Looking Backward*, composed his essay in the form of an imaginary letter written in 1998, explaining how the "Plague of 1893" shocked the nation into action.

7. *History and Report of the Work of the Anti-Tenement House League*, 19; *American Home Life* 3 (December 1893): 2, 7; Sarah Deutsch, *Women and the City: Gender, Space, and Power in Boston, 1870-1940* (New York: Oxford University Press, 2000), 165.

8. *History and Report of the Work of the Anti-Tenement House League*, 19-21.

9. U.S. House 52-2, S.S. 3140, Report 2309, "Investigation of the Sweating System," 1892, 112-17. Massachusetts Deputy Inspector John E. Griffin concluded in his testimony (173-81), and in a paper presented in September 1892 (see note 1), that the state's new laws did drive sweatshops out of business, since no merchant wanted to carry clothing labeled as made in a tenement house. Families and landlords worked together to improve living and working conditions, and business in the Boston industry increased as retailers rejected sweatshop garments from New York and elsewhere. Griffin did admit that the legislation did not address abuses of the contracting system where workers had to labor longer hours as piece rates declined sharply.

See also David Ward, *Cities and Immigrants: A Geography of Change in Nineteenth Century America* (New York: Oxford University Press, 1991), 101.

10. *History and Report of the Work of the Anti-Tenement House League*, 70-71; *American Home Life* 3 (December 1893): 7.

11. Letter from District Council No. 2, United Garment Workers of America, Boston, to Rev. A. A. Miner, January 5, 1894, Anti-Tenement House League Papers, State Historical Society of Wisconsin, Madison; Boris, *Home to Work*, 60. Crowley made his accusation that manufacturers were "buying up labor men at the present day" in his 1892 congressional testimony: see "Investigation of the Sweating System," 115.

12. Letter of John Crowley, Boston, to George McNeill, February 5, 1894, Anti-Tenement House League Papers.

13. Letter of John Crowley, Boston, to A. A. Carlton, February 5, 1894, Anti-Tenement House League Papers. There is no record of the league's internal investigation into accusations against Crowley. But the fact that he was sent back to Washington in April 1894 seems to indicate that the league's officers continued to have confidence in his work.

14. Summary of Massachusetts BLS data in "Investigation of the Sweating System," 230.

15. For more on the rhetorical evolution of the terms "sweatshops" and the "sweating system," see Daniel Bender, "Sweatshop Subjectivity and The Politics of Definition and Exhibition," *International Labor and Working Class History* 61 (Spring 2002): 13-23.

Another possible reason that the league made little effort to recruit recent immigrants may have been the obvious language barriers and low levels of literacy among many newcomers from southern and eastern Europe. Since so many labor reform groups based so much of their campaign efforts in print media—newspapers, reports, pamphlets—their strategies were premised on high literacy rates among workers as well as reformers.

16. Plunkett, "Sweat Shops in Massachusetts," 783; Horace Wadlin, "The Sweating System in Massachusetts," *Journal of Social Science* 30 (October 1892): 86–102, quotation on 95.

17. "How the Other Half Lives," *American Home Life* 3 (December 1893): 13.

18. Priscilla Murolo, *The Common Ground of Womanhood: Class, Gender, and Working Girls' Clubs, 1884–1928* (Urbana: University of Illinois Press, 1997), 107–10; Joanne Reitano, "Working Girls Unite," *American Quarterly* 36 (Spring 1984): 112–34. In the 1890s, some working girls' clubs were sponsored by the settlement houses scattered across the city. Denison House, however, seems to have focused more of its efforts on organizing women into their own union locals.

19. O. M. E. Rowe, "The Shorter Work-Day," *Report of the Proceedings of the Third National Convention of Working Women's Clubs*, Philadelphia, April 28–30, 1897, 69–70.

20. *Report of the Massachusetts Association of Working Women's Clubs from 1894 to 1897* (n.p., n.d.), 7–8.

21. *Report of the Massachusetts Association of Working Women's Clubs from 1894 to 1897*, 8; Rowe, "The Shorter Work-Day," 69; Edith M. Howes, "The Theory of the Club," *Report of the Proceedings of the Third National Convention of Working Women's Clubs*, 210; *A Directory of the Charitable and Beneficient Organizations of Boston*, 3rd edition (Boston: Darnrell and Upham, 1891), 135.

22. James Mooney, "John Graham Brooks," in *American National Biography*, vol. 3, ed. John Garraty and Mark Carnes (New York: Oxford University Press, 1999), 616–17; Minutes of Meetings of Consumers' League of Massachusetts [typescript], December 1897, Consumers' League of Massachusetts Papers, Schlesinger Library, Harvard University. Brooks and others also certainly knew that a Consumers' League had been active in New York City since 1890.

23. Minutes of Meetings of Consumers' League of Massachusetts, May 1897.

24. Minutes of Meetings of Consumers' League of Massachusetts, Thursday, September 23, 1897; Thursday, October 21, 1897.

25. John Graham Brooks, *The Consumer's League* (Cambridgeport, MA: Co-operative Press, 1897), 12–15, 18–20, 22, 24, 27, 31, 32.

26. Minutes of Meetings of Consumers' League of Massachusetts, January 20 and February 24, 1898.

27. Minutes of Meetings of Consumers' League of Massachusetts, March 1898; September 30, 1898; Deutsch, *Women and the City*, 181. For more on the often complex and conflicted relationship between Consumers' League labels and union labels, see Jacqueline K. Dirks, "Righteous Goods: Women's Production, Reform Publicity, and the National Consumers' League, 1891–1919" (PhD diss., Yale University, 1996), 113–29.

The league's executive committee, starting in 1898, met often at Edith Howes's home rather than the WEIU headquarters. Whether this change in location reflected strained relations between the two organizations is not clear.

28. Minutes of Meetings of Consumers' League of Massachusetts, November 30, 1898.

29. William Lyon MacKenzie King Diaries (MG26-J13) [typescript], Thursday, July 7, 1898; Friday, July 8, 1898 (quote); Saturday, July 9, 1898 (quote); Monday, July 11, 1898; Friday, July 28, 1898; Thursday, September 29, 1898, National Archives of Canada, Ottawa; W. L. MacKenzie King, *Report of Hours and Other Conditions in the Smaller Mercantile Establishments of Boston and Vicinity*, Consumers' League of Massachusetts, Bulletin No. 2, 1898, 38.

30. Minutes of Meetings of Consumers' League of Massachusetts, November 30 and December 15, 1898.

MacKenzie King, in his diary, noted his own concerns about the FLU's campaign for the sixty-hour law. He wrote on Tuesday, November 15, 1898, after having dinner at Denison House: "The Fed. Lab. Union decided to take up action of 60 hr. labor law for their winter's work—they are doing it, to have something to keep them together. Miss Dudley admitted so to me. They are not dealing squarely with the Consumers' League wh. has gone more fully into the matter.... I think this women's club etc. is all nonsense or largely so. Women trying to run labor problems is a mistake."

31. Minutes of Meetings of Consumers' League of Massachusetts, September 28, November 25, and December 14, 1899; Consumers' League of Massachusetts, Bulletin No. 31, March 1926, "The Consumers' League of Massachusetts and Legislation."

In December 1899 the executive committee convened back at the WEIU headquarters.

INDEX

abolitionists, 88, 95–96, 101, 107, 117, 120–21, 149, 159, 184, 194, 210, 220
Addams, Jane, 225, 231
Allen John, 54
American Federation of Labor (AFL), 230–31, 244
American Home Life, 251
American Workman, 117, 125, 127, 141, 159–60
Andover House, 21, 201–2, 214, 218, 224–27, 229, 232, 239. *See also* Woods, Robert A.
Andover Theological Seminary, 224–25, 227
Andrews, Jennie, 124
Andrews, John H., 92
Anti-Tenement House League, 21–22, 172, 240–45, 247–51, 261, 301n27, 303n13, 303n15; petition to U.S. Congress, 244–45
Associationists, 10, 13–14, 44–49, 55–57, 60–63, 66–69, 121, 125, 143, 271n24; and "attractive industry," 44. *See also* Brook Farm

Bagley, Sarah, 46–48, 52, 54
Balch, Emily Greene, 228, 230, 233, 259
Bellamy, Edward, 197, 295n35, 297n44, 297n46
Blanchard, J. G., 132
Bliss, William Dwight Porter, 173, 195–202, 204, 208, 217–18, 233–34, 243, 248, 262, 295n33, 296n37; and Wendell Phillips Union, 221–23
Boston Clothing Trade Advisory Board, 245
Boston Eight Hour League, 20, 26, 114–15, 128–29, 136–37, 139–40, 142–44, 147–49, 151, 153, 165–67, 174–75, 177–78, 283n41, 286n30, 287n38; constitution of, 136–37. *See also* Sylvis Hall

Boston Labor Council, 166
Boston Labor Reform Association (BLRA), 76–78, 85–86, 91, 93, 100, 278n24
Boston Printers' Protective Union, 68
Boston Tailors' Associative Union, 66–67
Boston Trades Union (BTU), 37, 40, 270n16; and "Ten Hour Circular," 37–38, 40
Boston Union of Associationists, 56, 67–68
Boston Workingmen's Assembly, 77, 81, 85, 88, 281n25
Boutwell, George, 71
Bowditch, Henry Ingersoll, 92
Brackett, John, 220, 243
Brook Farm, 42, 44–45, 47–48, 55–57, 62, 64
Brooks, John Graham, 217, 234–35, 253–57, 304n22
Brotherhood of the Carpenter, 222, 296n40. *See also* Church of the Carpenter
Bryant, David, 53–54
Bryant, S. N., 109–10
Bullock, Alexander, 102, 107, 282n32
Butler, Benjamin, 162, 220

Campbell, James, 60
Carlton, A. A., 248
Carlton, Frank, 9
Carruthers, John, 147
Casson, Herbert, 173, 204, 206, 208–11, 298nn52–53
Central Labor Union of Boston, 188, 222, 227, 230, 293n23

307

Chamberlin, Edwin, 109, 140, 154, 159, 165–66, 174, 180–83, 191, 196, 217, 219; on eight-hour law, 193–94; gubernatorial candidate of Massachusetts Labor Reform Party, 156, 161–62
child labor, 33
child labor laws, 97, 99, 103, 148, 151–52, 287n44
Christian Labor Union (CLU), 166, 173, 178–79, 181, 187, 195. *See also* Jones, Jesse
Christian Socialism, 20, 170, 173, 178, 181, 196–202, 217, 221, 227, 237; Casson's critique of, 208–9; and eight-hour movement, 194–95, 200
Church of the Carpenter, 173, 200–202, 208, 223, 262. *See also* Brotherhood of the Carpenter
Claflin, William, 150–51
Cluer, John, 53–54, 64, 124
Coddington, Edward, 68
College Settlements Association (CSA), 228
Collins, Jennie, 131, 166, 174
Coman, Kathleen, 228
Commons, John R., 9–11
consumer cooperatives, 49–50, 52–53, 61, 68, 76–77, 93
Consumers' League of Massachusetts, 21–22, 172, 240–42, 251, 253–54, 256–61, 304n27, 305nn30–31; constitution of, 256–57; and trade union labels, 257, 259; and "white list," 255
cooperatives. *See* consumer cooperatives; producer cooperatives
Coxey's Army, 206–7
Crane, W. Murray, 259
Crowley, John, 245–50, 302n6, 303n11, 303n13
Cummings, S. P., 122–23, 153–54, 158–59

Daily Evening Voice (*DEV*), 78–81, 84, 86, 95, 99–100, 105–7, 117, 132, 278n27, 281n25; and eight-hour day, 78–79; and eight-hour movement, 100
Dana, Charles, 47
Daniels, Elizabeth L., 109, 117, 121, 132
Daniels, Herbert, 109, 121, 132
The Dawn, 194, 196, 200, 202, 221–23, 295n33
Delano, Henry T., 165, 178
Denison House, 21, 214, 224, 227–31, 235–36, 238–39, 262, 304n18; Federal Labor Union (FLU) #5915, 233–35, 257–59, 305n30; Social Science Club, 232–33; and strike at Boston Gossamer Rubber Company, 234–35
Depression of 1870s, 145, 181, 216
Depression of 1893, 173, 202–3, 228–29, 231–32
Deutsch, Sarah, 14
Dickinson, Anna, 80–81, 107, 278n33
Douglas, Charles, 28, 34–37, 41, 69
Douglass, Frederick, 107
Dudley, Helena, 228–30, 232–33, 235–38, 257, 259, 305n30

Eastman, Mehitabel, 57–58, 60
eight-hour day, 3, 18–20, 25, 36, 38–39, 66, 76, 83, 86–88, 91–93, 111, 116, 126–27, 131, 136, 141, 149, 153, 165, 189, 211, 286n35; for Boston city employees, 109; in dry goods stores, 252, 257; and economic depressions, 145–48, 208
eight-hour law, 90–91, 94, 97–100, 103–6, 108, 111–13, 119, 123–24, 132, 138, 148, 157–58, 161, 163; for federal employees, 140, 166; for public employees in Massachusetts, 192–93
eight-hour leagues. *See* Boston Eight Hour League; Grand Eight Hour League of Massachusetts
eight-hour movement, 73, 76–77, 105, 131, 147–48, 156, 164, 182, 188, 202
eight-hour strikes (1886), 173, 188–89, 192, 196
Ely, Richard, 7, 223, 267n4
Emerson, Mary, 55, 59
Emerson, Ralph Waldo, 42, 107
Equity, 179
Equity Union, 205–6, 297n45
Evans, George Henry, 42, 47, 53

Factory Act, 148, 152
factory operatives, 34, 36, 43, 46, 111, 123, 156
Fall River Mechanics' Association, 41
Falls, William, 106, 109
Fincher's Trade Review, 86
Fisk, Theophilus, 38–40, 78
Fourierists. *See* Associationists
Frieze, Jacob, 28

Garrison, William Lloyd, 7, 28, 47, 88, 101, 106, 117
Goss, William S., 117
Grand Eight Hour League of Massachusetts, 100–101, 106

Index

Greeley, Horace, 45, 93
Greenbackers, 141–43, 145
Greene, William, 109
Greenhalge, Frederick, 204
Griffin, Martin, 85, 88–89, 100, 151, 163
Guarneri, Carl, 13–14
Guiney, Patrick, 102
Gunton, George, 165, 293n15, 295n35

Hatch, Joel, 52
Hewitt, Simon C., 41
Heywood, Angela, 133–43
Heywood, Ezra, 114–15, 117–24, 127–30, 132–36, 141–43, 147, 154, 164, 175, 284n3, 286n34, 287n38; condemns Massachusetts Bureau of the Statistics of Labor (BSL), 134; condemns Massachusetts Labor Reform Party, 132–33; condemns ten-hour law, 134–35; on railroad strikes of 1877, 184–86, 191. See also New England Labor Reform League (NELRL)
Hoar, George F., 245
Hoar, Sherman, 246
Holyoake, George, 164
Hosmer, Charles, 55–56
Howes, Edith, 252–54, 257, 259
Hull House, 225, 231
Hyde, William, 102–3, 282n32

immigrants, 28, 169, 172, 210, 216, 240, 249–50, 261, 301n28; Irish, 28, 71, 74–75
Institute Hall, 107, 139, 212, 283n44. See also Labor Reform Institute; Workingmen's Institute of Boston

Jaques, Daniel H., 57–60
Jones, Jesse, 165–66, 173, 175–81, 189, 197, 202, 219, 292n4, 293n15, 294n23; on eight-hour law, 192; on eight-hour movement, 177; on railroad strikes of 1877, 186–87, 191, 294n20

Kaulback, John G., 50
Kenney, Mary. See O'Sullivan, Mary Kenney
King, MacKenzie, 258, 305n30
Klaus, Henry, 234–35
Knights of Labor (District Assembly 30), 188, 199, 201, 222, 229, 294n23
Knights of St. Crispin, 117, 122, 127, 150, 158
Know-Nothing Party, 74–75

Labor Balance, 181
Labor Church, 21, 173, 204, 208–11, 298nn52–53
Labor Leader, 192–93, 197, 200, 220, 302n6
Labor Reform Institute, 84, 109–13, 117, 139, 212. See also Institute Hall; Workingmen's Institute of Boston
Labor Reform League of New England (LRLNE), 54–64. See also New England Workingmen's Association (NEWA)
land reform, 48, 52–54, 59–62, 158, 207. See also Evans, George Henry
Laurie, Bruce, 14
The Liberator, 7, 28, 88
Linton, Edward, 109–10, 117, 132, 140, 162, 166, 174, 180
Livermore, Charles, 76
Lloyd, Harry, 201, 232–34
Lowell Female Labor Reform Association (LFLRA), 46, See also Bagley, Sarah
Luther, Seth, 35, 37–38, 40, 53–54, 164, 274n40

Mahan, John, 85, 94
Manchester Female Labor Reform Association, 57
Massachusetts Association of Working Women's Clubs, 252–53
Massachusetts Board to Investigate the Subject of the Unemployed (1894), 204, 206, 297n46
Massachusetts Bureau of the Statistics of Labor (BSL), 20, 26, 116, 138, 142, 149–56, 165–67, 187, 228; annual reports of, 152; and eight-hour movement, 150–51; and ten-hour law, 152–53; and tenement-house labor, 240, 242, 249–50
Massachusetts Commission on the Hours of Labor (1866–67), 102, 149; report of, 103–6
Massachusetts House of Representatives, 85; Judiciary Committee (1865), 85
Massachusetts Labor Reform Party, 20, 26, 116, 153, 156–64, 166–67, 177, 289n53
Massachusetts legislature, 3, 14, 19, 56, 62, 66, 70–72, 74–75, 83–86, 99–100; Joint Special Committee (1865), 85–88, 97, 104, 279n6
Massachusetts Special Commission on the Hours of Labor (1865–66), 88, 92–93, 149; report of, 96–99
Massachusetts State Board of Arbitration, 233–35

Massachusetts State Labor Union, 110, 142
Massachusetts Workingmen's Party, 37
McLean, Charles, 85, 109, 111, 136, 151, 163
McNeill, George, 7–8, 113, 116, 120, 142, 148, 165–66, 174, 178, 180, 187–88, 191, 220, 222, 283n41, 288n50, 293n16, 294n23; and Anti-Tenement House League, 240, 243, 248, 250; and Boston Eight Hour League, 136, 139; and Christian Socialism, 173, 194–95; and Denison House, 232–34; as Deputy Chief of BSL, 151–54; on eight-hour law, 192–93; and Massachusetts Labor Reform Party, 156, 158, 162; and New England Labor Reform League (NELRL), 117, 121–23, 128–29; warden of Church of the Carpenter, 201–2; and Workingmen's Institute of Boston, 106–10
The Mechanic, 41
mill workers (textiles), 32, 36, 54, 71, 75, 123, 150, 158, 163
Miner, A. A., 247
Montgomery, David, 12–13, 15
Moxon, Philip, 189–91, 224, 243
Murphy, Teresa, 14

National Reform Association, 42, 52–53, 59
Nationalism, 197–98, 207–8, 222, 295n35, 297n44
New England Artisan, 28, 35
New England Association of Farmers, Mechanics, and other Working Men (NEA), 27–37, 41, 63, 261, 269n1; constitution of, 31–32; report on child labor, 33; and women workers, 36
New England Industrial League, 68–72
New England Labor Reform League (NELRL), 20, 26, 114–15, 117, 120–21, 127–36, 141–45, 150, 156, 164, 166, 184, 286n35; constitution of, 127–28; treasurer's report, 131
New England Protective Union, 50, 293n16
New England Workingmen's Association (NEWA), 9, 11, 14, 42–54, 60–61, 63–64, 70, 261, 271n24, 274n49; and ten-hour movement, 43, 45, 48, 53–55, 61–63. *See also* Labor Reform League of New England (LRLNE)
Norcross, Otis, 107

Oliver, Henry K., 116, 142, 151–55, 163
Orvis, John, 57–60, 64, 121, 124–28, 132, 140, 154, 156, 196, 293n16
O'Sullivan, John, 227, 230–34, 253
O'Sullivan, Mary Kenney, 231–36, 238

Paine, Robert Treat, Jr., 215–18
People's Reform Party of Massachusetts, 163
Persons, Charles, 8–9
Phillips, Wendell, 47, 77, 80, 94–96, 99, 101–2, 107, 109, 113, 117, 124, 132, 160–62, 164, 219–21, 281n21, 282n30, 286nn34–35, 291n71; and Boston Eight Hour League, 137–38; and eight-hour day, 95; and eight-hour movement, 96; gubernatorial candidate of Massachusetts Labor Reform Party, 158–59, 290n59, 290n65; criticizes Massachusetts Bureau of the Statistics of Labor (BSL), 151–54; split with Steward, Ira, 115, 140–43. *See also* Wendell Phillips Association; Wendell Phillips Hall; Wendell Phillips Union; Wendell Phillips Woman's Club
Pidgin, Charles, 228
Place, Edward, 109–10
Plunkett, John, 250
producer cooperatives, 44, 63, 66–69, 81, 93–94, 101, 104, 127, 136, 152–53, 160–61, 182–83, 188, 223, 272n27
Prohibition Party, 159
protective stores. *See* consumer cooperatives; New England Protective Union
Protective Union, 68

railroad strikes (1877), 173, 181, 183–84
Randall, George, 109–10
Reconstruction, 19, 82, 125
Republican Party, 116, 157, 159, 162, 177, 180, 293n15
Rice, Alexander, 148
Ripley, George, 47
Robinson, William, 71–72
Rogers, Edward H., 85–86, 95, 99–100, 102–5, 124, 140, 151, 165–66, 174, 217, 281n29, 282n32; and Christian Labor Union (CLU), 177–81; and eight-hour day, 104–5; critique of Massachusetts Labor Reform Party, 157; warden of Church of the Carpenter, 201
Rowe, O. M. E., 252

Russell, William, 242
Ryckman, Lewis, 45, 47–50

Sanborn, Franklin B., 92
Saxton, Henry L., 106, 117
Scudder, Vida, 202, 228–30, 232, 235, 238
seamstresses, 65
Seelye, Julius, 225
settlement houses, 21, 221, 223–25, 236–38.
 See also Andover House; Denison House
Shawmut Club, 252
Smart, W. G. H., 166
Smith, Gerrit, 101
Snelling, George H., 92
Social Gospel, 224, 227
Socialist Labor Party, 204, 210, 222
Society of Christian Socialists, 196, 295n33
Sorge, Friedrich, 8, 11, 147, 149, 165
South End, 170, 214, 216, 229, 261
South End House. See Andover House
Sovereigns of Industry, 181–82, 293n16
Spanish-American War, 210
Spenceley, C. J., 86
Steward, Ira, 3, 19–20, 25–26, 73, 83, 86–95, 102–3, 106, 111–13, 117, 127–29, 136, 138–43, 164–67, 170, 174, 177–78, 180, 192, 200, 202, 212, 217, 219, 281n29, 283n41, 286n35; and Boston Eight Hour League, 136, 138–43, 146–49; and Boston Labor Reform Association, 76–78, 86; leaves Boston, 148, 167; and eight-hour day, 120, 143; and eight-hour movement, 89–91, 102–3, 112; critique of financial reform, 143–45, 147, 291n71; and Grand Eight Hour League of Massachusetts, 100–101; and Massachusetts Bureau of the Statistics of Labor (BSL), 151–54; and Massachusetts Labor Reform Party, 156, 162–63; and New England Labor Reform League, 120–24; split with Wendell Phillips, 115, 140–43; and Workingmen's Institute of Boston, 108–10
Steward, Mary, 3, 108–10, 136, 151; death of, 148
Stone, Huldah, 47, 54, 59
Stone, James, 70, 72, 101
sweatshops. See tenement-house labor
Swift, Morrison, 204–8, 297nn44–45
Sylvis Hall, 139

Talbot, Thomas, 163
ten-hour day, 3, 25, 30, 32–33, 36, 39–41, 43, 73, 87, 105, 111, 123, 138, 161

ten-hour law, 3, 34, 43, 62, 70–72, 75, 111–12, 123, 127, 142, 148, 150, 155, 158, 166, 273n38; passage of law (1874), 163
ten-hour movement, 11, 14, 19, 66, 70, 75, 78, 81, 112, 116, 128, 162, 276n11
ten-hour petitions, 33–34, 43–45, 55–56, 59, 64, 70–71, 81, 97
ten-hour pledge, 32–34
Ten-Hour State Convention (1852), 72–73, 77, 89
ten-hour strikes, 33, 37, 40
tenement-house labor, 242, 249–51, 261; legislation regulating, 242, 249–51, 303n9
textile mills, 87
Thompson, William, 35
Tilden, William P., 92
Trades Assembly of Boston, 76
Trask, Henry, 68
Treanon, B. S., 66
Tucker, Benjamin, 117, 130, 140, 184
Tucker, William Jewett, 225

unemployment marches (1893–94), 203–4, 206–7
United Garment Workers of America (UGWA), 229–30; District Council No. 2, 247; Local 37, 230–31, 233
U.S. House of Representatives, Committee on Labor, 207–8
U.S. House of Representatives, Committee on Manufacturers, 246

Voice of Industry (VOI), 48–49, 52–53, 57, 59–60, 274n48

Wade, Rufus, 253
Wadlin, Horace Greeley, 250
Walker, Amasa, 102–3, 155
Walter, Francis Amasa, 155
Ware, Norman, 10–11
Washburn, William, 153, 163
Washingtonians, 58
Webb, Thomas, 122–24
Wells Memorial Association, 215, 222
Wells Memorial Building, 216, 218, 221
Wells Memorial Workingmen's Institute, 21, 214–19, 229, 238, 298n3, 301n31; and eight-hour day, 218
Wendell Phillips Association, 220–22
Wendell Phillips Hall, 219–21

Wendell Phillips Union, 21, 201, 214, 219–23, 238
Wendell Phillips Woman's Club, 223
woman suffrage, 131
Woman's Trade Union League, 238
Women Clerks' Benefit Association, 252
Women's Educational and Industrial Union (WEIU), 253, 301n31
Woods, Robert A., 201, 224–27, 300n21, 300n23; and Consumers' League of Massachusetts, 253, 257–59; and Denison House, 232–34; and Wells Memorial Workingman's Institute, 218. *See also* Andover House

Worcester Labor Reform League, 118
The Word, 135
working girls's (women's) clubs, 251–53, 257, 304n18
Workingmen's Institute of Boston, 106–9. *See also* Institute Hall; Labor Reform Institute
Working-people's Industrial Order, 124
Wright, Albert, 277n20
Wright, Carroll, 154–56, 163, 187, 289n52
Wright, Elizur, 92
Wyman, Rufus, 84, 99, 100

Young, William F., 49–54, 57, 60, 69, 72, 273n34

DAVID A. ZONDERMAN is a professor of history at North Carolina State University. Born and raised in Newton, Massachusetts, a suburb of Boston, he was educated at Amherst College and Yale University. He is also the author of *Aspirations and Anxieties: New England Workers and the Mechanized Factory System,* and he is currently writing a book on labor and the American Civil War. He lives in Raleigh, North Carolina, with his wife, Patty Williams; they have two sons and two dogs.